INTERNATIONAL MONETARY FUND

T0293267

WORLD ECONOMIC OUTLOOK

Recovery During a Pandemic

Health Concerns, Supply Disruptions,
and Price Pressures

2021
OCT

©2021 International Monetary Fund

Cover and Design: IMF CSF Creative Solutions Division
Composition: AGS, An RR Donnelley Company

Cataloging-in-Publication Data

Joint Bank-Fund Library

Names: International Monetary Fund.
Title: World economic outlook (International Monetary Fund)
Other titles: WEO | Occasional paper (International Monetary Fund) | World economic and
    financial surveys.
Description: Washington, DC : International Monetary Fund, 1980- | Semiannual | Some
    issues also have thematic titles. | Began with issue for May 1980. | 1981-1984: Occasional
    paper / International Monetary Fund, 0251-6365 | 1986-: World economic and financial
    surveys, 0256-6877.
Identifiers: ISSN 0256-6877 (print) | ISSN 1564-5215 (online)
Subjects: LCSH: Economic development—Periodicals. | International economic relations—
    Periodicals. | Debts, External—Periodicals. | Balance of payments—Periodicals. |
    International finance—Periodicals. | Economic forecasting—Periodicals.
Classification: LCC HC10.W79

HC10.80

ISBN 978-1-51357-752-4 (English Paper)
    978-1-55775-449-3 (English ePub)
    978-1-55775-442-4 (English Web PDF)

The *World Economic Outlook* (WEO) is a survey by the IMF staff published twice a
year, in the spring and fall. The WEO is prepared by the IMF staff and has benefited
from comments and suggestions by Executive Directors following their discussion of the
report on September 27, 2021. The views expressed in this publication are those of the
IMF staff and do not necessarily represent the views of the IMF's Executive Directors
or their national authorities.

Recommended citation: International Monetary Fund. 2021. *World Economic Outlook:
Recovery during a Pandemic—Health Concerns, Supply Disruptions, Price Pressures.*
Washington, DC, October.

Publication orders may be placed online, by fax, or through the mail:
International Monetary Fund, Publication Services
P.O. Box 92780, Washington, DC 20090, USA
Tel.: (202) 623-7430 Fax: (202) 623-7201
E-mail: publications@imf.org
www.imfbookstore.org
www.elibrary.imf.org

CONTENTS

Online Tables—Statistical Appendix

Figures

A number of assumptions have been adopted for the projections presented in the *World Economic Outlook* (WEO). It has been assumed that real effective exchange rates remained constant at their average levels during July 23, 2021, to August 20, 2021, except for those for the currencies participating in the European exchange rate mechanism II, which are assumed to have remained constant in nominal terms relative to the euro; that established policies of national authorities will be maintained (for specific assumptions about fiscal and monetary policies for selected economies, see Box A1 in the Statistical Appendix); that the average price of oil will be $65.68 a barrel in 2021 and $64.52 a barrel in 2022 and will remain unchanged in real terms over the medium term; that the six-month London interbank offered rate on US dollar deposits will average 0.2 percent in 2021 and 0.4 percent in 2022; that the three-month euro deposit rate will average –0.5 percent in 2021 and 2022; and that the six-month Japanese yen deposit rate will yield, on average, –0.1 percent in 2021 and 0.0 percent in 2022. These are, of course, working hypotheses rather than forecasts, and the uncertainties surrounding them add to the margin of error that would, in any event, be involved in the projections. The estimates and projections are based on statistical information available through September 27, 2021.

The following conventions are used throughout the WEO:

. . .   to indicate that data are not available or not applicable;

–   between years or months (for example, 2020–21 or January–June) to indicate the years or months covered, including the beginning and ending years or months; and

/   between years or months (for example, 2020/21) to indicate a fiscal or financial year.

"Billion" means a thousand million; "trillion" means a thousand billion.

"Basis points" refers to hundredths of 1 percentage point (for example, 25 basis points are equivalent to ¼ of 1 percentage point).

Data refer to calendar years, except in the case of a few countries that use fiscal years. Please refer to Table F in the Statistical Appendix, which lists the economies with exceptional reporting periods for national accounts and government finance data for each country.

For some countries, the figures for 2020 and earlier are based on estimates rather than actual outturns. Please refer to Table G in the Statistical Appendix, which lists the latest actual outturns for the indicators in the national accounts, prices, government finance, and balance of payments indicators for each country.

What is new in this publication:

- Data for Andorra have been added to the database and are included in the advanced economies group composites.

In the tables and figures, the following conventions apply:

- If no source is listed in tables and figures, data are drawn from the WEO database.

- When countries are not listed alphabetically, they are ordered on the basis of economic size.

- Minor discrepancies between sums of constituent figures and totals shown reflect rounding.

As used in this report, the terms "country" and "economy" do not in all cases refer to a territorial entity that is a state as understood by international law and practice. As used here, the term also covers some territorial entities that are not states but for which statistical data are maintained on a separate and independent basis.

Composite data are provided for various groups of countries organized according to economic characteristics or region. Unless noted otherwise, country group composites represent calculations based on 90 percent or more of the weighted group data.

The boundaries, colors, denominations, and any other information shown on maps do not imply, on the part of the IMF, any judgment on the legal status of any territory or any endorsement or acceptance of such boundaries.

FURTHER INFORMATION

Corrections and Revisions

The data and analysis appearing in the *World Economic Outlook* (WEO) are compiled by the IMF staff at the time of publication. Every effort is made to ensure their timeliness, accuracy, and completeness. When errors are discovered, corrections and revisions are incorporated into the digital editions available from the IMF website and on the IMF eLibrary (see below). All substantive changes are listed in the online table of contents.

Print and Digital Editions

Print

Print copies of this WEO can be ordered from the IMF bookstore at imfbk.st/460116.

Digital

Multiple digital editions of the WEO, including ePub, enhanced PDF, and HTML, are available on the IMF eLibrary at http://www.elibrary.imf.org/OCT21WEO.

Download a free PDF of the report and data sets for each of the charts therein from the IMF website at www.imf.org/publications/weo or scan the QR code below to access the WEO web page directly:

Copyright and Reuse

Information on the terms and conditions for reusing the contents of this publication are at www.imf.org/external/terms.htm.

DATA

This version of the *World Economic Outlook* (WEO) is available in full through the IMF eLibrary (www.elibrary.imf.org) and the IMF website (www.imf.org). Accompanying the publication on the IMF website is a larger compilation of data from the WEO database than is included in the report itself, including files containing the series most frequently requested by readers. These files may be downloaded for use in a variety of software packages.

The data appearing in the WEO are compiled by the IMF staff at the time of the WEO exercises. The historical data and projections are based on the information gathered by the IMF country desk officers in the context of their missions to IMF member countries and through their ongoing analysis of the evolving situation in each country. Historical data are updated on a continual basis as more information becomes available, and structural breaks in data are often adjusted to produce smooth series with the use of splicing and other techniques. IMF staff estimates continue to serve as proxies for historical series when complete information is unavailable. As a result, WEO data can differ from those in other sources with official data, including the IMF's *International Financial Statistics*.

The WEO data and metadata provided are "as is" and "as available," and every effort is made to ensure their timeliness, accuracy, and completeness, but these cannot be guaranteed. When errors are discovered, there is a concerted effort to correct them as appropriate and feasible. Corrections and revisions made after publication are incorporated into the electronic editions available from the IMF eLibrary (www.elibrary.imf.org) and on the IMF website (www.imf.org). All substantive changes are listed in detail in the online tables of contents.

For details on the terms and conditions for usage of the WEO database, please refer to the IMF Copyright and Usage website (www.imf.org/external/terms.htm).

Inquiries about the content of the WEO and the WEO database should be sent by mail, fax, or online forum (telephone inquiries cannot be accepted):

World Economic Studies Division

Research Department

International Monetary Fund

700 19th Street, NW

Washington, DC 20431, USA

Fax: (202) 623-6343

Online Forum: www.imf.org/weoforum

PREFACE

The analysis and projections contained in the *World Economic Outlook* are integral elements of the IMF's surveillance of economic developments and policies in its member countries, of developments in international financial markets, and of the global economic system. The survey of prospects and policies is the product of a comprehensive interdepartmental review of world economic developments, which draws primarily on information the IMF staff gathers through its consultations with member countries. These consultations are carried out in particular by the IMF's area departments—namely, the African Department, Asia and Pacific Department, European Department, Middle East and Central Asia Department, and Western Hemisphere Department— together with the Strategy, Policy, and Review Department; the Monetary and Capital Markets Department; and the Fiscal Affairs Department.

The analysis in this report was coordinated in the Research Department under the general direction of Gita Gopinath, Economic Counsellor and Director of Research. The project was directed by Petya Koeva Brooks, Deputy Director, Research Department; and Malhar Nabar, Division Chief, Research Department.

The primary contributors to this report are Philip Barrett, John Bluedorn, Christian Bogmans, Francesca Caselli, Sonali Das, Niels-Jakob Hansen, Christoffer Koch, Toh Kuan, Giacomo Magistretti, Prachi Mishra, Jean-Marc Natal, Diaa Noureldin, Andrea Pescatori, Ervin Prifti, Martin Stuermer, Nico Valckx, and Philippe Wingender.

Other contributors include Swapnil Agarwal, Itai Agur, Michal Andrle, Gavin Asdorian, Laurence Ball, Srijoni Banerjee, Eric Bang, Nina Biljanovska, Simon Black, Lukas Boer, Rachel Brasier, Mariya Brussevich, Chunya Bu, Luisa Calixto, Damien Capelle, Yaniv Cohen, Olivier Coibion, Mattia Coppo, Allan Dizioli, Romain Duval, Angela Espiritu, Rebecca Eyassu, Chenxu Fu, Vanda Guerreiro, Jinjin He, Mandy Hemmati, Keiko Honjo, Youyou Huang, Benjamin Hunt, Deniz Igan, Piyusha Khot, Eduard Laurito, Jungjin Lee, Daniel Leigh, Rui Mano, Susanna Mursula, Savannah Newman, Cynthia Nyanchama Nyakeri, Emory Oakes, Ilse Peirtsegaele, Evgenia Pugacheva, Yiyuan Qi, Daniela Rojas Fernandez, Max Rozycki, Damiano Sandri, Katrien Smuts, Antonio Spilimbergo, John Spray, Philip Stokoe, Susie Xiaohui Sun, Jim Tebrake, Nicholas Tong, Filiz Unsal, Shan Wang, Dong Wenchuan, Yarou Xu, Hannah Leheng Yang, Huiyuan Zhao, and Jiaqi Zhao.

Joseph Procopio from the Communications Department led the editorial team for the report, with production and editorial support from Christine Ebrahimzadeh, and additional assistance from Lucy Scott Morales, James Unwin, Harold Medina, and TalentMEDIA Services.

The analysis has benefited from comments and suggestions by staff members from other IMF departments, as well as by Executive Directors following their discussion of the report on September 28, 2021. However, estimates, projections, and policy considerations are those of the IMF staff and should not be attributed to Executive Directors or to their national authorities.

FOREWORD

The global recovery continues but the momentum has weakened, hobbled by the pandemic. Fueled by the highly transmissible Delta variant, the recorded global COVID-19 death toll has risen close to 5 million and health risks abound, holding back a full return to normalcy. Pandemic outbreaks in critical links of global supply chains have resulted in longer-than-expected supply disruptions, further feeding inflation in many countries. Overall, risks to economic prospects have increased, and policy trade-offs have become more complex.

Compared to our July forecast, the global growth projection for 2021 has been revised down marginally to 5.9 percent and is unchanged for 2022 at 4.9 percent. This modest headline revision, however, masks large downgrades for some countries. The outlook for the low-income developing country group has darkened considerably due to worsening pandemic dynamics. The downgrade also reflects more difficult near-term prospects for the advanced economy group, in part due to supply disruptions. Partially offsetting these changes, projections for some commodity exporters have been upgraded on the back of rising commodity prices. Pandemic-related disruptions to contact-intensive sectors have caused the labor market recovery to significantly lag the output recovery in most countries.

The dangerous divergence in economic prospects across countries remains a major concern. Aggregate output for the advanced economy group is expected to regain its pre-pandemic trend path in 2022 and exceed it by 0.9 percent in 2024. By contrast, aggregate output for the emerging market and developing economy group (excluding China) is expected to remain 5.5 percent below the pre-pandemic forecast in 2024, resulting in a larger setback to improvements in their living standards.

These economic divergences are a consequence of large disparities in vaccine access and in policy support. While almost 60 percent of the population in advanced economies are fully vaccinated and some are now receiving booster shots, about 96 percent of the population in low-income countries remain unvaccinated. Emerging and developing economies, faced with tighter financing conditions and a greater risk of de-anchoring inflation expectations, are withdrawing policy support more quickly despite larger shortfalls in output.

Supply disruptions pose another policy challenge. On the one hand, pandemic outbreaks and weather disruptions have resulted in shortages of key inputs and dragged manufacturing activity lower in several countries. On the other hand, these supply shortages, alongside the release of pent-up demand and the rebound in commodity prices, have caused consumer price inflation to increase rapidly in, for example, the United States, Germany, and many emerging market and developing economies. Food prices have increased the most in low-income countries where food insecurity is most acute, adding to the burdens of poorer households and raising the risk of social unrest.

The October 2021 *Global Financial Stability Report* highlights another challenge to monetary policy from increasing risk taking in financial markets and rising fragilities in the nonbank financial institutions sector.

A principal common factor behind these complex challenges is the continued grip of the pandemic on global society. The foremost policy priority is therefore to vaccinate adequate numbers in every country and prevent more virulent virus mutations. As Chapter 1 explains, this will require the Group of Seven and Group of Twenty countries to fulfill existing dose donation pledges, coordinate with manufacturers to prioritize deliveries to COVAX in the near term, and remove trade restrictions on the flow of vaccines and its inputs. At the same time, closing the $20 billion residual gap in grants to fund testing, therapeutics, and genomic surveillance will save lives now and keep vaccines fit for purpose. Looking ahead, vaccine manufacturers and high-income countries should support the expansion of regional production of COVID-19 vaccines in developing countries through financing and technology transfer solutions.

While reducing the likelihood of a prolonged pandemic is a key immediate global priority, another urgent priority is the need to slow the rise in global temperatures and contain the growing adverse health and economic effects of climate change. As Chapter 1 details, stronger concrete commitments are needed at the upcoming United Nations Climate Change Conference (COP26). A policy strategy that encompasses an international carbon price floor adjusted to country circumstances, a green public investment and research subsidy push, and compensatory, targeted transfers to households can help advance the energy transition in an equitable way. Just as importantly, advanced countries need to deliver on their earlier promises of mobilizing $100 billion of climate financing, annually, for developing nations.

The pandemic and climate change threaten to exacerbate the economic divergences among the world's economies. Concerted multilateral effort to ensure adequate international liquidity for constrained economies, and faster implementation of the Group of Twenty common framework to restructure unsustainable debt, will help limit these divergences. Building on the historic $650 billion special drawing right allocation, the IMF is calling on countries with strong external positions to voluntarily channel their special drawing rights into the Poverty Reduction and Growth Trust. Furthermore, it is exploring the establishment of a Resilience and Sustainability Trust that would provide long-term funding to support countries' investment in sustainable growth.

At the national level, the overall policy mix should be calibrated to local pandemic and economic conditions, aiming for maximum sustainable employment while protecting the credibility of policy frameworks. With fiscal space becoming more limited in many economies, health care spending should continue to be the priority, while lifelines and transfers will need to become increasingly targeted, reinforced with retraining and support for reallocation. As health outcomes improve, policy emphasis can increasingly focus on long-term structural goals. The analysis in Chapter 3 shows that investment in basic research can have far-reaching benefits through faster productivity growth, and it is important to promote the free flow of ideas and scientific collaboration across borders.

With debt levels at record highs, all initiatives should be rooted in credible medium-term frameworks, backed by feasible revenue and expenditure measures. The October 2021 *Fiscal Monitor* demonstrates that such credibility can lower financing costs for countries and increase fiscal space in the near term.

Monetary policy will need to walk a fine line between tackling inflation and financial risks and supporting the economic recovery. We project, amid high uncertainty, that headline inflation will likely return to pre-pandemic levels by mid-2022 for the group of advanced economies and emerging and developing economies. There is, however, considerable heterogeneity across countries, with upside risks for some, such as the United States, the United Kingdom, and some emerging market and developing economies. While monetary policy can generally look through transitory increases in inflation, central banks should be prepared to act quickly if the risks of rising inflation expectations become more material in this uncharted recovery. Central banks should chart contingent actions, announce clear triggers, and act in line with that communication.

More generally, clarity and consistent actions can go a long way toward avoiding unnecessary policy accidents that roil financial markets and set back the global recovery—ranging from a failure to lift the United States debt ceiling in a timely fashion, to disorderly debt restructurings in China's property sector, and escalations in cross-border trade and technology tensions.

Recent developments have made it abundantly clear that we are all in this together and the pandemic is not over *anywhere* until it is over *everywhere*. If Covid-19 were to have a prolonged impact into the medium term, it could reduce global GDP by a cumulative $5.3 trillion over the next five years relative to our current projection. It does not have to be this way. The global community must step up efforts to ensure equitable vaccine access for every country, overcome vaccine hesitancy where there is adequate supply, and secure better economic prospects for all.

Gita Gopinath
Economic Counsellor and Director of Research

The global economic recovery is continuing, even as the pandemic resurges. The fault lines opened up by COVID-19 are looking more persistent—near-term divergences are expected to leave lasting imprints on medium-term performance. Vaccine access and early policy support are the principal drivers of the gaps. Rapid spread of Delta and the threat of new variants have increased uncertainty about how quickly the pandemic can be overcome. Policy choices have become more difficult, confronting multidimensional challenges—subdued employment growth, rising inflation, food insecurity, the setback to human capital accumulation, and climate change—with limited room to maneuver.

The forecast: The global economy is projected to grow 5.9 percent in 2021 and 4.9 percent in 2022 (0.1 percentage point lower for 2021 than in the July 2021 *World Economic Outlook* (WEO) *Update*). The downward revision for 2021 reflects a downgrade for advanced economies—in part due to supply disruptions—and for low-income developing countries, largely due to worsening pandemic dynamics. This is partially offset by stronger near-term prospects among some commodity-exporting emerging market and developing economies. Employment is generally expected to continue lagging the recovery in output.

Beyond 2022 global growth is projected to moderate to about 3.3 percent over the medium term. Advanced economy output is forecast to exceed pre-pandemic medium-term projections—largely reflecting sizable anticipated further policy support in the United States that includes measures to increase potential. By contrast, persistent output losses are anticipated for the emerging market and developing economy group due to slower vaccine rollouts and generally less policy support compared to advanced economies.

Headline inflation rates have increased rapidly in the United States and in some emerging market and developing economies. In most cases, rising inflation reflects pandemic-related supply-demand mismatches and higher commodity prices compared to their low base from a year ago. As discussed in Chapters 1 and 2, for the most part, price pressures are expected to subside in 2022. In some emerging market and developing economies, price pressures are expected to persist because of elevated food prices, lagged effects of higher oil prices, and exchange rate depreciation lifting the prices of imported goods. However, great uncertainty surrounds inflation prospects—primarily stemming from the path of the pandemic, the duration of supply disruptions, and how inflation expectations may evolve in this environment.

Overall, the balance of risks for growth is tilted to the downside. The major source of concern is that more aggressive SARS-CoV-2 variants could emerge before widespread vaccination is reached.

Inflation risks are skewed to the upside and could materialize if pandemic-induced supply-demand mismatches continue longer than expected (including if the damage to supply potential turns out worse than anticipated), leading to more sustained price pressures and rising inflation expectations that prompt a faster-than-anticipated monetary normalization in advanced economies (see also the October 2021 *Global Financial Stability Report*).

Multilateral efforts to speed up global vaccine access, provide liquidity and debt relief to constrained economies, and mitigate and adapt to climate change remain essential. Speeding up the vaccination of the world population remains the top policy priority, while continuing the push for widespread testing and investing in therapeutics. This would save millions of lives, help prevent the emergence of new variants, and hasten the global economic recovery. As discussed in Chapter 1, an IMF proposal lays out concrete, cost-effective steps to vaccinate at least 40 percent of the population in every country by the end of 2021 and 70 percent by mid-2022.[1] It is also crucial to ensure that financially constrained countries can continue essential spending while meeting other obligations. The IMF's recent General Allocation of Special Drawing Rights, equivalent to $650 billion, provided much-needed international liquidity. Moreover, doubling down efforts to curb greenhouse gas emissions is critical—current actions and pledges are not enough to prevent a dangerous overheating of the planet. The international community should also resolve trade tensions and reverse the trade restrictions implemented in 2018–19, strengthen the rules-based multilateral trading system, and complete an agreement on a global minimum for corporate taxes that halts a race to the bottom and helps bolster finances to fund critical public investments.

At the national level, the policy mix should continue to be tailored to local pandemic and economic conditions, aiming for maximum sustainable employment while protecting the credibility of policy frameworks.

- *Fiscal policy:* The imperatives will depend on the stage of the pandemic (also see the October 2021 *Fiscal Monitor*). Health care-related spending remains the priority. As the pandemic persists and fiscal space is limited in some countries, lifelines and transfers will need to become increasingly targeted to the worst affected and provide retraining and support for reallocation. Where health metrics permit, emphasis should shift toward measures to secure the recovery and invest in longer-term structural goals.

[1]The 70 percent coverage target by mid-2022 is driven by the health and economic imperatives of stopping the pandemic as rapidly as possible. This is higher than the originally proposed 60 percent target for mid-2022 given the rise of more infectious variants. The revised target is consistent with the downside risk scenario envisioned in the original $50 billion IMF staff proposal released in May 2021, under which 1 billion *additional* doses were designated for low- and lower-middle income countries—and is aligned with the updated World Health Organization global vaccination strategy. The national targets may need to be adjusted based on age demographics and policy developments.

Initiatives should be embedded in medium-term frameworks with credible revenue and expenditure measures ensuring debt sustainability.

- *Monetary policy:* Although central banks can generally look through transitory inflation pressures and avoid tightening until there is more clarity on underlying price dynamics, they should be prepared to act quickly if the recovery strengthens faster than expected or risks of rising inflation expectations become tangible. In settings where inflation is rising amid still-subdued employment rates and risks of expectations de-anchoring are becoming concrete, monetary policy may need to be tightened to get ahead of price pressures, even if that delays the employment recovery. The alternative of waiting for stronger employment outcomes runs the risk that inflation increases in a self-fulfilling way, undermining the credibility of the policy framework and creating more uncertainty. A spiral of doubt could hold back private investment and lead to precisely the slower employment recovery central banks seek to avoid when holding off on policy tightening. By contrast, monetary policy can remain accommodative where inflation pressures are contained, inflation expectations are still below the central bank target, and labor market slack remains. The unprecedented conjuncture makes transparent and clear communication about the outlook for monetary policy even more critical.

- *Preparing for the post-pandemic economy:* Finally, it is important to deal with the challenges of the post-pandemic economy: reversing the pandemic-induced setback to human capital accumulation, facilitating new growth opportunities related to green technology and digitalization, reducing inequality, and ensuring sustainable public finances. Chapter 3 explores one dimension of this policy agenda—the importance of basic research investment for spurring productivity growth.

CHAPTER 1

GLOBAL PROSPECTS AND POLICIES

The global economic recovery continues amid a resurging pandemic that poses unique policy challenges (Figure 1.1). Vaccinations have proven effective at mitigating the adverse health impacts of COVID-19. However, unequal access to vaccines, vaccine hesitancy, and higher infectiousness have left many people still susceptible, providing fuel to the pandemic. The marked spread of the Delta variant and the threat of new variants that could undermine vaccine effectiveness make the future path of the pandemic highly uncertain. This has implications for the resilience of a recovery already in uncharted territory—characterized by pandemic-induced supply-demand mismatches that could worsen with a more protracted health crisis.

Gaps in expected recoveries across economy groups have widened since the July forecast, for instance between advanced economies and low-income developing countries. As recoveries proceed, the risks of derailments and persistent scarring in heavily impacted economies remain so long as the pandemic continues.

Meanwhile, inflation has increased markedly in the United States and some emerging market economies. As restrictions are relaxed, demand has accelerated, but supply has been slower to respond. Commodity prices have also risen significantly from their low levels of last year. Although price pressures are expected to subside in most countries in 2022, inflation prospects are highly uncertain. These increases in inflation are occurring even as employment is below pre-pandemic levels in many economies, forcing difficult choices on policymakers—particularly in some emerging market and developing economies.

The chapter first discusses the global outlook and risks, before turning to policies needed to address these challenges.

Near-Term Recovery Continues while the Pandemic Resurges

GDP growth in the first half of 2021 was broadly in line with expectations. Outturns for first quarter global GDP were stronger than anticipated, reflecting continued adaptation of economic activity to the pandemic

and associated restrictions as well as ongoing policy support in many countries. Momentum, however, weakened in the second quarter, weighed down by increasing infections in many emerging market and developing economies and by supply disruptions. Expenditure decompositions are consistent with input shortages contributing to weak investment in the second quarter (Figure 1.2). Recent high-frequency data are mixed. They suggest that the recovery continues, but with some softening in the third quarter, even while broadening across sectors. Services production is expanding, albeit prone to setbacks (Figure 1.3).

The global growth outlook is revised down for 2021 and is unchanged for 2022. The global economy is projected to grow 5.9 percent in 2021 and 4.9 percent in 2022. The 2021 forecast is revised down 0.1 percentage point relative to the July *World Economic Outlook* (WEO) *Update*, reflecting forecast downgrades to the advanced economy and low-income developing countries groups, as discussed below.

Vaccine access remains the principal driver of fault lines in the global recovery, reinforced by the resurgence of the pandemic. Many advanced economies have seen remarkable progress in vaccinations since the April 2021 WEO. By contrast, most emerging market and developing economies have had a much slower rollout, hampered by lack of supply and export restrictions.

- Advanced economies have achieved broad availability of vaccines, with hesitancy (rather than inadequate supply) being the main constraint on further gains. About 58 percent of the population in advanced economies has been fully vaccinated (Figure 1.4). By contrast, the rest of the world has starkly lower shares of population that are fully vaccinated against COVID-19, at about 36 percent in emerging market economies and less than 5 percent in low-income developing countries. In these economies, vaccine supply and distribution remain the primary constraints.

- The forecast assumes that some emerging market economies will join advanced economies in gaining broad vaccine access in 2021. Most countries are assumed to acquire broad access by the end of

Figure 1.1. New Confirmed COVID-19 Deaths
(Persons, seven-day moving average)

The pandemic began resurging over the summer.

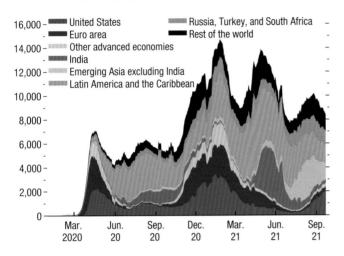

Sources: Our World in Data; and IMF staff calculations.
Note: Data as of September 22, 2021. Economy group and regional classifications are those in the *World Economic Outlook.* Other advanced economies in terms of International Organization for Standardization (ISO) country codes are AUS, CAN, CHE, CZE, DNK, GBR, HKG, ISL, ISR, JPN, KOR, MAC, NOR, NZL, SGP, SMR, SWE, and TWN.

Figure 1.2. Drivers of Global Growth
(Quarter-over-quarter growth contributions, percentage points)

Supply disruptions are weighing on private investment.

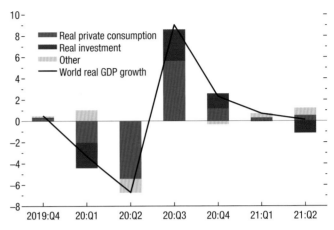

Sources: Haver Analytics; and IMF staff calculations.
Note: The estimate of world real GDP at the quarterly frequency is based on a sample of economies covering 79.4 percent of global economic activity in 2020. "Other" includes the sum of contributions from public consumption and a residual component, which mixes contributions from the sample's net exports to economies not covered and a statistical discrepancy.

Figure 1.3. Global Activity Indicators
(Three-month moving average, annualized percent change for industrial production; deviations from 50 for PMIs)

Higher-frequency indicators point to softening momentum.

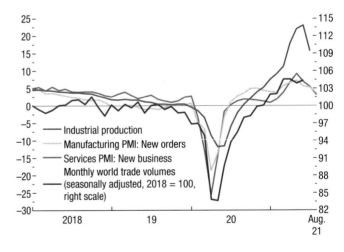

Sources: CPB Netherlands Bureau for Economic Policy Analysis; Haver Analytics; Markit Economics; and IMF staff calculations.
Note: PMI above 50 indicates expansion while below 50 indicates contraction. PMIs = purchasing managers' indexes.

2022 and some only in 2023. However, it seems likely that vaccinations alone will not be able to completely stamp out SARS-CoV-2 transmission, even though they remain effective against the most adverse health effects of the pandemic (severe illness and death). As a result, hospitalizations and deaths are expected to be brought to low levels everywhere by the end of 2022 through a combination of improved access to vaccines and therapies, combined with more highly targeted and effective precautions. Some countries may be able to reduce adverse public health outcomes sooner than others, depending on country-specific circumstances. The projections are tempered by the possibility of renewed outbreaks, particularly before vaccines become widely available.

• So long as the enormous differences in vaccine access persist, the inequalities in health and economic outcomes will increase, driving further divergences across two blocs of countries: those that can look forward to further normalization later this year (almost all advanced economies); and those that will struggle with the adverse health and economic impacts from resurgent infections. The pressure for booster shots in countries with already-high rates of vaccination could further delay access in others still at early stages of

Figure 1.4. The Great Vaccination Divide
(Percent of population)

Progress in vaccinations against COVID-19 remains highly unequal across the world.

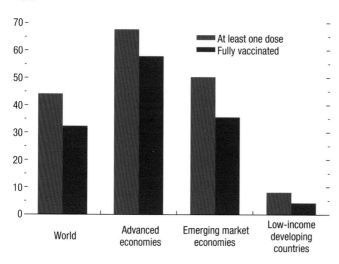

Sources: Our World in Data; and IMF staff calculations.
Note: Data as of September 22, 2021. "Fully vaccinated" are people who received all the doses prescribed for a full vaccination cycle (typically two, but one for Johnson&Johnson and CanSino). In a few cases, the recorded one-dose numbers are smaller than "fully vaccinated" numbers because of reporting lags. For these cases, we make a minimal consistency adjustment, setting one-dose numbers equal to "fully vaccinated" numbers.

Figure 1.5. Fiscal Stance, 2020–22
(Change in structural primary fiscal balance, percent of potential GDP)

Fiscal tightening is already under way in emerging market and developing economies and will pick up in advanced economies as well in 2022.

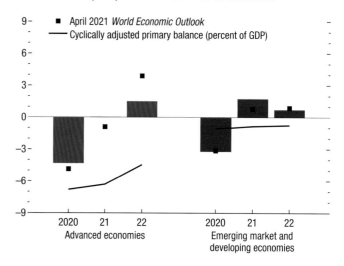

Source: IMF staff estimates.

getting first jabs into arms. The continuing wide circulation of the virus, particularly within countries and populations where vaccination rates are low, poses threats to health and economic recoveries everywhere. The World Health Organization is warning that more transmissible and deadly variants—which could escape protection from existing vaccines—are likely to evolve so long as a substantial share of the world population remains unprotected.

Differences in policy support across countries also underlay gaps in recovery speeds. Sizable fiscal support continues in advanced economies, while many emerging market economies are reducing policy support this year as policy space shrinks with the duration of the pandemic (Figure 1.5). Major advanced economy central banks are assumed to leave policy rates unchanged through late 2022 though, in some cases, asset purchases are expected to be scaled back before then—a process already underway, for example, in Australia and Canada. Meanwhile, some emerging market central banks—including in Brazil, Chile, Mexico, and Russia—have shifted to a less accommodative stance

over 2021, with tightening expected in more countries over the coming quarters.

- Policy support has helped create the conditions for a handoff to private demand in the recovery. Where deployed, extensive fiscal measures have provided insurance to households and firms, enabling many to replenish or build up their savings, and creating the conditions for private demand to propel the recovery, particularly in 2022 when the advanced economy group is projected to shift its fiscal stance toward tightening. Indeed, household savings accumulated in excess of the pre-pandemic trend shows a positive relationship vis-à-vis the extent of fiscal support.

- Moreover, there are signs that historically low-saving countries have tended to accumulate greater savings in the wake of the COVID-19 crisis, putting their finances on firmer footing going forward. The forecast assumes a smooth handoff from extraordinary policy support to private activity-led growth, with some of the additional savings buildup retained in places where previous saving rates were low. Demand is assumed to pick up as vaccination coverage rises—given that vaccines seem to protect against severe illness. The speed with which this happens—and excess savings are drawn down—will influence the pace of the recovery and inflationary pressures (if supply is unable to adjust quickly enough).

The forecast is predicated on financial conditions remaining supportive. Financial market sentiment has largely stayed attuned to the policy outlook as the recovery has proceeded (see the October 2021 *Global Financial Stability Report* and Figure 1.6). However, the high uncertainty around the conjuncture has also led to heightened sensitivity to any news, in particular about inflation prospects in advanced economies. The first quarter of 2021 and a brief period in June saw a bout of financial market volatility, with investors repositioning portfolio holdings as they reassessed the outlook for US inflation and monetary policy. Concerns about the spread of the Delta variant and associated implications for the recovery have also sparked episodes of volatility.

Even so, the overall picture is still one of broadly supportive financial conditions. Equity markets are buoyant, credit spreads remain tight, and net flows to emerging market economies have hitherto been broadly stable (particularly into hard currency bond funds). The global growth forecast is predicated on this support continuing.

Growth revisions: Vaccine rollout, policy support, and continued supportive financial conditions constitute the key considerations for the forecasts summarized in Table 1.1.

- *Advanced economies:* Growth prospects for 2021 are revised down compared to the July forecast, largely reflecting downgrades to the United States (due to large inventory drawdowns in the second quarter, in part reflecting supply disruptions, and softening consumption in the third quarter); Germany (in part because of shortages of key inputs weighing on manufacturing output); and Japan (reflecting the effect of the fourth State of Emergency from July to September as infections hit a record level in the current wave). The US outlook incorporates the infrastructure bill recently passed by the Senate and anticipated legislation to strengthen the social safety net, equivalent to about $4 trillion in spending over the next 10 years. The baseline also includes expected Next Generation European Union (EU) grants and loans for EU economies. Across advanced economies, an anticipated stronger rebound in the first half of next year, as vaccination proceeds, yields an upward revision to the growth forecast for 2022.

- *Emerging market and developing economies:* The forecast for the group is marked up slightly compared to the July 2021 WEO *Update*, reflecting upgrades across most regions. China's prospects

Figure 1.6. Monetary and Financial Conditions
(Percent, unless noted otherwise)

Financial conditions are supportive and attuned to the recovery.

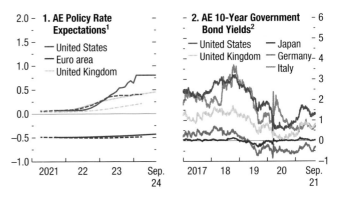

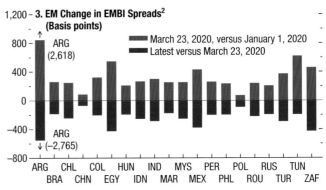

Sources: Bloomberg Finance L.P.; EPFR Global; Refinitiv Datastream; and IMF staff calculations.
Note: Data labels use International Organization for Standardization (ISO) country codes. Dashed lines in panel 1 are from the April 2021 *World Economic Outlook*. AE = advanced economy; EM = emerging market economy; EMBI = J.P. Morgan Emerging Markets Bond Index.
[1]Expectations are based on the federal funds rate futures for the United States, the sterling overnight interbank average rate for the United Kingdom, and the euro interbank offered forward rate for the euro area; updated September 22, 2021.
[2]Data are through September 21, 2021.

Table 1.1. Overview of the *World Economic Outlook* Projections
(Percent change, unless noted otherwise)

	2020	Projections		Difference from July 2021 WEO *Update*[1]		Difference from April 2021 WEO[1]	
		2021	2022	2021	2022	2021	2022
World Output	−3.1	**5.9**	**4.9**	**−0.1**	**0.0**	**−0.1**	**0.5**
Advanced Economies	−4.5	**5.2**	**4.5**	**−0.4**	**0.1**	**0.1**	**0.9**
United States	−3.4	6.0	5.2	−1.0	0.3	−0.4	1.7
Euro Area	−6.3	5.0	4.3	0.4	0.0	0.6	0.5
Germany	−4.6	3.1	4.6	−0.5	0.5	−0.5	1.2
France	−8.0	6.3	3.9	0.5	−0.3	0.5	−0.3
Italy	−8.9	5.8	4.2	0.9	0.0	1.6	0.6
Spain	−10.8	5.7	6.4	−0.5	0.6	−0.7	1.7
Japan	−4.6	2.4	3.2	−0.4	0.2	−0.9	0.7
United Kingdom	−9.8	6.8	5.0	−0.2	0.2	1.5	−0.1
Canada	−5.3	5.7	4.9	−0.6	0.4	0.7	0.2
Other Advanced Economies[2]	−1.9	4.6	3.7	−0.3	0.1	0.2	0.3
Emerging Market and Developing Economies	**−2.1**	**6.4**	**5.1**	**0.1**	**−0.1**	**−0.3**	**0.1**
Emerging and Developing Asia	−0.8	7.2	6.3	−0.3	−0.1	−1.4	0.3
China	2.3	8.0	5.6	−0.1	−0.1	−0.4	0.0
India[3]	−7.3	9.5	8.5	0.0	0.0	−3.0	1.6
ASEAN-5[4]	−3.4	2.9	5.8	−1.4	−0.5	−2.0	−0.3
Emerging and Developing Europe	−2.0	6.0	3.6	1.1	0.0	1.6	−0.3
Russia	−3.0	4.7	2.9	0.3	−0.2	0.9	−0.9
Latin America and the Caribbean	−7.0	6.3	3.0	0.5	−0.2	1.7	−0.1
Brazil	−4.1	5.2	1.5	−0.1	−0.4	1.5	−1.1
Mexico	−8.3	6.2	4.0	−0.1	−0.2	1.2	1.0
Middle East and Central Asia	−2.8	4.1	4.1	0.1	0.4	0.4	0.3
Saudi Arabia	−4.1	2.8	4.8	0.4	0.0	−0.1	0.8
Sub-Saharan Africa	−1.7	3.7	3.8	0.3	−0.3	0.3	−0.2
Nigeria	−1.8	2.6	2.7	0.1	0.1	0.1	0.4
South Africa	−6.4	5.0	2.2	1.0	0.0	1.9	0.2
Memorandum							
World Growth Based on Market Exchange Rates	−3.5	5.7	4.7	−0.3	0.1	−0.1	0.6
European Union	−5.9	5.1	4.4	0.4	0.0	0.7	0.5
Middle East and North Africa	−3.2	4.1	4.1	0.0	0.4	0.1	0.4
Emerging Market and Middle-Income Economies	−2.3	6.7	5.1	0.2	−0.1	−0.2	0.1
Low-Income Developing Countries	0.1	3.0	5.3	−0.9	−0.2	−1.3	0.1
World Trade Volume (goods and services)	**−8.2**	**9.7**	**6.7**	**0.0**	**−0.3**	**1.3**	**0.2**
Imports							
Advanced Economies	−9.0	9.0	7.3	−0.7	−0.3	−0.1	0.9
Emerging Market and Developing Economies	−8.0	12.1	7.1	0.7	0.0	3.1	−0.3
Exports							
Advanced Economies	−9.4	8.0	6.6	0.0	0.0	0.1	0.2
Emerging Market and Developing Economies	−5.2	11.6	5.8	0.8	−0.9	4.0	−0.2
Commodity Prices (US dollars)							
Oil[5]	−32.7	59.1	−1.8	2.5	0.8	17.4	4.5
Nonfuel (average based on world commodity import weights)	6.7	26.7	−0.9	0.2	−0.1	10.6	1.0
Consumer Prices							
Advanced Economies[6]	0.7	2.8	2.3	0.4	0.2	1.2	0.6
Emerging Market and Developing Economies[7]	5.1	5.5	4.9	0.1	0.2	0.6	0.5
London Interbank Offered Rate (percent)							
On US Dollar Deposits (six month)	0.7	0.2	0.4	−0.1	0.0	−0.1	0.0
On Euro Deposits (three month)	−0.4	−0.5	−0.5	0.0	0.0	0.0	0.0
On Japanese Yen Deposits (six month)	0.0	−0.1	0.0	−0.1	0.0	0.0	0.0

Source: IMF staff estimates.

Note: Real effective exchange rates are assumed to remain constant at the levels prevailing during July 23–August 20, 2021. Economies are listed on the basis of economic size. The aggregated quarterly data are seasonally adjusted. WEO = *World Economic Outlook*.

[1]Difference based on rounded figures for the current, July 2021 WEO *Update*, and April 2021 WEO forecasts.

[2]Excludes the Group of Seven (Canada, France, Germany, Italy, Japan, United Kingdom, United States) and euro area countries.

[3]For India, data and forecasts are presented on a fiscal year basis, and GDP from 2011 onward is based on GDP at market prices with fiscal year 2011/12 as a base year.

Table 1.1 Overview of the *World Economic Outlook* Projections *(continued)*
(Percent change, unless noted otherwise)

	Year over Year				Q4 over Q4[8]			
			Projections				Projections	
	2019	2020	2021	2022	2019	2020	2021	2022
World Output	**2.8**	**−3.1**	**5.9**	**4.9**	**2.7**	**−0.4**	**4.5**	**4.0**
Advanced Economies	**1.7**	**−4.5**	**5.2**	**4.5**	**1.6**	**−2.8**	**5.0**	**3.3**
United States	2.3	−3.4	6.0	5.2	2.6	−2.3	6.1	4.0
Euro Area	1.5	−6.3	5.0	4.3	1.1	−4.4	4.9	3.0
Germany	1.1	−4.6	3.1	4.6	0.9	−2.9	4.1	1.9
France	1.8	−8.0	6.3	3.9	0.9	−4.3	4.5	2.6
Italy	0.3	−8.9	5.8	4.2	−0.1	−6.5	5.6	2.9
Spain	2.1	−10.8	5.7	6.4	1.7	−8.8	7.4	3.1
Japan	0.0	−4.6	2.4	3.2	−1.3	−0.8	1.2	2.2
United Kingdom	1.4	−9.8	6.8	5.0	1.2	−7.3	7.2	2.2
Canada	1.9	−5.3	5.7	4.9	1.7	−3.1	4.9	4.0
Other Advanced Economies[2]	1.9	−1.9	4.6	3.7	2.1	−0.6	4.0	3.1
Emerging Market and Developing Economies	**3.7**	**−2.1**	**6.4**	**5.1**	**3.6**	**1.8**	**3.9**	**4.6**
Emerging and Developing Asia	5.4	−0.8	7.2	6.3	4.8	3.8	3.9	5.3
China	6.0	2.3	8.0	5.6	5.8	6.6	3.3	6.3
India[3]	4.0	−7.3	9.5	8.5	2.8	1.5	6.0	2.3
ASEAN-5[4]	4.9	−3.4	2.9	5.8	4.5	−2.6	3.2	5.7
Emerging and Developing Europe	2.5	−2.0	6.0	3.6	3.6	−0.1	4.6	3.7
Russia	2.0	−3.0	4.7	2.9	2.7	−1.9	3.9	2.8
Latin America and the Caribbean	0.1	−7.0	6.3	3.0	−0.4	−3.4	3.3	2.7
Brazil	1.4	−4.1	5.2	1.5	1.6	−1.2	2.1	1.4
Mexico	−0.2	−8.3	6.2	4.0	−0.9	−4.6	4.4	3.7
Middle East and Central Asia	1.5	−2.8	4.1	4.1	. . .	. . .	. . .	. . .
Saudi Arabia	0.3	−4.1	2.8	4.8	−0.3	−3.9	8.2	2.9
Sub-Saharan Africa	3.1	−1.7	3.7	3.8	. . .	. . .	. . .	. . .
Nigeria	2.2	−1.8	2.6	2.7	2.0	−0.5	2.4	1.9
South Africa	0.1	−6.4	5.0	2.2	−0.4	−3.4	1.5	3.2
Memorandum								
World Growth Based on Market Exchange Rates	2.5	−3.5	5.7	4.7	2.3	−1.0	4.6	3.9
European Union	1.9	−5.9	5.1	4.4	1.5	−4.2	5.3	2.9
Middle East and North Africa	1.0	−3.2	4.1	4.1	. . .	. . .	. . .	. . .
Emerging Market and Middle-Income Economies	3.5	−2.3	6.7	5.1	3.6	1.8	4.0	4.6
Low-Income Developing Countries	5.3	0.1	3.0	5.3	. . .	. . .	. . .	. . .
World Trade Volume (goods and services)	**0.9**	**−8.2**	**9.7**	**6.7**	**. . .**	**. . .**	**. . .**	**. . .**
Imports								
Advanced Economies	2.0	−9.0	9.0	7.3	. . .	. . .	. . .	. . .
Emerging Market and Developing Economies	−0.9	−8.0	12.1	7.1	. . .	. . .	. . .	. . .
Exports								
Advanced Economies	1.2	−9.4	8.0	6.6	. . .	. . .	. . .	. . .
Emerging Market and Developing Economies	0.4	−5.2	11.6	5.8	. . .	. . .	. . .	. . .
Commodity Prices (US dollars)								
Oil[5]	−10.2	−32.7	59.1	−1.8	−6.1	−27.6	54.1	−6.2
Nonfuel (average based on world commodity import weights)	0.8	6.7	26.7	−0.9	5.0	15.4	16.3	−1.7
Consumer Prices								
Advanced Economies[6]	1.4	0.7	2.8	2.3	1.4	0.4	3.6	1.9
Emerging Market and Developing Economies[7]	5.1	5.1	5.5	4.9	5.1	3.2	5.2	4.3
London Interbank Offered Rate (percent)								
On US Dollar Deposits (six month)	2.3	0.7	0.2	0.4	. . .	. . .	. . .	. . .
On Euro Deposits (three month)	−0.4	−0.4	−0.5	−0.5	. . .	. . .	. . .	. . .
On Japanese Yen Deposits (six month)	0.0	0.0	−0.1	0.0	. . .	. . .	. . .	. . .

[4]Indonesia, Malaysia, Philippines, Thailand, Vietnam.

[5]Simple average of prices of UK Brent, Dubai Fateh, and West Texas Intermediate crude oil. The average price of oil in US dollars a barrel was $41.29 in 2020; the assumed price, based on futures markets, is $65.68 in 2021 and $64.52 in 2022.

[6]The inflation rates for 2021 and 2022, respectively, are as follows: 2.2 percent and 1.7 percent for the euro area, −0.2 percent and 0.5 percent for Japan, and 4.3 percent and 3.5 percent for the United States.

[7]Excludes Venezuela. See the country-specific note for Venezuela in the "Country Notes" section of the Statistical Appendix.

[8]For world output, the quarterly estimates and projections account for approximately 90 percent of annual world output at purchasing-power-parity weights. For Emerging Market and Developing Economies, the quarterly estimates and projections account for approximately 80 percent of annual emerging market and developing economies' output at purchasing-power-parity weights.

Table 1.2. Overview of the *World Economic Outlook* Projections at Market Exchange Rate Weights
(Percent change)

	2020	Projections		Difference from July 2021 WEO *Update*[1]		Difference from April 2021 WEO[1]	
		2021	2022	2021	2022	2021	2022
World Output	−3.5	5.7	4.7	−0.3	0.1	−0.1	0.6
Advanced Economies	−4.6	5.2	4.5	−0.5	0.2	0.0	0.9
Emerging Market and Developing Economies	−1.9	6.5	5.0	0.1	−0.1	−0.1	0.1
Emerging and Developing Asia	0.1	7.4	6.0	−0.2	−0.2	−1.0	0.2
Emerging and Developing Europe	−2.2	5.8	3.7	0.9	0.0	1.5	−0.3
Latin America and the Caribbean	−7.1	6.3	3.0	0.6	−0.1	1.8	−0.1
Middle East and Central Asia	−4.2	3.9	3.9	0.1	0.4	0.3	0.3
Sub-Saharan Africa	−2.2	3.7	3.7	0.3	−0.3	0.3	−0.1
Memorandum							
European Union	−6.0	5.0	4.3	0.4	0.0	0.7	0.5
Middle East and North Africa	−4.7	3.8	3.9	0.0	0.4	0.0	0.4
Emerging Market and Middle-Income Economies	−2.0	6.7	5.0	0.1	−0.1	−0.1	0.1
Low-Income Developing Countries	−0.1	3.1	5.2	−0.8	−0.2	−1.2	0.1

Source: IMF staff estimates.

Note: The aggregate growth rates are calculated as a weighted average, in which a moving average of nominal GDP in US dollars for the preceding three years is used as the weight. WEO = *World Economic Outlook.*

[1]Difference based on rounded figures for the current, July 2021 WEO *Update*, and April 2021 WEO forecasts.

for 2021 are marked down slightly due to stronger-than-anticipated scaling back of public investment. Outside of China and India, emerging and developing Asia is downgraded slightly as the pandemic has picked up. Growth forecasts in other regions have been revised up slightly for 2021. The revisions in part reflect improved assessments for some commodity exporters outweighing drags from pandemic developments (Latin America and the Caribbean, Middle East and Central Asia, sub-Saharan Africa). Elsewhere, stronger-than-anticipated domestic demand in key regional economies further lifts the 2021 forecast (emerging and developing europe).

- The growth forecast for the *low-income developing country* group is marked down 0.6 percentage point relative to July, with the continuing slow rollout of vaccines as the main factor weighing on the recovery. IMF staff analysis indicates that low-income developing countries will require close to $200 billion in spending to combat the pandemic and $250 billion to regain the convergence paths they were on prior to the pandemic. Labor market prospects for low-skilled workers and youth continue to be relatively bleak compared to other demographic groups, pointing to increasing inequality and higher vulnerability to incomes falling below extreme poverty thresholds within countries in this group. About 65–75 million additional people are estimated to be in extreme poverty in 2021 compared to pre-pandemic projections.

Employment Growth Projected to Lag the Output Recovery

Labor market recovery is underway, but is uneven. Labor markets are recovering from a catastrophic hit in 2020. According to the International Labour Organization (see ILO 2021a), the decline in hours worked was equivalent to 255 million full-time jobs lost. But the pace is uneven across economies and workers. Employment around the world remains below its pre-pandemic levels, reflecting a mix of negative output gaps, worker fears of on-the-job infection in contact-intensive occupations, childcare constraints, labor demand changes as automation picks up in some sectors, replacement income through furlough schemes or unemployment benefits helping to cushion income losses, and frictions in job searches and matching.

Emerging market and developing economies have been hit harder than advanced economies, on average. International Labour Organization estimates (see ILO 2021b) suggest that Latin America and the Caribbean and South Asia were among the regions where declines in working hours in 2020 were particularly large.

Within economies, employment of youth and lower-skilled workers remains weaker than that of prime-age and higher-skilled workers (Figure 1.7). Women's employment in emerging market and developing economies remains more adversely impacted than men's, while in advanced economies, earlier differences by gender have largely subsided. Some of these asymmetric impacts reflect differences in

Figure 1.7. Labor Markets, by Economy and Worker Groups
(Average percent difference from 2019:Q4 to 2021:Q1)

Employment and participation in labor markets are still below their pre-pandemic levels, with emerging market and developing economies hit harder than advanced economies, on average. Developments have been highly unequal across worker groups, with youth and lower-skilled workers still more impacted.

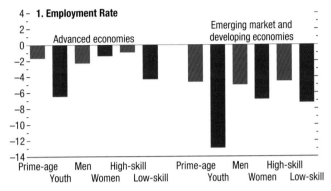

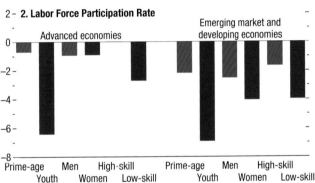

Sources: International Labour Organization; Organisation for Economic Co-operation and Development; and IMF staff calculations.
Note: The bars are derived from year fixed effects in a regression of each employment rate/labor force participation rate class on time and country fixed effects to account for sample changes (see Karbarbounis and Neiman 2014). High-skill = tertiary education and above; Low-skill = above secondary and nontertiary education and below; Prime-age = ages 25 to 54; Youth = ages 15 to 24. Value for the average labor force participation rate difference for high-skilled workers in advanced economies is 0.01 percent.

sectoral employment across worker groups. Youth and lower-skilled workers tend to be employed in sectors that are more contact-intensive and vulnerable to automation. These sectors have been more impacted by the pandemic and are experiencing an acceleration of the long-term trend toward greater automation (see Chapter 3 of the April 2021 WEO).

On the supply side of labor markets, participation is also troublingly lower than pre-pandemic, with historically more disadvantaged groups again exhibiting worse outcomes. Youth participation rates are more than 6 percent lower as of early 2021 in both advanced and emerging market economies, on average—much greater than the decline for prime-age workers (Figure 1.7, panel 2).

Lower-skilled workers' participation is also depressed. Similar to the differences in employment by gender, women's participation in emerging market and developing economies still shows a larger relative decline than men's, while in advanced economies they are roughly similar. If these participation gaps persist, they could have severe medium-term implications for economic inequalities across worker groups. Moreover, if participation does not rebound and firms cannot substitute with machines undertaking more tasks, it may put greater upward pressure on wages and prices as employers compete for scarcer workers.

Employment growth is expected to lag the output recovery. While recent developments are encouraging, the employment recovery is expected to lag output for a large share of economies—reflecting possible lingering health concerns, replacement income under furlough schemes or unemployment benefits cushioning income loss, and the accelerated shift to automation. All advanced economies are expected to regain pre-COVID-19 output levels by the end of 2022, but only two-thirds are projected to regain their earlier employment. Emerging market and developing economies show a similar pattern (Figure 1.8). This differential between projected output and employment recoveries suggests that COVID-19–related structural shifts may cause an increase in inequality and social tension, as discussed below.

Rises in Inflation, High Uncertainty

Even as employment rates remain below pre-pandemic levels—suggesting substantial labor market slack—headline inflation rates have increased rapidly in the United States and in some emerging market and developing economies in recent months, although there are differences in the extent of pressures across countries. In some countries in sub-Saharan Africa and the Middle East and Central Asia, food prices have increased significantly amid local shortages and the rise in global food prices. Core inflation—which removes the influence of food and energy prices—has also risen in many countries, but to a lesser extent (Figure 1.9).

To a large degree, the increase in inflation reflects a combination of pandemic-induced supply-demand mismatches, rising commodity prices, and policy-related developments (such as the expiration of last year's temporary value-added tax cut in Germany and the increase in the shelter component of US consumer prices as rent and mortgage moratoriums expire in some

Figure 1.8. Share of Economies Projected to Regain Pre-Pandemic Employment and Output Levels by 2022
(Percent)

Almost all advanced economies and a large fraction of emerging market and developing economies are expected to regain or surpass their pre-pandemic output levels by the end of 2022. The recovery in employment is instead expected to lag that of output in a number of countries.

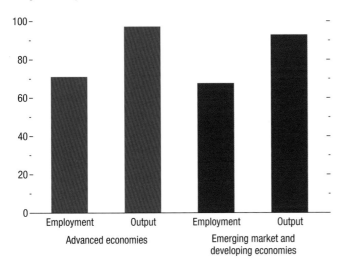

Source: IMF staff estimates.
Note: For employment, the bars measure the fraction of countries expected to regain 2019 employment by 2022. For output, the comparison is of real GDP between 2019:Q4 and 2022:Q4.

Figure 1.9. Inflation Trends
(Three-month moving average; annualized percent change)

Headline inflation has picked up on average, with advanced economies seeing a sharper rise. Core inflation has also increased, but more moderately.

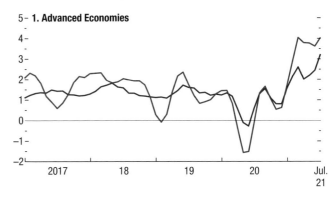

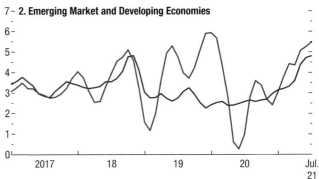

Sources: Consensus Economics; Haver Analytics; and IMF staff calculations.
Note: Average inflation rates by economy group are purchasing power parity GDP-weighted averages. In terms of International Organization for Standardization (ISO) country codes, advanced economies comprise AUT, BEL, CAN, CHE, CZE, DEU, DNK, ESP, EST, FIN, FRA, GBR, GRC, HKG, IRL, ISR, ITA, JPN, KOR, LTU, LUX, LVA, NLD, NOR, PRT, SGP, SVK, SVN, SWE, TWN, USA; emerging market and developing economies comprise BGR, BRA, CHL, CHN, COL, HUN, IDN, IND, MEX, MYS, PER, PHL, POL, ROU, RUS, THA, TUR, ZAF.

jurisdictions), rather than a sharp drop-off in spare capacity. In some countries, exchange rate depreciations have contributed to higher import goods prices.

Supply bottlenecks: The sharp contraction in demand in 2020 led many businesses to slash orders of inter-mediate inputs. As the recovery picked up steam in 2021, some producers found themselves flatfooted and unable to ramp up sufficient supply again quickly; for example, microchip production relative to demand remains hampered. Moreover, the world distribution of shipping containers became highly distorted during the pandemic, leaving many stranded off their usual routes. Temporary disruptions (such as the closure of the Suez Canal, restrictions in ports in China's Pearl River Delta following COVID-19 outbreaks, and con-gestion in the ports of Los Angeles and Long Beach) exacerbated delays in delivery times. Analysis of the Baltic Dry Index—an index of expenditures related to international shipping—suggests that the bulk of its rise over the past few months has been due to supply factors (Figure 1.10).

Rising commodity prices: Commodity prices have continued their upward tear with strengthening

economic activity (Figure 1.11). Oil prices are expected to increase in 2021, close to 60 percent above their low base for 2020. Non-oil commodity prices are expected to rise almost 30 percent above their 2020 levels, reflecting particularly strong increases in the price of metals and food over recent months (see also the Commodity Special Feature for further discussion, including on the impact of the energy transition on the markets for metals). Food price rises have unfor-tunately tended to concentrate in places where food insecurity is high, putting poorer households under greater stress and raising the specter of greater social unrest (Figure 1.12).

Figure 1.10. Supply and Demand Drivers of Shipping Expenditure Growth
(Percent)

Increases in the Baltic Dry Index were driven mostly by supply factors in 2021:Q1 and 2021:Q2.

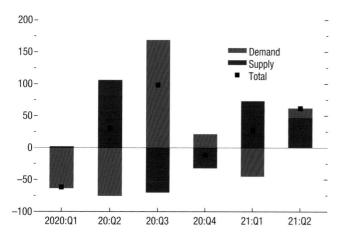

Sources: Haver Analytics; and IMF staff calculations.
Note: The decomposition is derived from a global dynamic factor model (GDFM) that includes 20 variables, including purchasing managers' index, industrial production, world trade, house prices, confidence indicators, and the Baltic Dry index. The GDFM was inspired by the Federal Reserve Bank of New York's nowcasting model. The decomposition is based on the Baltic Dry Index's average quarterly growth rate, and the demand component is what is explained by the model.

Figure 1.11. Commodity Prices
(Deflated using US consumer price index; 2014 = 100)

Commodity prices have risen markedly from their pandemic recession troughs.

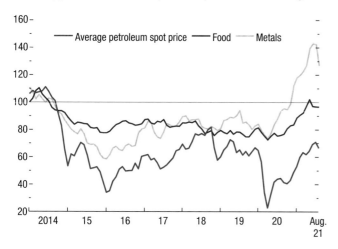

Sources: IMF, Primary Commodity Price System; and IMF staff calculations.

Figure 1.12. Food Price Inflation and Food Insecurity
(Percent)

Food price increases in the past two years have been more substantial in countries where food insecurity is more prevalent.

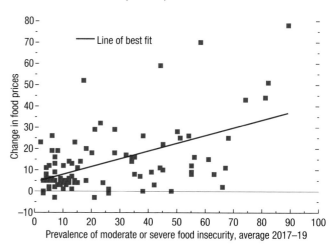

Sources: Food and Agriculture Organization of the United Nations; and IMF staff calculations.
Note: Each square corresponds to one country. Five countries with changes in prices larger than 100 percent are not shown in the figure to enhance readability. The change in food prices is the percent change between March 2019 and March 2021.

Wage growth has been high in some sectors. As the recovery continues, labor markets have tightened, making it more difficult for employers in some countries to fill positions quickly. For example, the ratio of job openings to unemployed workers is close to 1 in the United States. Consistent with a resumption of greater activity, there are signs of higher wage growth in some sectors—for instance, leisure and hospitality, retail, and transportation in the United States (Figure 1.13). At the same time, wages for individuals with either lower incomes or lower levels of educational attainment have improved better-than-average compared to a year ago, according to the Federal Reserve Bank of Atlanta's Wage Growth Tracker—which follows the same employed individuals over time, thereby correcting for compositional changes due to entry and exit. Overall, average, economy-wide nominal wage inflation remains contained (Canada, Germany, Spain, United Kingdom, United States).

Inflation expectations appear contained across most economies. Some household survey-based measures, for example in the United States, have registered a recent increase in inflation expectations—possibly linked to rising fuel prices. Moreover, market-implied measures

Figure 1.13. US Average Hourly Earnings: Overall and Selected Sectors
(Annualized percent change of three-month moving average)

Wages in the United States are rising, markedly in sectors hit harder by the pandemic.

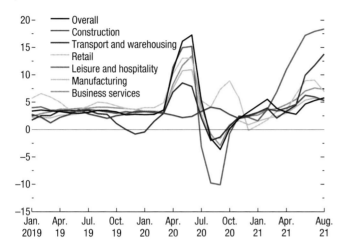

Sources: Haver Analytics; and IMF staff calculations.
Note: Hourly earnings are seasonally adjusted.

Figure 1.14. Five-Year, Five-Year Inflation Swaps
(Percent)

Inflation in the United States and euro area is expected to be slightly higher over the medium term, but it remains contained.

Sources: Bloomberg Finance L.P.; and IMF staff calculations.
Note: Market-implied average inflation rate expected over the five-year period starting five years from date shown.

also point to inflation pressure over a two- to three-year horizon, consistent with the Federal Reserve's Average Inflation Targeting policy framework. However, market-implied medium-term inflation expectations have so far remained well behaved, hovering around the levels seen just before the pandemic struck in early 2020 (Figure 1.14).

Inflation outlook: The various indicators discussed above point to a highly uncertain outlook for inflation (see Chapter 2 for a more in-depth analysis). In the baseline projections, across most economies, inflation is expected to come down to its pre-pandemic range in 2022, once supply-demand mismatches resolve. This is motivated by three pieces of evidence: (1) labor market slack remains large, even as job postings have increased, with employment rates typically below their pre-shock levels; (2) in large, advanced economies, inflation expectations are still well anchored, according to benchmark market-based measures; and (3) structural factors that have lowered the sensitivity of prices to shrinking labor market slack—such as increasing automation—continue to operate or are even intensifying. However, the lagged pass-through to broader inflation from higher food and oil prices for importers means that price pressures are anticipated to stay elevated into 2022 in some emerging market and developing economies. In economies where the

stock of vacant dwellings is low, the pandemic shock and low borrowing costs have also spurred an increase in house prices. This has already directly impacted headline inflation in these economies through its impact on imputed rents and could contribute to more persistent inflationary pressures if demand remains high, as it takes time to increase the housing stock (see Box 1.1 for a detailed look at real estate price dynamics and inflation).

The evolution of inflation expectations in this uncharted recovery will prove decisive for the inflation outlook. The aftershocks from the upheaval of 2020 and the prospect of renewed restrictions to slow virus transmission could translate into more persistent supply disruptions. Faced with continued rising demand, firms may increase prices and workers may bid up wages more broadly than has occurred so far. More generally, should households, businesses, and investors begin anticipating that price pressures from pent-up demand and the many factors outlined above will persist, there is a risk that medium-term inflation expectations could drift upward and lead to a self-fulfilling further rise in prices (as prices and wages are reset in line with higher inflation expectations). As noted, there are no signs of such a shift, with expectations still tightly bound to central banks' stated targets.

Large Differences in Medium-Term Economic Losses Linger

The differential recovery speeds across economy groups are likely to leave long-lasting imprints. The pattern of emerging market and developing economies suffering larger medium-term damages compared to advanced economies on average—discussed in Chapter 2 of the April 2021 WEO—persists in the latest projections.

Output losses: Activity is generally expected to remain below its pre-pandemic path through 2023 across economy groups (Figure 1.15, panel 1). Output in the advanced economy group is projected to return to pre-pandemic trends by 2022 and rise slightly above it thereafter, mainly because of the anticipated additional policy support in the United States. The other income groups, however, are expected to remain below their pre-pandemic paths throughout the forecast horizon. Moreover, negative output gaps—indicative of slack—are expected across many economies over the next three years (Figure 1.15, panel 2). In other words, scarring— defined as medium-term economic performance below pre-shock projections—is expected to be pervasive outside of the advanced economy group (Figure 1.15, panel 3).

As discussed in Chapter 2 of the April 2021 WEO, the pattern of medium-term damages across economy groups is different from what was observed after the 2008–09 global financial crisis. Then, advanced economies were hit hard and emerging market and developing economies fared better. Today the reverse appears likely, consistent with the greater protection against further COVID-19 shocks from more widespread vaccinations in many advanced economies and sizable policy support. The better-than-expected performance in the United States, for example— where output is anticipated to end up above its pre-pandemic trend—reflects the impacts of the new structural investments planned by the government, upgrading dilapidated infrastructure, and hastening a green energy transition.

Labor market scarring: A similar picture of lasting effects emerges when looking at labor markets, suggesting that employment is a major channel through which economic scarring manifests. As with output, worse-than-expected employment prospects are concentrated in emerging market and developing economies (Figure 1.15, panel 4).

Figure 1.15. Medium-Term Prospects: Output and Employment
(Percent, unless noted otherwise)

Output and employment over the medium term are expected to remain below pre-pandemic trends in many places.

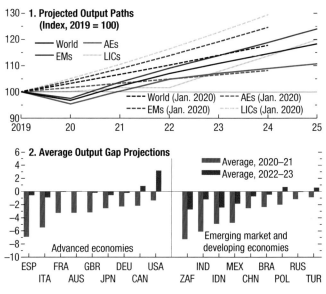

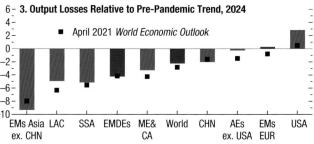

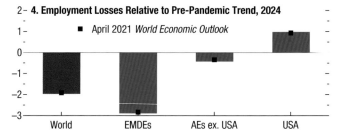

Source: IMF staff calculations.
Note: Data labels use International Organization for Standardization (ISO) country codes. Output in panels 1 and 3 is real GDP. Output gap in panel 2 is the difference between real and potential GDP as a percent of potential GDP. Medium-term losses in panels 3 and 4 are the difference between forecasts of the indicated variable for 2024 from the October 2021 WEO and January 2020 WEO *Update* vintages. The sample of countries in panel 4 comprises those which have comparable employment projections in both vintages. The EMDE employment aggregate excludes China and India due to changes in employment definitions across vintages. AEs = advanced economies; AEs ex. USA = advanced economies (excluding the United States); EMs = emerging market economies; EMs Asia ex. CHN/EUR = emerging market economies (in Asia excluding China, in Europe); EMDEs = emerging market and developing economies; LAC = Latin American and Caribbean economies; LICs = low-income countries; ME&CA = Middle Eastern and Central Asian economies; SA = sub-Saharan African economies; WEO = *World Economic Outlook*.

Early responses to the health and economic crisis are expected to limit persistent losses. When unpacking these patterns further, high persistence in output and employment shocks is anticipated, with revisions this year passing through almost one-for-one with expectations five years out. Such persistence—particularly of adverse shocks—has been well-documented in the recent literature. This feature suggests that actions to improve output and employment outcomes today are very likely to pay out dramatically through reduced scarring. This is especially true when it comes to the speed of vaccinations—a key driver of medium-term growth upgrades since April 2021 (Figure 1.16). Forecasts for medium-term output have been revised up more for countries with higher vaccination rates. Additional fiscal support to households and firms in response to the pandemic since April 2021 is associated with a small downgrade to output, suggesting that recent countercyclical support has been concentrated in economies where the recovery lags.

Trade Growing, Imbalances Projected to Narrow over the Medium-Term

Global trade: Despite temporary disruptions, trade volumes are expected to grow almost 10 percent in 2021, moderating to about 7 percent in 2022—in line with the projected broader global recovery. Trade growth is projected to moderate to about 3.5 percent over the medium term. The overall trade recovery masks a subdued outlook for tourism-dependent economies and cross-border services more generally. As noted in the October 2020 WEO, countries where tourism and travel account for a larger share of GDP are projected to suffer larger declines in activity compared to pre–COVID-19 forecasts. Travel restrictions and lingering fears of contagion are likely to weigh on cross-border tourist activity until virus transmission declines durably.

Global current account balances: As noted in the 2021 *External Sector Report*, global current account balances—the sum of absolute deficits and surpluses—are set to widen for the second successive year in 2021 following an increase in 2020. The widening in 2020 reflected the impact of the pandemic—seen in elevated exports of some goods (medical equipment, work-from-home electronics, consumer durables), subdued travel, and lower

Figure 1.16. Correlates of Projected Output Revisions
(Percentage points)

Higher COVID-19 vaccination rates are associated with improved output expectations across horizons since April 2021, while increased fiscal support measures since then appear more concentrated in places where the recovery is lagging. Infections rates do not exhibit a relationship to recent output revisions.

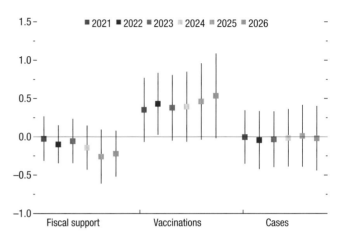

Sources: IMF, Database of Country Fiscal Measures in Response to the COVID-19 Pandemic; Our World In Data; and IMF staff calculations.
Note: Figure shows point estimates and 90 percent confidence intervals (with heteroscedasticity-consistent standard errors) for coefficients of a cross-sectional, cross-country regression (unweighted) of forecast revisions at different horizons since the April 2021 *World Economic Outlook* on the set of explanatory variables (shown) and region fixed effects (not shown). The Seychelles are excluded from the estimation sample as an extreme outlier as identified by Cook's distance metric. Fiscal support refers to additional above-the-line spending and forgone revenues and liquidity support in response to COVID-19 between March 17, 2021, and June 5, 2021, as a share of GDP. Vaccinations and cases are the difference in the cumulative share of population either fully vaccinated or diagnosed with COVID-19, respectively, between March 31, 2021, and September 28, 2021. Explanatory variables are standardized to have zero mean and unit standard deviation.

oil prices. For 2021 the widening reflects a larger deficit in the United States from the increased fiscal support and corresponding increases in surpluses. Current account balances are expected to narrow over 2022–26, reflecting anticipated declines in the US deficit and China's surplus (Figure 1.17, panel 1).

Global creditor and debtor positions: Stocks of external assets and liabilities are close to historic highs, even after allowing for the fact that the substantial widening as a share of global GDP in 2020 reflects the large drop in the denominator and valuation changes (Figure 1.17, panel 2). As noted in the 2021 *External Sector Report*, this poses risks to both debtor and creditor economies. The stocks are expected to decline somewhat in 2021 and shrink modestly thereafter, consistent with the gradual narrowing of global current account balances.

Figure 1.17. Current Account and International Investment Positions
(Percent of global GDP)

Current account balances are expected to narrow over 2022–26, while global stocks of external assets and liabilities are anticipated to remain near their historical highs.

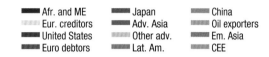

■ Afr. and ME	■ Japan	■ China
Eur. creditors	■ Adv. Asia	Oil exporters
■ United States	Other adv.	■ Em. Asia
■ Euro debtors	■ Lat. Am.	CEE

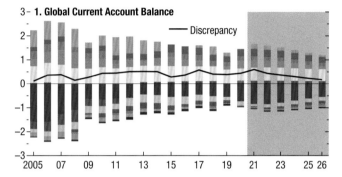

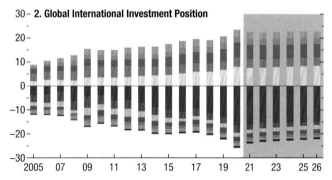

Source: IMF staff estimates.
Note: Adv. Asia = advanced Asia (Hong Kong SAR, Korea, Singapore, Taiwan Province of China); Afr. and ME = Africa and the Middle East (Democratic Republic of the Congo, Egypt, Ethiopia, Ghana, Jordan, Kenya, Lebanon, Morocco, South Africa, Sudan, Tanzania, Tunisia); CEE = central and eastern Europe (Belarus, Bulgaria, Croatia, Czech Republic, Hungary, Poland, Romania, Slovak Republic, Turkey, Ukraine); Em. Asia = emerging Asia (India, Indonesia, Pakistan, Philippines, Thailand, Vietnam); Eur. creditors = European creditors (Austria, Belgium, Denmark, Finland, Germany, Luxembourg, The Netherlands, Norway, Sweden, Switzerland); Euro debtors = euro area debtors (Cyprus, Greece, Ireland, Italy, Portugal, Spain, Slovenia); Lat. Am. = Latin America (Argentina, Brazil, Chile, Colombia, Mexico, Peru, Uruguay); Oil exporters = Algeria, Azerbaijan, Iran, Kazakhstan, Kuwait, Nigeria, Oman, Qatar, Russia, Saudi Arabia, United Arab Emirates, Venezuela; Other adv. = other advanced economies (Australia, Canada, France, Iceland, New Zealand, United Kingdom).

Uncertainty Grows as Variants Threaten the Recovery's Resilience

The baseline forecast is subject to high uncertainty regarding the evolution of the pandemic, the outlook for inflation, and the associated shifts in global financial conditions. The balance of risks suggests that growth outcomes—over both the near and medium

term—are more likely to disappoint than to register positive surprises.

On the *downside*, the main risk factors are the following (some of these aspects are explored in alternative scenarios using the IMF's G20 Model—see the Scenario Box):

- *Emergence of more transmissible and deadlier SARS-CoV-2 variants* could further re-energize the pandemic's spread and intensity, prolonging the pandemic and precipitating pullbacks of economic activity. Trade disruptions and supply-demand mismatches could increase with port closures due to renewed lockdowns. Early studies suggest that existing vaccines may show reduced efficacy against the Delta variant, although their levels of protection against severe disease still remain high. Roadblocks in the global distribution of vaccines to countries still lacking sufficient access, high levels of vaccine hesitancy in countries with advanced vaccination campaigns, and any other factors that delay broad vaccine coverage of the world population, heighten these risks. Each infection represents another opportunity for the virus to mutate into an even more detrimental pathogen.

- *More persistent supply-demand mismatches, price pressures, and faster-than-anticipated monetary policy normalization:* Pandemic-induced supply-demand mismatches could persist longer than expected, leading to sustained price pressures and rising inflation expectations. In response, a faster-than-anticipated monetary normalization in advanced economies could lead to a sudden tightening of global financial conditions. Compressed volatility and elevated equity price valuations point to the possibility of rapid repricing of financial assets in the event of a reassessment of the outlook (see the October 2021 *Global Financial Stability Report*). As discussed in the April 2021 WEO, vulnerable emerging market and developing economies with large foreign currency debt and financing needs would be particularly exposed. Difficulties with rolling over their external obligations could force abrupt adjustments in these economies, leading to adverse growth outcomes.

- *Financial market volatility:* More generally, in a context of stretched asset valuations, investor sentiment could shift rapidly because of adverse news on the pandemic or policy developments. A pressing concern is the ongoing impasse over the US debt ceiling. Failure to lift the ceiling before the US Treasury runs out of resources to meet its spending and debt repayment obligations (estimated by the US

Treasury to occur around mid-October) could have serious implications for financial markets. Similarly, large-scale disorderly corporate debt defaults or restructuring, for instance in China's property sector, could reverberate widely.

- *Smaller US fiscal package:* The baseline forecast assumes a fiscal impulse in the United States broadly consistent with the infrastructure bill recently passed by the Senate and the administration's blueprint to remake the US social safety net. Any significant change in the size or composition of the fiscal package will have repercussions for US growth prospects and those of its trading partners.

- *Greater social unrest:* Instances of social unrest had declined during the early phases of the pandemic but rose in the second half of 2020 and at the beginning of 2021 (Barrett and Chen 2021). The causes vary across countries. Frustration with the handling of the pandemic is juxtaposed in some cases with the increase in food prices, slow employment growth, and long-standing erosion of trust in government institutions. A further intensification could damage sentiment and weigh on the recovery. Recent turmoil in Afghanistan has worsened the humanitarian situation in the region and is fueling a wave of refugees, with the potential to further increase regional tensions, economic spillovers, and fiscal strains on host countries.

- *More adverse climate shocks:* Climate change, a principal driver of more frequent and intense weather-related disasters, already has had visible immediate impacts, with spillovers beyond the regions where the disasters strike. Cross-border migration pressures, financial stresses (including among creditors and insurers in countries not directly impacted by a given event), and health care burdens may rise, with implications that persist long after the event itself. Against the backdrop of the ongoing pandemic, climate shocks may pose further challenges to the global recovery.

- *Cyberattacks:* An increase in the spread and destructiveness of cyberattacks involving critical infrastructure could act as further drags on the recovery (as evinced by recent and damaging ransomware cases), particularly as telework and automation increase.

- *Intensification of trade and technology tensions:* Geopolitical risks remain elevated. An escalation of trade and technology tensions, notably between the United States and China, could weigh on investment and productivity growth, raising additional roadblocks in the recovery path.

On the *upside*:

- *Faster vaccine production and distribution:* Large amounts of new vaccine supplies are expected to come online over the coming months, both in terms of production of existing vaccines and deployment of completely new vaccines. Pledges have also been made by countries with large stocks of unused vaccines to donate them. A faster pace of vaccinations than what is assumed in the baseline projections would have a direct positive effect on economic activity. It could also boost the confidence of consumers and firms, triggering a rise in spending and investment that would strengthen the economic recovery.

- *Productivity growth spurt:* The pandemic has accelerated change across many sectors of the economy through greater automation and a transformation of workplaces that can rely more on technology platforms to conduct work remotely. Productivity growth could accelerate as a result of these changes in production, distribution, and payment systems. More specifically, faster and more effective deployment and implementation of structural investment plans (for example, in the context of the anticipated public investment push in the United States and the Next Generation EU plan) could lift the medium-term growth outlook for regions where subdued long-term prospects have long been a concern. In turn, this could lead to stronger investment and more robust near-term growth.

Policy Actions to Strengthen the Recovery

The large divergences in economic losses and the sizable downside risks surrounding the conjuncture discussed above call for strong policy effort at both multilateral and national levels to strengthen global economic prospects. This section first discusses multilateral priority actions to address the pandemic (highlighting vaccine deployment), climate policy, and international liquidity. It then turns to national policies to complement the multilateral effort. These will require much more tailoring to country-specific conditions and better targeting, as policy space constraints become more binding the longer the pandemic lasts.

Multilateral Actions with Positive Spillovers

Global vaccine deployment: The global community needs to increase its efforts to vaccinate adequate numbers everywhere. This would save millions of lives by reducing risks of severe health outcomes and deaths, lower the risks of new variants emerging, and thereby add trillions of dollars to the global economic recovery. It would also reduce the expected divergence in recoveries between advanced and emerging market and developing economy groups.

- Most of the currently approved vaccines markedly lower the risk of severe disease from all current COVID-19 variants and thus limit hospitalizations and deaths. The case of the United Kingdom is instructive in the effectiveness of large-scale vaccination campaigns, even against highly contagious variants. Although the number of confirmed daily COVID-19 cases in July 2021 was higher than that seen in December 2020 for most of the month (reflecting the greater infectiousness of the Delta variant), hospitalization and death rates were only 10–20 percent of the levels registered last winter (Figure 1.18). The key difference between the two points in time is that the United Kingdom had fully vaccinated about half of its population (two-thirds at least partially vaccinated) by July 2021, whereas in 2020 there was no vaccine protection available.

- In addition to preventing severe health outcomes, recent evidence from the United States suggests that widespread vaccinations can also have powerful, positive economic effects, bolstering the recovery. US counties where first-dose vaccinations went up showed a simultaneous boost in weekly credit card spending and a decline in weekly unemployment claims (Figure 1.19).

- The IMF has proposed a plan—jointly endorsed by the World Health Organization, the World Bank, and the World Trade Organization—to vaccinate at least 40 percent of the population in every country by the end of 2021 and 70 percent by mid-2022, alongside ensuring adequate diagnostics and therapeutics (Agarwal and Gopinath 2021).[1] At an estimated cost of about $50 billion, the plan has the potential to yield massive social and economic

[1]The 70 percent coverage target by mid-2022 is driven by the health and economic imperatives of stopping the pandemic as rapidly as possible. This is higher than the originally proposed 60 percent target for mid-2022 given the rise of more infectious variants. The revised target is consistent with the downside risk scenario envisioned in the original $50 billion IMF staff proposal released in May 2021, under which 1 billion *additional* doses were designated for low- and lower-middle income countries—and is aligned with the updated World Health Organization global vaccination strategy. The national targets may need to be adjusted based on age demographics and policy developments.

Figure 1.18. COVID-19 Vaccine Rollouts and Health Outcomes: The Case of the United Kingdom
(Per million)

Despite similar COVID-19 infection rate paths in July 2021 and December 2020 in the United Kingdom, hospitalization and death rates were substantially lower in July 2021, reflecting widespread vaccinations.

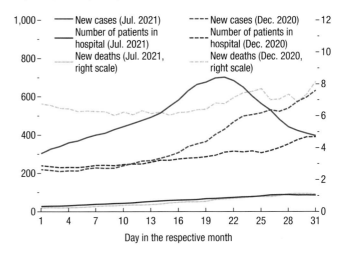

Sources: Airfinity; Our World in Data; and IMF staff calculations.
Note: As of July 31, 2021, 56.5 percent of the UK population was fully vaccinated and 69 percent had received at least one dose. In December 2020, rates were effectively zero as the mass vaccination effort had yet to start.

Figure 1.19. COVID-19 Vaccinations and Economic Activity in US Counties
(Percent change, year over year, relative to pre-pandemic levels)

Counties in the United States that had increased vaccination rates saw higher spending and reduced unemployment.

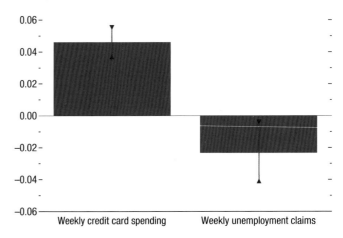

Sources: Centers for Disease Control and Prevention; Opportunity Insights Economic Tracker; and IMF staff calculations.
Note: The figure shows the average effect of a 10-percentage-point rise in the fully vaccinated population share. For spending, the estimation sample covers 1,608 counties in weeks 12–21 in 2021. For unemployment claims, the estimation sample covers 378 counties in weeks 12–24 in 2021. Credit card spending is the year-over-year change as percent of the January 2020 level. Unemployment claims are expressed as percent of the 2019 labor force. Regressions control for county and state time fixed effects.

Figure 1.20. Gaps in Vaccination Rates across Economies
(Percent)

Over half of the countries in the world are not on track to reach the goal of vaccinating 40 percent of their population by the end of 2021.

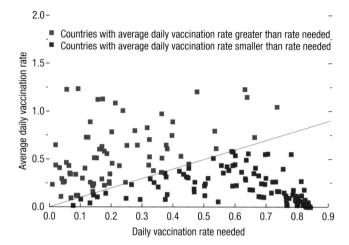

Sources: Our World in Data; and IMF staff calculations.
Note: Data are as of September 22, 2021. *X*-axis shows daily vaccination rates needed to reach 40 percent of population fully vaccinated by end-2021, assuming two-dose vaccines. *Y*-axis shows average daily vaccination rates in the preceding seven days. Each square corresponds to a country. Countries that have already reached the 40 percent threshold are not shown. The line indicates the 45-degree line.

returns. Over half of the countries in the world—accounting for 35 percent of global population—are not on track to achieve the 40 percent mark by the end of 2021 (Figure 1.20). There is an urgent need for *vaccine donations* by countries with large shares of their population already vaccinated. The IMF proposal estimates that at least 1 billion doses could be shared by the end of 2021 without jeopardizing national vaccination targets. Recent pledges by China, the Group of Seven, and other countries in that direction are welcome steps, though donations should be accelerated to rapidly fulfill the commitments (by mid-September, only about 19 percent of the 850 million doses pledged by the Group of Seven to COVAX in June has been delivered). It is also crucial to *prioritize vaccine deliveries* to countries that still lack wide access—including by enhancing supply to collective procurement vehicles, such as COVAX. Quickly *removing remaining restrictions on exports* of medical equipment, raw materials, and finished vaccines is another priority. *Diversifying and increasing vaccine production and distribution capabilities* (including via at-risk investments in doses on behalf of low-income developing countries)

are important to speed up the broad coverage of the world population. Such actions would enhance readiness to react and adapt to unexpected turns in the pandemic, including the potential need for booster shots if immunity wanes or new variants emerge. More generally, it remains crucial to increase funding for *testing, tracing, and therapeutics* to improve diagnostics and treatment *while scaling up genomic surveillance* for early detection of new variants. Any actions that help contain and mitigate the health effects from SARS-CoV-2 increase further in importance as the likelihood that the virus becomes endemic rises with the persistence of the pandemic.

Mitigating and adapting to climate change: The past few months have witnessed a panoply of extreme weather-related events, including the heat domes and intense wildfires in Canada and the United States, high precipitation and flooding in Europe, drought in Brazil, and floods in eastern and south Asia. Combined with evidence from the Intergovernmental Panel on Climate Change that the world is experiencing the warmest period in over 100,000 years, these events have further raised fears that the highly adverse consequences of climate change may arise sooner rather than later, increasing the urgency of actions to reduce these risks and improve resilience.

- Greenhouse gas emissions due to human activity are on a steep upward trajectory—with the dip due to the acute pandemic rapidly reversing. Commitments and realized actions to reduce emissions must be ramped up. The existing nationally determined contributions for reductions in greenhouse gas emissions are insufficiently ambitious, remaining far above the level consistent with capping the average global temperature increase at 2 degrees Celsius above pre-industrial levels—a commonly agreed limit to contain the risks of catastrophic effects from warming (Figure 1.21, panel 1).
- Moreover, there are still few signs of concrete actions in aggregate policy measures—tax revenue related to environmental policy objectives as a share of GDP have tended to decline on average over the past 15 years, while public expenditures on environmental policy objectives as a share of GDP have stayed largely flat (Figure 1.21, panel 2). Similarly, even though there has been a sizable increase in the coverage of greenhouse gas emissions subject to control under emissions trading schemes or similar carbon pricing measures in recent years, only about

Figure 1.21. Climate Change Policy Gaps

World greenhouse gas emissions are far in excess of current national commitments to reduce emissions, which in turn are not ambitious enough to cap global temperature increase at well below 2 degrees Celsius.

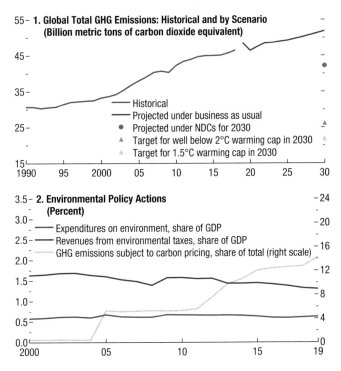

1. Global Total GHG Emissions: Historical and by Scenario
   (Billion metric tons of carbon dioxide equivalent)

— Historical
— Projected under business as usual
● Projected under NDCs for 2030
▲ Target for well below 2°C warming cap in 2030
▲ Target for 1.5°C warming cap in 2030

2. Environmental Policy Actions
   (Percent)

— Expenditures on environment, share of GDP
— Revenues from environmental taxes, share of GDP
⋯ GHG emissions subject to carbon pricing, share of total (right scale)

Sources: IMF, Climate Change Indicators Dashboard; World Bank, Carbon Pricing Dashboard; and IMF staff calculations.
Note: Total GHG emissions are calculated excluding potential effects from land use, land-use change, and forestry. IMF estimates of NDCs are based on commitments as of August 2021. Expenditures and revenues related to environmental policies at the country level are aggregated using purchasing-power-parity GDP weights for a constant composition country sample, covering countries that account for about 30 percent (expenditures) and 65 percent (revenues) of world GDP. More detailed descriptions of all the variables in the figure and their calculations are included in Box A.2 in the Statistical Appendix. GHG = greenhouse gas; NDCs = nationally determined contributions.

one-fifth of emissions are covered, even after the adoption by China of its national emission trading scheme in July this year.

- The global and multifaceted nature of the climate change challenge requires a well-coordinated policy response, for which the upcoming United Nations Climate Change Conference (COP26) is an excellent opportunity to negotiate and make concrete. An ideal policy mix would include: (1) an international carbon price floor adjusted to country circumstances—a transparent and effective instrument that can tilt the balance of incentives away from the most polluting energy sources; (2) a green public investment program and research subsidies to support the development and deployment of

new clean energies and low-carbon technologies—from renewables to hydrogen and longer-lasting and faster-charging batteries to carbon capture, utilization, and storage systems; and (3) targeted transfer schemes that ensure a fair and equitable transition by channeling back some of the revenues from carbon pricing to households adversely affected by the climate policies implemented while maintaining the behavioral incentives to shift their consumption bundle. As discussed in Chapter 3 of the October 2020 WEO, a green infrastructure push at the current conjecture is a win-win strategy that can strengthen the recovery from the pandemic through investment with high returns—both in terms of output and employment—while tackling one of the major challenges of our times (also see Chapter 3 of the October 2021 *Global Financial Stability Report* on the role of sustainable finance in facilitating the energy transition). At the same time, multilateral support via cross-border technology transfer and climate finance initiatives can help ensure that the transition is not limited only to countries that can afford such mitigation measures. An analysis of employment according to the tasks involved in occupations and whether they would be directly impacted by the green transformation of the economy suggests that the green task intensity of the average job has picked up slightly over the past 10 years, to just under 2.5 percent. Green jobs are present in all sectors, but more so in industry, with workers in those jobs having higher skills and incomes, pointing to complementarities between investing in people and greening the economy (Box 1.2).

Easing financial constraints of struggling countries and tackling debt vulnerabilities: The months of health emergency and subdued global economic activity have entailed substantial public finance interventions, stretching budgets and posing enormous challenges to countries that entered the pandemic with already-limited fiscal space. The IMF has stepped in by providing more than $110 billion in new financing to 86 countries since the early phases of the pandemic. A further boost to countries' reserve assets came from the *General Allocation of Special Drawing Rights* equivalent to $650 billion that took place in late August, with emerging market and developing economies receiving about 40 percent of the allocation (and potentially more through voluntary channeling of special drawing rights from countries with stronger external positions). These and other initiatives by the IMF and the international community—including the Debt Service Suspension Initiative (DSSI) by the Group of Twenty, extended to December 2021—are helping countries avoid even larger reductions in essential health care–related spending while meeting their external payment obligations (see the October 2021 *Fiscal Monitor*). Nevertheless, in cases where sovereign debt is not sustainable or where financing needs are large, liquidity relief may not be enough. The Common Framework for Debt Treatments beyond the DSSI endorsed by the Group of Twenty last year aimed to provide a mechanism for timely and orderly debt restructurings that can prevent the higher costs of protracted debt crises, but its implementation in the initial country cases has been too slow, calling for urgent improvements in this area given the expiry of the DSSI at the end of 2021.

Defusing trade and technology tensions and instituting an international minimum corporate tax: Many of the cross-border trade and technology frictions that predate the pandemic continue to fester. The increased trade restrictions implemented in 2018–19, for example, remain in place and risk impeding the recovery. Countries should cooperate to remove these restrictions, address the grievances at the root of long-standing disputes, and strengthen the rules-based multilateral trading system—including by resolving the impasse over appointments to the World Trade Organization's Appellate Body. In parallel, they should finalize an agreement on a global minimum for corporate taxes, avoiding a race to the bottom and helping bolster public finances to fund critical investments.

National-Level Policies Adjusted to Pandemic Conditions and Policy Space Constraints

Quick and strong policy actions at the national level thwarted even worse economic outcomes through last year's recession and have fostered the recovery from that unprecedented collapse. As discussed in the April 2021 WEO, without the direct fiscal actions and liquidity support policies implemented across Group of Twenty economies in 2020, the contraction in global activity could have been at least three times worse than the actual outcome. Moreover, extraordinary monetary policy actions—including, for the first time, asset purchases by many emerging market central banks—and

regulatory efforts to support credit helped prevent a systemic financial crisis.

Reduced policy space, tighter constraints: These actions have, however, reduced policy space in many countries, leaving them with limited room to address any further setbacks. Public debt has gone up significantly across all income groups (see the October 2021 *Fiscal Monitor*), while inflation has also increased sharply in many countries. However, the pandemic is far from over and its path subject to high uncertainty—the prospects for a protracted stop-and-go recovery cannot be excluded. National-level policies to support the recovery confront difficult choices in this environment and, especially for emerging market and developing economies, generally must work within tighter constraints than at the onset of the crisis.

A policy approach tailored to a country's pandemic and economic conditions: The priority must remain critical health care spending—on the rollout of vaccines, testing, and treatments—with targeted emergency support to households and firms most impacted by public health measures to contain the spread of the virus. International aid may be required in those economies where fiscal constraints or local capacities do not permit more action to safeguard lives. The longer the pandemic persists, resources will also need to be increasingly devoted to worker retraining and support for reallocation away from sectors struggling to regain pre-pandemic vitality. Even when the pandemic's ferocity abates, the steady rollout of vaccines and investments to fortify human health must proceed to help secure the recovery against future resurgences. Broad-based demand support and remedial measures to address the scars from the shock can be deployed to further bolster the economy, as policy space allows. This will also be the time to invest in the future, taking the opportunity to advance long-term goals and improve the economy's potential and resilience. Health metrics—such as infection, hospitalization, and mortality rates, as well as the population share protected by vaccines—can help policymakers recognize how and when to adapt policies.

Recognizing the constraints by country: Beyond the recurring ups and downs of the pandemic, the uncharted nature of the recovery further complicates policymaking. Standard dashboard measures to assess the cyclical position—such as the output gap—are subject to even greater uncertainty than in a typical business cycle. Near-term macroeconomic policies should aim for the maximum level of employment without compromising the credibility of policymaking institutions while ensuring fiscal sustainability and financial stability. At the same time, near-term policies should be designed to work seamlessly alongside measures to promote longer-term objectives of stronger and more equitable growth and resilience. Specifically:

- *Fiscal policies* should be undertaken within medium-term frameworks to improve tradeoffs between providing cyclical support now, building buffers to address future shocks, and advancing long-term structural goals. Fiscal frameworks featuring a clear operational rule, a medium-term debt anchor reinforced with pre-approved revenue and expenditure measures to be implemented after the acute phase of the crisis fades, and well-articulated escape clauses can enhance countercyclical stabilization while strengthening credibility (October 2021 *Fiscal Monitor*).

- Fiscal policymakers should continue to prioritize spending to end the pandemic—including on vaccine production and distribution infrastructure; storage and dispensing facilities; campaigns to boost take-up; and health workers to implement vaccinations, testing, and therapies. The longer the pandemic persists, fiscal space constraints will bind tighter in some countries. Lifelines, transfers, and short-time work programs will need to become better targeted. To facilitate worker reallocation from shrinking to growing sectors, hiring subsidies, job search and matching assistance, and training, alongside critical income support for displaced workers, will need to be deployed. As the pandemic is brought under control, the emphasis can be shifted toward measures to secure the recovery and invest in the future, as fiscal space allows.

- Where fiscal space is more limited—particularly in some emerging market and developing economies—poorly targeted subsidies and recurrent expenditure will need to be pared back to create room for needed health care and social spending and infrastructure outlays. These efforts can be reinforced with initiatives to strengthen tax compliance and improve revenue administration. As noted, strong international support, particularly for vulnerable economies, will be needed to supplement domestic initiatives.

- *Monetary policy* should not lose sight of central bankers' hard-won credibility for maintaining price stability. As the recent experience with large-scale asset purchases has demonstrated, independent central banks with credible policy frameworks can implement countercyclical support more effectively in downturns, highlighting their value in responding to shocks (Box 1.3). The unprecedented conjuncture makes transparent and clear communication about the outlook for monetary policy even more critical. In particular, clear central bank communications about the persistence of inflation drivers, any changes in views about inflation, and the monetary policy outlook will continue to be critical to shaping expectations.

- Although central banks can generally look through transitory inflation pressures and avoid tightening until there is more clarity on underlying price dynamics, they should be prepared to act quickly if the recovery strengthens faster than expected—as the Bank of Canada did when it scaled back its asset purchase programs in April and July. Early preemptive action will be required where there is a tangible risk of rising inflation expectations and more persistent price increases.

- Central banks with dual mandates in economies confronting rising inflation against the backdrop of still-subdued employment rates and labor market slack face particularly difficult choices. The response in such a setting, where the risks of inflation expectations de-anchoring rise significantly, may be to tighten monetary policy to get ahead of price pressures, even if that means the employment recovery is delayed. The alternative of waiting for stronger employment outcomes while allowing price pressures to build runs the risk that inflation increases in a self-fulfilling way, creating more uncertainty and undermining the credibility of the central bank—which could hold back private investment and lead to precisely the slower employment recovery that the central bank hopes to avoid by waiting to tighten policy.

- In economies where the recovery is strengthening, inflation has risen, and health protections—such as widespread vaccinations—are an effective bulwark against the pandemic, central banks can more forcefully signal forthcoming monetary policy normalization. In the United States, the baseline forecast is for a strong, sustained recovery with output expected to exceed potential over much of the forecast horizon. As this solidifies, the Federal Reserve should communicate a scaling back of asset purchases and begin tapering in late 2021 to prepare for a policy rate liftoff in late 2022. By contrast, where inflation pressures are contained, inflation expectations are still below the central bank target, and labor market slack remains—for instance, in the euro area and Japan—monetary policy can remain accommodative.

Financial sector policies and resolution frameworks: Measures to support credit and stabilize balance sheets—including credit guarantees, debt moratoria, and release of capital and liquidity buffers—should become more targeted (see the October 2021 *Global Financial Stability Report*). Support can be focused, for example, on smaller but viable banks and firms in sectors where the recovery is lagging because of ongoing health-related concerns. At the same time, policymakers should strengthen out-of-court mechanisms to expedite resolution of debt overhangs—facilitating capital reallocation and reducing the risk of keeping low-productivity zombie firms afloat.

Preparing for a possible tightening of external financial conditions: Although the exact timing may be hard to predict, the strengthening recovery in advanced economies presages an eventual end to the extraordinary monetary support and rising yields. Emerging market and developing economies should prepare for a possible increase in advanced economy interest rates through debt maturity extensions where feasible, thereby reducing their rollover needs. Regulators should also focus on limiting the buildup of balance sheet mismatches. In countries with deep financial markets and low balance sheet mismatches, exchange rate flexibility can help absorb shocks while also permitting monetary policy to address domestic macroeconomic conditions. Foreign exchange intervention and temporary capital flow management measures may be useful, however, in some circumstances in countries with balance sheet vulnerabilities and market frictions. These measures can increase the autonomy of monetary policy to respond to domestic inflation and output developments (Adrian, Gopinath, and Pazarbasioglu 2020), but they should not substitute for needed macroeconomic adjustment.

Preparing and Investing for the Longer-Term, Post-Pandemic Economy

Even as the pandemic re-intensifies and its duration is highly uncertain, the challenges policymakers will face in the economy after the health crisis fades are becoming increasingly visible. If downside risks to the pandemic's evolution materialize, there could be a need for permanently higher health care spending

Figure 1.22. Internet Access around the World
(Individuals using the internet, percent of population)

Although improving over the five years before the pandemic, there are still large gaps across economy groups in the share of individuals with internet access.

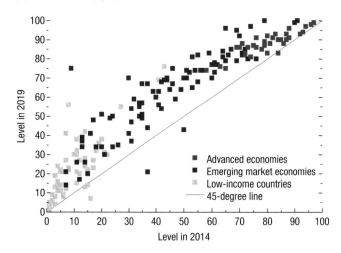

Sources: International Telecommunication Union, World Telecommunication/ICT Indicators Database; and IMF staff calculations.
Note: Each square in the figure corresponds to a country. For countries where data for 2019 are not available, the latest available value is shown on the *y*-axis, and the value for the preceding five years is shown on the *x*-axis.

(including medical infrastructure) to adapt to a more adverse disease environment. Outside of these potential changes, key challenges include facilitating new growth and productivity opportunities related to green technology and digitalization, reversing the setback to human capital accumulation, and containing increases in inequality. At the same time, elevated debt levels in many countries will require efforts to place public finances on a sustainable footing. Once economies are more firmly on durable recovery paths, policies will need to more strongly address these challenges.

- *Facilitating new growth opportunities by greening the economy and through digitalization:* As discussed earlier, a green investment push would aid the transition to a cleaner economy while catalyzing new growth opportunities, for example, in the construction and energy sectors. Moreover, investing in broadband to improve access to the internet can help bridge the digital divide (Figure 1.22). Building on the policies to secure the recovery, structural reforms that reduce labor market rigidities, repair balance sheets, and improve competition can also help reallocate resources toward growing sectors and raise long-term productivity.
- *Reversing the setback to human capital accumulation:* The pandemic-induced global loss of learning

Figure 1.23. School Closures and Enrollment
(Percent of students)

Although there have been recent increases in the share of schools open, the pandemic's impact on schooling persists, hurting students' future prospects.

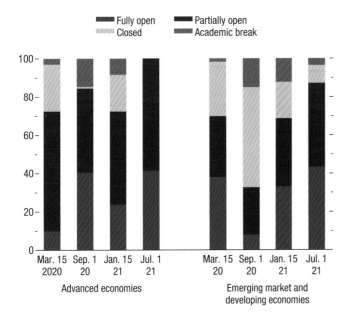

Sources: United Nations Educational, Scientific and Cultural Organization (https://en.unesco.org/covid19/educationresponse); and IMF staff calculations.

from temporary school closures (Figure 1.23) could potentially have long-lasting effects on individual earnings and aggregate productivity growth. To reverse the setback to human capital accumulation and long-term potential, policymakers may need to try a variety of strategies, including greater time in school over the next few years, additional teacher training on methods to aid catch-up, and expansion of extracurricular tutoring programs (see J-PAL 2019 and World Bank 2020a for examples of strategies and tools). Furthermore, educational and vocational programs may need to be adapted to evolving post-pandemic labor demand, with facility with digital technologies becoming a feature of more jobs and greater anticipated employment needs in sectors requiring more specialized skills (such as health care).

- *Reducing inequality:* The setback to human capital accumulation is one dimension along which inequality is likely to increase as a result of the pandemic. Beyond policies to improve educational achievement, spending measures that can improve the resilience of individuals and households and lower inequality include greater coverage of social assistance—via conditional cash transfers, in-kind food benefits, and medical coverage for low-income households—and expanded social insurance (including unemployment benefits for the self-employed and gig workers and greater availability of paid family and sick leave).

- *Addressing sovereign debt overhangs:* The room for initiatives to address the challenges of the post-pandemic economy is limited in many instances, particularly among emerging market and developing economies. Even with relatively low interest rates, emerging market economies' overall debt service burdens are set to rise because of the large increase in the stock of debt over the pandemic. Governments with large debt stocks and high interest burdens will need to institute both revenue and expenditure measures to alleviate the situation. On the revenue side, these include increasing progressive income taxes, reducing loopholes and deductions, adopting well-designed value-added taxes, and expanding the tax base—by relying more on e-filing, for instance, and building capacity for property taxation. These initiatives can be complemented with efforts to scale back poorly targeted subsidies and improve the governance of public investment (for instance, through greater transparency and disclosure of procurements, instituting specific budget lines, and subjecting the projects to regular audits). Such measures will be particularly relevant for low-income developing countries where advancing toward their Sustainable Development Goals remains an overarching challenge. As noted earlier, the international community will need to play a more active role in supporting these countries, including through debt restructuring and reprofiling where needed.

Scenario Box 1. Downside Scenarios

This box examines two downside scenarios: first, US inflation expectations rising more than expected over the next three years; second, the implications of living with endemic COVID-19 well into the medium term.

Risk of rising US inflation expectations: Although inflation expectations have been relatively well anchored in most industrial countries for an extended period, a confluence of factors are starting to line up, as discussed in Chapters 1 and 2. These factors appear to be particularly pressing in the case of the United States. High current US inflation, a real risk that inflation could remain persistently high, and some uncertainty about exactly how tolerant the Federal Reserve will be of this high inflation could lead to a persistent shift upward in inflation expectations.

The IMF's G20 Model is used here to consider the implications of a sequence of unexpected ½-percentage-point shocks to US inflation expectations over 2022–24. The shocks then fade out over 2025–26. The expectations-driven inflation surprises are assumed to overshoot the Federal Reserve's comfort zone suggested by its new average-inflation-targeting framework, causing it to respond. Higher policy rates and an increase in the term premium yield higher long-term rates in the United States (almost 100 basis points above baseline at its peak). These are transmitted globally, based on empirical spillover analysis. Monetary policy in Japan and the euro area is assumed not to respond (because space is exhausted); the same is assumed for emerging market economies (for fear of triggering capital outflows). The simulated impact is shown in the blue line in Scenario Figure 1.1. Furthermore, country-specific risk premiums are assumed to increase, based on the IMF staff assessment of relative vulnerabilities (peaking at 150 basis points on average in 2024). The impact is shown in the red line.

These factors lead to US output below baseline by almost 1¼ percent by 2026. At the global level, output is also below baseline by roughly 1¼ percent by 2026. Emerging market economies suffer disproportionally: GDP falls by just over 1½ percent at its trough, roughly four times more than the decline in GDP in advanced economies excluding the United States.

The authors of this box are Allan Dizioli, Keiko Honjo, Benjamin Hunt, and Susanna Mursula.

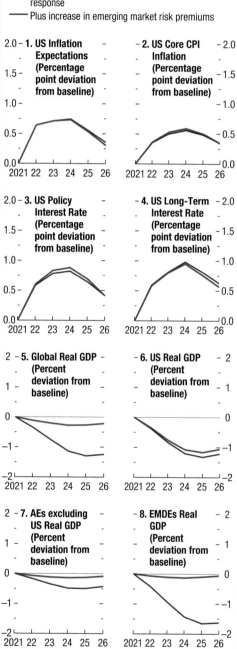

Scenario Figure 1.1. Increase in United States Inflation Expectations

——— Increase in US inflation expectations and US policy response
——— Plus increase in emerging market risk premiums

1. US Inflation Expectations (Percentage point deviation from baseline)
2. US Core CPI Inflation (Percentage point deviation from baseline)
3. US Policy Interest Rate (Percentage point deviation from baseline)
4. US Long-Term Interest Rate (Percentage point deviation from baseline)
5. Global Real GDP (Percent deviation from baseline)
6. US Real GDP (Percent deviation from baseline)
7. AEs excluding US Real GDP (Percent deviation from baseline)
8. EMDEs Real GDP (Percent deviation from baseline)

Sources: IMF, Group of 20 model simulation; and IMF staff estimates.
Note: AEs = advanced economies; CPI = consumer price index; EMDEs = emerging market and developing economies.

Scenario Box 1 *(continued)*

Endemic COVID-19: The second downside scenario explores the possible implications of having to live with COVID-19 well into the medium term. The motivation for this scenario is twofold. First, vaccinations, although critical in the fight, will not, on their own, put an end to the virus's circulation. Second, constraints on vaccine availability and vaccine hesitancy mean that there is likely to be a significant number of unvaccinated people for an extended period.

Constantly having to live with COVID-19 means that activity in many contact-intensive sectors may never return to pre-pandemic levels and that significant adjustments are likely to be required. To estimate how this adjustment might unfold, the standard SEIRD model with vaccines was extended in several dimensions to incorporate recent news about the effectiveness of vaccines and vaccine penetration.

The analysis assumes that vaccine efficacy against infections wanes over time to only 50 percent after six months; infected nonvaccinated people are 40 percent more infectious than infected vaccinated people; infectiousness of the virus is as high as the Delta variant; vaccines are 100 percent effective against deaths in the first six months and then 90 percent effective after that; and vaccine hesitancy will limit the fully vaccinated share, even once the virus becomes endemic. Surveys are used to estimate final shares of populations fully vaccinated. Further, it is assumed that people would voluntarily reduce their mobility so that deaths are 50 percent lower than they would be with pre-pandemic levels of mobility. Moreover, as companies improve their hybrid work models and teleworking technologies improve, the elasticity of GDP to mobility is further reduced and is only one-third of the elasticity observed in 2021:Q1.

The estimated declines in domestic demand from the SEIRD model-based analysis under the above assumptions are mapped into the IMF's G20 Model to estimate the global impact including spillovers via trade. The simulated results are presented in the blue line in Scenario Figure 1.2. In addition to the direct demand impact of reduced mobility, structural changes will be needed to minimize the impact of the virus over the medium term. Some of the existing capital stock will no longer be viable, and new capital will need to be put in place. Productivity growth will be temporarily reduced as firms adjust to the additional constraints. The natural rate of unemployment will likely rise as labor is reallocated. The scenario assumes these forces will be roughly half as large as has been

Scenario Figure 1.2. Living with COVID-19
(Percent deviation from baseline)

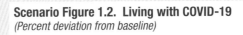

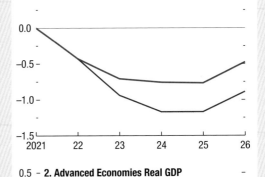

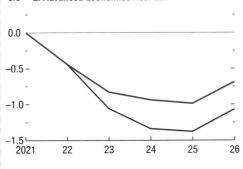

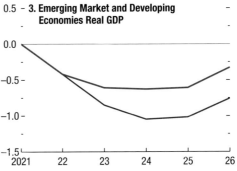

Sources: G20 model simulation; and IMF staff estimates.

assumed for baseline scarring effects. The estimated additional impact of these structural changes is given by the red line in Scenario Figure 1.2.

These factors are estimated to take more than 1 percent off the level of global GDP by 2025, with a gradual recovery back toward baseline starting subsequently. Advanced economies are more negatively impacted than emerging market economies owing to the estimates of vaccine hesitancy.

Box 1.1. House Prices and Consumer Price Inflation

Steady as She Goes

Contrary to the expectation that house prices would decline during recessions (Igan and others 2011; Duca, Muellbauer, and Murphy, forthcoming), real house prices rose by 5.3 percent, on average, globally in 2020 as the pandemic-induced economic downturn took hold. Perhaps more strikingly, this was the highest annual growth rate observed in the past 15 years (Figure 1.1.1). While house price growth has breezed ahead, residential rents have grown at a slower rate, rising by 1.8 percent, on average, across countries over the same period.[1]

Figure 1.1.1. Global Housing Indicators
(GDP-weighted indices, 2015 = 100)

Sources: Bank for International Settlements; Haver Analytics; and IMF staff calculations.
Note: The sample covers 57 countries. Nominal house price data are deflated by the consumer price index.

The authors of this box are Nina Biljanovska, Chenxu Fu, and Deniz Igan.

[1]Rents are proxied by the rent expenditure component of the national consumer price index (CPI) due to lack of data availability on market rents across countries. It is worth noting that the proxy used for the CPI could diverge from the rental rates asked by landlords. In the United States, for instance, the rent index (based on data from apartmentlist.com) recorded a monthly average increase of 0.18 percent in 2017–19, compared to the 0.3 percent average monthly increase in the rent of primary residence component in the CPI (as published by the Bureau of Labor Statistics). The two series diverged considerably in 2020, with the rent index declining by 1.2 percent and the rent of primary residence component increasing by 1.8 percent. This large divergence in part may reflect the policy support measures banning evictions during the pandemic.

Implications of a hot housing market for consumer prices

The house price surge comes at a time when questions are mounting over post-pandemic inflation dynamics (see Chapter 2). House prices matter for inflation because—through an asset pricing equation—they are linked to two measures of housing costs that could enter the CPI. One is the actual rent paid by tenants. The other is the imputed rent, or owner's equivalent rent, which is an estimate of how much homeowners would need to pay were they to rent their own house.[2,3] Overall, the rent component accounts, on average, for about 20 percent of the CPI.[4]

How much of an increase in inflation is expected?

To what extent house prices feed into the rent-based components in the CPI is a question of the nature and persistence of the observed dynamics.[5] A cross-country estimate of the link between nominal house price growth and CPI rent inflation suggests

[2]There is variation in how different countries incorporate either of these components in their inflation measures. Some include only the actual rent; others also include imputed rent. Data on these subcomponents of the national CPI series are available for 45 countries, of which only one-third consider *imputed* rental cost in addition to *actual* rental costs in the calculation of the CPI. House prices themselves are not included in the CPI because house purchases are regarded as investment, not consumption. Also, while many countries use the rental equivalence method to estimate the cost of owner-occupied housing, a few (for example, Australia and New Zealand) use the net acquisition approach with the aim of capturing the cost of purchasing a dwelling, excluding the land component but including transfer, insurance, and maintenance costs.

[3]From a theoretical perspective, owner's equivalent rent overstates the cost of owner-occupied housing because it fails to account for capital gains from, and the favorable tax treatment of, homeownership (Dougherty and van Order 1982; Muellbauer 2011). The theoretically superior alternative of *user cost* is difficult to implement in practice given challenges in measuring expected capital gains and risk premiums.

[4]This weight ranges from 14 to 49 percent across countries, with 15 percent and 23 percent being the 25th and 75th percentiles, respectively. In most cases where owner-occupied costs are approximated by the rental equivalence method, this excludes other shelter-related expenditures, such as maintenance and utilities.

[5]Rents are not as procyclical as prices (see, for example, Glaeser and Nathanson 2015). Plausible explanations include the non-forward-looking nature and stickiness of rents (for example, due to long-term rental contracts or regulatory limits on annual rent increases to protect tenants).

Box 1.1 *(continued)*

that a 1-percentage-point, year-on-year increase in nominal house prices in the quarter ahead is associated with a cumulative increase of 1.4 percentage points in annual rent inflation over a period of two years (Figure 1.1.2).[6] The effect is strongest in the fourth quarter following the increase and persists for about three years. Then, considering that rent costs account for about 20 percent of the consumer basket, a 5.3 percent increase in nominal house prices—corresponding to the nominal house price growth rate over 2019:Q4–20:Q4—would translate to a cumulative increase of 1.5 percentage points in inflation over a period of two years. The pass-through to overall inflation and the degree of persistence remain uncertain and depend on how the factors behind house price increases will evolve: the ultra-low-for-long interest rate environment, which has pushed mortgage rates to very low levels; low housing inventory,[7] induced by production shortfalls and sellers' hesitancy to put houses on the market;

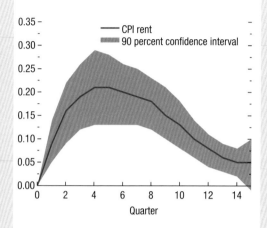

Figure 1.1.2. Response of CPI Rent Inflation to a 1-Percentage-Point Shock to Nominal House Prices
(Percentage points)

Sources: Haver Analytics; national statistics offices; and IMF staff calculations.
Note: CPI = consumer price index.

[6]The econometric specification used to estimate the impact of movements in house prices on CPI rent inflation is:
$\Delta ln\left(rent_{i,t}^{h}\right) = \sum_{k=1}^{4} \alpha_{k}^{h} \Delta ln\left(rent_{i,t-k}\right) + \sum_{k=1}^{4} \beta_{k}^{h} \Delta ln\left(nhp_{i,t-k}\right) + \sum_{k=1}^{4} \gamma_{k}^{h} \Delta ln\left(cpi\_exp_{i,t-k}\right) + \delta_{i}^{h} + \theta_{t}^{h} + \varepsilon_{i,t}^{h}$, where i indexes countries and t indexes quarters, $\Delta ln\left(rent_{i,t}^{h}\right)$ is the annualized growth rate in CPI rent, $\Delta ln\left(nhp_{i,t-k}\right)$ is the annualized growth rate in nominal house prices, $\Delta ln\left(cpi\_exp_{i,t-k}\right)$ is inflation expectations for the current year, δ_{i}^{h} are country fixed effects, θ_{t}^{h} are time fixed effects, and $\varepsilon_{i,t}^{h}$ are standard errors clustered at the country level. The regression equation is estimated using local projections over a horizon $h = 14$, and the coefficient of interest is β_{1}^{h}, plotted in the figure. The sample is a (unbalanced) panel of 45 countries over 1970:Q1–2020:Q4.

[7]In the United States, for example, days on market fell sharply in 2021 from about 45 days to 35 days for condominiums while the drop for single-family homes was even sharper—to only 20 days.

and shifts in consumption patterns toward housing and away from, for example, travel, dining, and entertainment (see Chapter 1 of the October 2021 *Global Financial Stability Report* for a discussion on house prices at risk). And, beyond translation to inflation through the rent component, policymakers have other reasons to monitor and take actions in response to rising house prices where necessary: the impact on affordability and cost of living; potential resource misallocation and risk of overheating, even in the absence of visible inflationary pressures; and implications for financial stability.

Box 1.2. Jobs and the Green Economy

Achieving the reductions in greenhouse gas emissions needed to mitigate global warming will require a transformation of the global economy. This green economic transformation will likely necessitate a shift of workers away from carbon-intensive and environmentally destructive production processes toward jobs that help reduce greenhouse gas emissions and improve environmental sustainability. These "green" or "greener" jobs include newer occupations using emerging technologies, which are expected to see increased demand with the greening of the economy (such as jobs related to solar and wind power installation and maintenance) as well as existing occupations with markedly enhanced or changed skill sets required for a low-carbon economy (such as jobs in automotive repair, power plants, and mining operations).[1] But how prevalent are these jobs in the economy, what sectors and kinds of workers have them, and what have been the recent trends in their growth? This box examines these questions and provides some perspectives on how the job market could be impacted by the green transition.

A key question for policymakers is how the transition to a greener economy will affect employment, both in the aggregate and across sectors and skill levels. A first step in answering this question is defining what green jobs are. In this box, green jobs are identified using the O*NET Resource Center (2021) taxonomy of green occupations. This taxonomy enables occupations to be sorted into three categories: (1) new occupations based on tasks that use emerging technologies to green the economy; (2) occupations that are expected to undergo significant changes in the kind and composition of tasks they do, owing to the greening of the economy; and (3) other occupations, which do not involve green tasks. For each occupation, a green-task-intensity measure is computed as the ratio of green to total tasks, following Vona and others (2018). For remaining occupations (in the third category), their green task intensity is set to zero. Aggregate green-task-intensity indices are computed as employment-weighted averages for the relevant workforce. At the economy level, this index can be thought of as proxying the share of tasks undertaken by

Figure 1.2.1. Green Tasks in Jobs across Countries and Worker Groups
(Share of green tasks in employment)

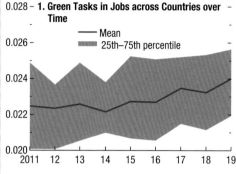

1. Green Tasks in Jobs across Countries over Time

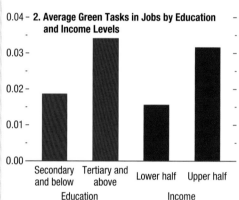

2. Average Green Tasks in Jobs by Education and Income Levels

Sources: European Union Labor Force Survey; O*NET; US Current Population Survey; and IMF staff calculations.
Note: The figure shows the 25th percentile, mean, and 75th percentile across countries. The indicator for green tasks is computed as the employment-weighted average share of tasks that are green across occupations in an economy (Vona, Marin, and Consoli 2019). Sample comprises AUT, BEL, CHE, CYP, CZE, DEU, DNK, ESP, FIN, FRA, GBR, GRC, HRV, HUN, IRL, ISL, ITA, LTU, LUX, NLD, NOR, POL, PRT, ROU, SVK, SWE, and USA. International Organization for Standardization (ISO) codes are used to indicate the country. The share of workers with secondary education and below is 79 percent. The share with tertiary and above is 21 percent.

the workforce that are directly contributing to the green economic transition.[2]

Figure 1.2.1, panel 1, shows how the aggregate green task index has evolved during 2011–19. The index is computed using micro-level data for the

---

The authors of this box are John Bluedorn and Niels-Jakob Hansen, with support from Savannah Newman.

[1]See O*NET Resource Center (2021) for details on the task-based classification of occupations according to the relationship to the greening of the economy. For examples of studies applying this taxonomy to the United States, see Consoli and others (2016); Bowen, Kuralbayeva, and Tipoe (2018); and, particularly, Vona and others (2018).

[2]Jobs that *only* do green tasks include "Wind Energy Operation Managers," "Brownfield Redevelopment Specialists and Site Managers," "Hazardous Material Removal Workers," and "Weatherization Installers and Technicians." Examples of other jobs with high shares of green tasks (40–50 percent) include "Automotive Specialty Technicians," "Civil Engineers," and "Plumbers."

Box 1.2 *(continued)*

United States and a selected group of European Union member countries.[3] The figure suggests that the share of green tasks in the average job has increased marginally since 2014, from about 2.2 percent to about 2.4 percent, with some variation across countries. A growing proportion of workers is employed in greening occupations, caused by employment shifts either within or between sectors. But the pace of increase is slow, with no marked evidence for greening of jobs. The urgency of the climate change threat suggests that a faster transformation will be needed in the future.

Figure 1.2.2 shows both the average green task index by sector and the distribution across occupations within each sector. The two sectors with the largest share of green tasks are "Water and Waste Management" and "Professional and Scientific Activities." However, green tasks are also being performed in other sectors, including those usually associated with higher carbon emissions, such as heavy industry. Moreover, jobs with workers at higher levels of educational attainment or income tend to involve more green tasks (Figure 1.2.1, panel 2).

Overall, the evidence presented in this box suggests that jobs have become greener over the past decade. In addition, green tasks are being performed across all sectors—an important nuance about the potential impact of the green transition only evident from examining employment through the lens of occupations and tasks. Finally, workers with higher educational attainment and higher incomes are more likely to be in jobs involving greener tasks. In other words, greener jobs tend to be higher-skill and higher-income jobs, highlighting the complementarity between investing in people and boosting the green economic transition. Lower-skilled workers should receive the training and support needed to ensure that the green transition is inclusive.

[3]The individual-level EU microdata used come from Eurostat: EU Labour Force Survey 2011–19. The responsibility for all conclusions drawn from the data lies entirely with the authors. The individual-level data for the United States come from IPUMS CPS.

Figure 1.2.2. Green Tasks in Jobs across Sectors
(Share of green tasks in employment)

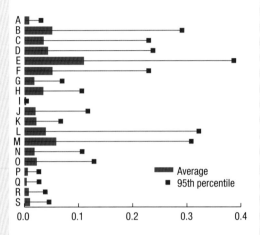

Sources: European Union Labor Force Survey; O*NET; US Current Population Survey; and IMF staff calculations.
Note: The indicator for green tasks is computed as the employment-weighted share of tasks that are green across occupations by sector (Vona, Marin, and Consoli 2019). A = agriculture, forestry and fishing; B = mining and quarrying; C = manufacturing; D = electricity and gas, steam, and air-conditioning supply; E = water supply and sewage, waste management and remediation; F = construction; G = wholesale and retail trade; H = transportation and storage; I = accommodation and food service; J = information and communication; K = financial and insurance; L = real estate; M = professional, scientific, and technical; N = administrative and support services; O = public administration and defense; P = education; Q = human health and social work; R = arts, entertainment, and recreation; S = other service activities. Sample comprises AUT, BEL, CHE, CYP, CZE, DEU, DNK, ESP, EST, FIN, FRA, GBR, GRC, HRV, HUN, IRL, ISL, ITA, LTU, LUX, LVA, NLD, NOR, POL, PRT, ROU, SVK, SWE, and USA. International Organization for Standardization (ISO) codes are used to indicate the country.

Box 1.3. Monetary Expansions and Inflationary Risks

The COVID-19 pandemic has prompted various central banks to cut policy rates close to zero and has pushed fiscal authorities to massive fiscal expansions, leading to sharp increases in public debt and, in some countries, casting doubts about debt sustainability. Given the constraints faced by conventional monetary policy and fiscal policy, central banks in various countries will likely remain under pressure to use unconventional policy tools to support the economic recovery and react to possible adverse shocks.

Besides using forward guidance and, in a few cases, resorting to negative interest rates, central banks in advanced economies have increasingly relied on refinancing operations and large-scale purchases of government bonds and even private securities. During the pandemic, central banks in several emerging market and developing economies have undertaken similar, albeit modest, asset purchases, sometimes with the explicit goal to provide fiscal support.

Asset purchases by central banks are generally financed through an expansion of the monetary base. These operations have at times blurred the demarcation between monetary and fiscal policies, raising the specter of fiscal dominance. The concern is that monetary base expansions may de-anchor inflation expectations and trigger severe price pressures if they are perceived as responding to fiscal pressures rather than to macroeconomic stabilization goals. To shed light on this issue, Agur and others (forthcoming) analyze the association between increases in the monetary base and changes in inflation up to 10 years in the future using a large panel of countries with data going back to the 1950s. The analysis uses local projections that control for the real growth rate of GDP and lagged values of money growth and inflation.

The association between money growth and inflation depends heavily on economic conditions and institutional factors, especially in the first few years after the monetary expansion. An expansion of the monetary base is followed by only a modest increase in inflation if the initial level of inflation is low (Figure 1.3.1 panel 1), the central bank operates under strong independence (Figure 1.3.1, panel 2), and the fiscal deficit is modest (Figure 1.3.1, panel 3). On the contrary, a monetary expansion tends to be followed by sharp increases in inflation if the initial

The authors of this box are Itai Agur, Damien Capelle, and Damiano Sandri.

Figure 1.3.1. Change in Inflation after a 10 Percent Increase in the Monetary Base
(Percentage points)

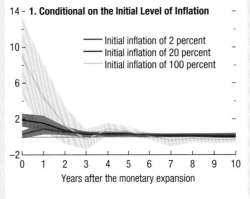

1. Conditional on the Initial Level of Inflation
- Initial inflation of 2 percent
- Initial inflation of 20 percent
- Initial inflation of 100 percent

Years after the monetary expansion

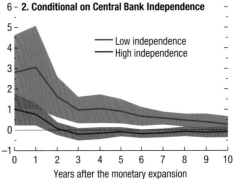

2. Conditional on Central Bank Independence
- Low independence
- High independence

Years after the monetary expansion

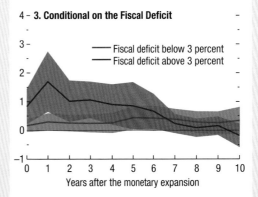

3. Conditional on the Fiscal Deficit
- Fiscal deficit below 3 percent
- Fiscal deficit above 3 percent

Years after the monetary expansion

Sources: Agur and others (2021); and IMF staff estimates.
Note: Lines correspond to impulse response function coefficients. Shaded areas correspond to 90 percent confidence intervals.

level of inflation is high, central bank independence is weak, and the fiscal deficit is large.

These results suggest that asset purchases financed via an increase in the monetary base are unlikely to trigger sharp inflation responses if they are deployed

Box 1.3 *(continued)*

by credible central banks when inflation is below target and the fiscal position is sustainable. Nonetheless, central banks should remain vigilant about the possible inflationary effects of recent monetary expansions because their balance sheets have reached historically high levels in several countries and due to the concomitant effects of large fiscal stimulus during the

COVID-19 pandemic. Central banks should instead refrain from asset purchases if they operate under weak independence and in the context of high inflation and precarious fiscal positions. In these circumstances, monetary expansions are much more likely to fuel sharp price responses, possibly reflecting heightened risks of fiscal dominance.

Special Feature: Commodity Market Developments and Forecasts

Primary commodity prices rose 16.6 percent between February and August 2021. The sharp, broad-based increase, led by metals and energy commodities, was buoyed by a strong recovery in commodity demand, loose financial conditions, and supply-side and weather disruptions. A resurgence of COVID-19 is the major risk factor. This special feature also analyzes how the soaring demand for metals may delay the energy transition.

Market Developments

Oil prices rose 13.9 percent between February and August 2021 on the rapid economic recovery in advanced economies. In light of falling global inventories (Figure 1.SF.1, panel 4), OPEC+ (Organization of the Petroleum Exporting Countries, plus Russia and other non-OPEC oil exporters) agreed in July to gradually phase out their remaining 5.8 million barrel per day production curbs by September 2022.

Futures prices point to *backwardation* (a downward sloping curve), with oil prices at $65.7 per barrel in 2021—59 percent higher than the 2020 average—falling to $56.3 in 2026. Market tightness is expected to continue—in line with the International Energy Agency's (IEA) oil demand recovery projections. Risks to oil prices are balanced in the near term. Upside risks include lower global production capacity (because investment has fallen over the past year) and prolonged price support by OPEC+. The rise of the Delta variant of SARS-CoV-2 and higher output from uncommitted OPEC+ members (Iran, Libya, Venezuela) and US shale oil producers are the major downside risks to oil prices in the near term (Figure 1.SF.1, panels 2 and 3).

Natural gas prices spiked globally. Asian liquefied natural gas prices rose 132.2 percent to $16.6 a million British thermal units between February and August 2021, spilling over to European and US prices. The price spike was driven mainly by depleted natural gas stocks after a harsh winter, coupled with hot summer weather in the Northern Hemisphere, rebounding industrial activity, and idiosyncratic factors, such as low hydropower output in Brazil. High natural gas prices sustained the power sector's demand for coal, although surging coal prices—caused in part by supply disruptions and China's restrictions on Australian coal imports—and higher carbon prices narrowed coal's

Figure 1.SF.1. Commodity Market Developments

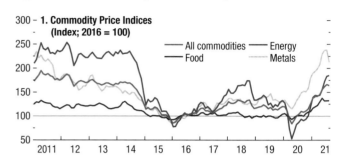
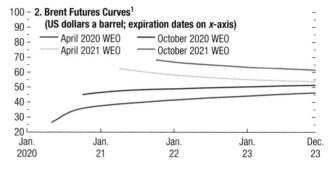
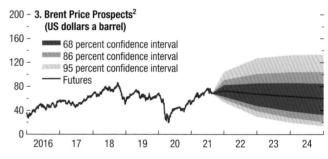
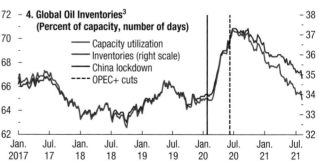

Sources: Bloomberg Finance L.P.; IMF, Primary Commodity Price System; Kpler; Refinitiv Datastream; and IMF staff estimates.
Note: OPEC+ = Organization of the Petroleum Exporting Countries, including Russia and other non-OPEC oil exporters; WEO = *World Economic Outlook.*
[1]Baseline assumptions for each WEO and are derived from futures prices. October 2021 WEO prices are based on August 18, 2021, closing.
[2]Derived from prices of futures and options on August 18, 2021.
[3]Inventories are expressed in days of 2019 oil consumption.

Figure 1.SF.2. Rising Pressure on Consumer Food Prices
(Percent)

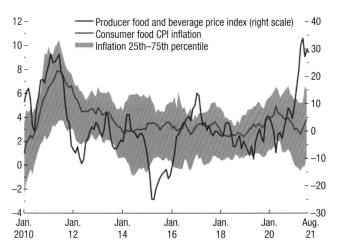

Sources: Haver Analytics; and IMF staff calculations.
Note: Global food inflation represents the average level of consumer food price inflation in 91 countries. CPI = consumer price index.

cost advantage. Over the long term, phaseout plans and rising emission costs may negatively weigh on the demand outlook for coal, possibly benefiting natural gas demand in the coming years as the capacity for renewables ramps up.

The IMF base metal price index rose 9.7 percent between February and August 2021, while precious metal prices decreased by 1.8 percent. Base metals reached a 10-year high in July but have retreated somewhat since then. Prices were buoyed by the recovery in global manufacturing, improved prospects for infrastructure investment in advanced economies, and supply disruptions due to COVID-19. Expectations of higher metal demand during the energy transition supported prices for copper, cobalt, and other metals. Loose financial conditions provided additional price support.

The base metal price index in 2021 is projected to be 57.7 percent higher than the previous year average and to decrease 1.5 percent in 2022. Risks to the outlook are balanced, but the rise of the Delta variant is a major source of uncertainty as the resurgence of the virus may suppress demand for metals as well as disrupt supply. The pace of the energy transition adds uncertainty to the demand for some metals (see below). Precious metal prices are expected to rise 5.1 percent in 2021 and 0.2 percent in 2022.

Food prices: During the first half of 2021 prices of many staple crops surged, continuing the trend noted in the April 2021 *World Economic Outlook.* The

IMF's food and beverage price index rose 11.1 percent between February and August, peaking in May 2021 at the highest price in real terms since the 2010–11 world food price crisis—led by meat (up 30.1 percent), coffee (29.1 percent), and cereals (5.4 percent).

Continued increases in international food producer prices pose upside risks to consumer food price inflation (Figure 1.SF.2), especially in emerging markets, where the pass-through from producer to consumer prices is higher than in advanced economies (26 percent versus 14 percent). The lag and magnitude of the pass-through vary according to regional factors, such as dependence of food imports and the strength of the local currency against the US dollar.

Clean Energy Transition and Metals: Blessing or Bottleneck?

To limit global temperature increases from climate change to 1.5 degrees Celsius, countries and firms increasingly pledge to reduce carbon dioxide emissions to net zero by 2050. Reaching this goal requires a transformation of the energy system that could substantially raise the demand for metals. Low-greenhouse-gas technologies—including renewable energy, electric vehicles, hydrogen, and carbon capture—require more metals than their fossil-fuel-based counterparts.

If metal demand ramps up and supply is slow to react, a multiyear price rally may follow—possibly derailing or delaying the energy transition. To shed light on the issue, this Special Feature introduces "energy transition" metals, estimates price elasticity of supply, and presents price scenarios for major metals. It also provides estimates for revenues and identifies which countries may benefit.

Critical Metals for Green Technologies

The metals required for clean energy transition are quite diverse (Table 1.SF.1). Some, such as copper and nickel (major *established* metals), have been traded for more than a century on metal exchanges. Others, such as lithium and cobalt (minor but *rising* metals), are thinly or not yet traded on metal exchanges but have gained popularity because they are used in energy transition technologies. In addition, the demand for some metals would increase with more certainty because they are used across a range of low-carbon technologies (copper, nickel, and manganese, for example) while

Table 1.SF.1. Key Indicators for Energy Transition Metals

Metal	Exchange Traded	Energy Transition Usage				Production (2020, $ billion)
		Renewable	Network	Battery	Hydrogen	
Copper	✓	✓	✓	✓		123.0
Aluminum	✓	✓	✓	✓	✓	107.0
Nickel	✓	✓		✓	✓	28.0
Zinc	✓	✓				28.0
Lead	✓	✓		✓	✓	26.0
Silver	✓	✓				13.0
Manganese	No	✓		✓	✓	25.0
Chromium	Recent	✓				19.0
Silicon	No	✓				14.0
Molybdenum	Recent	✓			✓	5.0
Cobalt	Recent			✓		4.1
Lithium	Recent			✓		1.8
Vanadium	No			✓		1.3
Graphite	No			✓		1.3

Sources: IEA (2021); World Bank (2020b); and IMF staff calculations.
Note: The column "Production" is the value of refined and unrefined mining production.

the use of others, such as cobalt and lithium, is limited to batteries.

The four representative metals chosen for in-depth analysis are copper, nickel, cobalt, and lithium. Copper and nickel are well-established metals. Cobalt and lithium are probably the most promising *rising* metals.

In the IEA's *Net Zero by 2050* emissions scenario, total consumption of lithium and cobalt rises by a factor of more than six, driven by clean energy demand, while copper shows a twofold and nickel a fourfold increase in total consumption (see Figure 1.SF.3).[1] The scenario also implies that the growth in metal demand would initially be very high between now and 2030 and slow down over time because the switch from fossil fuels to renewables requires large initial investments (Figure 1.SF.4). The increase in demand for metals is more modest in the IEA's *Stated Policies Scenario*.

Where Will Energy Transition Metals Be Produced? Who Will Benefit?

The supply of metals is quite concentrated, implying that a few top producers may stand to benefit. In most cases, countries that have the largest production have the highest level of reserves and, thus, are likely prospective producers. The Democratic Republic of the Congo, for example, accounts for about 70 percent of global cobalt output and 50 percent of reserves (Figure 1.SF.5).

[1]The IEA's *Net Zero by 2050* scenario assumes that policies and behavioral changes bring carbon emissions to net zero by 2050. The IEA's *Stated Policies Scenario* assumes a more gradual energy transition, resulting in insufficient action on climate change (IEA 2021).

Other countries that stand out in production and reserves include Australia (for lithium, cobalt, and nickel); Chile (for copper and lithium); and, to lesser extent, Peru, Russia, Indonesia, and South Africa.

The economic benefits of higher prices for metal exporters could be substantial. Econometric analysis identifies the impact of price shocks, exploiting the different responses of GDP and government balances

Figure 1.SF.3. Demand for Critical Energy Transition Metals May Increase Sharply in the Next Two Decades
(Ratios, 2030s average consumption relative to 2010s average)

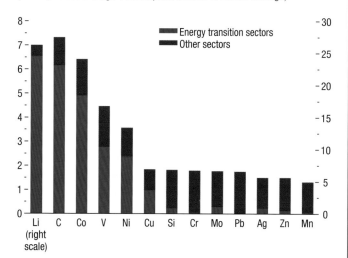

Sources: International Energy Agency (IEA); Schwerhoff and Stuermer (2020); and IMF staff estimates.
Note: The bars represent decade ratios: consumption of each metal in the 2030s divided by consumption in the 2010s, under the IEA's *Net Zero by 2050* emissions scenario. See Online Annex 1.SF.1 for the selection of metals and abbreviations.

Figure 1.SF.4. Historical Metal Production and IEA Energy Transition Scenarios
(Million metric ton)

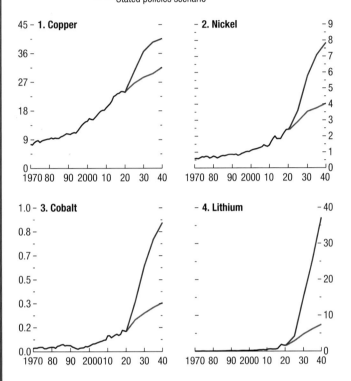

Sources: International Energy Agency (IEA); Schwerhoff and Stuermer (2020); US Geological Survey; and IMF staff calculations.
Note: Copper and nickel refer to refined production, while cobalt and lithium refer to mine production.

between the 15 largest metal exporters and importers. A 15 percent persistent increase in the IMF metal price index adds an extra 1 percentage point of real GDP growth (fiscal balance) for metal exporters compared with metal importers (Figure 1.SF.6).

Metal Prices and Supply Elasticities in a *Net Zero by 2050* Scenario[2]

Supply elasticities summarize how fast firms raise output in reaction to a price increase. In the short term, supply grows thanks to more recycling and higher utilization rates of mining capacity. In the long term, firms build new mines, innovate in extraction

[2]The econometric analysis of this section and subsequent sections is based on Boer, Pescatori, and Stuermer (forthcoming).

Figure 1.SF.5. Top Three Countries, by Share of Global Production and Reserves for Selected Metals
(Percentage points)

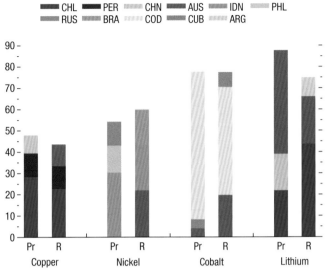

Sources: United States Geological Survey; and IMF staff calculations.
Note: Data labels use International Organization for Standardization (ISO) country codes. Pr = Production; R = Reserves.

Figure 1.SF.6. Impact of Metal Price Shocks on Exporters
(Basis points)

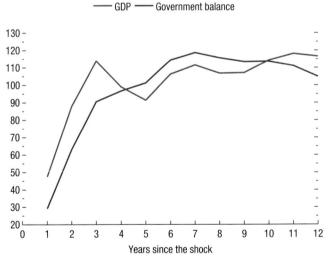

Source: IMF staff calculations.
Note: The figure shows panel vector autoregression generalized impulse responses following Pesaran and Shin (1998) for the differences in GDP growth and the general government-balance-to-GDP ratio of the 15 largest metals exporters relative to the 15 largest importers for a 1-standard-deviation shock to metal prices (about 15 percent).

Figure 1.SF.7. Supply Elasticities for Selected Metals

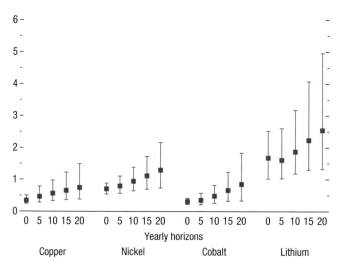

Sources: Schwerhoff and Stuermer 2020; and IMF staff calculations.
Note: Supply elasticities are the ratio of the change in price and output from horizon 0 to 20 years, derived from metal-specific demand shocks. Lower and upper bounds are the 16th and 84th percentiles, respectively. See Online Annex 1.SF.1 for methodology.

technologies, and conduct exploration.[3] To estimate the elasticity at different horizons, data are used for global economic activity, output, and real prices from 1879 to 2020, where available.

Results show that supply is quite inelastic over the short term but more elastic over the long term (Figure 1.SF.7). A demand-induced positive price shock of 10 percent increases the same-year output of copper by 3.5 percent, nickel 7.1 percent, cobalt 3.2 percent, and lithium 16.9 percent. After 20 years, the same price shock raises the output of copper by 7.5 percent, nickel 13.0 percent, cobalt 8.6 percent, and lithium 25.5 percent.

The elasticities correspond to the four metals' different production methods. Copper, nickel, and cobalt are extracted in mines, which often require capital-intensive investment and take as long as 19 years to construct. In contrast, lithium is often extracted from mineral springs and brine as salty water is pumped from the earth. As such, lead times to open new production facilities—up to seven years—are shorter. Innovation in extraction technology, market concentration, and regulations also influence supply elasticities.

---

[3]Geological reserves are not fixed but dynamic. Firms can increase their reserves by investing in exploration and extraction technologies. The amount of metals in the Earth's crust is quite abundant compared to human extraction in any time frame relevant for economic considerations (see Schwerhoff and Stuermer 2020).

Metal Price Scenarios

Based on historical data and the estimated supply elasticities, the algorithm by Antolin-Diaz, Petrella, and Rubio-Ramirez (2021) pins down a series of exogenously- and demand-driven price shocks that incentivize the production path needed for the energy transition in the IEA scenarios (see Online Annex 1.SF.1, available at www.imf.org/en/Publications/WEO). A price path implied by these shocks is then derived. Compared with conditional forecasts, this methodology can distinguish between demand and supply shocks driving the price.

Results show that prices would reach historical peaks for an unprecedented, sustained period under the *Net Zero by 2050* emissions scenario. The prices of cobalt, lithium, and nickel would rise several hundred percent from 2020 levels and could delay the energy transition (Figure 1.SF.8). In contrast, copper is less in danger of a bottleneck as it faces

Figure 1.SF.8. Price Scenarios for the IEA's *Stated Policies Scenario* and the *Net Zero by 2050* Emissions Scenario
(Thousands of 2020 US dollars a metric ton)

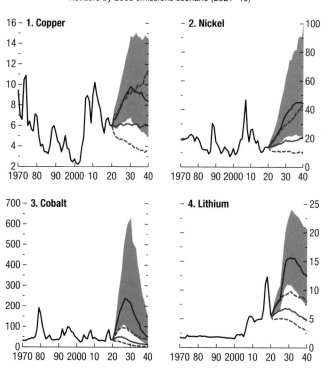

Sources: International Energy Agency (IEA); Schwerhoff and Stuermer (2020); US Bureau of Labor Statistics; US Geological Survey; and IMF staff calculations.
Note: Prices are adjusted for inflation using the US consumer price inflation index. The scenarios are based on a metal-specific demand shock. See Online Annex 1.SF.1 for the data descriptions and methodology.

less steep demand increases. Estimated prices reach a peak, roughly such as the one in 2011, although for a longer period. Prices for all four metals would broadly stay in the current range in the *Stated Policies Scenario*. Results are subject to high uncertainty, reflected in the large bounds.

Prices peak mostly around 2030 for two reasons: first, the steep rises in demand are frontloaded in the *Net Zero by 2050* emissions scenario. Unlike fossil-fuel-based energy production, renewable energy production uses metals up front; for example, to build wind turbines or batteries. Second, the price boom induces a supply reaction, reducing market tightness after 2030.

Revenue and Policy Implications

In the *Net Zero by 2050* emissions scenario, the demand boom would lead to a sixfold increase in the value of metal production—totaling $12.9 trillion over the next two decades for the four energy transition metals alone, providing significant windfalls to producers. This would rival the potential value of global oil production in that scenario (see Table 1.SF.2).

High uncertainty surrounds the demand scenarios. First, technological change is hard to predict. Second, the speed and direction of the energy transition depend on policy decisions.

High policy uncertainty, in turn, may hinder mining investment and increase the chances that high metal prices will derail or delay the energy transition.

Table 1.SF.2. Estimated Cumulated Real Revenue for the Global Production of Selected Energy Transition Metals: 2021–40
(Billions of 2020 US dollars)

	Historical (1999 to 2018)	Stated Policies Scenario	Net Zero Scenario
Selected Metals	**3,043**	**4,974**	**13,007**
Copper	2,382	3,456	6,135
Nickel	563	1,225	4,147
Cobalt	80	152	1,556
Lithium	18	141	1,170
Fossil Fuels	**70,090**	**. . .**	**19,101**
Oil	41,819	. . .	12,906
Natural Gas	17,587	. . .	3,297
Coal	10,684	. . .	2,898

Sources: International Energy Agency; and IMF staff calculations.
Note: For 2021–40, prices of $30 a barrel for oil, $1.50 a million British thermal unit for natural gas, and $40 a metric ton for coal are assumed.

A credible, globally coordinated climate policy; high environmental, social, labor, and governance standards; and reduced trade barriers and export restrictions would allow markets to operate efficiently, directing investment to sufficiently expand metal supply—thus avoiding unnecessarily increasing the cost of low-carbon technologies and supporting the clean energy transition.

Finally, a new international institution focused on metals—analogous to the IEA for energy and the Food and Agricultural Organization for agricultural goods—could play a pivotal role in data dissemination and analysis, industry standards, and international cooperation.

Annex Table 1.1.1. European Economies: Real GDP, Consumer Prices, Current Account Balance, and Unemployment
(Annual percent change, unless noted otherwise)

	Real GDP			Consumer Prices[1]			Current Account Balance[2]			Unemployment[3]		
		Projections			Projections			Projections			Projections	
	2020	2021	2022	2020	2021	2022	2020	2021	2022	2020	2021	2022
Europe	**−5.0**	**5.4**	**4.1**	**2.0**	**4.2**	**3.6**	**1.7**	**2.3**	**2.3**	...	...	...
Advanced Europe	**−6.5**	**5.2**	**4.4**	**0.4**	**2.1**	**1.8**	**2.0**	**2.5**	**2.5**	**7.0**	**7.3**	**7.3**
Euro Area[4,5]	−6.3	5.0	4.3	0.3	2.2	1.7	2.2	2.6	2.7	7.9	8.0	8.1
Germany	−4.6	3.1	4.6	0.4	2.9	1.5	6.9	6.8	6.9	3.8	3.7	3.6
France	−8.0	6.3	3.9	0.5	2.0	1.6	−1.9	−1.7	−1.4	8.0	8.1	8.3
Italy	−8.9	5.8	4.2	−0.1	1.7	1.8	3.5	3.7	3.6	9.3	10.3	11.6
Spain	−10.8	5.7	6.4	−0.3	2.2	1.6	0.7	0.4	1.4	15.5	15.4	14.8
The Netherlands	−3.8	3.8	3.2	1.1	1.9	1.7	7.0	7.9	8.7	3.8	3.6	4.0
Belgium	−6.3	5.6	3.1	0.4	2.4	2.2	−0.2	0.0	−0.6	5.6	6.3	6.1
Austria	−6.2	3.9	4.5	1.4	2.5	2.4	2.5	1.6	2.0	5.4	6.4	6.0
Ireland	5.9	13.0	3.5	−0.5	1.9	1.9	−2.7	11.1	8.8	5.8	7.8	7.0
Portugal	−8.4	4.4	5.1	−0.1	1.2	1.3	−1.1	−1.7	−2.1	7.0	6.9	6.7
Greece	−8.2	6.5	4.6	−1.3	−0.1	0.4	−7.4	−7.4	−5.1	16.4	15.8	14.6
Finland	−2.9	3.0	3.0	0.4	1.9	1.6	0.8	−0.1	0.4	7.8	7.8	6.8
Slovak Republic	−4.8	4.4	5.2	2.0	2.4	3.0	−0.4	−0.9	−1.3	6.7	6.8	6.1
Lithuania	−0.9	4.7	4.1	1.1	3.0	2.8	8.3	6.7	4.7	8.5	6.5	6.1
Slovenia	−4.2	6.3	4.6	−0.1	1.4	1.8	7.4	6.4	6.3	5.0	4.5	4.3
Luxembourg	−1.3	5.5	3.8	0.0	2.7	1.4	4.3	4.7	4.3	6.3	5.6	5.5
Latvia	−3.6	4.5	5.2	0.1	2.6	3.0	3.0	−1.0	−1.1	8.1	7.7	7.2
Estonia	−3.0	8.5	4.2	−0.6	3.8	4.9	−0.6	−1.8	−2.0	6.8	6.5	6.0
Cyprus	−5.1	4.8	3.6	−1.1	1.7	1.0	−11.9	−9.3	−7.4	7.6	7.5	6.9
Malta	−8.3	5.7	6.0	0.8	0.7	1.8	−3.5	−2.4	−0.3	4.3	3.6	3.5
United Kingdom	−9.8	6.8	5.0	0.9	2.2	2.6	−3.7	−3.4	−3.4	4.5	5.0	5.0
Switzerland	−2.5	3.7	3.0	−0.7	0.4	0.6	3.8	7.2	7.5	3.1	3.1	3.0
Sweden	−2.8	4.0	3.4	0.7	2.0	1.6	5.7	4.8	4.3	8.3	8.9	7.9
Czech Republic	−5.8	3.8	4.5	3.2	2.7	2.3	3.6	1.6	0.8	2.5	3.4	3.2
Norway	−0.8	3.0	4.1	1.3	2.6	2.0	2.0	7.2	7.0	4.6	4.3	4.0
Denmark	−2.1	3.8	3.0	0.3	1.4	1.6	8.2	7.0	6.8	5.6	5.4	5.3
Iceland	−6.5	3.7	4.1	2.9	4.3	3.1	0.9	1.0	1.2	6.4	7.0	5.0
Andorra	−12.0	5.5	4.8	0.3	1.7	1.5	14.3	14.7	15.7	2.9	3.1	2.2
San Marino	−6.5	5.5	3.7	0.2	0.8	0.9	1.8	1.1	1.0	7.3	6.7	6.4
Emerging and Developing Europe[6]	**−2.0**	**6.0**	**3.6**	**5.4**	**8.4**	**7.1**	**0.1**	**1.6**	**1.0**	...	...	...
Russia	−3.0	4.7	2.9	3.4	5.9	4.8	2.4	5.7	4.4	5.8	4.9	4.6
Turkey	1.8	9.0	3.3	12.3	17.0	15.4	−5.2	−2.4	−1.6	13.1	12.2	11.0
Poland	−2.7	5.1	5.1	3.4	4.4	3.3	3.4	2.3	1.6	3.2	3.5	3.2
Romania	−3.9	7.0	4.8	2.6	4.3	3.4	−5.2	−5.7	−5.5	5.0	4.9	4.9
Ukraine[7]	−4.0	3.5	3.6	2.7	9.5	7.1	4.0	−0.7	−2.4	9.2	9.7	8.7
Hungary	−5.0	7.6	5.1	3.3	4.5	3.6	−0.1	0.6	0.9	4.1	4.1	3.8
Belarus	−0.9	2.1	0.5	5.5	9.2	8.3	−0.4	0.4	−0.7	4.1	4.3	4.2
Bulgaria[5]	−4.2	4.5	4.4	1.2	2.1	1.9	−0.7	0.5	0.3	5.2	5.2	4.7
Serbia	−1.0	6.5	4.5	1.6	3.0	2.7	−4.3	−4.1	−4.4	9.5	9.3	9.3
Croatia	−8.0	6.3	5.8	0.1	2.0	2.0	−0.4	−0.1	−0.8	9.0	8.4	8.0

Source: IMF staff estimates.

Note: Data for some countries are based on fiscal years. Please refer to Table F in the Statistical Appendix for a list of economies with exceptional reporting periods.

[1]Movements in consumer prices are shown as annual averages. Year-end to year-end changes can be found in Tables A5 and A6 in the Statistical Appendix.

[2]Percent of GDP.

[3]Percent. National definitions of unemployment may differ.

[4]Current account position corrected for reporting discrepancies in intra-area transactions.

[5]Based on Eurostat's harmonized index of consumer prices except for Slovenia.

[6]Includes Albania, Bosnia and Herzegovina, Kosovo, Moldova, Montenegro, and North Macedonia.

[7]See the country-specific note for Ukraine in the "Country Notes" section of the Statistical Appendix.

Annex Table 1.1.2. Asian and Pacific Economies: Real GDP, Consumer Prices, Current Account Balance, and Unemployment
(Annual percent change, unless noted otherwise)

	Real GDP			Consumer Prices[1]			Current Account Balance[2]			Unemployment[3]		
		Projections			Projections			Projections			Projections	
	2020	2021	2022	2020	2021	2022	2020	2021	2022	2020	2021	2022
Asia	**−1.3**	**6.5**	**5.7**	**2.5**	**2.1**	**2.4**	**2.6**	**2.2**	**2.0**	...	...	...
Advanced Asia	**−2.9**	**3.8**	**3.5**	**0.2**	**1.0**	**1.2**	**4.6**	**4.9**	**4.5**	**3.6**	**3.5**	**3.1**
Japan	−4.6	2.4	3.2	0.0	−0.2	0.5	3.3	3.5	3.3	2.8	2.8	2.4
Korea	−0.9	4.3	3.3	0.5	2.2	1.6	4.6	4.5	4.2	3.9	3.8	3.7
Australia	−2.4	3.5	4.1	0.9	2.5	2.1	2.7	3.6	1.3	6.5	5.2	4.8
Taiwan Province of China	3.1	5.9	3.3	−0.2	1.6	1.5	14.2	15.6	15.2	3.9	3.8	3.6
Singapore	−5.4	6.0	3.2	−0.2	1.6	1.5	17.6	15.9	15.7	3.0	2.7	2.5
Hong Kong SAR	−6.1	6.4	3.5	0.3	1.9	2.1	6.5	6.0	5.6	5.8	5.6	4.6
New Zealand	−2.1	5.1	3.3	1.7	3.0	2.2	−0.8	−3.3	−2.5	4.6	4.3	4.4
Macao SAR	−56.3	20.4	37.6	0.8	−0.3	2.0	−34.2	−18.5	8.9	2.6	2.9	2.5
Emerging and Developing Asia	**−0.8**	**7.2**	**6.3**	**3.1**	**2.3**	**2.7**	**1.6**	**1.1**	**0.9**	...	...	...
China	2.3	8.0	5.6	2.4	1.1	1.8	1.8	1.6	1.5	4.2	3.8	3.7
India[4]	−7.3	9.5	8.5	6.2	5.6	4.9	0.9	−1.0	−1.4	...	...	...
ASEAN-5	**−3.4**	**2.9**	**5.8**	**1.4**	**2.0**	**2.4**	**2.0**	**0.6**	**0.7**	...	...	...
Indonesia	−2.1	3.2	5.9	2.0	1.6	2.8	−0.4	−0.3	−1.0	7.1	6.6	6.0
Thailand	−6.1	1.0	4.5	−0.8	0.9	1.3	3.5	−0.5	2.1	2.0	1.5	1.0
Vietnam	2.9	3.8	6.6	3.2	2.0	2.3	3.7	1.8	3.2	3.3	2.7	2.4
Philippines	−9.6	3.2	6.3	2.6	4.3	3.0	3.6	0.4	−1.8	10.4	7.8	6.8
Malaysia	−5.6	3.5	6.0	−1.1	2.5	2.0	4.2	3.8	3.7	4.5	4.7	4.5
Other Emerging and Developing Asia[5]	**−1.3**	**1.7**	**6.3**	**5.2**	**4.9**	**5.6**	**−2.0**	**−2.1**	**−2.2**	...	...	...
Memorandum												
Emerging Asia[6]	**−0.8**	**7.5**	**6.3**	**3.0**	**2.2**	**2.6**	**1.7**	**1.2**	**1.0**	...	...	...

Source: IMF staff estimates.

Note: Data for some countries are based on fiscal years. Please refer to Table F in the Statistical Appendix for a list of economies with exceptional reporting periods.

[1]Movements in consumer prices are shown as annual averages. Year-end to year-end changes can be found in Tables A5 and A6 in the Statistical Appendix.

[2]Percent of GDP.

[3]Percent. National definitions of unemployment may differ.

[4]See the country-specific note for India in the "Country Notes" section of the Statistical Appendix.

[5]Other Emerging and Developing Asia comprises Bangladesh, Bhutan, Brunei Darussalam, Cambodia, Fiji, Kiribati, Lao P.D.R., Maldives, Marshall Islands, Micronesia, Mongolia, Myanmar, Nauru, Nepal, Palau, Papua New Guinea, Samoa, Solomon Islands, Sri Lanka, Timor-Leste, Tonga, Tuvalu, and Vanuatu.

[6]Emerging Asia comprises the ASEAN-5 economies, China, and India.

Annex Table 1.1.3. Western Hemisphere Economies: Real GDP, Consumer Prices, Current Account Balance, and Unemployment
(Annual percent change, unless noted otherwise)

	Real GDP			Consumer Prices[1]			Current Account Balance[2]			Unemployment[3]		
		Projections			Projections			Projections			Projections	
	2020	2021	2022	2020	2021	2022	2020	2021	2022	2020	2021	2022
North America	**−4.0**	**6.0**	**5.0**	**1.4**	**4.3**	**3.4**	**−2.6**	**−3.0**	**−3.1**	...	...	...
United States	−3.4	6.0	5.2	1.2	4.3	3.5	−2.9	−3.5	−3.5	8.1	5.4	3.5
Mexico	−8.3	6.2	4.0	3.4	5.4	3.8	2.4	0.0	−0.3	4.4	4.1	3.7
Canada	−5.3	5.7	4.9	0.7	3.2	2.6	−1.8	0.5	0.2	9.6	7.7	5.7
Puerto Rico[4]	−3.9	−0.6	−0.3	−0.5	4.0	1.9	...	...	...	8.9	8.7	8.5
South America[5]	**−6.6**	**6.3**	**2.3**	**8.1**	**11.5**	**9.9**	**−0.9**	**−0.7**	**−1.3**	...	...	...
Brazil	−4.1	5.2	1.5	3.2	7.7	5.3	−1.8	−0.5	−1.7	13.5	13.8	13.1
Argentina	−9.9	7.5	2.5	42.0	...	...	0.9	1.0	0.8	11.6	10.0	9.2
Colombia	−6.8	7.6	3.8	2.5	3.2	3.5	−3.4	−4.4	−4.0	16.1	14.5	13.8
Chile	−5.8	11.0	2.5	3.0	4.2	4.4	1.4	−2.5	−2.2	10.8	9.1	7.4
Peru	−11.0	10.0	4.6	1.8	3.1	2.5	0.8	0.4	0.1	13.0	8.7	6.5
Ecuador	−7.8	2.8	3.5	−0.3	0.0	2.1	2.5	1.7	1.7	5.3	4.6	4.2
Venezuela	−30.0	−5.0	−3.0	2,355	2,700	2,000	−4.3	0.3	−0.7	...	...	...
Bolivia	−8.8	5.0	4.0	0.9	1.3	2.7	−0.5	−2.2	−2.8	8.3	7.8	6.0
Paraguay	−0.6	4.5	3.8	1.8	3.5	4.0	2.2	3.5	2.1	6.5	6.1	5.9
Uruguay	−5.9	3.1	3.2	9.8	7.5	6.1	−0.7	−1.3	−0.3	10.4	10.4	9.2
Central America[6]	**−7.1**	**7.7**	**4.6**	**2.0**	**4.4**	**3.4**	**1.3**	**−0.9**	**−1.1**	...	...	...
Caribbean[7]	**−4.2**	**3.6**	**11.3**	**8.0**	**8.3**	**6.8**	**−4.3**	**−3.1**	**1.5**	...	...	...
Memorandum												
Latin America and the Caribbean[8]	−7.0	6.3	3.0	6.4	9.3	7.8	0.0	−0.6	−1.0	...	...	...
Eastern Caribbean Currency Union[9]	−16.4	1.0	9.6	−0.6	1.6	1.7	−14.8	−17.0	−12.7	...	...	...

Source: IMF staff estimates.

Note: Data for some countries are based on fiscal years. Please refer to Table F in the Statistical Appendix for a list of economies with exceptional reporting periods.

[1]Movements in consumer prices are shown as annual averages. Year-end to year-end changes can be found in Tables A5 and A6 in the Statistical Appendix. Aggregates exclude Venezuela.

[2]Percent of GDP.

[3]Percent. National definitions of unemployment may differ.

[4]Puerto Rico is a territory of the United States, but its statistical data are maintained on a separate and independent basis.

[5]See the country-specific notes for Argentina and Venezuela in the "Country Notes" section of the Statistical Appendix.

[6]Central America refers to CAPDR (Central America, Panama, and the Dominican Republic) and comprises Costa Rica, Dominican Republic, El Salvador, Guatemala, Honduras, Nicaragua, and Panama.

[7]The Caribbean comprises Antigua and Barbuda, Aruba, The Bahamas, Barbados, Belize, Dominica, Grenada, Guyana, Haiti, Jamaica, St. Kitts and Nevis, St. Lucia, St. Vincent and the Grenadines, Suriname, and Trinidad and Tobago.

[8]Latin America and the Caribbean comprises Mexico and economies from the Caribbean, Central America, and South America. See the country-specific notes for Argentina and Venezuela in the "Country Notes" section of the Statistical Appendix.

[9]Eastern Caribbean Currency Union comprises Antigua and Barbuda, Dominica, Grenada, St. Kitts and Nevis, St. Lucia, and St. Vincent and the Grenadines as well as Anguilla and Montserrat, which are not IMF members.

Annex Table 1.1.4. Middle East and Central Asia Economies: Real GDP, Consumer Prices, Current Account Balance, and Unemployment

(Annual percent change, unless noted otherwise)

	Real GDP			Consumer Prices[1]			Current Account Balance[2]			Unemployment[3]		
		Projections			Projections			Projections			Projections	
	2020	2021	2022	2020	2021	2022	2020	2021	2022	2020	2021	2022
Middle East and Central Asia	−2.8	4.1	4.1	10.1	11.7	8.5	−2.4	1.7	1.5	...	...	...
Oil Exporters[4]	−4.2	4.5	3.9	8.1	10.8	8.2	−1.9	3.5	3.4	...	...	...
Saudi Arabia	−4.1	2.8	4.8	3.4	3.2	2.2	−2.8	3.9	3.8	7.4	...	...
Iran	3.4	2.5	2.0	36.4	39.3	27.5	−0.1	1.3	1.0	9.6	10.0	10.5
United Arab Emirates	−6.1	2.2	3.0	−2.1	2.0	2.2	3.1	9.7	9.4	...	...	...
Algeria	−4.9	3.4	1.9	2.4	6.5	7.6	−12.7	−7.6	−5.5	14.0	14.1	14.7
Kazakhstan	−2.6	3.3	3.9	6.8	7.5	6.5	−3.7	−0.9	−1.4	4.9	4.8	4.7
Iraq	−15.7	3.6	10.5	0.6	6.4	4.5	−10.8	6.2	4.0	...	...	...
Qatar	−3.6	1.9	4.0	−2.7	2.5	3.2	−2.4	8.2	11.6	...	...	...
Kuwait	−8.9	0.9	4.3	2.1	3.2	3.0	16.7	15.5	13.3	1.3	...	...
Azerbaijan	−4.3	3.0	2.3	2.8	4.4	3.2	−0.5	7.8	7.7	7.2	6.4	6.3
Oman	−2.8	2.5	2.9	−0.9	3.0	2.7	−13.7	−5.8	−0.9	...	...	...
Turkmenistan[6]	−3.4	4.5	1.7	7.6	12.5	13.0	−2.6	0.6	−1.2	...	...	...
Oil Importers[5]	−0.6	3.6	4.3	13.2	13.2	8.9	−3.6	−3.7	−4.0	...	...	...
Egypt	3.6	3.3	5.2	5.7	4.5	6.3	−3.1	−3.9	−3.7	8.3	9.3	9.2
Pakistan	−0.5	3.9	4.0	10.7	8.9	8.5	−1.7	−0.6	−3.1	4.5	5.0	4.8
Morocco	−6.3	5.7	3.1	0.6	1.4	1.2	−1.5	−3.1	−3.3	12.2	12.0	11.5
Uzbekistan	1.7	6.1	5.4	12.9	11.0	10.9	−5.0	−6.0	−5.6	...	...	...
Sudan	−3.6	0.9	3.5	163.3	194.6	41.8	−17.5	−10.1	−9.4	26.8	28.0	27.7
Tunisia	−8.6	3.0	3.3	5.6	5.7	6.5	−6.8	−7.3	−8.4	17.4	...	...
Jordan	−1.6	2.0	2.7	0.4	1.6	2.0	−8.0	−8.9	−4.4	22.7	...	...
Lebanon[6]	−25.0	...	...	84.9	...	...	−17.8	...	...	...	...	...
Afghanistan[6]	−2.4	...	...	5.6	...	...	11.2	...	...	...	...	...
Georgia	−6.2	7.7	5.8	5.2	9.3	5.4	−12.5	−10.0	−7.6	18.5	...	...
Armenia	−7.4	6.5	4.5	1.2	6.9	5.8	−3.8	−2.9	−4.0	18.0	18.5	18.3
Kyrgyz Republic	−8.6	2.1	5.6	6.3	13.0	7.8	4.5	−7.7	−7.6	6.6	6.6	6.6
Tajikistan	4.5	5.0	4.5	8.6	8.0	6.5	4.2	1.9	−1.9	...	...	...
Memorandum												
Caucasus and Central Asia	−2.2	4.3	4.1	7.5	8.5	7.5	−3.4	−0.9	−1.4	...	...	...
Middle East, North Africa, Afghanistan, and Pakistan	−2.9	4.1	4.1	10.5	12.1	8.6	−2.3	2.0	1.8	...	...	...
Middle East and North Africa	−3.2	4.1	4.1	10.5	12.7	8.6	−2.4	2.1	2.2	...	...	...
Israel[7]	−2.2	7.1	4.1	−0.6	1.4	1.8	5.4	4.5	3.8	4.3	5.1	4.6
Maghreb[8]	−7.9	14.0	2.8	2.3	6.0	5.6	−7.9	−4.0	−3.6	...	...	...
Mashreq[9]	1.4	2.7	4.7	8.3	8.0	7.8	−4.3	−4.9	−3.9	...	...	...

Source: IMF staff estimates.

Note: Data for some countries are based on fiscal years. Please refer to Table F in the Statistical Appendix for a list of economies with exceptional reporting periods.

[1]Movements in consumer prices are shown as annual averages. Year-end to year-end changes can be found in Tables A5 and A6 in the Statistical Appendix.

[2]Percent of GDP.

[3]Percent. National definitions of unemployment may differ.

[4]Includes Bahrain, Libya, and Yemen.

[5]Includes Djibouti, Mauritania, Somalia, and West Bank and Gaza. Excludes Syria because of the uncertain political situation.

[6]See the country-specific notes for Afghanistan, Lebanon, and Turkmenistan in the "Country Notes" section of the Statistical Appendix.

[7]Israel, which is not a member of the economic region, is included for reasons of geography but is not included in the regional aggregates.

[8]The Maghreb comprises Algeria, Libya, Mauritania, Morocco, and Tunisia.

[9]The Mashreq comprises Egypt, Jordan, Lebanon, and West Bank and Gaza. Syria is excluded because of the uncertain political situation.

Annex Table 1.1.5. Sub-Saharan African Economies: Real GDP, Consumer Prices, Current Account Balance, and Unemployment

(Annual percent change, unless noted otherwise)

	Real GDP			Consumer Prices[1]			Current Account Balance[2]			Unemployment[3]		
		Projections			Projections			Projections			Projections	
	2020	2021	2022	2020	2021	2022	2020	2021	2022	2020	2021	2022
Sub-Saharan Africa	**−1.7**	**3.7**	**3.8**	**10.3**	**10.7**	**8.6**	**−3.0**	**−2.2**	**−2.7**	...	...	...
Oil Exporters[4]	**−2.5**	**2.1**	**2.5**	**13.8**	**16.8**	**12.8**	**−3.5**	**−1.9**	**−1.3**	...	...	...
Nigeria	−1.8	2.6	2.7	13.2	16.9	13.3	−4.0	−3.2	−2.2	...	...	...
Angola	−5.4	−0.7	2.4	22.3	24.4	14.9	1.5	7.3	5.7	...	...	...
Gabon	−1.8	1.5	3.9	1.3	2.0	2.0	−6.0	−3.8	−2.0	...	...	...
Chad	−0.8	0.9	2.4	4.5	2.6	2.8	−8.1	−5.2	−4.7	...	...	...
Equatorial Guinea	−4.9	4.1	−5.6	4.8	0.5	3.1	−6.3	−4.2	−5.2	...	...	...
Middle-Income Countries[5]	**−4.2**	**4.8**	**3.6**	**4.3**	**5.4**	**5.2**	**−0.5**	**0.2**	**−1.7**	...	...	...
South Africa	−6.4	5.0	2.2	3.3	4.4	4.5	2.0	2.9	−0.9	29.2	33.5	34.4
Ghana	0.4	4.7	6.2	9.9	9.3	8.8	−3.1	−2.2	−3.5	...	...	...
Côte d'Ivoire	2.0	6.0	6.5	2.4	3.0	2.5	−3.5	−3.8	−3.4	...	...	...
Cameroon	−1.5	3.6	4.6	2.4	2.3	2.0	−3.7	−2.8	−2.2	...	...	...
Zambia	−3.0	1.0	1.1	15.7	22.8	19.2	10.4	13.5	14.9	...	...	...
Senegal	1.5	4.7	5.5	2.5	2.4	2.0	−10.2	−12.2	−11.6	...	...	...
Low-Income Countries[6]	**1.9**	**4.1**	**5.3**	**13.1**	**10.6**	**8.3**	**−5.2**	**−5.7**	**−5.3**	...	...	...
Ethiopia[7]	6.1	2.0	...	20.4	25.2	...	−4.6	−2.9	...	...	...	...
Kenya	−0.3	5.6	6.0	5.2	6.0	5.0	−4.4	−5.0	−5.1	...	...	...
Tanzania	4.8	4.0	5.1	3.3	3.2	3.4	−1.8	−3.2	−3.8	...	...	...
Uganda	−0.8	4.7	5.1	2.8	2.2	5.0	−9.6	−8.9	−7.3	...	...	...
Democratic Republic of the Congo	1.7	4.9	5.6	11.4	9.4	6.4	−2.2	−2.1	−1.8	...	...	...
Mali	−1.6	4.0	5.3	0.5	3.0	2.0	−0.2	−5.3	−5.0	...	...	...
Burkina Faso	1.9	6.7	5.6	1.9	3.0	2.6	−0.1	−2.5	−4.1	...	...	...

Source: IMF staff estimates.

Note: Data for some countries are based on fiscal years. Please refer to Table F in the Statistical Appendix for a list of economies with exceptional reporting periods.

[1]Movements in consumer prices are shown as annual averages. Year-end to year-end changes can be found in Table A6 in the Statistical Appendix.

[2]Percent of GDP.

[3]Percent. National definitions of unemployment may differ.

[4]Includes Republic of Congo and South Sudan.

[5]Includes Botswana, Cabo Verde, Eswatini, Lesotho, Mauritius, Namibia, and Seychelles.

[6]Includes Benin, Burundi, Central African Republic, Comoros, Eritrea, The Gambia, Guinea, Guinea-Bissau, Liberia, Madagascar, Malawi, Mozambique, Niger, Rwanda, São Tomé and Príncipe, Sierra Leone, Togo, and Zimbabwe.

[7]See the country-specific note for Ethiopia in the "Country Notes" section of the Statistical Appendix.

Annex Table 1.1.6. Summary of World Real per Capita Output

(Annual percent change; in constant 2017 international dollars at purchasing power parity)

	Average 2003–12	2013	2014	2015	2016	2017	2018	2019	2020	Projections 2021	Projections 2022
World	**2.5**	**2.0**	**2.1**	**2.1**	**1.9**	**2.5**	**2.4**	**1.7**	**−4.3**	**4.8**	**3.8**
Advanced Economies	**1.0**	**0.9**	**1.5**	**1.7**	**1.2**	**2.0**	**1.8**	**1.3**	**−4.9**	**5.0**	**4.3**
United States	1.0	1.1	1.6	2.0	0.9	1.6	2.4	1.8	−3.8	5.7	4.8
Euro Area[1]	0.5	−0.4	1.2	1.7	1.6	2.4	1.6	1.3	−6.6	4.9	4.2
Germany	1.3	0.2	1.8	0.6	1.4	2.3	0.8	0.8	−4.6	2.9	4.4
France	0.6	0.1	0.5	0.6	0.8	2.2	1.5	1.6	−8.2	6.0	3.6
Italy	−0.7	−2.1	−0.1	0.9	1.5	1.8	1.2	0.5	−8.6	5.9	4.3
Spain	−0.2	−1.1	1.7	3.9	2.9	2.8	1.9	1.3	−10.8	5.6	5.9
Japan	0.7	2.2	0.5	1.7	0.8	1.8	0.8	0.2	−4.3	2.7	3.6
United Kingdom	0.7	1.5	2.1	1.6	0.9	1.1	0.6	0.9	−10.2	6.4	4.4
Canada	0.8	1.3	1.8	−0.1	0.0	1.8	1.0	0.4	−6.4	5.1	3.8
Other Advanced Economies[2]	2.6	1.8	2.2	1.5	1.8	2.5	2.0	1.3	−2.5	4.2	3.3
Emerging Market and Developing Economies	**4.8**	**3.5**	**3.1**	**2.8**	**2.9**	**3.3**	**3.3**	**2.3**	**−3.4**	**5.1**	**4.0**
Emerging and Developing Asia	7.4	5.8	5.8	5.9	5.8	5.7	5.6	4.5	−1.7	6.4	5.6
China	9.9	7.1	6.7	6.5	6.2	6.4	6.3	5.6	2.0	7.7	5.4
India[3]	6.3	5.1	6.2	6.8	7.1	5.7	5.4	2.9	−8.0	8.4	7.5
ASEAN-5[4]	4.1	3.7	3.4	3.7	3.9	4.3	4.3	3.7	−4.6	2.0	4.8
Emerging and Developing Europe	4.5	2.8	1.5	0.5	1.6	3.9	3.3	2.3	−1.9	5.8	3.4
Russia	4.9	1.5	−1.1	−2.2	0.0	1.8	2.9	2.1	−2.6	4.7	3.0
Latin America and the Caribbean	2.6	1.8	0.1	−0.7	−1.8	0.2	0.2	−1.3	−8.2	5.5	2.2
Brazil	2.7	2.1	−0.3	−4.4	−4.1	0.5	1.0	0.6	−4.8	4.8	0.9
Mexico	0.8	0.1	1.6	2.1	1.5	1.0	1.1	−1.2	−9.2	5.3	3.1
Middle East and Central Asia	2.5	0.3	0.5	0.5	2.3	0.0	0.0	−0.5	−5.0	1.7	2.2
Saudi Arabia	2.2	0.0	2.5	1.7	−0.6	−3.3	0.0	−2.0	−6.3	1.5	2.8
Sub-Saharan Africa	2.7	2.1	2.3	0.5	−1.2	0.3	0.6	0.5	−4.3	1.2	1.2
Nigeria	4.9	2.6	3.5	0.0	−4.2	−1.8	−0.7	−0.4	−4.3	0.1	0.1
South Africa	2.0	0.9	−0.1	−0.2	−0.8	−0.3	0.0	−1.3	−7.8	3.4	0.6
Memorandum											
European Union	1.0	−0.1	1.5	2.1	1.9	2.8	2.1	1.7	−6.1	4.9	4.3
Middle East and North Africa	1.7	−0.4	−0.1	0.2	2.6	−0.9	−0.7	−1.1	−5.6	1.6	2.2
Emerging Market and Middle-Income Economies	5.1	3.7	3.2	3.0	3.3	3.6	3.5	2.5	−3.3	5.7	4.3
Low-Income Developing Countries	3.6	3.4	3.8	2.1	1.5	2.6	2.7	2.9	−2.1	0.7	3.0

Source: IMF staff estimates.

Note: Data for some countries are based on fiscal years. Please refer to Table F in the Statistical Appendix for a list of economies with exceptional reporting periods.

[1]Data calculated as the sum of individual euro area countries.

[2]Excludes the Group of Seven (Canada, France, Germany, Italy, Japan, United Kingdom, United States) and euro area countries.

[3]See the country-specific note for India in the "Country Notes" section of the Statistical Appendix.

[4]Indonesia, Malaysia, Philippines, Thailand, Vietnam.

References

Abdul Latif Jameel Poverty Action Lab (J-PAL). 2019. "Case Study: Teaching at the Right Level to Improve Learning."

Adrian, Tobias, Gita Gopinath, and Ceyla Pazarbasioglu. 2020. "Navigating Capital Flows—An Integrated Approach." IMF blog. https://blogs.imf.org/2020/12/09/navigating-capital -flows-an-integrated-approach/.

Agarwal, Ruchir, and Gita Gopinath. 2021. "A Proposal to End the COVID-19 Pandemic." IMF Staff Discussion Note 21/04, International Monetary Fund, Washington, DC.

Agur, Itai, Damien Capelle, Giovanni Dell'Ariccia, and Damiano Sandri. Forthcoming. "Monetary Finance: Do Not Touch or Handle with Care?" Departmental Paper, Research Department, International Monetary Fund, Washington, DC.

Antolin-Diaz, Juan, Ivan Petrella, and Juan F. Rubio-Ramirez. 2021. "Structural Scenario Analysis with SVARs." *Journal of Monetary Economics* 117: 798–815.

Barrett, Philip, and Sophia Chen. 2021. "The Economics of Social Unrest." *Finance and Development Online*. August.

Boer, Lukas, Andrea Pescatori, and Martin Stuermer. Forthcoming. "Energy Transition Metals" IMF Working Paper, International Monetary Fund, Washington, DC.

Bowen, Alex, Karlygash Kuralbayeva, and Eileen L. Tipoe. 2018. "Characterising Green Employment: The Impacts of 'Greening' on Workforce Composition." *Energy Economics* 72 (2018): 263–75.

Carrillo-Tudela, Carlos, Bart Hobijn, Powen She, and Ludo Visschers. 2016. "The Extent and Cyclicality of Career Changes: Evidence for the UK." *European Economic Review* 84: 18–41.

Consoli, Davide, Giovanni Marin, Alberto Marzucchi, and Francesco Vona. 2016. "Do Green Jobs Differ from Non-Green Jobs in Terms of Skills and Human Capital?" *Research Policy* 45 (2016): 1046–60.

Dougherty, Ann, and Robert van Order. 1982. "Inflation, Housing Costs, and the Consumer Price Index." *American Economic Review* 72 (1): 154–64.

Duca, John V., John Muellbauer, and Anthony Murphy. Forthcoming. "What Drives House Price Cycles? International Experience and Policy Issues." *Journal of Economic Literature.*

Glaeser, Edward L., and Charles G. Nathanson. 2015. "Housing Bubbles." In *Handbook of Regional and Urban Economics*, edited by Gilles Duranton, Vernon Henderson, and William Strange, (5): 701–51. North Holland: Elsevier.

Igan, Deniz, Alain Kabundi, Francisco Nadal De Simone, Marcelo Pinheiro, and Natalia Tamirisa. 2011. "Housing,

Credit, and Real Activity Cycles: Characteristics and Comovement." *Journal of Housing Economics* 20 (3): 210–31.

International Energy Agency (IEA). 2021. "The Role of Critical Minerals in Clean Energy Transitions." World Energy Outlook Special Report, IEA, Paris.

International Labour Organization (ILO). 2021a. "ILO Monitor: COVID-19 and the World of Work, Seventh Edition, Updated Estimates and Analysis." ILO, Geneva.

International Labour Organization (ILO). 2021b. "World Employment and Social Outlook: Trends 2021." ILO Flagship Report, ILO, Geneva.

Karabarbounis, Loukas, and Brent Neiman. 2014. "The Global Decline of the Labor Share." *The Quarterly Journal of Economics* 129 (1): 61–103.

Muellbauer, John. 2011. "Housing and the Macroeconomy." In the *International Encyclopedia of Housing and Home*, edited by Susan J. Smith, 301–14. Elsevier Science.

O*NET Resource Center. 2021. "Green Occupations." Version 22.0. https://www.onetcenter.org/dictionary/22.0/excel/green _occupations.html, accessed May 17.

Parry, Ian, Simon Black, and James Roaf. 2021. "Proposal for an International Carbon Price Floor among Large Emitters." IMF Staff Climate Notes 21/01, International Monetary Fund, Washington, DC.

Pesaran, H. Hashem, and Yongcheol Shin. 1998. "Generalized Impulse Response Analysis in Linear Multivariate Models." *Economics Letters* 58 (1): 17–29.

Schwerhoff, Gregor, and Martin Stuermer. 2020. "Non-Renewable Resources, Extraction Technology, and Endogenous Technological Change." Working Paper 1506, Federal Reserve Bank of Dallas, TX.

Vona, Francesco, Giovanni Marin, and Davide Consoli. 2019. "Measures, Drivers, and Effects of Green Employment: Evidence from US Local Labor Markets, 2006–2014." *Journal of Economic Geography* 19 (5): 1021–48.

Vona, Francesco, Giovanni Marin, Davide Consoli, and David Popp. 2018. "Environmental Regulation and Green Skills: An Empirical Exploration." *Journal of the Association of Environmental and Resource Economists* 5 (4): 713–53.

World Bank Group. 2020a. "The COVID-19 Pandemic: Shocks to Education and Policy Responses." Washington, DC.

World Bank Group. 2020b. "Minerals for Climate Action: The Mineral Intensity of the Clean Energy Transition." Washington, DC.

Since the beginning of 2021, headline consumer price index (CPI) inflation has increased in advanced and emerging market economies, driven by firming demand, input shortages, and rapidly rising commodity prices. Despite large uncertainty about the measurement of output gaps around the pandemic, a significant relationship remains between economic slack and inflation. Long-term inflation expectations have stayed relatively anchored so far, with little evidence that recent exceptional policy measures have de-anchored those expectations. Looking ahead, headline inflation is projected to peak in the final months of 2021, with inflation expected back to pre-pandemic levels by mid-2022 for both advanced economies and emerging markets country groups, and with risks tilted to the upside. Long-term inflation expectations are projected to remain anchored in the baseline forecast. Given the recovery's uncharted nature, considerable uncertainty remains, particularly relating to the assessment of economic slack. Prolonged supply disruptions, commodity and housing price shocks, longer-term expenditure commitments, and a de-anchoring of inflation expectations could lead to significantly higher inflation than predicted in the baseline. Clear communication, combined with appropriate monetary and fiscal policies tailored to country-specific contexts, however, could prevent "inflation scares" from unhinging inflation expectations.

Introduction

Headline inflation has risen rapidly in advanced economies and emerging market and developing economies since the beginning of 2021, though it has been relatively stable in low-income countries (Figure 2.1). While core inflation—the change in the prices of goods and services excluding food and energy—has risen less than headline rates, it has also ticked up in

The authors of this chapter are Francesca Caselli (co-lead), Sonali Das, Christoffer Koch, Prachi Mishra (co-lead), and Philippe Wingender, with contributions from Chunya Bu and support from Youyou Huang and Cynthia Nyakeri. Swapnil Agarwal and Mattia Coppo also provided data support. The chapter benefited from discussions with Rodrigo Valdés and from comments by internal seminar participants and reviewers. Olivier Coibion provided valuable guidance and suggestions.

recent months. These developments have occurred amid still-substantial policy support as economies recover from the deep contraction of 2020. Moreover, as economies reopen, the release of excess savings accumulated during the pandemic could further fuel private spending. This combination of unprecedented factors has led to concern about the possibility of persistently high inflation.

From a macroeconomic perspective, a sustained rise in inflation in advanced economies leading to an unanticipated withdrawal of monetary accommodation could disrupt financial markets. Emerging market and developing economies would be especially affected from the resulting spillover effects through capital outflows and exchange rate depreciations, as seen during the taper tantrum episode in 2013. High inflation would also tend to hurt those who rely primarily on labor income (generally lower-income individuals) but could also benefit debtors while hurting lenders. Inflation can, therefore, have complex distributional consequences.

This chapter assesses the outlook for inflation and evaluates the risks around it. It first takes stock of inflation trends during the pandemic and then examines the drivers of inflation using the Phillips curve, which relates inflation to domestic slack—a key framework central banks use to form their views on inflation and, in turn, on monetary policy. It also examines whether there has been a change in the overall relationship between economic slack and inflation with inclusion of the pandemic period. This could have major implications for evaluating the effect of accelerating demand during the recovery and for the conduct of monetary policy (see, for example, Draghi 2017 and Powell 2018).

Inflation expectations and supply shocks are also crucial to understanding the inflation process. A key concern is identifying the conditions that could cause recent inflation spikes to persist, leading to unanchored expectations and self-fulfilling inflation spirals. Policymakers worry that the unprecedented policy support enacted in response to the COVID-19 crisis may have reduced the room for monetary policy to maneuver,

Figure 2.1. Consumer Price Inflation, by Country Group
(Median, year-over-year percent change)

Broad-based rise in headline inflation.

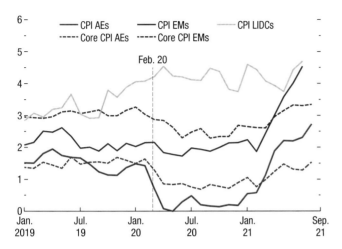

Sources: Haver Analytics; IMF, CPI database; and IMF staff calculations.
Note: The vertical line indicates February 2020. AEs = advanced economies;
CPI = consumer price index; EMs = emerging market economies;
LIDCs = low-income developing countries.

thereby impacting the credibility of central banks and leading to possible de-anchoring of inflation expectations. This chapter examines how robust the anchor was during the pandemic and assesses the potential risk of de-anchoring during the recovery phase. Finally, the analysis zooms in on sectoral and commodity price movements, asking how supply shocks could contribute to the inflation outlook.

The key findings of the chapter suggest the following:

Inflation is expected to revert to pre-pandemic levels by mid-2022. The analysis indicates that headline inflation and medium-term inflation expectations are projected to revert to pre-pandemic levels by mid-2022. Although much uncertainty remains, particularly regarding measurement of output gaps, recovering demand is expected to have only a small impact on future inflation. The IMF staff's baseline forecasts suggest that, for the advanced economy country group, on average, headline inflation will peak in the final months of 2021 and will decline to about 2 percent by mid-2022. Risks remain tilted slightly to the upside over the medium term. The outlook for emerging market and developing economies similarly shows headline inflation declining to about 4 percent after a peak of 6.8 percent later this year, with risks tilted to the upside over the medium term. A key feature of the outlook is the significant

cross-country heterogeneity across advanced and emerging market and developing economies—and even within advanced economies. While the United States drives the strong inflation dynamics in advanced economies in the short term, with near-term risks tilted to the upside, underlying inflation dynamics in the euro area and Japan remain weak.

Risks: Inflation expectations have stayed relatively anchored so far, and risks of de-anchoring appear limited for advanced economies despite frequent monetary and fiscal policy announcements during the pandemic. The density forecast in the baseline also indicates anchored inflation expectations in emerging market and developing economies over the next two years. However, considerable uncertainty surrounds these forecasts, particularly related to the assessment of economic slack and reflected in the distribution around the baseline and in the counterfactual scenarios. Sharply rising housing prices and prolonged input supply shortages in both advanced economies and emerging market and developing economies and continued food price pressures and currency depreciations in the latter group could keep inflation elevated for longer. Simulations of a tail risk scenario with continued sectoral disruptions and large swings in commodity prices show that headline inflation could rise significantly higher than the baseline. Simulations including a temporary de-anchoring of inflation expectations lead to even higher, more persistent, and volatile inflation.

Policy implications: Selected case studies complement the statistical analysis and confirm that persistent "inflation scares" could lead to higher inflation expectations. While strong, sustained policy action was often needed to bring down inflation and inflation expectations in the past, these actions were accompanied by—and helped reinforce the credibility of—sound and clear communication. Importantly, longer-term expenditure commitments could be associated with unhinged expectations and underscore the importance of credible medium-term fiscal frameworks in keeping expectations anchored (see Chapter 2 of the October 2021 *Fiscal Monitor*). It is important that policymakers be on the lookout and be prepared to act, especially if some of the risks highlighted in this chapter should materialize at the same time—prolonged supply disruptions, rising commodity and housing prices, permanent and unfunded fiscal commitments, a de-anchoring of expectations, combined with mismeasurement of output gaps.

The rest of the chapter starts with an overview of recent inflation developments before assessing the implications of recovering demand on the inflation outlook through the lens of a Phillips curve. It then explores the conditions under which inflation spikes have tended to persist and inflation expectations to become de-anchored in the past. Next, the chapter examines the implications of the recent sectoral price shocks for overall inflation and inflation expectations. The chapter concludes with a discussion of the analysis's main policy implications.

Inflation Dynamics: Recent Drivers

The framework employed here sheds light on three broad drivers of increases in headline inflation: (1) a pickup in economic activity or closing output gaps supported by accommodative fiscal and monetary policies, along with the release of pent-up demand and accumulated savings (Figure 2.2, panel 1); (2) rapidly rising commodity prices (Figure 2.2, panel 2); and (3) input shortages and supply chain disruptions (Figure 2.2, panel 3). Some have suggested that the fiscal expansion—unprecedented as it was, especially in advanced economies—may push unemployment low enough to cause overheating, possibly de-anchoring inflation expectations and resulting in a self-fulfilling inflation spiral (Blanchard 2021; Summers 2021). Others see a persistent surge in price pressures from a "one-time surge in spending" as unlikely (Powell 2021).

An Uncertain Outlook

The contrasting views on inflation prospects point to the high uncertainty surrounding the outlook for price movements. Factors behind the uncertain inflation outlook—not necessarily covered explicitly in this chapter—include the evolution of housing (see Box 1.1 in Chapter 1), structural transformation in labor markets, and food prices. Global food prices are up by about 40 percent since the start of the pandemic. This has implications especially for low-income countries, where the share of food in consumption baskets is high (see Box 2.1).

Another source of uncertainty is wage processes coming out of the pandemic, with accelerating labor demand hitting up against likely temporary shortages, leading to worries about fueling a wage-price spiral. Consistent with a resumption of greater activity, signs

Figure 2.2. Excess Savings, Commodity Prices, and Supply Chain Disruptions

Rise in headline inflation amid pent-up demand, commodity price pressures, and supply chain disruptions.

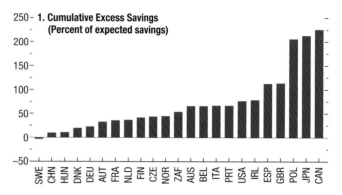

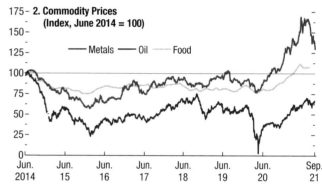

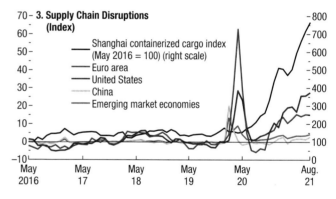

Sources: Baltic Exchange; Haver Analytics; IMF, Primary Commodity Price System; Organisation for Economic Co-operation and Development; and IMF staff calculations.
Note: Cumulative excess savings are household savings from 2020:Q1–21:Q1 or the latest quarter available, exceeding expected savings based on a calculated linear trend from 2017:Q1–19:Q4 for each country. In panel 3, the composite emerging market economy data are from IHS Markit. Supply chain disruptions are calculated as the difference between the supply delivery times subindex in the purchasing managers' index (PMI) and a counterfactual, cyclical measure of supply delivery times based on the manufacturing output subindex in the PMI. Data labels use International Organization for Standardization (ISO) country codes.

Figure 2.3. Labor Demand in Advanced Economies
(Year-over-year percent change)

While wages increased in 2020, this was concomitant with a decline in hours.

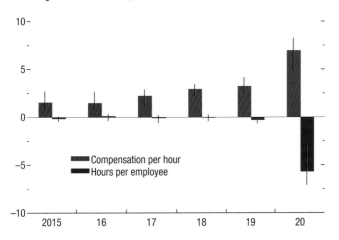

Sources: Eurostat; Haver Analytics; Organisation for Economic Co-operation and Development; and IMF staff calculations.
Note: The bars represent medians; vertical lines represent the interquartile ranges of corresponding variables across 24 advanced economies. See Online Annex 2.1 for further details.

of higher wage growth are apparent in sectors that were hurt the most by the COVID-19 shock early on—for instance, there have been notable upticks in wages for jobs in leisure and hospitality and retail, among other sectors, in the United States. Evidence from a sample of 23 advanced economies also suggests that the average compensation per hour went up significantly in 2020. However, this wage growth happened at the same time as a decline in hours (Figure 2.3), and the brunt of the reduction was disproportionately borne by low-skilled workers and youth, who tend to earn less. Despite sectoral wage pressures, and a slight uptick in economy-wide nominal wage inflation in the United States, few signs of acceleration in economies are visible where data are available through the middle of the year (Canada, Germany, Spain, United Kingdom). Even after adjusting for composition effects, overall wage growth has remained within normal ranges, according to the Federal Reserve of Atlanta's US Wage Growth Tracker. As health metrics improve and exceptional income support measures expire, hiring difficulties in certain sectors could abate. That said, substantial uncertainty remains—and depends on whether firms can hold off filling the vacancies, their views on how long current worker shortages will persist, and how workers' health-risk-adjusted reservation wages evolve (see Chapter 1).

To take into account exceptionally large changes in prices of items other than food and energy—such as tourism and travel—during this crisis, alternative measures (such as trimmed means or medians that filter out these unusual movements) point to a more muted increase in underlying inflation (see Box 2.2). While some of the current price pressures could indeed be transitory (for example, because of droughts, export restrictions, and stockpiling of food stocks), much uncertainty remains regarding the evolution of several factors.

Economic Slack and the Inflation Outlook— Evidence from the Phillips Curve

A key element of central banks' policy frameworks is the Phillips curve relationship. This describes a trade-off between low slack (for instance, low cyclical unemployment) and high inflation.[1] In the Phillips curve, the inflation process is also related to cost-push shocks driven by supply disturbances and to long-term inflation expectations. As inflation-targeting regimes have become more prevalent, long-term inflation expectations have played a greater role in explaining inflation outcomes.[2]

This section focuses on evaluating the strength of the relationship between inflation and economic slack to assess the extent to which expanding demand could contribute to inflation in the period ahead. A Phillips curve that includes forward-looking inflation expectations, lagged inflation, foreign price pressures, and output gaps is estimated on a large sample of advanced economies and emerging markets for 2000–20. Figure 2.4 reports the estimates for the pooled sample and the group of advanced economies

[1]Monetary policymakers typically use the "New Keynesian" framework comprising (1) an aggregate demand relationship, (2) optimal monetary policy, and (3) a Phillips curve relationship (see Clarida, Galí, and Gertler 1999). Alternative approaches to understanding the inflation process consider monetary aggregates as potential predictors of inflation (see, for instance, Pradhan and Goodhart 2021 for a review). In the context of the current crisis, Agur and others (2021) documents that large increases in the money supply because of major fiscal and monetary stimulus have led to only modest short-term pass-through from money growth to inflation, especially in countries with credible central banks.
[2]Major central banks, such as the European Central Bank and the US Federal Reserve, have recently adjusted their frameworks to guide long-term inflation expectations and mitigate deflationary risks, among other objectives. Thus far, the evolution of inflation expectations is consistent with the intended objectives of the frameworks' adjustment.

Figure 2.4. Unemployment Gap–Inflation Phillips Correlation
(Percentage points)

Unemployment changes away from the natural rate are associated with softer inflation, more so in emerging market economies.

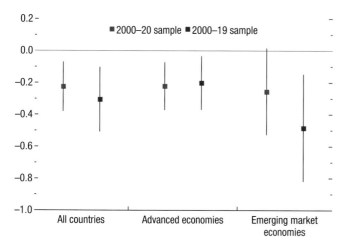

Sources: Haver Analytics; and IMF staff calculations.
Note: The squares represent the coefficient estimates of the unemployment gap-inflation Phillips correlation. The vertical bars represent the 90 percent confidence intervals. See Online Annex 2.1 for further details.

and emerging markets separately (see Online Annex 2.2 for details of the sample composition and estimation).[3] A 1-percentage-point widening of the unemployment gap—that is, unemployment higher than the natural rate of unemployment—is associated with a decline in core inflation of 0.22 percentage point, on average. A similar point estimate is seen for advanced economies when splitting the sample by income groups. The coefficient for emerging markets is broadly similar, but not statistically distinguishable from zero.

The COVID-19 period, however, poses many challenges to estimating this relationship. There is much uncertainty about unemployment and output gaps during the pandemic (see Chapter 1). A massive, unprecedented fiscal and monetary policy response to the economic shock may also obscure the relationship between slack and inflation to a greater extent than would be seen over the course of a typical business cycle. Moreover, supply chain disruptions, sectoral dislocation associated with the pandemic, commodity price volatility, changing weights in consumer baskets (Cavallo 2020; Reinsdorf 2020), and extreme base effects also contribute to measurement challenges beyond those related to potential output.

[3]All annexes are available at www.imf.org/en/Publications/WEO.

Comparison with the Phillips curve relationship prior to the pandemic can shed light on the extent to which the unusually sharp fall and rebound in effective potential output induced by lockdown and reopening in 2020 might have affected the estimates. Figure 2.4 reports the response of core inflation to the changes in the unemployment gap estimated up to the fourth quarter of 2019 for advanced economies. The unprecedented pandemic disturbances do not seem to have altered the Phillips curve relationship for advanced economies. Estimates for emerging markets instead seem to be more sensitive to the inclusion of the pandemic period.[4] The results also point to mixed evidence on nonlinear effects at different levels of slack (see Online Annex 2.2).

A Causal Phillips Curve Confirms the Relevance of the Inflation-Activity Trade-Off

Although these results are based on a model that includes country-specific indicators and several controls, they could still be confounded by omitted variables and reverse causality. A widening output gap and weakening of inflation, for example, could induce central banks to reduce interest rates to boost demand, and so blunt what might have otherwise shown up as pronounced movement in the data (for a detailed discussion of the endogeneity issues in this setting, see McLeay and Tenreyro 2020). To address such concerns, an alternative estimation based on a treatment effect methodology is performed.[5] As proposed by Barnichon and Mesters (2021), well-identified demand shocks can be used to instrument for changes in unemployment. In particular, monetary policy shocks are used to proxy for demand shocks, to recover a causal relationship between inflation and activity. Causal estimates of the Phillips coefficient can be recovered by taking the

[4]The larger magnitude of the estimated coefficient for emerging markets in the pre-COVID-19 sample could be driven by different policies and shocks and could point to measurement errors too, especially in measuring slack, attenuating the estimates in the 2000–20 sample toward zero.

[5]This involves estimating central banks' monetary policy reaction functions and using inverse probability weighting to identify the impact of unexpected changes in short-term rates. The methodology proposed by Angrist, Jordà, and Kuersteiner (2018) is extended here to a panel setting. Recent macroeconomic studies that use this methodology to achieve identification include Jordà and Taylor (2016), Serrato and Wingender (2016), Acemoglu and others (2019), and Caselli and Wingender (2021). Willems (2020) instead constructs a measure of monetary policy tightening based on large and unexpected interest rate hikes for 162 countries.

ratio of these impulse response functions of inflation to unemployment at the relevant horizon.[6] A negative and statistically significant slope coefficient of minus 0.22 is estimated for advanced economies, providing reassurance of the validity of the reduced form results. These findings provide further evidence of strength in the relationship between inflation and slack.[7]

The Impact of Recovering Demand on Inflation Dynamics

What role will the closing of output gaps play in the inflation outlook while the recovery is under way? The previous causal relationship is used to back out the contribution of the projected closing of the unemployment gap in advanced economies on inflation dynamics for the next six years.[8] This year and the next exhibit a moderately positive inflation impulse of about 0.23 percentage point and 0.14 percentage point, respectively (Figure 2.5). This impact softens in 2023 and 2024 before turning into a negligible disinflation impulse in 2026. These aggregate figures

[6]Online Annex 2.2 presents the details of the impulse responses of inflation and unemployment to contractionary monetary policy surprises and discusses their dynamics. Online Annex Figure 2.2.2, panel 1, shows that the unemployment rate increases by 1 percentage point, on average, in response to a cumulative 40-basis-point surprise tightening, compared with a neutral stance, and the full impact takes about 12 quarters to materialize. Online Annex Figure 2.2.2, panel 2, shows that core inflation significantly decreases by about 0.2 percentage point after 15 quarters to the same sequence of monetary policy tightening. While the estimated impulse response function for the unemployment rate is at the higher end, it is consistent with the empirical literature that exploits narrative approaches to estimate the effects of monetary policy shocks on real activity (Ramey 2016). Moreover, it is important to stress the differences in terms of sample period and composition and estimation approach compared with the bulk of the literature, which focuses on linear models in the United States. See Online Annex 2.2 for a more detailed discussion.

[7]Results are reported for advanced economies only. Data limitations and variability in policy reaction functions for emerging market central banks result in a weak first stage for these countries.

[8]The literature points to mixed evidence about the strength of the Phillips curve. Several explanations have been offered for a potential flattening of the Phillips curve. For instance, since the mid-1990s inflation expectations have become increasingly more important in explaining current inflation (Chapter 3 of the April 2013 *World Economic Outlook* [WEO]; Yellen 2015). Second, globalization forces have been mentioned as potential drivers of a weakening relationship between inflation and domestic slack (Borio and Filardo 2007; Auer, Borio, and Filardo 2017; Chapter 3 of the October 2018 WEO; Bems and others, forthcoming). Third, other long-term structural changes, such as workers' declining bargaining power and automation, greater employer concentration, and higher wage rigidity reduced the sensitivity of inflation to the level of slack (Yellen 2012; Daly, Hobijn, and Pyle 2016; Hooper, Mishkin, and Sufi 2019).

Figure 2.5. Slack-Induced Inflation Dynamics from Structural Phillips Curve in Advanced Economies
(Percentage points)

Changes in advanced economies' unemployment gaps lead to a small inflation impulse from slack.

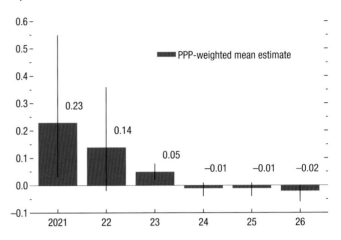

Sources: Haver Analytics; and IMF staff calculations.
Note: The bars represent the inflation impulse from changes in the unemployment gap based on the October 2021 *World Economic Outlook* vintage and the structural Phillips curve estimation described in the chapter. The vertical lines represent the interquartile ranges. PPP = purchasing power parity.

mask a significant degree of heterogeneity, as shown by the interquartile ranges, with the United States and its extraordinary policy support driving short-term inflation dynamics. Results for emerging markets using reduced-form estimates show a stronger impulse toward inflation as a result of recovering labor markets equal to 0.5 percentage point in 2021, but moderate contributions through the forecast horizon (see Online Annex 2.2).[9] These calculations crucially rely on the projected unemployment paths and estimates of the potential scarring from the crisis (see Chapter 1). Given the recovery's uncharted nature, considerable uncertainty around these economic-slack-induced dynamics remains because of the difficulties in quantifying the extent of potential scarring and the effects of the crisis on potential output.

The Role of Anchoring of Inflation Expectations

The previous section presented evidence that expanding demand is likely to have a muted impact on future inflation. Nevertheless, other factors, such as the

[9]The calculation for emerging markets is presented in Online Annex Figure 2.2.3, and is based on ordinary least squares coefficients.

anchoring of inflation expectations and supply shocks, are also crucial to understanding the inflation process. A key question is the conditions under which recent inflation spikes could persist, including because expectations become unanchored and lead to self-fulfilling inflation spirals. This section explores the conditions under which expectations can become unanchored. It then examines what countries have done in the past to successfully keep expectations anchored or bring them down once they rose.

Anchoring: The literature proposes various indicators to measure the degree of anchoring. Chapter 3 of the October 2018 WEO and Bems and others (2021) construct a synthetic indicator that includes four subcomponents capturing either operational or practical characteristics associated with stable and anchored inflation expectations.[10] Inflation expectations are considered anchored if they are stable over time, exhibit little cross-sectional dispersion, are insensitive to macroeconomic news, and are close to the central bank target. As shown in Figure 2.6, panel 1, although advanced economies presented a relatively stable degree of anchoring during the past two decades, consistent with early adoption of inflation-targeting regimes, emerging markets have seen significant improvements since the beginning of the 2000s. These economies have achieved anchoring comparable to that of advanced economies in recent years. Nevertheless, among emerging market economies, significant variability remains—as shown by the wider interquartile range in Figure 2.6, panel 1.

Institutional characteristics and anchoring of inflation expectations: The extent of anchoring is closely associated with institutional characteristics, such as the credibility of monetary and fiscal policy as well as the general macroeconomic situation and structural characteristics. In this regard, an independent and transparent central bank and sound and sustainable fiscal policy are key prerequisites for credible policies (Mishkin 2000; Mishkin and Savastano 2001). The cross-country variation in the degree of anchoring is positively correlated

---

[10]These include (1) the variability of long-term inflation forecasts over time—if expectations are anchored, revisions to long-term forecasts should be small, and thus the average forecast relatively stable over time; (2) the dispersion of expectations across agents; (3) the sensitivity of long-term expectations to expectations about short-term inflation or macroeconomic surprises; and (4) the deviation of medium- or longer-term inflation expectations from the central bank's target. For details on the construction of the index, see Bems and others (2021). The index is constructed using professional forecasters' long-term (three-year and longer) inflation expectations.

Figure 2.6. Inflation Anchoring
(Index)

Anchoring has improved, particularly in emerging market economies, but it still varies across countries. Sound and suitable monetary and fiscal policies are associated with more anchored expectations.

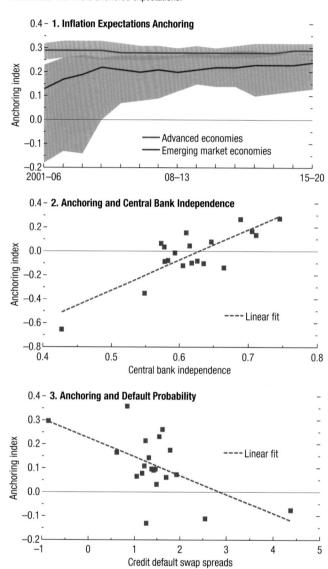

Sources: Bems and others (2021); Concensus Economics; Dincer and Eichengreen (2014); Garriga (2016); Haver Analytics; and IMF staff calculations.
Note: In panel 1, lines represent the median; shaded areas represent the interquartile range of anchoring index by country group. See Online Annex 2.1 for further details.

with the degree of independence of the central bank (Figure 2.6, panel 2) and negatively associated with the probability of default (Figure 2.6, panel 3).

Benefits of anchoring: What are the benefits of anchored inflation expectations? If long-term inflation expectations are not anchored, shocks that weaken economic activity could present the central bank with a policy dilemma. Although loose monetary policies might be appropriate to boost demand, they could accelerate price pressure and increase uncertainty, which would hold back private investment and employment growth. By contrast, if inflation expectations are anchored, the central bank has more scope to pursue the appropriate countercyclical policy response to stimulate demand (Chapter 3 of the October 2018 WEO; Bems and others 2020).

When Have Expectations Become Unanchored in the Past?

Analysis of past inflation episodes can help shed light on conditions that contribute to de-anchoring of inflation expectations. The exercise identifies turning points in inflation—"inflation accelerations or scares"—following the approach used in Hausmann, Pritchett, and Rodrik (2005) (for growth performance). Fifty-five episodes distributed equally across advanced economies and emerging markets are identified (Figure 2.7).

Inflation accelerations are associated with sharp exchange rate depreciations in emerging markets. On average, the nominal effective exchange rate depreciated by about 8 percent in the quarter the episode began.[11] Inflation accelerations were also preceded by an upsurge in fiscal and current account deficits in emerging markets. Unlike the full sample or emerging market and developing economy estimates, fiscal balances in advanced economies rose prior to high inflation episodes, on average, which suggests that aggregate demand shocks could have driven both fiscal performance and inflation in advanced economies. Short- and medium-term inflation expectations rose sharply too during inflation scares. More persistent episodes, defined as those during which inflation remained elevated for six quarters or more, were associated with a steeper rise in three-year-ahead inflation expectations (see Online Annex 2.3).

Given the difficulty of quantifying some important policy variables, such as communication from the central bank, this section also applies a narrative approach to selected case studies (Box 2.3). An analysis of macroeconomic outcomes in the case studies confirms many of the findings of the statistical analysis and offers additional insights. Longer-term expenditure

[11]The exchange rate depreciation is the only factor that appears as statistically significant.

Figure 2.7. Inflation Episodes

Episodes of high inflation are associated with large exchange rate depreciations.

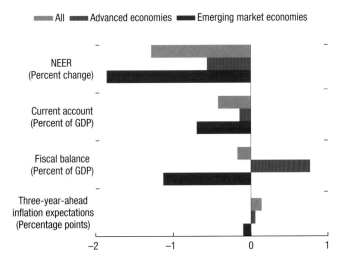

Sources: Bloomberg Finance L.P.; Consensus Economics; Haver Analytics; and IMF staff calculations.
Note: The chart presents the difference in the three-quarter averages just prior to the start of an inflation acceleration episode (from $t-3$ to $t-1$) compared with the previous six-quarter averages ($t-9$ to $t-4$). NEER = nominal effective exchange rate.

commitments (for example, financing the Vietnam War and Great Society programs in the 1960s in the United States, and soaring subsidy bills and agricultural debt waivers in India in the late 2000s) could be associated with unhinged expectations.[12] External shocks combined with sharp exchange rate depreciations (for example, in Brazil in the early 2000s) could also trigger a de-anchoring of expectations, especially in countries starting from an environment of low monetary policy credibility. Moreover, even when expectations are well anchored, a prolonged deviation of inflation from target could cause expectations to move (such as in Chile before the global financial crisis).

Expectations Anchoring during the COVID-19 Pandemic

How robust has the inflation anchor been during the COVID-19 pandemic? If inflation expectations are well anchored, they should not respond to inflation surprises. To zoom in on the pandemic

[12]Coibion, Gorodnichenko, and Weber (2021) finds that US households anticipate higher short-term and long-term inflation following news about future debt but do not in response to information about current debt, suggesting that households are able to distinguish between transitory fiscal changes and those that are more permanent.

period, a daily market-based measure of long-term inflation expectations, the five-year, five-year forward breakeven inflation rate, is analyzed for a sample of 14 countries.[13] Inflation surprises are proxied by oil price shocks, measured as the change in the price of one-year-ahead oil futures contracts. Consistent with the previous literature (Gürkaynak, Sack, and Wright 2010; Beechey, Johannsen, and Levin 2011; Celasun, Mihet, and Ratnovski 2012), the results indicate a small but significant effect of oil price shocks on expectations (Figure 2.8, panel 1). The introduction of an interaction term of oil futures prices with an indicator for the pandemic period (starting in March 2020) reveals that, on average, in the limited sample, there was no significant change in the relationship between oil price surprises and the breakeven rate during the pandemic compared with normal times (Figure 2.8, panel 2). Breakeven inflation rates in the United States, however, overshot their pre-pandemic levels in January 2021.[14] An analysis of daily monetary and fiscal policy announcements reveals no evidence of de-anchoring in response to the exceptionally large policy responses to the pandemic (see Online Annex Figure 2.3.2). Overall, these findings suggest that the anchor has remained relatively stable so far during the COVID-19 pandemic crisis.

Sectoral Shocks and the Inflation Outlook

The COVID-19 crisis triggered large price movements in some sectors, notably transportation, food, clothing, and communications (see Online Annex 2.4). However, overall sectoral price dispersion so far has remained relatively subdued by recent historical standards, especially compared with the global

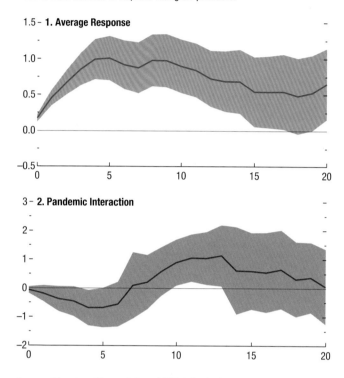

Figure 2.8. Response of Five-Year, Five-Year Forward Breakeven Inflation to Oil Price Shocks
(Basis points)

Market-based inflation expectations respond to oil price surprises but have not become more sensitive to surprises during the pandemic.

1. Average Response

2. Pandemic Interaction

Sources: Bloomberg Finance L.P.; and IMF staff calculations.
Note: The solid lines represent the estimated response; shaded areas represent 95 percent confidence intervals. The *x*-axis indicates the number of days after the shock starts.

---

[13]See Online Annex 2.3 for country coverage, variable definitions, and estimation details. In addition to reflecting expectations about future inflation, breakeven rates include both liquidity risk premiums and inflation risk premiums, reflecting uncertainty about future inflation, which could have important policy implications (Chapter 1 of the October 2021 *Global Financial Stability Report*). Countries for which breakeven inflation rates are available are mostly advanced economies or major emerging markets with high central bank credibility and well-anchored inflation expectations. Robustness exercises with liquidity-adjusted measures are implemented following Gürkaynak, Sack, and Wright (2010). The time-varying effect of liquidity on inflation compensation is measured as the fitted values from a regression of the breakeven rate on liquidity proxies for both bonds.

[14]Consistent with the shift to the flexible average inflation-targeting framework, breakeven inflation rates in the United States rose, particularly at shorter horizons, primarily due to an increase in the risk-adjusted expected inflation component (Chapter 1 of the October 2021 *Global Financial Stability Report*).

financial crisis (Figure 2.9, panel 1). As illustrated in Figure 2.9, panel 2, this is driven by somewhat smaller and shorter-lived swings in fuel (transport), food, and housing prices, which are the three largest components of consumption baskets, on average.

In addition, a case study of the semiconductor industry in the United States points to only a modest increase in overall inflation, given a potential doubling of semiconductor input prices (see Online Annex Figure 2.4.2). This is because categories with the highest potential increase in inflation, as a result of the doubling input price of semiconductors, have a very small weight in personal consumption expenditures (such as personal computers and photographic equipment).[15] An important caveat though is, while

---

[15]In contrast, consumption items with the highest weights in the consumption basket (for example, housing) exhibit negligible price increases from higher semiconductor input prices. The analysis makes use of US input-output tables.

Figure 2.9. Sectoral Inflation Dynamics

Sectoral inflation dispersion during the pandemic does not stand out by historical standards. This is largely due to smaller and shorter-lived swings in fuel, food, and housing prices.

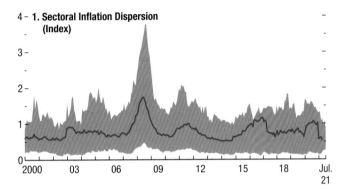

1. Sectoral Inflation Dispersion
   (Index)

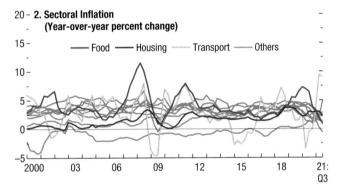

2. Sectoral Inflation
   (Year-over-year percent change)

Food ─── Housing ─── Transport ─── Others

Sources: Haver Analytics; IMF, CPI database; and IMF staff calculations.
Note: In panel 1, the solid line represents the cross-country mean of sectoral inflation dispersion; shaded area represents the 10th–90th percentile range. The sectoral inflation dispersion index is calculated as the standard deviation of sectoral inflation weighted by consumption shares. Panel 2 presents averages weighted by country's purchasing-power-parity GDP.

it is possible that the shortage in semiconductor chips may not directly translate into higher prices, it could still lead to lower output of products that rely on chips as inputs, for instance cars, which in turn could lead to higher prices for these goods or their substitutes.

The Inflation Outlook

To assess how sectoral price dynamics could affect the inflation outlook, a structural quantile vector autoregression model is estimated for advanced economies and emerging market and developing economies to gauge the balance of risks by looking at broader moments of the density forecast (Koenker and Xiao 2006; Ghysels, Iania, and Striuakas 2018; Montes-Rojas 2019; Chavleishvili and Manganelli 2020; Boire, Duprey, and

Ueberfeldt 2021).[16] Online Annex 2.4 provides details and definitions of the variables.

Density forecasts show a sharp rise in inflation in the near term. Headline inflation among advanced economies is expected to peak at 3.6 percent in the final months of 2021 (Figure 2.10, panel 1). The forecast then drops to 3.2 percent by the end of the year and reaches about 2 percent by mid-2022. Risks are tilted slightly to the upside over the medium term for advanced economies. These findings also suggest a 10 percent probability of inflation remaining above 3.4 percent through the end of 2021. While the density forecasts suggest that inflation is likely to peak later this year in advanced economies, uncertainty remains related to the factors mentioned earlier.

The outlook for emerging market and developing economies indicates a return to trend headline inflation of about 4 percent by mid-2022 (Figure 2.10, panel 3). Risks remain tilted to the upside over the medium term for emerging markets, as evidenced by the wider interquartile range at the top of the density forecast than at the bottom.[17]

Inflation expectations: Long-term inflation expectations present a relatively strong degree of anchoring. They gradually trend back to about 2 percent, on average, in the baseline forecast for advanced economies, with little risk of de-anchoring (Figure 2.10, panel 2). For emerging market and developing economies, expectations are projected to remain anchored over the medium term, but with upside risks, as shown by the mean forecast lying above the median forecast starting in mid-2023 (Figure 2.10, panel 4).

Assessing the Impact of Continued Strong Increases in Commodity Prices and Sectoral Price Dispersion

The previous results are based on the historical relationship between inflation dynamics and its determinants, including the reaction function of central banks to incoming data. Given the uniqueness of the current episode, any attempt to extrapolate lessons from experience into the future must be approached with caution. In particular, policymakers wonder about the effect of continued and sustained sectoral disruptions on the inflation outlook. Could sectoral price volatility, for example from housing or food prices,

---

[16]Following Lenza and Primiceri (2020), the estimation of parameters of the model excludes the pandemic period.

[17]Reversion to trend may be delayed if monetary policy does not respond as quickly to higher inflation as it has in the past.

Figure 2.10. Headline Inflation and Inflation Expectations Baseline Outlook
(Percent)

In the baseline forecast, headline inflation exhibits a short-lived increase in both advanced economies and emerging market and developing economies, and inflation expectations are projected to remain anchored over the medium term.

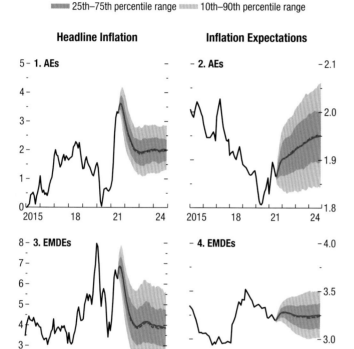

Figure 2.11. Headline Inflation and Inflation Expectations Outlook with Adverse Sectoral and Commodity Price Shocks
(Percent)

A sharp rise in commodity prices and sectoral inflation dispersion over the next 12 months would have a strong but temporary impact on headline inflation. Inflation expectations could overshoot but revert to trend over the medium term.

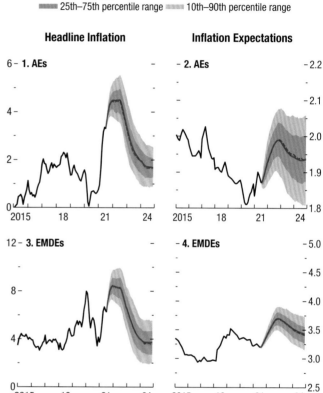

Sources: Consensus Economics; Haver Analytics; IMF, CPI database; and IMF staff estimates.
Note: The lines are averages weighted by countries' purchasing-power-parity GDP. Central tendencies for headline inflations are adjusted to ensure consistency with mean *World Economic Outlook* inflation forecasts. AEs = advanced economies; EMDEs = emerging market and developing economies. See Online Annex 2.1 for further details about the list of countries included in the samples.

Sources: Consensus Economics; Haver Analytics; IMF, CPI database; and IMF staff estimates.
Note: The lines are averages weighted by countries' purchasing-power-parity GDP. Sectoral dispersion and commodity price shocks are assumed to be drawn from the top 75 percent of the predictive distributions for 12 consecutive months from July 2021 to June 2022. AEs = advanced economies; EMDEs = emerging market and developing economies. See Online Annex 2.1 for further details about the list of countries included in the samples.

spill over into headline inflation and lead to higher, more persistent, and volatile inflation? Could this lead to an inflation spiral propelled by the de-anchoring of inflation expectations?

Tail-risk scenario: A forward-looking exercise is used to answer these questions. The exercise simulates inflation developments assuming a tail scenario which, according to the model employed here, has less than 0.01 percent probability of materializing. This scenario is marked by strong rises in commodity prices and sectoral inflation dispersion over the next 12 months and

allows an assessment of the potential impacts of continued supply disruptions or mismatches as the recovery proceeds. In this scenario, headline inflation would increase significantly, peaking at 4.4 percent, on average, in advanced economies by mid-2022 and 8.4 percent in emerging markets by early 2022 (Figure 2.11, panels 1 and 3). The forecasts in this scenario show broadly balanced risks over the medium term. However, even in this extreme scenario, headline inflation goes back to trend by early 2024. A look at inflation expectations

Figure 2.12. Headline Inflation with Adverse Sectoral and Commodity Price Shocks and Adaptive Expectations Shock
(Percent)

Sectoral and commodity, price shocks with unanchored expectations would lead to higher, more persistent, and volatile inflation.

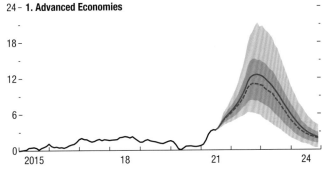

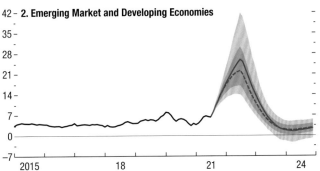

Sources: Consensus Economics; Haver Analytics; IMF, CPI database; and IMF staff estimates.
Note: The lines are averages weighted by countries' purchasing-power-parity GDP. Adaptive expectations assume that inflation is driven by one-year-ahead inflation expectations instead of the conventional three-year-ahead horizon for 12 consecutive months from July 2021 to June 2022. See Online Annex 2.1 for further details about the list of countries included in the samples.

points to fairly strong anchoring of about 2 percent in advanced economies, with little risk of de-anchoring (Figure 2.11, panel 2). For emerging market and developing economies, there is overshooting of expectations in the short term (Figure 2.11, panel 4). However, inflation expectations are projected to remain anchored over the medium term.

In summary, sectoral disruptions and large swings in commodity prices could mean upside risks for headline inflation, with higher peaks and a delayed return to trend inflation. The medium-term outlook, nevertheless, would likely still be driven by fundamentals, including the speed of the recovery and the continued anchoring of inflation expectations.

Potential effects of an additional de-anchoring shock: Importantly, the preceding scenario assumes inflation expectations remain anchored. While plausible—sectoral inflation dispersion reached very high levels after the global financial crisis without having long-lasting effects on headline inflation—the possibility of expectations deviating from target and creating a self-fulfilling inflationary spiral is a serious concern for policymakers. To evaluate the potential effects of a de-anchoring shock on the outlook, the previous scenario is extended to allow for inflation expectations to become adaptive for a period of 12 months, meaning expectations are no longer forward-looking but rather react to incoming data.[18] In Figure 2.12, inflation increases substantially in this extreme scenario and becomes more persistent and volatile, as indicated by the much wider interquartile ranges—pointing to the serious implications of inflation expectations becoming de-anchored.

Conclusions

Rising commodity prices and supply chain bottlenecks are putting upward pressure on headline inflation rates. Moreover, the unprecedented nature of the current recovery has raised questions about how long supply will take to catch up with accelerating demand. These uncertainties are fueling worries that inflation could persistently overshoot central bank targets and de-anchor expectations, leading to a self-fulfilling inflation spiral.

The analysis in this chapter suggests that likely will not be the case. Although the overall findings imply an increase in headline inflation in both advanced and emerging markets, it is expected to subside to pre-pandemic ranges by mid-2022 in the baseline.

However, this assessment is subject to significant uncertainty, given the uncharted nature of the recovery. Simulations of scenarios characterized by strong rises in commodity prices, continued sectoral shocks, and adaptive expectations suggest significant risks to the inflation outlook. More persistent supply disruptions and sharply rising housing prices in both advanced economies and emerging market and developing economies, or currency depreciations and food price

---

[18]The simulations assume that the expectations relevant for price formation in advanced economies are the one-year-ahead inflation expectations instead of the conventional three-year-ahead horizon. For emerging market and developing economies, expectations are assumed to be equal to the previous month's inflation.

pressure in the latter group emerging market and developing economies, could all lead inflation to remain elevated for longer than currently expected.

In terms of policy implications, there are four key lessons.

First, the narrative account of selected case studies and scenario analyses suggest that when expectations become de-anchored, inflation can quickly take off and be costly to rein back in. Ultimately, policy credibility and setting of inflation expectations are an endogenous, and possibly nonlinear, process that is hard to pin down precisely; moreover, any assessment of inflation anchoring cannot be decided entirely on the basis of relationships observed in historical data. Policymakers therefore must be ready to act and, more importantly, ensure that sound monetary frameworks are in place, including triggers that could require action. Such triggers could comprise early signs of de-anchoring inflation expectations—from forward-looking surveys, unsustainable fiscal and current accounts, or sharp movements in the exchange rate. In particular, policymakers must be alert to triggers for a perfect storm of inflation risks that could be relatively benign when considered individually but that, by materializing together, could lead to significantly higher inflation than predicted in the baseline forecasts.

Second, case studies demonstrate that, while strong policy action was often successful in bringing down inflation and inflation expectations, sound and credible communication also played a crucial role in keeping expectations anchored. In this context, clear and state-contingent forward guidance and communication (with well-articulated triggers for action) from advanced economy central banks are key during periods of policy normalization to avoid taper-tantrum-like scenarios. Similarly, a well-communicated plan for a gradual exit from exceptional monetary policy and liquidity support as the recovery strengthens would foster orderly market transitions in emerging markets, too. The case studies

also highlight the importance of maintaining strong fiscal credibility for inflation anchoring.

Third, policymakers need to walk a tightrope between acting patiently to support the recovery and at the same time preparing to act quickly if inflation expectations show signs of de-anchoring. Central banks could look beyond temporary inflationary pressures and avoid tightening policies prematurely until there is more clarity on underlying price dynamics (conditional on expectations remaining firmly anchored). At the same time, central banks should also prepare to act quickly if the need arises and chart contingent actions that reveal their true preferences. Fiscal policies should adhere to sustainable medium-term frameworks. However, uncertainty about medium-term output gaps is still high and could affect the optimal timing for removal of policy support while the recovery is still under way. Policies, therefore, should be mindful of the unusual short-term dynamics and uncertainties surrounding potential output.

Fourth, a key feature of the outlook is the significant degree of cross-country heterogeneity among advanced economies and emerging market and developing economies and even within advanced economies. While the United States is projected to drive much of the slack-induced inflation dynamics in the baseline for advanced economies, with near-term risks tilted to the upside, underlying inflation dynamics in the euro area and Japan remain weak. Policy recommendations should be tailored to economies' particular vulnerabilities and business cycle phases. Yet, spillovers from asynchronous monetary and fiscal tightening must be at the core of multilateral policy discussions. For emerging markets, medium-term expectations rose sharply during inflation scare episodes, which were preceded by growing internal and external imbalances—all of which underscores the role of strong macroeconomic fundamentals and credible medium-term fiscal frameworks in keeping expectations anchored.

Box 2.1. Food Insecurity and Prices during COVID-19

Nominal global food prices have risen more than 40 percent since the start of the pandemic.[1] The prices of goods sold in a local market—a more relevant indicator, especially if the good is produced domestically (for example, cassava in central and western Africa)—were influenced by numerous local factors, including supply and demand, government policies, exchange rates, transportation costs, and income levels. Data for monthly market food prices across locations for seven staples (wheat, rice, sugar, maize, milk, poultry, cassava), which

contribute about 60 percent of average daily consumption, from 259 markets in 73 emerging markets are used. The real local price of staples in emerging markets has increased by 4.0 percent since the pandemic began.[2] Significant price surges in staple foods in several countries are observed. By contrast, a number of food-producing countries that experienced favorable weather conditions have avoided upward price pressure.

In the absence of frictions, such as transportation costs, prices tend to equalize across markets.

The authors of this box are Katrien Smuts, John Spray, and Filiz Unsal.

[1] IMF Primary Commodity Price System and authors' calculations; May 2020–May 2021 year-over-year change.

[2] The values are calculated as the regional median of consumption share$_{ij}$ * change in real prices in local currency$_{ij}$, in which i = country and j = staple: 2020:Q1–2021:Q1 year-over-year change.

Figure 2.1.1. Selected Countries' Commodity Price Surges
(Year-over-year percent change, unless noted otherwise)

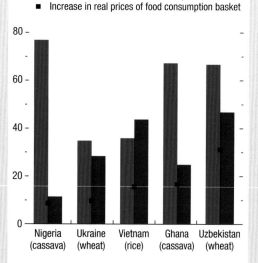

Sources: FAOSTAT New Food Balances; GIEWS FPMA Tool; and IMF staff calculations.
Note: The real increase in consumption baskets includes all staples, not just the ones listed here. The data are from 2020:Q1–2021:Q1.

Figure 2.1.2. Food Staples Contribution to CPI Inflation; Median, by Income
(Percentage points; percent on right scale)

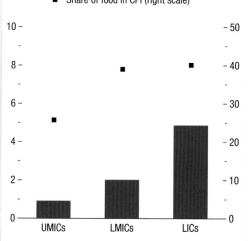

Sources: FAOSTAT New Food Balances; GIEWS FPMA Tool; IMF, International Financial Statistics; and IMF staff calculations.
Note: The staples included in the calculations are wheat, maize, rice, milk, poultry, sugar, and cassava. The countries included in the data set are those for which at least one staple price was available over the sample period. Missing prices are imputed from regional and income group averages. CPI = consumer price index; LICs = low-income countries; LMICs = lower-middle-income countries; UMICs = upper-middle-income countries. The data are from 2020:Q1–2021:Q1.

Box 2.1 *(continued)*

The pandemic, however, coincided with a sharp—20 percent, on average—increase in within-country variation in food prices.[3] This could indicate growing local supply shortages, likely because of pandemic-related declines in mobility—a

greater concern for regions far from food production centers.

The dual shock of rising food prices and falling incomes will exacerbate inequality. In low-income countries, where food makes up about 40 percent of the consumption basket, staple food price growth raised consumer price index inflation 5 percentage points. Within countries, the poorest households spend proportionately more on food (people in sub-Saharan Africa with consumption below $2.97 a day spend about 58 percent of their income on food).

---

[3]Variations in food prices are calculated as $(\max(price_{ijct})_{jct} - \min(price_{ijct})_{jct})/\max(price_{ijct})_{jct}$ for commodity j, market i, in country c in quarter t. An average across commodities and countries within each region is then taken. Commodities that are not present in at least three markets are excluded. 2020:Q1–2021:Q1 year-over-year change.

Box 2.2. Core Inflation in the COVID-19 Crisis

US headline inflation has risen sharply since the start of the pandemic. To interpret such developments, economists distinguish between underlying or "core" inflation, which reflects macroeconomic conditions and is especially salient for monetary policy deliberations, and transitory fluctuations around the core arising from changes in relative prices caused by microeconomic factors. But making this distinction is challenging in the current environment because different measures of core inflation give different signals.

A common measure of core personal consumption expenditure inflation that excludes food and energy prices has recently spiked even higher than headline inflation. But simply removing food and energy prices is not the best way to measure core inflation: transitory movements can arise in different industries (Dolmas 2005). These concerns have led to core measurement based on median inflation (the price change at the 50th percentile of all prices each month) or on trimmed mean inflation (stripping out a fixed share of price changes).

Based on median or trimmed mean inflation, recent developments are less alarming. This difference reflects the large sectoral shocks to industries other than food

The authors of this box are Laurence Ball, Daniel Leigh, Prachi Mishra, and Antonio Spilimbergo.

and energy, which caused the traditional measure to rise sharply but are filtered out of median or trimmed mean inflation. For example, the April 2021 inflation spike reflected the prices of light trucks, hotel rooms, air transportation, spectator sports, and car rentals, which more than doubled at a monthly annualized rate, while median inflation was only 2.8 percent (Figure 2.2.1).

Which of these core measures is more relevant for understanding the current situation? Historical data suggest that it is median or trimmed mean inflation. Figure 2.2.2 compares the volatility of inflation and the strength of its relationship with unemployment using different measures. Trimming more extreme price movements increases the stability of the underlying inflation measure and strengthens its relationship with macroeconomic conditions. Inflation excluding food and energy has been 70 percent more volatile than median inflation and has had a much weaker relationship with unemployment. The COVID-19 crisis has strengthened the case for median or trimmed mean inflation.

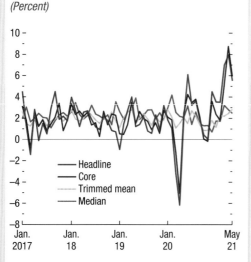

Figure 2.2.1. Headline and Underlying Inflation in the United States
(Percent)

Sources: Haver Analytics; and IMF staff calculations.
Note: Inflation rates are based on the personal consumption expenditure chain-type price index. Trimmed mean is produced by the Federal Reserve Bank of Dallas.

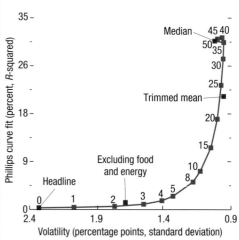

Figure 2.2.2. Inflation Rates in the United States; by Industry, April 2021

Sources: Haver Analytics; and IMF staff calculations.
Note: Points along the line indicate different trimming percentages from monthly distribution of all price changes. Volatility is defined as standard deviation of change in monthly annualized inflation for each measure (January 1990–May 2021). Phillips curve fit indicates R-squared of estimated relationship between quarterly annualized inflation for each measure in deviation from 10-year-ahead Survey of Professional Forecasters expectations and four-quarter average gap between unemployment and its Congressional Budget Office natural rate, estimated based on quarterly data for 1990:Q1–2019:Q4.

Box 2.3. Policy Responses and Expectations in Inflation Acceleration Episodes

United States 1965–83

Background: After two decades of low inflation following World War II, inflation started to increase gradually in the mid-1960s. Inflation continued to drift upward during the 1970s amid several external price shocks, high fiscal deficits due to military engagements and rising social spending, a likely overestimation of productivity growth and potential output, and dovish destabilizing monetary policy.

Policy response and results: The 1978 Humphrey-Hawkins Act amended the Federal Reserve's mandate and enabled then-Federal Reserve Board Chair Paul Volcker to aggressively raise interest rates. The federal funds rate averaged 11.2 percent in 1979, the first year of Volcker's tenure, and rose to 20 percent in June 1981. Inflation peaked in March 1980 at almost 15 percent and fell to 3 percent by 1983. The drop was induced by a sharp demand-led recession that raised the unemployment rate from 5.6 percent in May 1979 to 10.8 percent in November 1982.

Policy conclusions: Important policy lessons were learned from the US Great Inflation of the 1970s and its demise. Central bank independence as a potential mitigant to inflationary bias, as well as central bank transparency, prudent medium-term fiscal planning, and adherence to stabilizing monetary rules and inflation targeting became central.

Brazil 2002–05

Background: Currency depreciations coupled with domestic and external shocks in 2001 triggered a sudden stop in 2002. Brazil experienced a reversal in capital flows and cuts to trade credit lines, and the *real* depreciated by 53 percent in 2002. Inflation expectations rose along with the increase in inflation.

Policy response and results: Starting from low monetary policy credibility and concerns about fiscal dominance, policymakers decided against a gradual tightening. A cumulative increase of 550 basis points was implemented by February 2003, accompanied by an increase in banks' reserve requirements. Expectations began to lower only after the country's monetary policy committee kept the policy rate at 26.5 percent in April 2003 for a third month in a row, despite public outcry. Inflation expectations remained stable until mid-2004. In September 2004, the committee

responded to rising inflation concerns by starting another tightening cycle and clearly laying out conditions under which they would act. They committed to a forward-looking inflation objective for 2005 and announced that policy would respond asymmetrically to inflation-increasing and -decreasing shocks. Expectations fell afterward, even as inflation continued to rise, and expectations indeed converged to the target by the end of 2005. The new government also made efforts to assert a fiscally prudent policy.

Policy conclusions: Considered a stress test of a new inflation-targeting framework, the experience showed (1) the need for larger monetary policy action to counter unanchored expectations and establish credibility, and (2) how clear and state-contingent guidance could complement the initial response.

Chile 2007–09

Background: The Banco Central de Chile (BCC) formally adopted a flexible inflation-targeting framework in 1999. Inflation expectations were well anchored thereafter at about 3 percent. The new monetary policy regime was accompanied by a credible fiscal rule, sound financial sector regulation, and supervision. From mid-2007 to late 2008, however, Chile experienced upward inflation pressure from international factors—rising copper, food, and energy prices. Headline inflation exceeded the target range in August 2007. Inflation expectations began to increase and moved above the 3 percent target by late 2008.

Policy response and results: In the second half of 2007 the BCC tightened monetary policy, raising the policy rate by 25 basis points in July 2007. Despite a cumulative rate increase of 325 basis points by September 2008, two-year-ahead expectations increased to 3.9 percent. The BCC was somewhat slow to act on the rise in inflation for several reasons: (1) the degree of slack in the economy did not rise as high as was estimated, (2) the pass-through from the appreciating exchange rate was lower than expected, and (3) the size and persistence of the increase in agricultural commodity prices was unanticipated. The global financial crisis then led to a recession and reversal of commodity prices rises, while inflation declined sharply and expectations came down to target through 2009.

Policy conclusions: Even when expectations are well anchored, risks to credibility could arise when inflation moves far from its target or when it remains above its band for an extended period.

The authors of this box are Sonali Das, Christoffer Koch, and Prachi Mishra.

Box 2.3 *(continued)*

India 2010–14

Background: Following a rebound after the global financial crisis, growth began to slow in 2011 because of domestic and external factors. The 2003 fiscal rule was abandoned, leading to internal and external imbalances. Inflation expectations were not anchored during this time. At the first hint of US monetary policy tapering on May 22, 2013, India's large current account deficit and excessive dependence on portfolio flows stood badly exposed. A plunging rupee heightened concerns of even higher inflation and risks of a ratings downgrade.

Policy response and results: A new central banker was appointed and laid out several priorities on the first day, September 2, 2013. Two things stood out: (1) a pledge to restore confidence, and (2) a commitment to make the central bank more transparent and predictable. A new inflation-targeting framework began guiding policy and communications in January 2014. Foreign exchange interventions to address commodity price volatility accompanied this strategy. Confidence in the country's economy was achieved as rupee expectations became firmly anchored and inflation and inflation expectations were brought under control.

Policy conclusions: Monetary policy operations improvements and communication strategies, along with a transparent and credible commitment to reducing inflation, worked to disinflate from high levels. The central bank's success on this front opened up the space to pursue other objectives without disturbing inflation expectations.

References

Acemoglu, Daron, Suresh Naidu, Pascual Restrepo, and James A. Robinson. 2019. "Democracy Does Cause Growth." *Journal of Political Economy* 127 (1): 47–100.

Agur, Itai, Damien Capelle, Giovanni Dell'Ariccia, and Damiano Sandri. Forthcoming. "Monetary Finance: Do Not Touch or Handle with Care?" Departmental Paper, Research Department, International Monetary Fund, Washington, DC.

Angrist, Joshua D., Òscar Jordà, and Guido M. Kuersteiner. 2018. "Semiparametric Estimates of Monetary Policy Effects: String Theory Revisited." *Journal of Business & Economic Statistics* 36 (3): 371–87.

Auer, Raphael, Claudio Borio, and Andrew Filardo. 2017. "The Globalization of Inflation: The Growing Importance of Global Value Chains." CEPR Discussion Paper 11905, Centre for Economic Policy Research, London.

Ball, Laurence, Gita Gopinath, Daniel Leigh, Prachi Mishra, and Antonio Spilimbergo. 2021. "Underlying US Inflation: Set for Take-Off? VoxEU, May 7.

Barnichon, Regis, and Geert Mesters. 2021. "The Phillips Multiplier." *Journal of Monetary Economics* 117: 689–705.

Beechey, Meredith, Benjamin Johannsen, and Andrew Levin. 2011. "Are Long-Run Inflation Expectations Anchored More Firmly in the Euro Area than in the United States?" *American Economic Journal: Macroeconomics* 3: 104–29.

Bems, Rudolfs, Francesca G. Caselli, Francesco Grigoli, and Bertrand Gruss. 2020. "Gains from Anchoring Inflation Expectations: Evidence from the Taper Tantrum Shock." *Economics Letters*, Volume 188, March 2020, 108820.

Bems, Rudolfs, Francesca G. Caselli, Francesco Grigoli, and Bertrand Gruss. 2021. "Expectations Anchoring and Inflation Persistence." *Journal of International Economics* 132: 103516.

Bems, Rudolfs, Francesca G. Caselli, Francesco Grigoli, and Bertrand Gruss. Forthcoming. "Is Inflation Domestic or Global?" *International Journal of Central Banking*.

Blanchard, Olivier. 2021. "In Defense of Concerns over the $1.9 Trillion Relief Plan." *Real Time Economic Issues Watch*, Peterson Institute for International Economics, Washington, DC.

Boire, François-Michel, Thibaut Duprey, and Alexander Ueberfeldt. 2021. "Shaping the Future: Policy Shocks and the GDP Growth Distribution." Bank of Canada Working Paper 2021–24, Ottawa.

Borio, Claudio, and Andrew Filardo. 2007. "Globalization and Inflation: New Cross-Country Evidence on the Global Determinants of Domestic Inflation." BIS Working Paper 227, Bank for International Settlements, Basel.

Carrière-Swallow, Yan, Bertrand Gruss, Nicolás E. Magud, and Fabián Valencia. 2021. "Monetary Policy Credibility and Exchange Rate Pass-Through." *International Journal of Central Banking* 17 (3): 61–94.

Caselli, Francesca, and Philippe Wingender. 2021. "Heterogeneous Effects of Fiscal Rules: The Maastricht Fiscal Criterion and the Counterfactual Distribution of Government Deficits." *European Economic Review* 136.

Cavallo, Alberto. 2020. "Inflation with COVID Consumption Baskets." NBER Working Paper 27352, National Bureau of Economic Research, Cambridge, MA.

Celasun, Oya, Roxana Mihet, and Lev Ratnovski. 2012. "Commodity Prices and Inflation Expectations in the United States." IMF Working Paper 12/89, International Monetary Fund, Washington, DC.

Chavleishvili, Sulkhan, and Simone Manganelli. 2020. "Forecasting and Stress Testing with Quantile Vector Autoregression." ECB Working Paper 2330, European Central Bank, Frankfurt.

Chernozhukov, Victor, Iván Fernández-Val, and Alfred Galichon. 2010. "Quantile and Probability Curves without Crossing." *Econometrica* 78 (3): 1093–125.

Clarida, Richard, Jordi Galí, and Mark Gertler. 1999. "The Science of Monetary Policy: A New Keynesian Perspective." *Journal of Economic Literature* 37 (4): 1661–707.

Coibion, Olivier, and Yuriy Gorodnichenko. 2015. "Is the Phillips Curve Alive and Well after All? Inflation Expectations and the Missing Disinflation." *American Economic Journal: Macroeconomics* 7 (1): 197–232.

Coibion, Olivier, Yuriy Gorodnichenko, Saten Kumar, and Mathieu Pedemonte. 2020. "Inflation Expectations as a Policy tool?" *Journal of International Economics* 124.

Coibion, Olivier, Yuriy Gorodnichenko, and Michael Weber. 2021. "Fiscal Policy and Households' Inflation Expectations: Evidence from a Randomized Control Trial." CESifo Working Paper Series 8905, Center of Economic Studies, Munich.

Daly, Mary C., Bart Hobijn, and Benjamin Pyle. 2016. "What's Up with Wage Growth?" Federal Reserve Bank of San Francisco Economic Letter 2016-07, March 7.

Dincer, N. Nergiz, and Barry Eichengreen. 2014. "Central Bank Transparency and Independence: Updates and New Measures." *International Journal of Central Banking*. 10 (1): 189–259.

Dolmas, Jim. 2005. "Trimmed Mean PCE Inflation." Research Department Working Paper 0506, Federal Reserve Bank of Dallas.

Draghi, Mario. 2017. "Accompanying the Economic Recovery." Speech at the European Central Bank Forum on Central Banking, Sintra, June 27.

Galí, Jordi, and Mark Gertler. 1999. "Inflation Dynamics: A Structural Econometric Analysis." *Journal of Monetary Economics* 44 (2): 195–222.

Galí, Jordi, Mark Gertler, and David Lopez-Salido. 2001. "European Inflation Dynamics." *European Economic Review* 45 (7): 1237–270.

Galí, Jordi, Mark Gertler, and David Lopez-Salido. 2005. "Robustness of the Estimates of the Hybrid New Keynesian Phillips Curve." *Journal of Monetary Economics* 52 (6): 1107–118.

Galí, Jordi, Frank Smets, and Rafael Wouters. 2012. "Unemployment in an Estimated New Keynesian Model." *NBER Macroeconomics Annual* 26: 329–60.

Garriga, Ana Carolina. 2016. Central Bank Independence in the World: A New Dataset. *International Interactions* 42 (5):849–868.

Ghysels, Eric, Leonardo Iania, and Jonas Striaukas. 2018. "Quantile-Based Inflation Risk Models." National Bank of Belgium Working Paper 34, Brussels.

Goel, Rohit, and Sheheryar Malik. 2021. "What Is Driving the Rise in Advanced Economy Bond Yields?" IMF Global Financial Stability Note 2021/03, International Monetary Fund, Washington, DC.

Gopinath, Gita. 2015. "The International Price System." NBER Working Paper 21646, National Bureau of Economic Research, Cambridge, MA.

Gürkaynak, Refet S., Brian Sack, and Jonathan H. Wright. 2010. "The TIPS Yield Curve and Inflation Compensation." *American Economic Journal: Macroeconomics* 2 (1): 70–92.

Hausmann, Ricardo, Lant Pritchett, and Dani Rodrik. 2005. "Growth Accelerations." *Journal of Economic Growth* 10 (4): 303–29.

Hooper, Peter, Frederic Mishkin, and Amir Sufi. 2019. "Prospects for Inflation in a High-Pressure Economy: Is the Phillips Curve Dead or Is It Just Hibernating?" NBER Working Paper 25792, National Bureau of Economic Research, Cambridge, MA.

Imbens, G. W., and J. M. Wooldridge. 2009. "Recent Developments in the Econometrics of Program Evaluation." *Journal of Economic Literature* 47 (1): 5–86.

Jordà, Òscar. 2005. "Estimation and Inference of Impulse Responses by Local Projections." *American Economic Review* 95 (1): 161–82.

Jordà, Òscar, and Alan Taylor. 2016. "The Time for Austerity: Estimating the Average Treatment Effect of Fiscal Policy." *Economic Journal* 126 (590): 219–55.

Koenker, Roger, and Zhijie Xiao. 2006. "Quantile Autoregression." *Journal of the American Statistical Association* 101 (475): 980–90.

Kumar, Anil, and Orrenius, Pia M. 2016. "A Closer Look at the Phillips Curve Using State-Level Data." *Journal of Macroeconomics* 47 (Part A): 84–102.

Lenza, Michele, and Giorgio Primiceri. 2020. "How to Estimate a VAR after March 2020." NBER Working Paper 27771, National Bureau of Economic Research, Cambridge, MA.

Lopez-Salido, David, and Francesca Loria. 2020. "Inflation at Risk." Finance and Economics Discussion Series 2020-013, Board of Governors of the Federal Reserve System, Washington, DC.

Mavroeidis, Sophocles, Mikkel Plagborg-Møller, and James H. Stock. 2014. "Empirical Evidence on Inflation Expectations in the New Keynesian Phillips Curve." *Journal of Economic Literature* 52 (1): 124–88.

McLeay, Michael, and Silvana Tenreyro. 2020. "Optimal Inflation and the Identification of the Phillips Curve." *NBER Macroeconomics Annual 2020* 34: 199–255.

Mihailov, Alexander, Giovanni Razzu, and Zhe Wang. 2019. "Heterogeneous Effects of Single Monetary Policy on Unemployment Rates in the Largest EMU Economies." Economics Discussion Papers em-dp2019-07, Department of Economics, University of Reading.

Mishkin, Frederic S. 2000. "Inflation Targeting in Emerging Market Countries." *American Economic Review* 90 (2): 105–9.

Mishkin, Frederic S. 2007. "Inflation Dynamics." *International Finance* 10 (3): 317–34.

Mishkin, Frederic S., and Miguel A. Savastano. 2001. "Monetary Policy Strategies for Latin America." *Journal of Development Economics* 66 (2): 415–44.

Montes-Rojas, Gabriel. 2019. "Multivariate Quantile Impulse Response Functions." *Journal of Time Series Analysis* 40 (5): 739–52.

Powell, Jerome H. 2018. "Monetary Policy at a Time of Uncertainty and Tight Labor Markets." Remarks at Price and Wage-Setting in Advanced Economies, European Central Bank Forum on Central Banking, Sintra, Portugal, June 20.

Powell, Jerome H. 2021. "Virtual Hearing—Oversight of the Treasury Department's and Federal Reserve's Pandemic Response." March 23.

Pradhan, Manoj, and Charles Goodhart. 2021. "Friedman vs Phillips: A Historic Divide." *VoxEU* column, February 26.

Ramey, Valerie A. 2016. "Macroeconomic Shocks and Their Propagation." In *Handbook of Macroeconomics* 2A, edited by John B. Taylor and Harald Uhlig, 71–162.

Reinsdorf, Marshall. 2020. "COVID-19 and the CPI: Is Inflation Underestimated?" IMF Working Paper 20/224, International Monetary Fund, Washington, DC.

Romer, Christina D., and David H. Romer. 2004. "A New Measure of Monetary Shocks: Derivation and Implications." *American Economic Review* 94 (4): 1055–84.

Serrato, J. C., and P. Wingender. 2016. "Estimating Local Fiscal Multipliers." NBER Working Paper 22425, National Bureau of Economic Research, Cambridge, MA.

Strohsal, Till, and Lars Winkelmann. 2015. "Assessing the Anchoring of Inflation Expectations." *Journal of International Money and Finance* 50 (C): 33–48.

Summers, Laurence H. 2021. "The Biden Stimulus Is Admirably Ambitious. But It Brings Some Big Risks, Too." Opinion, *Washington Post,* February 4.

Willems, Tim. 2020. "What Do Monetary Contractions Do? Evidence from Large Tightenings." *Review of Economic Dynamics* 38: 41–58.

Yellen, Janet L. 2012. "Perspectives on Monetary Policy." Speech at the Boston Economic Club, Boston, MA, June 6.

Yellen, Janet L. 2015. "Inflation Dynamics and Monetary Policy." Speech at the Philip Gamble Memorial Lecture, University of Massachusetts, Amherst, September 24.

Yellen, Janet L. 2016. "Macroeconomic Research after the Crisis." Speech at the 60th Annual Economic Conference, The Elusive "Great" Recovery: Causes and Implications for Future Business Cycle Dynamics, sponsored by the Federal Reserve Bank of Boston, October 14.

RESEARCH AND INNOVATION: FIGHTING THE PANDEMIC AND BOOSTING LONG-TERM GROWTH

How can policymakers boost long-term growth in the post–COVID-19 global economy? This chapter looks at the role of basic research—undirected, theoretical, or experimental work. Using rich new data that draw on connections from individual innovations to scientific articles, it shows that basic research is an essential input into innovation, with wide-ranging international spillovers and long-lasting impacts. International spillovers are particularly important for emerging market and developing economies, where institutional factors—including better education and deeper financial markets—help convert innovation into economic growth, making rapid technology transfer, the free flow of ideas, and collaboration across borders key priorities. Model-based analysis reveals that advanced economies could raise long-term growth by increasing research funding, targeting basic research, and developing closer connections between public and private research. By lifting the growth potential and future tax base of the economy, these investments tend to pay for themselves within a decade. Investments in basic research may also have green benefits, as cleaner technological innovations rely on newer, more fundamental research.

Introduction

Few concepts have implications as far reaching for economic policy as long-term growth. Growth—namely, the increase in an economy's *potential* to produce goods and services—is of central importance not only for improving living standards, but also for addressing inequality, debt sustainability, and the cost of climate change mitigation.

Yet, the past few decades have seen a long and persistent decline in long-term growth. Policymakers face an urgent and essential question: how can this trend be reversed to build a more buoyant post-pandemic global economy? Although this has so far been mostly an advanced-economy phenomenon, demographic trends

in China and other emerging markets make the need for an answer more urgent. With fewer active workers, aging populations will require more output per worker to maintain living standards.

Addressing this question requires an understanding of the underlying drivers of growth. The earliest explanations emphasized the role of *productivity*—the ability to create more outputs with the same inputs.[1] More recent work emphasizes the role of *innovation*—the emergence and adoption of new technologies that improve the production of goods and services—as a driver of productivity.[2] But the data present something of a challenge to this idea. Productivity growth has slowed, even amid increased spending on research and development—a common proxy for innovation effort (Figure 3.1, panels 1 and 2). This apparent conflict with leading theories makes formulating policies to boost long-term growth rather difficult.

One possible answer is that the type of research matters. Innovations, great and small, occur not in a vacuum but draw on the stock of *basic* scientific knowledge. The invention of the cardiac pacemaker required a scientific understanding of both human anatomy and electronics. The GPS technology familiar to many smartphone users relies on Einstein's theories of relativity to account for how time passes at different rates on fast-moving satellites and the Earth's surface. More recently, the extraordinarily rapid development of COVID-19 vaccines, based on decades of prior basic scientific research, has had the massive economic payoff of bringing forward the reopening of many economies, perhaps by years (Box 3.1). Growth in research inputs has been increasingly *applied*, even as innovation depends more on basic scientific advances (Figure 3.1, panels 3 and 4), which may help resolve part of this puzzle.

The character of basic scientific research also suggests that policies to encourage it might be particularly

The authors of this chapter are Philip Barrett (co-lead), Niels-Jakob Hansen, Jean-Marc Natal (co-lead), and Diaa Noureldin, with support from Evgenia Pugacheva, Max Rozycki, and Xiaohui Sun.

---

[1]As opposed to population growth or capital accumulation; see Ramsey (1928), Solow (1956), Cass (1965), and Koopmans (1965).

[2]See the April 2018 *World Economic Outlook*; Grossman and Helpman (1991); Aghion and Howitt (1992); Mankiw, Romer, and Weil (1992); and Aghion and others (2005).

Figure 3.1. Measures of Research and Productivity

Productivity growth has been declining for decades despite a steady increase in research effort. The increasing importance of science, combined with a focus on more commercial research, could explain this decline.

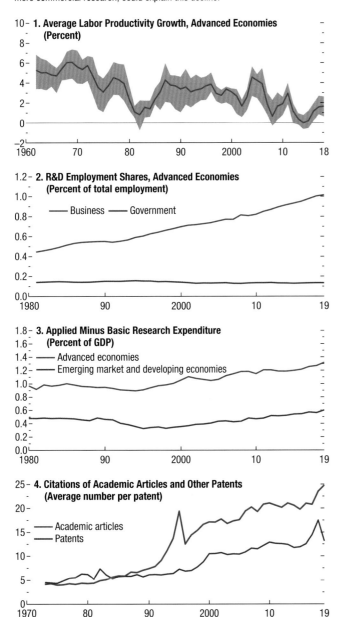

1. Average Labor Productivity Growth, Advanced Economies
(Percent)

2. R&D Employment Shares, Advanced Economies
(Percent of total employment)
— Business — Government

3. Applied Minus Basic Research Expenditure
(Percent of GDP)
— Advanced economies
— Emerging market and developing economies

4. Citations of Academic Articles and Other Patents
(Average number per patent)
— Academic articles
— Patents

Sources: OECD Science and Technology Indicators; Penn World Table 10.0; Reliance on Science; United States Patent and Trademark Office; and IMF staff calculations.
Note: In panel 1, labor productivity growth is reported as a three-year moving average. The shaded area denotes the 25th to 75th percentile. Sample is restricted to be balanced throughout the period. In panel 3, the figure shows the average difference in funding for applied minus basic research over time. In panel 4, average citations from patents to academic articles and other patents are shown by year of application. The spike in 1995 is likely associated with a legislative change prompting an increase in patent applications (Byrne 1995).
R&D = research and development.

potent—something relevant to aspirations to build a better post–COVID-19 economy (see Chapter 1). In contrast to applied innovation, basic research can have very broad economic applications. While this likely means that social returns from basic research are high, it also means that firms may struggle to internalize the gains from basic science, undermining private incentives. No firm could fully capture the gains from the invention of, say, the jet engine or the internet. As a result, private firms are likely to underprovide the most basic, far-reaching, and economically impactful types of research (Nelson 1959)—suggesting a role for public policy to bridge this gap.

This chapter explores whether public policy should support basic scientific research to boost growth during the exit from the global pandemic, addressing the following questions:

- *What is the progression from basic science to innovation and productivity growth?* How does basic scientific knowledge diffuse internationally? And how do the economic roles of basic and more applied research differ?
- *What is the global economic benefit of scientific integration?* How might a reverse in scientific integration of major economies, such as the United States and China, affect global growth?
- *Is basic research under- or overprovided?* Can policy intervene to correct socially inefficient levels of basic research? If so, what is the appropriate policy mix? How should these policies balance returns from public and private basic research? And what are the potential gains from such policies? Can basic scientific research help in the fight against climate change? And if so, how might those benefits manifest?

These are the chapter's main findings:
- Basic scientific research is a key driver of innovation and productivity, and basic scientific knowledge diffuses internationally farther than applied knowledge. A 10 percent increase in domestic (foreign) basic research is estimated to raise productivity by about 0.3 (0.6) percent, on average. International knowledge spillovers are more important for innovation in emerging market and developing economies than in advanced economies. Easy technology transfer, collaboration, and the free flow of ideas across borders should be key priorities.
- A decoupling of basic scientific research between the United States and China could have big negative

effects on global productivity, with an estimated first-round decline of up to 0.8 percent.

- Basic scientific research in advanced economies is underfunded. As a result, policies that fund public research and subsidize private research will have positive payoffs. A model estimated on three advanced economies suggests that subsidy rates for private research should be approximately doubled and public research expenditure increased by about one-third. Targeting support to basic scientific research will deliver the greatest return but, where this is not possible, more public-private partnerships may be a partial substitute. While such policies pay for themselves in the long term, optimal research funding may be lower in countries with immediate fiscal constraints. Science also plays a larger role in green innovation than in dirty technological change, suggesting that policies to boost science can help tackle climate change.

Conceptual Framework

The chapter's conceptual framework draws on innovation-driven endogenous growth theory (Romer 1990; Grossman and Helpman 1991; Aghion and Howitt 1992; Akcigit and Kerr 2018), in which knowledge creation plays a central role in driving productivity growth.

In its simplest form, economic output can be thought of as produced by two interlinked production functions (Figure 3.2). In the first, the production function for ideas, research inputs—both basic and applied—are combined with preexisting knowledge to produce economically relevant innovations that add to the stock of common knowledge. The key difference

between basic and applied research is that the former is undirected, theoretical, or experimental, whereas the latter is aimed at bringing products to market. In the second production function (the one for goods and services), standard macroeconomic inputs (capital and labor) are combined to produce output. The productivity of this process depends on the current stock of ideas and other country-specific institutional factors. Thus, research increases knowledge, knowledge enhances productivity, and productivity determines how much final output is generated from real inputs.

Although the analysis in the chapter adds finer details to this picture, the basic structure remains the same throughout. The empirical analysis unpacks these two production functions and estimates the direct impact and international spillovers of investing in basic science. Subsequent model-based policy analysis complements the empirical evidence by allowing for richer interactions, including between basic and applied research in general equilibrium. Given that the analysis of the more basic types of research is novel, the chapter's focus is naturally on basic research. For more on applied research, see the April 2016 *Fiscal Monitor* and the April 2018 *World Economic Outlook*.

Connecting Basic Science to Growth

This section presents an empirical investigation into the two production functions outlined in Figure 3.2, extending it to include an international dimension, distinguishing the impact not only of basic and applied research but also the extent of international spillovers. An important first step is to construct measures of the stock of foreign knowledge accessible to each country.

The Diffusion of Basic and Applied Knowledge

The relevance of knowledge in one country for an innovator in another may depend on a variety of factors, including proximity, language, and so forth, and might be different for basic and applied knowledge. Cross-country citations in patent applications, from the Reliance on Science database (RoS, for basic research) and from PATSTAT (for applied research), provide valuable clues about the drivers of the international transmission of knowledge.

The RoS database is a rich data set that tracks citations of some 38 million US and European patents to scientific articles (Marx and Fuegi 2020). By providing unique identifiers for patents issued by the US Patent

Figure 3.2. Stylized Conceptual Framework

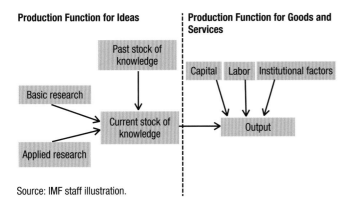

Source: IMF staff illustration.

Figure 3.3. Geography of International Basic Knowledge Flows
(Citation share)

Most scientific citations within patent applications are to the United States, although Europe and Asia have become increasingly important.

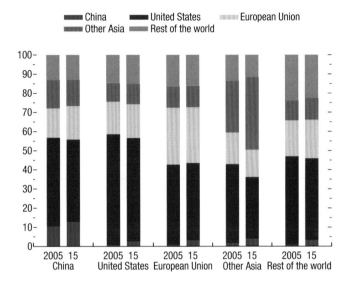

Sources: Reliance on Science; United States Patent and Trademark Office; and IMF staff calculations.
Note: Bars correspond to the country or region of the citing patent; legend items correspond to the country or region of the cited research article.

and Trademark Office, RoS can identify the countries both of the patent's inventor(s) and of the authors of cited scientific articles. PATSTAT, maintained by the European Patent Office, provides global coverage of patent applications, with 105 million records from more than 190 patenting offices. These sources illuminate two inputs to the production function for ideas, basic and applied research, and are discussed in Online Annex 3.1.[3]

A key assumption in the empirical work is that citations to scientific articles capture dependence on basic research and that citations to patents capture reliance on applied research. This draws a sharp distinction, whereas reality is more blurred; some articles may cover applied topics, and patentable work may spur major scientific breakthroughs.[4]

Figure 3.3 shows the main patterns of international citations of basic knowledge, using cross-border citations in the RoS. The United States is the main source

of cited works—a constant in recent decades. However, citations to Chinese science have grown strongly since 2005 (albeit from a low base), as have citations across Asian countries. In general, regions tend to exhibit home bias, citing their own scientific works more than others do. This suggests that diffusion of knowledge from its source is partial—a point explored more formally in the next section.

Across Space

To harness this information, the chapter estimates a gravity-type model of international knowledge flows. The outcome variable is the number of citations from one country to another. For example, for basic research, this would be the number of citations by, say, Malaysian inventors to scientific articles with Spanish authors (for applied research, the citations are to other patents). The explanatory variables are: whether the two countries share a border, whether they have a common official language, how specialization in their economies differs (scientific specialization for science citations, technological for patent citations), and geographic distance in kilometers. Citing and cited country fixed effects capture differences in the knowledge mass, intellectual property rights, and other factors that may influence a country's propensity to patent or to cite other patents. Further details are in Online Annex 3.2.

Panel 1 of Figure 3.4 shows the estimated cumulative impact of these various barriers, calculated separately for basic and applied knowledge. These show that basic knowledge diffuses more strongly than applied knowledge, with the red line staying above the blue line across most barriers. Country borders, lack of a common language, and specialization distance all present a larger impediment to the diffusion of applied knowledge. The marginal effect of geographic distance is negative for basic knowledge but insignificant for applied knowledge. Patent-to-patent citation intensity for applied knowledge is instead likely more dependent on other factors, such as tough competition. One example is the recent 5G technology race among China, the European Union, and the United States. However, the cumulative effect differs only over very long distances. These findings are unaffected by a variety of robustness checks, including controlling for cross-country differences in scientific and technological output, as detailed in Online Annex 3.2.

---

[3]All annexes are available at www.imf.org/en/Publications/WEO.
[4]Ahmadpoor and Jones (2017) gives examples of how the two types of research mutually reinforce their role in innovation.

Figure 3.4. Diffusion of Basic and Applied Knowledge

Basic knowledge diffuses farther than applied and remains relevant longer.

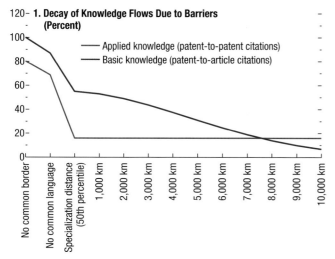

1. Decay of Knowledge Flows Due to Barriers
(Percent)

— Applied knowledge (patent-to-patent citations)
— Basic knowledge (patent-to-article citations)

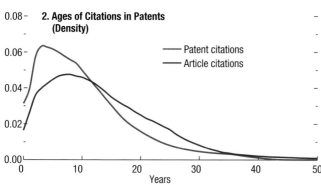

2. Ages of Citations in Patents
(Density)

— Patent citations
— Article citations

Sources: PATSTAT; Reliance on Science; and IMF staff calculations.
Note: In panel 1, the baseline knowledge flow equals 100 in the absence of barriers. In panel 2, the sample is restricted to patents applied for during 2010–19. Axis truncated at 50 years. Specialization distance is measured as one minus the uncentered correlation coefficient between the specialization vectors of country i and country j, where the vectors are the share of patents falling within internationally classified scientific/technological fields. km = kilometers. See Online Annexes 3.1 and 3.2 for details.

This sort of exercise has a long history in the academic literature on international trade. Earlier attempts to adapt the framework to knowledge diffusion typically focused on applied knowledge flows using patent-to-patent citations.[5] The extension to basic knowledge flows using patent-to-science citations

is new. Predictions of the estimated models can also be used as a measure of how relevant knowledge in one country is for research elsewhere. This point is important for the empirical analysis of the production function for ideas, which uses this measure to create country-specific aggregate foreign knowledge stocks for each country (more on this later).

Over Time

Knowledge diffuses over time as well as across space. Panel 2 of Figure 3.4 illustrates this point, showing the density of the age of scientific articles (red line) and patents (blue line) cited by various patents. As such, they approximate the influence of basic and applied knowledge over the years. Basic knowledge displays a long-lasting impact, with the density for the age of cited scientific articles reaching a peak at about eight years versus three years for cited patents. This evidence suggests that scientific ideas can still be economically influential for long periods of time.[6]

Of course, using patent-induced knowledge flows to understand innovation drivers is subject to some caveats. Some research and development may have a direct impact on productivity without necessarily resulting in new patents, and new patent applications may be more reflective of strategic patenting practices than of authentic innovation. Yet, when using only patents filed in at least two distinct national offices—a likely control for these effects—the findings are similar (Online Annex Table 3.2.3).

Knowledge Stocks and the Production Function for Ideas

The empirical production function for ideas explains how the flow of new productive ideas—as captured by patents—depends on foreign and domestic applied and basic research stocks.

Given that these stocks are measures of research expenditure (that is, research inputs), they are true inputs to a production function. Domestic stocks are computed by summing past expenditures, with 10 percent annual depreciation. Construction of the foreign stocks follows Peri (2005). For each country, a weighted average of the domestic research stocks in all the other countries is calculated, with the weights

[5]The spatial diffusion of knowledge spillovers using patent data has been widely studied, starting with Jaffe, Trajtenberg, and Henderson (1993). See Peri (2005) for a more recent example. While advances in communication have improved accessibility to scientific articles, there is still evidence of the localization of scientific knowledge (for example, Belenzon and Schankerman 2013), partly explained by national policies aimed at fostering collaboration among local universities, firms, and government funding agencies (Etzkowitz and Leydesdorff 2000).

[6]A back-of-the-envelope calculation of tail decay rates reveals that, in the long term, basic (applied) knowledge decays at 7 (11) percent annually.

determined by the gravity model presented in this chapter. For example, Mexico's constructed foreign basic research stock puts weight on the United States that is proportional to the average Mexican inventor's citations to science from the United States, as predicted by the determinants of the gravity model—geography, language, and technological mix. In this sense, construction of the data measures how accessible foreign research stocks are to a given country.

The estimated impact of research and development stocks on innovation is plotted in panel 1 of Figure 3.5. The main estimates use dynamic ordinary least squares, which efficiently utilize the cointegration of the data.[7] The point estimates show the effect of a 1-percentage-point increase in the respective research stocks on the annual flow of patents, along with 95 percent confidence bands. For "own" basic research, the impact is 0.67 percentage point, and for applied research 0.77 percentage point, each having tight confidence bands. This suggests that domestic basic and applied research each have positive effects on patenting activity and are of similar magnitudes.

Foreign basic research also has a sizable effect, leading annual patent flows to increase 1.36 percentage points. In contrast, foreign applied knowledge has a negative estimated impact on patenting activity. However, this is very imprecisely estimated. Indeed, the magnitude of imprecision prohibits any confidence about even the direction of the true effect. That said, a negative impact of foreign applied research on domestic innovation is not completely implausible and would at least be consistent with the idea that some applied research and development leads to "business stealing" by competitors (as opposed to the nonrival and nonexcludable nature of foreign basic research; see Bloom, Schankerman, and Van Reenen 2013).[8]

Online Annex 3.3 shows the estimates of alternative specifications of the ideas production function. While the details vary, the estimates consistently reveal a strong and significant relationship between basic research and innovation and positive spillovers from foreign research (although the relative roles of foreign basic and applied research are not always as clear).

[7]See column (7) in Table 3.3.1 in Online Annex 3.3.

[8]Note that foreign research stocks are an order of magnitude larger than domestic stocks and even larger for emerging market and developing economies. This affects the interpretation of the estimated coefficients: a 1-percentage-point increase in foreign research is a much larger change in the total knowledge. Further, the results in panel 1 of Figure 3.5 are robust to the exclusion of the United States (as a key driver of the technological frontier) from the sample.

Figure 3.5. Estimated Ideas Production Function

Basic research expenditures correlate significantly with patent creation, and spillovers from foreign research stocks are larger for emerging markets than advanced economies.

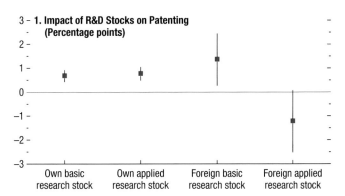

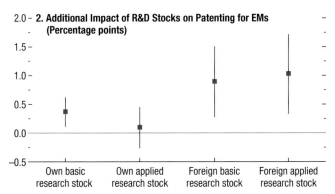

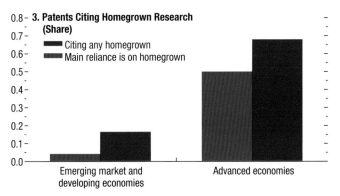

Sources: PATSTAT; Penn World Table 10.0; Reliance on Science; World Bank; and IMF staff calculations.
Note: Panel 1 shows the response of patent flows (log scale) to a 1-percentage-point change in each covariate (log scale) along with the 95 percent confidence interval. Panel 2 shows the additional estimated effect of research stocks on innovation in emerging markets. See Online Annex 3.3 for details. EMs = emerging markets; R&D = research and development.

Box 3.2 extends this analysis to look at a particular type of innovation—clean technologies—and finds that basic research has larger green spillovers, suggesting that spending on basic research can play an important role in combating global climate change.

Differences in the Ideas Production Function: Advanced versus Emerging Market and Developing Economies

The estimates presented so far reflect those for an average economy in the data set. However, the estimated effects of basic and applied research stocks on innovations may differ by country. To get a sense of the size of these differences and what drives them, Figure 3.5 (panel 2) presents the estimated difference between advanced economies and emerging market and developing economies (see Table 3.3.2 in Online Annex 3.3). Two findings are apparent:

- First, access to foreign research has a larger estimated effect on innovation in emerging markets than in advanced economies. This is true for both applied and basic research. Consistent with this difference, inventors from emerging markets are also less likely to cite homegrown research (Figure 3.5, panel 3). The results suggest that foreign technology adoption is more important for emerging markets than for advanced economies, consistent with the April 2018 *World Economic Outlook*. Learning-by-doing is one possible channel; adoption of foreign technologies (for example, through trade links; see Chuang 1998) may provide local workers the opportunity to learn new processes, forming the basis for innovation.
- Second, evidence for the role of domestic research is mixed. While the estimated effect of applied research on innovation is not significantly different across emerging markets and advanced economies, basic research seems to play a larger role in emerging markets.[9] It is possible that this reflects the larger impact of basic science in niche fields that receive less attention in advanced economies but may be relevant in emerging markets.

Overall, these results emphasize the importance of foreign knowledge for emerging market and developing economies. Although domestic basic research is more productive than for advanced economies in generating innovation, the effect is even larger for foreign research.

The Production Function for Goods and Services

Building on the estimates of the ideas production function presented earlier, this section examines the link between innovation and productivity.

The analysis relies on a production function for output and estimates the long-term relationship between productivity (real output per worker) and the country-specific stock of innovation.[10] This is the empirical analogue of the production function for output in Figure 3.2.

In this setting, the stock of innovations is measured using cumulated annual flows of new patents, assuming an annual depreciation rate of 10 percent. The regression also takes in the usual factors of production, such as capital per worker and human capital, along with country and time fixed effects. Finally, the regression includes interactions between innovation and institutional factors to allow institutions to affect the transmission from innovation to productivity. Constant returns to scale are imposed, and the estimation uses data covering 138 countries during 1980–2017.[11]

The estimated relationship between innovation and productivity is strong and significant (Figure 3.6). An increase in the stock of patents by 1 percent is associated with an increase in productivity per worker of 0.04 percent,[12] in line with estimates reported in Ulku (2004) and dependent on the institutional features of a country (Figure 3.6). The relationship is stronger for countries with higher financial development and more years of schooling, consistent with the idea that deeper financial markets and more educated workforces help transform innovation into productivity. Together with the findings on strong spillovers from foreign research (Figure 3.5, panel 2), these findings are relevant for emerging market and developing markets, as these results suggest that financial market and educational reforms can allow countries to better absorb the stock of foreign research.

Putting It All Together

This section combines the exercises of the previous sections to trace the path to the final impact of increases in basic research stocks on productivity.

Specifically, Figure 3.7 (panel 1) shows that the estimated effect of a 10 percent permanent increase in the stock of a country's own basic research is to increase

---

[9]Note, however, that the coefficient becomes insignificant (although still positive) when China is excluded from the sample (see Online Annex 3.3).

[10]See also Ulku (2004) for a similar exercise.

[11]Online Annex 3.4 reports the full econometric specification and details on the analysis.

[12]Results from alternative specifications in Online Annex 3.4 show this to be robust to averaging over multiyear intervals, which is strongly suggestive of a long-term relationship.

Figure 3.6. Estimated Output Production Function
(Percentage points)

Innovation correlates with productivity, and more so in countries with deeper financial markets and a better-educated population.

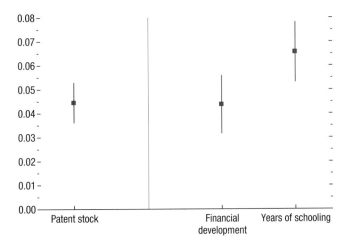

Sources: PATSTAT; Penn World Table 10.0; Reliance on Science; World Bank; and IMF staff calculations.
Note: Patent stock shows the estimated effect of a 1 percent increase in the stock of patents on productivity. The other coefficients show the additional estimated effect (estimated in separate equations) of innovation on productivity from moving from the middle to the upper tercile of countries in financial development and years of schooling, respectively. See Online Annex 3.4 for details.

Figure 3.7. Implications of the Empirical Findings
(Percent)

Investment in research boosts productivity, while scientific decoupling would be detrimental for global innovation and productivity.

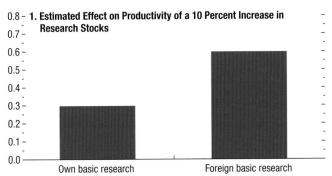

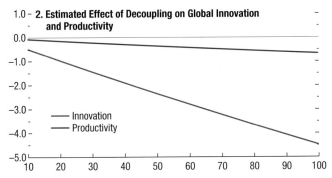

Source: IMF staff calculations.
Note: Panel 1 shows the estimated effect of a permanent 10 percent increase in research stocks on real GDP per worker. An estimated elasticity of 0.674/1.358 for patents with respect to own basic research/foreign basic research is used. An estimated elasticity of 0.044 for productivity with respect to the stock of patents is used. Panel 2 shows the estimated effect on global innovation (measured as flow of new patents) and productivity of a given reduction (in percent) in citations between the United States and China. See Online Annex 3.5 for details.

productivity by 0.30 percent, while a similar increase in the stock of foreign basic research is estimated to have a larger impact, increasing productivity by about 0.6 percent. The impact on productivity of own applied research is estimated to be of the same order as the impact of own basic research, and international spillovers are insignificant. The differences are driven by the respective elasticities estimated from the production function for ideas (Figure 3.5).

Overall, the evidence suggests that international productivity spillovers are significant, particularly from basic research. This is in line with the earlier evidence on the extent of international spillovers in Figure 3.4, which also suggests that basic knowledge diffuses more widely and for a longer time than applied knowledge. Hence, the type of research does seem to matter for productivity growth. Quantitatively, however, large confidence bands around those estimates suggest caution in interpreting these results, especially on the impact of foreign research (Figure 3.5). In addition, the linear regression approach measures only the direct effect of basic research on innovation and

productivity growth. The true effect may be even larger due to nonlinear relationships linking applied research to the stock of basic knowledge.[13]

Policy Experiment: Scientific Decoupling between the United States and China

In recent years, concern has been growing that rising tensions between China and the United States could lead to technological decoupling, with detrimental effects on innovation capacity and growth at the global level. This section uses the empirical

[13]See the "Policy Analysis" section for general equilibrium effects of policies stimulating basic research.

framework described in this chapter to do a back-of-the-envelope calculation of the cost for global innovation of increased scientific decoupling between the two countries.

The empirical framework can be used to model scientific decoupling, implemented as a reduction in the citation intensity between the two countries. This reduces the foreign stock of basic research available to each country, which in turn decreases innovation and productivity. This is consistent with, for example, differences in technology standards inducing changes across the two countries, such that research done in one becomes less relevant for the other. Limits on knowledge flows might also arise if ongoing geopolitical tensions make it harder for researchers in the two countries to interact or work together. For instance, restriction on travel might prohibit the all-important personal contacts that can occur at seminars, conferences, and the like.

Figure 3.7 shows the estimated impact on global innovation as measured by the annual flow of new patents for various degrees of scientific decoupling. As a purely illustrative example, full decoupling, as modeled by citations between the two countries shrinking to zero, is estimated to reduce global patent flows by 4.4 percent and global productivity by 0.8 percent.[14]

These estimates are likely a lower bound of the impact of decoupling, for two reasons. First, they assume that only foreign stocks of basic research, innovation, and productivity for the United States and China are affected in a decoupling scenario. In reality, stocks in other countries are likely to be affected too, creating an extra dimension to the shock. Second, these estimates are partial insofar as they do not include any general equilibrium effects that could affect the impact of the initial shock on global innovation and productivity. Given the evidence presented previously on the magnitude of global basic research spillovers, these could be substantial.[15]

Policy Analysis

Earlier sections established the empirical links between basic research, innovation, and economic activity. This raises an obvious question: how can

[14]Online Annex 3.5 provides further details and a full breakdown of these effects.
[15]See Cerdeiro and others (2021) for a more structural approach to the decoupling issue.

public policy best exploit these links to boost living standards? An important aspect of this empirical work is that it measures only the direct part of these links, holding all else fixed. But in reality, many indirect channels exist. For instance, policies that boost basic science spill over to increase returns to applied innovation, and changes in productivity feed back into wages, driving demand and influencing research incentives. To assess the impact of policy, a framework articulating these links is required.

The Model

Recent work by Akcigit, Hanley, and Serrano-Velarde (2021) provides a theoretical framework for answering this question. It analyzes a setting in which firms conduct two types of research: basic, which builds the stock of knowledge; and applied, which converts knowledge into products. These correspond closely to the basic and applied expenditure concepts used in the empirical analysis. The government has three policy levers: subsidies for each of the two types of research; and direct funding for public basic research, such as universities and public research labs.

The key feature of this approach is that basic research is modeled as having applications in many different fields. This captures an essential aspect of basic research—that, because individual firms typically operate in only a few sectors, they cannot profit fully from the range of economic applications opened up by the most fundamental and basic discoveries. As a result, private incentives for basic research are outstripped by its social benefits. Without a public policy response, this will result in inefficiently low levels of innovation and productivity.

Despite the special character of basic research, it is not the only potential target of public policy in this framework. Applied research—which is complementary to basic research, adapting knowledge to produce marketable products—also generates spillovers, which could also motivate public support. This is because innovations that bring a product to market can be superseded by competitors' innovations. This introduces a "quality ladder" mechanism: firms may not be able to fully internalize the social value of applied innovation, leading to underprovision of applied research as well. Whether applied or basic research is more desirable is not hardwired into the model

Figure 3.8. Optimal Policy

Public and private research are underfunded; where different subsidies to basic and applied research are impossible, public-private partnerships may be a good substitute.

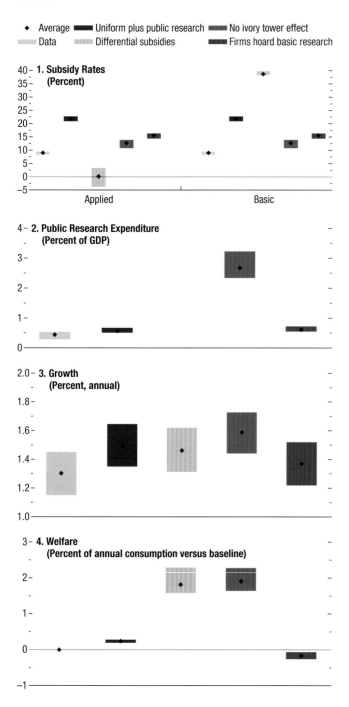

Sources: Organisation for Economic Co-operation and Development; and IMF staff calculations.
Note: Range shows optimal policies across the model reestimated for France, the United Kingdom, and the United States. In the differential subsidies case, public research is assumed fixed at the level in the data. See Online Annex 3.6 for details.

but is instead a function of parameters estimated from the data.

The model is estimated for three countries: France, the United Kingdom, and the United States. Although estimating for more countries would be ideal, the data requirements needed to maintain the important distinction between basic and applied research preclude this. Still, this exercise gives some sense of the impact of country-specific factors, at least within advanced economies.

Optimal Policies

Figure 3.8 shows optimal policies and the resultant outcomes from several experiments. The first, shown in red, is the case when governments cannot subsidize applied and basic research separately and, so, must apply the same rate to both. This is not an unreasonable approximation of reality, as deciding which of firms' individual activities are "applied" and which are "basic" is often challenging and, so, being able to target them separately may be difficult. Indeed, many data sources for such subsidies cannot make this distinction.

This exercise suggests that research, in general, is funded below its socially optimal level. Subsidy rates for private research should be doubled, and public research expenditure increased by about one-third. Although country-specific caveats (see "Policy Conclusions" below) might caution against a too-literal interpretation of these findings, they are at least broadly supportive of the notion that there are likely underexploited spillovers from research that can leave room for policy to make households better off. Increasing subsidies and public research expenditures as recommended would raise productivity growth in the order of about 0.2 percentage point a year. This would start to pay for itself within about a decade. If applied over the period shown in panel 1 of Figure 3.1, this would have resulted in current per capita incomes about 12 percent higher than in the data. Moreover, in an era of low real interest rates, small increases in economic growth can have very large impacts on debt sustainability.

Under this policy program, the stocks of both applied and basic knowledge increase. But because public expenditure is purely basic, the stock of basic knowledge increases by more—with an increase about several times the size of that for applied knowledge. This increase in the knowledge stock also varies across countries and is largest in the United States, where higher corporate entry and exit rates mean that firms do not internalize the social benefits of research, leaving more room for policy to play a positive role. The level of wages also rises under optimal policy, with increases of between 2.5 percent and 3 percent, depending on the country.

Of course, assuming that no scope exists for targeting subsidies might seem somewhat restrictive and, so, the results of separately subsidizing applied and basic research are also shown in Figure 3.8, in yellow. This policy clearly dominates the previous one, which implies that, where possible, governments should target subsidies aggressively toward basic research. This policy recommendation matches the earlier empirical evidence, which shows that basic research is an important determinant of productivity growth.

Although targeting has only a minor additional impact on growth, it reduces the cost of subsidies, lowering taxes and making households substantially better off. The intuition for this is that basic research is a smaller sector than applied research. Given that the subsidy is smaller, and growth spillovers from basic research are larger than for applied research, this achieves a similar growth effect but with a much smaller subsidy. Lower subsidy spending can translate into lower taxes, boosting household disposable income and consumption permanently.

Exploring the Assumptions

As with any model-based analysis, the results depend on the modeling assumptions. Here, two important assumptions are explored in detail.

The first is the substitutability of public and private research. In the baseline, this substitutability is imperfect; public research requires extra work to be useful for commercial innovation—the "ivory tower" effect. If this is turned off, public basic research can be commercialized more easily and can take on more of the qualities of a public-private partnership.

The most obvious effect of this experiment is that optimal research expenditure increases considerably, to about 3 percent of GDP (Figure 3.8, panel 2, in green). This is not surprising: a public sector that can deliver more commercially adaptable innovations means better use of resources. Optimal subsidies fall, and growth increases by an average of another 0.1 percentage point. The policy implication is that, even if discrimination between basic and applied research

subsidies is not possible, governments might be able to achieve something similar by encouraging greater collaboration between public and private basic researchers.

The second experiment investigates how sensitive these results are to assumptions about private basic research spillovers. It is conceivable that spillovers from private firms may decrease if, for example, recent technological change allows for more market power or other abilities to privatize breakthroughs. To proxy this, the blue bars in Figure 3.8 show what happens if the spillovers from private basic research shrink by one-quarter. This limits public gains from research and, so, optimal public subsidy rates are increased only by half relative to the data (versus doubling in the baseline).

Policy Conclusions

The preceding experiments highlight four key policy lessons.
- First, public funding for research is too low. Gains can be made from both subsidizing more private research and doing more public research.
- Second, the ability to discriminate among various types of research is very valuable. If possible, governments could achieve similar outcomes to the baseline at roughly half the cost.
- Third, better connections between public and private researchers might be able to substitute for targeted subsidies, which can be hard to implement.
- Fourth, regarding firms' ability to protect their discoveries, if basic research spillovers decline, then the social gains from research will fall. This suggests that reducing overbearing market power or excessively broad patenting can boost productivity and growth (Box 3.3 discusses this issue more broadly).

As with any model-based analysis, tractability demands that this assessment leave out a number of other factors that could affect the policy conclusions. As such, these conclusions should be treated as a baseline, from which country-specific considerations could require some deviation.

One such issue is the absence of distorting taxation. In this setting, taxes are raised by collecting a lump sum from households. In reality, though, most tax instruments, such as labor or capital taxes, induce some sort of inefficiency. Such instruments introduce an extra cost to policy interventions. Because these costs typically increase with the size of the tax, countries with high tax distortions may find policies to support basic research to be more costly. A similar caveat applies to countries with high debt burdens or inefficient revenue collection systems. In these cases, a better source of funding might be to reprioritize expenditure or improve revenue mobilization.

Moreover, these policy conclusions are perhaps most directly relevant to advanced economies: the model lacks a channel (such as trade) for the international diffusion of knowledge, which earlier sections show to be important in emerging market and developing economies. As such, these countries may find that policies to better adapt foreign knowledge to local conditions are a better avenue for development than investing directly in homegrown basic research (Acemoglu, Aghion, and Zilibotti 2006). Other unmodeled factors, such as political constraints, may also hinder the kind of tax-funded innovation-boosting policies presented here.

Conclusions: Investment in Basic Science Boosts Productivity and Pays for Itself over the Long Term

The development of COVID-19 mRNA vaccines acts as a stark reminder of the importance of science for innovation and growth. In common with other technological breakthroughs, past scientific discoveries in unrelated fields typically laid the foundation for today's technological advances, driving future productivity and economic growth (Box 3.1).

Improving growth outcomes will be essential to post-pandemic economies, helping finance higher public debt and additional post-pandemic social expenditures. It is therefore worrisome that the share of basic research has been steadily declining over the past three decades.

That the private sector underinvests in basic research is not surprising. As shown in this chapter, the benefits of basic research are diffuse and long-lasting, making it an unattractive proposition for private firms. This creates an opportunity for policy intervention. The chapter shows that doubling subsidies to private research and boosting public research expenditure by one-third could increase annual growth per capita by around 0.2 percent. Better targeting of subsidies and closer public-private cooperation could boost this further, at lower public expense. Such investments could start to pay for themselves within a decade or so.

The chapter also shows that scientific knowledge travels far over time and distance and that it is a key driver of innovation in both advanced economies and emerging markets. Spillovers from advanced economies to emerging markets are particularly large. Deep financial markets and better educational systems are key facilitators for cross-border technology adoption.

It is also important to ensure the free flow of ideas and scientific collaboration across borders, especially for emerging markets. The technological trajectories of China and the United States have been closely linked in the past two decades. Rising political tensions could lead to scientific decoupling, with detrimental effects on innovation capacity and global economic growth.

Beyond its impact on growth, basic science is likely to be a key contributor to a greener future. The fight against climate change requires drastic cuts in global emissions. New clean technologies will be central to this effort. Evidence presented in this chapter suggests that investment in frontier science—especially in natural sciences and engineering—could help speed the transition toward a cleaner economy.

Box 3.1. mRNA Vaccines and the Role of Basic Scientific Research

Vaccines using new mRNA technology are key to the fight against COVID-19; the most well-known are those developed by Pfizer/BioNTech and Moderna.[1] This technology uses genetic code known as messenger RNA (or mRNA) to instruct human cells to make part of the virus's protective shell. These fragments help train the body's immune system to attack the real virus. Compared with conventional approaches, mRNA technology can deliver better-performing vaccines with shorter research and production times. Their social and economic impact has been enormous, likely shortening the pandemic by years, and looks set to revolutionize medical treatments in years to come.

This technology was built on waves of prior scientific discoveries. To track these discoveries, Figure 3.1.1 shows the publication dates of scientific articles cited by five of the seven Moderna COVID-19 vaccine patents (in blue). This distribution captures the direct dependence of vaccine development on

The authors of this box are Philip Barrett and Xiaohui Sun.
[1] While the reliance of the Moderna vaccine on just a few patents makes it easy to trace through the links from basic research, the main conclusions likely hold for other vaccines. This applies both to those using new immunization technologies (such as Johnson & Johnson and Oxford/AstraZeneca) and more traditional approaches (such as Sinopharm); they all require scientific knowledge that was once new.

past scientific discoveries and is concentrated around breakthroughs on the function of mRNA in the early 2010s. To measure the indirect influence of science, the yellow line shows the scientific citations of the vaccine's "parent" patents—other patents referenced in the five original vaccine patents. These peak in the early 2000s, tracking discoveries in editing genetic codes. Earlier advances in reading genetic codes drove a similar wave of citations from "grandparent" patents in the early 1990s. These waves of scientific influence illustrate how policies that help incentivize advances in basic science today influence the building blocks of future technologies and yield long-lasting economic payoffs.

Developing mRNA vaccines relied on a broad base of scientific knowledge. On average, the Moderna vaccine patents are in the same technological category as only 55 percent of their parent patents—a number that falls further as citation chains lengthen (Figure 3.1.2). This shows how wide-ranging basic science contributed to mRNA

Figure 3.1.1. mRNA Technology Was Built on Waves of Previous Scientific Discoveries
(Percent of citations)

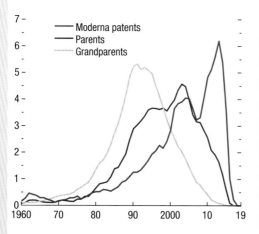

Sources: Moderna; Reliance on Science; United States Patent and Trademark Office; and IMF staff calculations.
Note: The *y*-axis shows the scientific citations by Moderna's mRNA patents and their ancestors. Parent patents are those cited by Moderna's mRNA vaccine patents. Grandparents are those cited by parent patents.

Figure 3.1.2. mRNA Vaccines Relied on a Broad Base of Scientific Knowledge
(Percent)

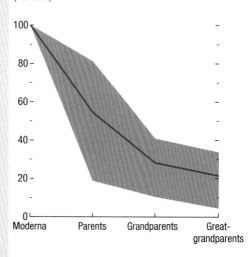

Sources: Moderna; United States Patent and Trademark Office; and IMF staff calculations.
Note: The *y*-axis shows the fraction of patents in the same technological categories as the seven Moderna vaccine patents. The blue line is the averaged percentage for each ancestor. The shaded area shows the range of each ancestor of citation across the seven Moderna vaccine patents. Total number of categories is 7,523 based on the International Patent Classification. Parent patents are those cited by Moderna's mRNA vaccine patents. Grandparents are those cited by parent patents. Great-grandparents are those cited by grandparent patents.

Box 3.1 *(continued)*

vaccines, indicating that policies to develop a broad scientific base can pay off in many and unexpected ways.

The development of COVID-19 vaccines was encouraged by unprecedented public support. This included regulatory forbearance (emergency use authorization of COVID-19 vaccines), at-risk up-front investment and subsidies for vaccine production (Operation Warp Speed), help in scaling up manufacturing (Indian government grants to vaccine producers), joint licensing agreements with local producers (India, South Africa), and advance public purchase commitments (Israel, United Kingdom, United States). A distinguishing feature of public support for a COVID-19 vaccine was its continuation throughout the development process. Typically, public funding is most generous for early trials, falling

as products near market. For COVID-19 vaccines, public and academic funding for clinical trials stayed high, even at the latest stages of development (Figure 3.1.3). This highlights how support throughout the production process can incentivize research by forward-looking firms.

Global distribution of vaccines remains a challenge. Although reliable data are hard to come by, global supply seems sufficient. World production of COVID-19 vaccines is likely to hit almost two doses per capita by the end of 2021—slightly less than demand. Although supply disruptions and capacity constraints can hamper delivery of vaccines, even planned purchases are unevenly distributed, with outsized demand in the United States and Europe (Figure 3.1.4). Fair distribution of vaccines will require adjustment of planned allocations, irrespective of where they are produced.

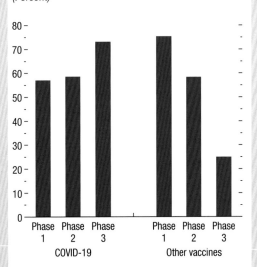

Figure 3.1.3. Unprecedented Public Support for COVID-19 Vaccine Clinical Trials
(Percent)

Sources: US National Library of Medicine; and IMF staff calculations.
Note: The *y*-axis shows the fraction of clinical trials with no private support. The three bars on the left show the clinical trial data for the COVID-19 vaccine. Support may include activities related to funding, design, implementation, data analysis, or reporting. Funder type is defined as private if support comes only from organizations in industry. Phases are based on the US Food and Drug Administration definition.

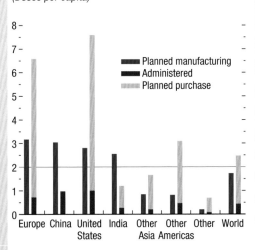

Figure 3.1.4. Global Distribution of Vaccines Remains a Key Policy Challenge
(Doses per capita)

Sources: Duke Global Health Innovation Center; Our World in Data; and IMF staff calculations.
Note: Blue bars show the planned doses of manufactured vaccines by region by the end of 2021, which also includes doses in contracts under discussion. Red bars show the number of administered vaccines by region. Yellow bars show the differences between the number of planned purchase of vaccines by the end of 2021 and the number administered. Other Americas = Americas excluding the United States; Other Asia = Asia excluding China and India.

Box 3.2. Clean Tech and the Role of Basic Scientific Research

Avoiding catastrophic climate change requires a rapid reduction in emissions of greenhouse gases. This will be possible only if global energy consumption transitions to predominantly clean (zero carbon emissions) energy sources. Technological advances to drive down the cost of clean energy are a key part of any strategy to minimize the economic impact of that switch. This box shows how investment in basic research is especially important to foster innovation in clean technologies and thus spur emission reductions.

This question is addressed using the patent-level Reliance on Science data set. This includes detailed information on the industrial category of its constituent patents, which is used to classify the technology covered in each patent as a clean or a dirty innovation (following Dechezleprêtre, Muckley, and Neelakantan 2020). Clean innovations include renewable energy technology and electric vehicles; dirty innovations cover gas turbines, furnaces, and the like. Comparing the properties of clean and dirty innovations against all other patents (as a benchmark) can help uncover the relationship between scientific research and the direction of technical change.[1]

The first dimension for comparing clean and dirty patents is their relative citations to prior patents and scientific articles. This contains information on how various types of innovation depend on applied and basic knowledge stocks. Figure 3.2.1 summarizes the results of this exercise. The first panel shows that both clean and dirty innovations cite less prior research than other sorts of innovation. Clean innovations cite more research than dirty innovations, but mainly within scientific articles. With a sample of several million patents, these differences are very precisely estimated.

The second panel compares the age of the research used by clean and dirty innovation, which can be thought of as a proxy for distance to the technological frontier. Clean innovations cite newer patents and scientific articles than both dirty innovations and other types of innovations. However, the difference is largest for scientific articles, which are, on average, 0.8 years newer than those cited

The authors of this box are Philip Barrett and Niels-Jakob Hansen.

[1]This comparison is done via regression, allowing for results that account for third factors that might otherwise influence this relationship. This includes the year that the patent is issued and the country of the inventor.

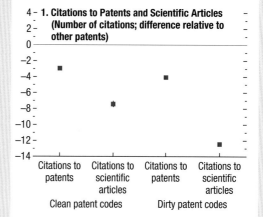

Figure 3.2.1. Clean Innovation Relies Relatively More on Basic and Newer Research

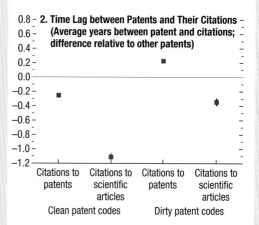

Sources: Reliance on Science; United States Patent and Trademark Office; and IMF staff calculations.
Note: Panel 1 (panel 2) shows coefficients from regression of citations (citation lag) on dummies for patent type, year, and country of inventor. Error bars represent 95 percent confidence intervals. Because the sample is very large, confidence intervals are sometimes so small as to be narrower than the width of the marker for the point estimate.

by dirty innovation. In other words, clean breakthroughs rely more on scientific research closer to the frontier than dirty innovation.

Figure 3.2.2 shows the fraction of scientific research in various fields, relative to other patents. It shows that clean innovation is particularly likely to rely on research in engineering and technology and unlikely to rely on medical research. Interestingly, dirty innovations cite the natural sciences much less frequently

Box 3.2 *(continued)*

than do clean ones. Unsurprisingly, neither clean nor dirty innovation seems to depend much on research in agriculture, social science, or the humanities.

Overall, the evidence presented here suggests that clean innovations depend more than dirty ones on frontier science, particularly natural sciences and engineering. Accordingly, basic research investment

in these fields is likely to have a positive impact in the fight against climate change. That said, public promotion of basic research in these fields will be only part of the solution. Other factors, such as incentives to bring new clean technologies to market, as well as addressing stranded assets associated with dirty fuels, will also be important.

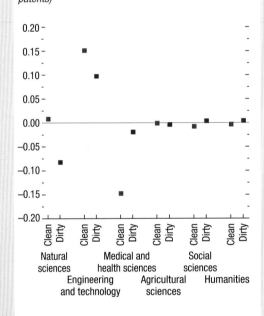

Figure 3.2.2. Clean Innovation, in Particular, Cites Engineering and Technology
(Fraction of citations; difference relative to other patents)

Sources: Reliance on Science; United States Patent and Trademark Office; and IMF staff calculations.
Note: Figure shows coefficients from regression of research field dummies on dummies for patent type. Error bars represent 95 percent confidence intervals. Because the sample is very large, confidence intervals are sometimes so small as to be narrower than the width of the marker for the point estimate.

Box 3.3. Intellectual Property, Competition, and Innovation

Intellectual property rights are among several public policy tools to foster private innovation. Innovation requires costly and risky up-front investments in research and development. Thus, would-be innovating firms may undertake them only with some guarantee that their ideas can be protected from potential imitators, at least for some time. Intellectual property rights are designed to do just that. By granting temporary monopoly power to inventors, intellectual property rights make it profitable to invest in research and development and incentivize a continuous flow of innovation. Strong intellectual property rights also complement growth-enhancing pro-competition policies, such as reduced market entry barriers and tougher antitrust frameworks (Aghion, Howitt, and Prantl 2015). Competition is generally good for innovation but, when too strong, it can weaken firms' prospective monopoly rents and therefore their incentive to innovate (April 2019 *World Economic Outlook*; IMF 2021), unless these future rents are well protected by patent laws.

However, there is a limit to how strong intellectual property rights should be. If overly protective they can cement leading firms' position and weaken their incentive to innovate, discouraging lagging firms from doing so as well (Akcigit and Ates 2021). This is particularly likely if patents excessively reward incremental innovations, or if market leaders use them as barriers to competition. "Patent thickets"—overly complicated legal setups that require a firm to seek agreements with many parties to use a technology—are an example (Shapiro 2001).

The authors of this box are Romain Duval and Jean-Marc Natal.

In sum, intellectual property rights should be neither too weak nor too strong and they should reward disruptive innovations far more than those that are incremental. Yet, even when well calibrated, intellectual property rights confer temporary monopoly power, which delays the widespread dissemination of innovation to competitors and the general public. This could, at times, run counter to society's broader goals. In a pandemic, for example, any delay in widespread vaccine production has enormous human and economic costs. Therefore, during a public emergency, and when the use of a targeted innovation is clearly identified, governments should consider alternative, less distortive approaches. Tax credits for specific research and development, direct government support, and innovation prizes, in particular, have been proposed in such situations (Kremer and Williams 2010; Maskin 2020). These policies better align society's goals with private incentives when the targeted innovation (for example, a new vaccine) and success criteria (such as effectiveness and safety) are well identified.

By covering costs and risks *up front*, Operation Warp Speed generated the necessary incentives for pharmaceutical companies to develop effective vaccines in record time. Intellectual property rights also likely helped stimulate the development of vaccines, but at the risk of slowing global production in the near future. In response, a proposal—supported by China, Russia, and the United States—to temporarily waive these rights for vaccines is currently under discussion at the World Trade Organization. In future pandemics, alternative policy support, such as well-designed innovation prizes, could be considered, which would stimulate vaccine development just as powerfully while *also* facilitating rapid vaccine dissemination.

References

Acemoglu, Daron, Philippe Aghion, and Fabrizio Zilibotti. 2006. "Distance to Frontier, Selection, and Economic Growth." *Journal of the European Economic Association* 4 (1): 37–74.

Aghion, Philippe, and Peter Howitt. 1992. "A Model of Growth through Creative Destruction." *Econometrica* 60 (2): 323–51.

Aghion, Philippe, Nicholas Bloom, Richard Blundell, and Rachel Griffith. 2005. "Competition and Innovation: An Inverted-U Relationship." *The Quarterly Journal of Economics,* 120 (2): 701–28.

Aghion, Philippe, Peter Howitt, and Susanne Prantl. 2015. "Patent Rights, Product Market Reforms, and Innovation." *Journal of Economic Growth* 20 (3): 223–62.

Aghion, Philippe, Ufuk Akcigit, and Peter Howitt. 2013. "What Do We Learn from Schumpeterian Growth Theory?" In *Handbook of Economic Growth* 2, edited by Philippe Aghion and Steven Durlauf. Amsterdam: North-Holland.

Ahmadpoor, Mohammad, and Benjamin F. Jones. 2017. "The Dual Frontier: Patented Inventions and Prior Scientific Advance." *Science* 357 (6351): 583–87.

Akcigit, Ufuk, and Sina T. Ates. 2021. "Ten Facts on Declining Business Dynamism and Lessons from Endogenous Growth Theory." *American Economic Journal: Macroeconomics* 13 (1): 257–98.

Akcigit, Ufuk, Wenjie Chen, Federico J. Diez, Romain Duval, Philipp Engler, Jiayue Fan, Chiara Maggi, Marina Mendes Tavares, Daniel A Schwartz, Ippei Shibata, and Carolina Villegas-Sánchez. 2021. "Rising Corporate Market Power: Emerging Policy Issues." IMF Staff Discussion Note 2021/001, International Monetary Fund, Washington, DC.

Akcigit, Ufuk, Douglas Hanley, and Nicolas Serrano-Velarde. 2021. "Back to Basics: Basic Research Spillovers, Innovation Policy, and Growth." *The Review of Economic Studies* 88 (1): 1–43.

Akcigit, Ufuk, and William R. Kerr. 2018. "Growth through Heterogeneous Innovations." *Journal of Political Economy* 126 (4): 1374–443.

Belenzon, Sharon, and Mark Schankerman. 2013. "Spreading the Word: Geography, Policy, and Knowledge Spillovers." *The Review of Economics and Statistics* 95 (3): 884–903.

Bloom, Nicholas, Mark Schankerman, and John Van Reenen. 2013. "Identifying Technology Spillovers and Product Market Rivalry." *Econometrica* 81 (4): 1347–93.

Blundell, Richard, and Stephen Bond. 1998. "Initial Conditions and Moment Restrictions in Dynamic Panel Data Models." *Journal of Econometrics* 87 (1): 115–43.

Byrne, John G. 1995. "Changes on the Frontier of Intellectual Property Law: An Overview of the Changes Required by GATT." *Duquesne Law Review* 34 (1): 121.

Cass, David. 1965. "Optimum Growth in an Aggregative Model of Capital Accumulation." *The Review of Economic Studies* 32: 233–40.

Cerdeiro, Diego A., Johannes Eugster, Rui C. Mano, Dirk Muir, and Shanaka J. Peiris. 2021. "Sizing Up the Effects of Technological Decoupling." IMF Working Paper 21/69, International Monetary Fund, Washington, DC.

Chuang, Yih-Chyi. 1998. "Learning by Doing, the Technology Gap, and Growth." *International Economic Review* 39 (3): 697–721.

Dechezleprêtre, Antoine, Cal B. Muckley, and Parvati Neelakantan. 2020. "Is Firm-Level Clean or Dirty Innovation Valued More?" *The European Journal of Finance,* July 2. doi: 10.1080/1351847X.2020.1785520.

Etzkowitz, Henry, and Loet Leydesdorff. 2000. "The Dynamics of Innovation: From National Systems and 'Mode 2' to a Triple Helix of University–Industry–Government Relations." *Research Policy* 29 (2): 109–23.

Grossman, Gene M., and Elhanan Helpman. 1991. *Innovation and Growth in the Global Economy.* Cambridge, MA: MIT Press.

Jaffe, Adam B., Manuel Trajtenberg, and Rebecca Henderson. 1993. "Geographic Localization of Knowledge Spillovers as Evidenced by Patent Citations." *The Quarterly Journal of Economics* 108 (3): 577–98.

Koopmans, Tjalling C. 1965. "On the Concept of Optimal Economic Growth." In *Study Week on the Econometric Approach to Development Planning*, 225–87. Amsterdam: North-Holland.

Kremer, Michael, and Heidi Williams. 2010. "Incentivizing Innovation: Adding to the Toolkit." In *Innovation Policy and the Economy* 10. Cambridge, MA: National Bureau of Economic Research.

Mankiw, Gregory N., David Romer, and David N. Weil. 1992. "A Contribution to the Empirics of Economic Growth." *The Quarterly Journal of Economics* 107 (2): 407–37.

Marx, Matt, and Aaron Fuegi. 2020. "Reliance on Science: Worldwide Front-Page Patent Citations to Scientific Articles." *Strategic Management Journal* 41 (9): 1572–94.

Maskin, Eric. 2020. "Mechanism Design for Pandemics." Talk at the Santa Fe Institute Webinar on the Complexity of COVID-19, April 14.

Nelson, Richard R. 1959. "The Simple Economics of Basic Scientific Research." *Journal of Political Economy* 67 (3): 297–306.

Peri, Giovanni. 2005. "Determinants of Knowledge Flows and Their Effect on Innovation." *The Review of Economics and Statistics* 87 (2): 308–22.

Ramsey, Frank. 1928. "A Mathematical Theory of Saving." *The Economic Journal* 38 (152): 543–59.

Romer, Paul. 1990. "Endogenous Technological Change." *Journal of Political Economy* 98 (5): S71–S102.

Santos Silva, João, and Silvana Tenreyro. 2006. "The Log of Gravity." *The Review of Economics and Statistics* 88 (4): 641–58.

Shapiro, Carl. 2001. "Navigating the Patent Thicket: Cross Licenses, Patent Pools, and Standard Setting." *Innovation Policy and the Economy* (1): 119–50.

Solow, Robert M. 1956. "A Contribution to the Theory of Economic Growth." *The Quarterly Journal of Economics* 70 (1): 65–94.

Ulku, Hulya. 2004. "R&D, Innovation, and Economic Growth: An Empirical Analysis." IMF Working Paper 04/185, International Monetary Fund, Washington, DC.

The Statistical Appendix presents historical data as well as projections. It comprises eight sections: Assumptions, What's New, Data and Conventions, Country Notes, Classification of Countries, General Features and Composition of Groups in the *World Economic Outlook*, Key Data Documentation, and Statistical Tables.

The first section summarizes the assumptions underlying the estimates and projections for 2021–22. The second section briefly describes the changes to the database and statistical tables since the April 2021 *World Economic Outlook* (WEO). The third section offers a general description of the data and the conventions used for calculating country group composites. The fourth section presents selected key information for each country. The fifth section summarizes the classification of countries in the various groups presented in the WEO. The sixth section provides information on methods and reporting standards for the member countries' national account and government finance indicators included in the report.

The last, and main, section comprises the statistical tables. (Statistical Appendix A is included here; Statistical Appendix B is available online at www.imf.org/en/Publications/WEO).

Data in these tables have been compiled on the basis of information available through September 27, 2021. The figures for 2021–22 are shown with the same degree of precision as the historical figures solely for convenience; because they are projections, the same degree of accuracy is not to be inferred.

Assumptions

Real effective *exchange rates* for the advanced economies are assumed to remain constant at their average levels measured during July 23, 2021–August 20, 2021. For 2021 and 2022 these assumptions imply average US dollar–special drawing right (SDR) conversion rates

of 1.431 and 1.444, US dollar–euro conversion rates[1] of 1.194 and 1.208, and yen–US dollar conversion rates of 108.5 and 106.7, respectively.

It is assumed that the *price of oil* will average $65.68 a barrel in 2021 and $64.52 a barrel in 2022.

National authorities' established *policies* are assumed to be maintained. Box A1 describes the more specific policy assumptions underlying the projections for selected economies.

With regard to *interest rates*, it is assumed that the London interbank offered rate (LIBOR) on six-month US dollar deposits will average 0.2 percent in 2021 and 0.4 percent in 2022, the LIBOR on three-month euro deposits will average –0.5 percent in 2021 and 2022, and the LIBOR on six-month yen deposits will average –0.1 percent in 2021 and 0.0 percent in 2022.

What's New

- Data for Andorra have been added to the database and are included in the advanced economies group composites.

Data and Conventions

Data and projections for 196 economies form the statistical basis of the WEO database. The data are maintained jointly by the IMF's Research Department and regional departments, with the latter regularly updating country projections based on consistent global assumptions.

Although national statistical agencies are the ultimate providers of historical data and definitions,

---

[1] In regard to the introduction of the euro, on December 31, 1998, the Council of the European Union decided that, effective January 1, 1999, the irrevocably fixed conversion rates between the euro and currencies of the member countries adopting the euro are as described in Box 5.4 of the October 1998 WEO. See Box 5.4 of the October 1998 WEO as well for details on how the conversion rates were established. For the most recent table of fixed conversion rates, see the Statistical Appendix of the October 2020 WEO.

international organizations are also involved in statistical issues, with the objective of harmonizing methodologies for the compilation of national statistics, including analytical frameworks, concepts, definitions, classifications, and valuation procedures used in the production of economic statistics. The WEO database reflects information from both national source agencies and international organizations.

Most countries' macroeconomic data as presented in the WEO conform broadly to the 2008 version of the *System of National Accounts* (2008 SNA). The IMF's sector statistical standards—the sixth edition of the *Balance of Payments and International Investment Position Manual* (BPM6), the *Monetary and Financial Statistics Manual and Compilation Guide* (MFSMCG), and the *Government Finance Statistics Manual 2014* (GFSM 2014)—have been aligned with the SNA 2008. These standards reflect the IMF's special interest in countries' external positions, financial sector stability, and public sector fiscal positions. The process of adapting country data to the new standards begins in earnest when the manuals are released. However, full concordance with the manuals is ultimately dependent on the provision by national statistical compilers of revised country data; hence, the WEO estimates are only partly adapted to these manuals. Nonetheless, for many countries, conversion to the updated standards will have only a small impact on major balances and aggregates. Many other countries have partly adopted the latest standards and will continue implementation over a number of years.[2]

The fiscal gross and net debt data reported in the WEO are drawn from official data sources and IMF staff estimates. While attempts are made to align gross and net debt data with the definitions in the GFSM, as a result of data limitations or specific country circumstances, these data can sometimes deviate from the formal definitions. Although every effort is made to ensure the WEO data are relevant and internationally comparable, differences in both sectoral and instrument coverage mean that the data are not universally comparable. As more information becomes available, changes in either data sources or instrument coverage can give rise to data revisions that can sometimes

be substantial. For clarification on the deviations in sectoral or instrument coverage, please refer to the metadata for the online WEO database.

Composite data for country groups in the WEO are either sums or weighted averages of data for individual countries. Unless noted otherwise, multiyear averages of growth rates are expressed as compound annual rates of change.[3] Arithmetically weighted averages are used for all data for the emerging market and developing economies group—except data on inflation and money growth, for which geometric averages are used. The following conventions apply:

Country group composites for exchange rates, interest rates, and growth rates of monetary aggregates are weighted by GDP converted to US dollars at market exchange rates (averaged over the preceding three years) as a share of group GDP.

Composites for other data relating to the domestic economy, whether growth rates or ratios, are weighted by GDP valued at purchasing power parity as a share of total world or group GDP.[4] Annual inflation rates are simple percentage changes from the previous years, except in the case of emerging market and developing economies, for which the rates are based on logarithmic differences.

Composites for real GDP per capita in *purchasing power parity* terms are sums of individual country data after conversion to the international dollar in the years indicated.

Unless noted otherwise, composites for all sectors for the euro area are corrected for reporting discrepancies in intra-area transactions. Unadjusted annual GDP data are used for the euro area and for the majority of individual countries, except for Cyprus, Ireland, Portugal, and Spain, which report calendar-adjusted data. For data prior to 1999, data aggregations apply 1995 European currency unit exchange rates.

---

[2] Many countries are implementing the SNA 2008 or European System of National and Regional Accounts (ESA) 2010, and a few countries use versions of the SNA older than that from 1993. A similar adoption pattern is expected for the BPM6 and GFSM 2014. Please refer to Table G, which lists the statistical standards each country adheres to.

[3] Averages for real GDP, inflation, GDP per capita, and commodity prices are calculated based on the compound annual rate of change; averages for the unemployment rate are based on the simple arithmetic average.

[4] See Box 1.1 of the October 2020 WEO for a summary of the revised purchasing-power-parity-based weights as well as "Revised Purchasing Power Parity Weights" in the July 2014 WEO *Update*, Appendix 1.1 of the April 2008 WEO, Box A2 of the April 2004 WEO, Box A1 of the May 2000 WEO, and Annex IV of the May 1993 WEO. See also Anne-Marie Gulde and Marianne Schulze-Ghattas, "Purchasing Power Parity Based Weights for the *World Economic Outlook*," in *Staff Studies for the World Economic Outlook* (Washington, DC: International Monetary Fund, December 1993), 106–23.

Composites for fiscal data are sums of individual country data after conversion to US dollars at the average market exchange rates in the years indicated.

Composite unemployment rates and employment growth are weighted by labor force as a share of group labor force.

Composites relating to external sector statistics are sums of individual country data after conversion to US dollars at the average market exchange rates in the years indicated for balance of payments data and at end-of-year market exchange rates for debt denominated in currencies other than US dollars.

Composites of changes in foreign trade volumes and prices, however, are arithmetic averages of percent changes for individual countries weighted by the US dollar value of exports or imports as a share of total world or group exports or imports (in the preceding year). Unless noted otherwise, group composites are computed if 90 percent or more of the share of group weights is represented.

Data refer to calendar years, except in the case of a few countries that use fiscal years; Table F lists the economies with exceptional reporting periods for national accounts and government finance data for each country.

For some countries, the figures for 2020 and earlier are based on estimates rather than actual outturns; Table G lists the latest actual outturns for the indicators in the national accounts, prices, government finance, and balance of payments indicators for each country.

Country Notes

For *Afghanistan*, all projections for 2021–26 are omitted due to an unusually high degree of uncertainty.

For *Albania*, projections were prepared prior to the 2021 Article IV mission that ended on October 11, 2021, and thereby do not reflect updates during the mission.

For *Argentina*, fiscal and inflation variables are excluded from publication for 2021–26 as these are to a large extent linked to still-pending program negotiations. The official national consumer price index (CPI) for Argentina starts in December 2016. For earlier periods, CPI data for Argentina reflect the Greater Buenos Aires Area CPI (prior to December 2013), the national CPI (IPCNu, December 2013 to October 2015), the City of Buenos Aires CPI (November 2015 to April 2016), and the Greater Buenos Aires Area CPI (May 2016 to December 2016). Given limited comparability of these series on account of differences in geographical coverage, weights, sampling, and methodology, the average CPI inflation for 2014–16 and end-of-period inflation for

2015–16 are not reported in the October 2021 WEO. Also, Argentina discontinued the publication of labor market data in December 2015 and new series became available starting in the second quarter of 2016.

Data and forecasts for *Bangladesh* are presented on a fiscal year basis starting with the October 2020 WEO. However, the real GDP and purchasing-power-parity GDP aggregates that include Bangladesh are based on calendar year estimates.

For *Costa Rica*, the central government definition has been expanded as of January 1, 2021, to include 51 public entities as per Law 9524. Data are adjusted back to 2019 for comparability.

The fiscal series for the *Dominican Republic* have the following coverage: public debt, debt service, and the cyclically adjusted/structural balances are for the consolidated public sector (which includes central government, the rest of the nonfinancial public sector, and the central bank); and the remaining fiscal series are for the central government.

The fiscal data for *Ecuador* reflect net lending/borrowing for the nonfinancial public sector. Ecuadorian authorities, with technical support from the IMF, are undertaking revisions of the historical fiscal data for the net lending/borrowing of the nonfinancial public sector over 2012–17, with the view of correcting recently identified statistical errors in data compilation at the subnational level and the consistency between above-the-line and financing data by subsectors.

For *Ethiopia*, projections for 2022–26 are omitted due to an unusually high degree of uncertainty.

India's real GDP growth rates are calculated as per national accounts: for 1998 to 2011, with base year 2004/05 and, thereafter, with base year 2011/12.

For *Lebanon*, projections for 2021–26 are omitted due to an unusually high degree of uncertainty. Official GDP numbers are available only through 2019.

Against the backdrop of a civil war and weak capacity, the reliability of *Libya*'s data, especially regarding national accounts and medium-term projections, is low.

Data for *Syria* are excluded from 2011 onward because of the uncertain political situation.

For *Turkmenistan*, national accounts data are IMF staff estimates compiled in line with international methodologies (SNA), using official estimates and sources as well as United Nations and World Bank databases. The Turkmenistan authorities' estimate of real GDP growth in 2020 is 5.9 percent. Estimates and projections of the fiscal balance exclude receipts from domestic bond issuances as well as privatization operations, in line with GFSM 2014.

The authorities' official estimates on fiscal accounts, which are compiled using domestic statistical methodologies, include bond issuance and privatization proceeds as part of government revenues.

Ukraine's revised national accounts data are available beginning in 2000 and exclude Crimea and Sevastopol from 2010 onward.

In December 2020 the *Uruguay* authorities began reporting the national accounts data according to SNA 2008, with the base year 2016. The new series begin in 2016. Data prior to 2016 reflect the IMF staff's best effort to preserve previously reported data and avoid structural breaks.

Starting in October 2018 *Uruguay*'s public pension system has been receiving transfers in the context of a new law that compensates persons affected by the creation of the mixed pension system. These funds are recorded as revenues, consistent with the IMF's methodology. Therefore, data and projections for 2018–21 are affected by these transfers, which amounted to 1.2 percent of GDP in 2018, 1.1 percent of GDP in 2019, and 0.6 percent of GDP in 2020, and are projected to be 0.3 percent of GDP in 2021, and 0.0 percent thereafter. See IMF Country Report 19/64 for further details.[5] The disclaimer about the public pension system applies only to the revenues and net lending/borrowing series.

The coverage of the fiscal data for *Uruguay* was changed from consolidated public sector to nonfinancial public sector with the October 2019 WEO. In Uruguay, nonfinancial public sector coverage includes central government, local government, social security funds, nonfinancial public corporations, and Banco de Seguros del Estado. Historical data were also revised accordingly. Under this narrower fiscal perimeter—which excludes the central bank—assets and liabilities held by the nonfinancial public sector where the counterpart is the central bank are not netted out in debt figures. In this context, capitalization bonds issued in the past by the government to the central bank are now part of the nonfinancial public sector debt. Gross and net debt estimates for 2008–11 are preliminary.

Projecting the economic outlook in *Venezuela*, including assessing past and current economic developments as the basis for the projections, is complicated by the lack of discussions with the authorities (the last Article IV consultation took place in 2004), incomplete understanding of the reported data, and difficulties in interpreting certain reported economic indicators given economic developments. The fiscal accounts include the budgetary central government; social security; FOGADE (insurance deposit institution); and a sample of public enterprises, including Petróleos de Venezuela, S.A. (PDVSA); and data for 2018–21 are IMF staff estimates. The effects of hyperinflation and the paucity of reported data mean that the IMF staff's projected macroeconomic indicators need to be interpreted with caution. For example, nominal GDP is estimated assuming the GDP deflator rises in line with the IMF staff's projection of average inflation. Public external debt in relation to GDP is projected using the IMF staff's estimate of the average exchange rate for the year. Wide uncertainty surrounds these projections. Venezuela's consumer prices are excluded from all WEO group composites.

In 2019 *Zimbabwe* authorities introduced the Real Time Gross Settlement dollar, later renamed the Zimbabwe dollar, and are in the process of redenominating their national accounts statistics. Current data are subject to revision. The Zimbabwe dollar previously ceased circulating in 2009, and during 2009–19, Zimbabwe operated under a multicurrency regime with the US dollar as the unit of account.

Classification of Countries
Summary of the Country Classification

The country classification in the WEO divides the world into two major groups: advanced economies and emerging market and developing economies.[6] This classification is not based on strict criteria, economic or otherwise, and it has evolved over time. The objective is to facilitate analysis by providing a reasonably meaningful method of organizing data. Table A provides an overview of the country classification, showing the number of countries in each group by region and summarizing some key indicators of their relative size (GDP valued at purchasing power parity, total exports of goods and services, and population).

Some countries remain outside the country classification and therefore are not included in the analysis. Cuba and the Democratic People's Republic of Korea are examples of countries that are not IMF members, and the IMF therefore does not monitor their economies.

[5]*Uruguay: Staff Report for the 2018 Article IV Consultation,* Country Report 19/64 (Washington, DC: International Monetary Fund, February 2019).

[6]As used here, the terms "country" and "economy" do not always refer to a territorial entity that is a state as understood by international law and practice. Some territorial entities included here are not states, although their statistical data are maintained on a separate and independent basis.

General Features and Composition of Groups in the *World Economic Outlook* Classification

Advanced Economies

Table B lists the 40 advanced economies. The seven largest in terms of GDP based on market exchange rates—the United States, Japan, Germany, France, Italy, the United Kingdom, and Canada—constitute the subgroup of major advanced economies, often referred to as the Group of Seven. The members of the euro area are also distinguished as a subgroup. Composite data shown in the tables for the euro area cover the current members for all years, even though the membership has increased over time.

Table C lists the member countries of the European Union, not all of which are classified as advanced economies in the WEO.

Emerging Market and Developing Economies

The group of emerging market and developing economies (156) includes all those that are not classified as advanced economies.

The regional breakdowns of emerging market and developing economies are emerging and developing Asia; emerging and developing Europe (sometimes also referred to as "central and eastern Europe"); Latin America and the Caribbean; Middle East and Central Asia (which comprises the regional subgroups Caucasus and Central Asia; and Middle East, North Africa, Afghanistan, and Pakistan); and sub-Saharan Africa.

Emerging market and developing economies are also classified according to *analytical criteria* that reflect the composition of export earnings and a distinction between net creditor and net debtor economies. Tables D and E show the detailed composition of emerging market and developing economies in the regional and analytical groups.

The analytical criterion *source of export earnings* distinguishes between the categories *fuel* (Standard International Trade Classification [SITC] 3) and

nonfuel and then focuses on *nonfuel primary products* (SITCs 0, 1, 2, 4, and 68). Economies are categorized into one of these groups if their main source of export earnings exceeded 50 percent of total exports on average between 2016 and 2020.

The financial and income criteria focus on *net creditor economies*, *net debtor economies*, heavily indebted poor countries (HIPCs), *low-income developing countries* (LIDCs), and *emerging market and middle-income economies* (EMMIEs). Economies are categorized as net debtors when their latest net international investment position, where available, was less than zero or their current account balance accumulations from 1972 (or earliest available data) to 2020 were negative. Net debtor economies are further differentiated on the basis of *experience with debt servicing*.[7]

The HIPC group comprises the countries that are or have been considered by the IMF and the World Bank for participation in their debt initiative known as the HIPC Initiative, which aims to reduce the external debt burdens of all the eligible HIPCs to a "sustainable" level in a reasonably short period of time.[8] Many of these countries have already benefited from debt relief and have graduated from the initiative.

The LIDCs are countries that have per capita income levels below a certain threshold (set at $2,700 in 2016 as measured by the World Bank's Atlas method), structural features consistent with limited development and structural transformation, and external financial linkages insufficiently close for them to be widely seen as emerging market economies.

The EMMIEs group comprises emerging market and developing economies that are not classified as LIDCs.

[7] During 2016–20, 32 economies incurred external payments arrears or entered into official or commercial bank debt-rescheduling agreements. This group is referred to as *economies with arrears and/or rescheduling during 2016–20*.

[8] See David Andrews, Anthony R. Boote, Syed S. Rizavi, and Sukwinder Singh, "Debt Relief for Low-Income Countries: The Enhanced HIPC Initiative," IMF Pamphlet Series 51 (Washington, DC: International Monetary Fund, November 1999).

Table A. Classification by *World Economic Outlook* Groups and Their Shares in Aggregate GDP, Exports of Goods and Services, and Population, 2020[1]
(Percent of total for group or world)

	Number of Economies	GDP Advanced Economies	World	Exports of Goods and Services Advanced Economies	World	Population Advanced Economies	World
Advanced Economies	**40**	**100.0**	**42.4**	**100.0**	**63.0**	**100.0**	**14.0**
United States		37.3	15.8	15.3	9.6	30.7	4.3
Euro Area	19	28.4	12.1	42.4	26.7	31.6	4.4
Germany		8.1	3.4	12.0	7.5	7.7	1.1
France		5.4	2.3	5.4	3.4	6.1	0.9
Italy		4.4	1.9	4.0	2.5	5.6	0.8
Spain		3.2	1.4	2.8	1.8	4.4	0.6
Japan		9.5	4.0	5.7	3.6	11.7	1.6
United Kingdom		5.3	2.2	5.3	3.3	6.2	0.9
Canada		3.3	1.4	3.4	2.2	3.5	0.5
Other Advanced Economies	17	16.2	6.9	27.9	17.6	16.2	2.3
Memorandum							
Major Advanced Economies	7	73.2	31.1	51.1	32.2	71.5	10.0

	Number of Economies	Emerging Market and Developing Economies	World	Emerging Market and Developing Economies	World	Emerging Market and Developing Economies	World
Emerging Market and Developing Economies	**156**	**100.0**	**57.6**	**100.0**	**37.0**	**100.0**	**86.0**
Regional Groups							
Emerging and Developing Asia	30	55.9	32.2	53.3	19.7	56.0	48.1
China		31.8	18.3	33.3	12.3	21.5	18.5
India		11.8	6.8	6.1	2.3	21.0	18.0
ASEAN-5	5	9.8	5.7	12.3	4.6	8.8	7.6
Emerging and Developing Europe	16	13.4	7.7	16.4	6.1	5.8	5.0
Russia		5.4	3.1	4.6	1.7	2.2	1.9
Latin America and the Caribbean	33	12.6	7.3	13.1	4.9	9.7	8.3
Brazil		4.2	2.4	2.9	1.1	3.2	2.8
Mexico		3.2	1.8	5.3	2.0	1.9	1.7
Middle East and Central Asia	32	12.5	7.2	13.1	4.8	12.7	10.9
Saudi Arabia		2.1	1.2	2.2	0.8	0.5	0.5
Sub-Saharan Africa	45	5.5	3.2	4.1	1.5	15.9	13.7
Nigeria		1.4	0.8	0.5	0.2	3.1	2.7
South Africa		1.0	0.6	1.1	0.4	0.9	0.8
Analytical Groups[2]							
By Source of Export Earnings							
Fuel	26	10.0	5.8	12.3	4.5	9.5	8.2
Nonfuel	128	89.9	51.8	87.7	32.5	90.4	77.7
Of Which, Primary Products	36	5.7	3.3	5.4	2.0	9.7	8.3
By External Financing Source							
Net Debtor Economies	121	51.0	29.3	46.5	17.2	67.8	58.3
Net Debtor Economies by Debt-Servicing Experience							
Economies with Arrears and/or Rescheduling during 2016–20	32	4.6	2.6	3.2	1.2	9.9	8.5
Other Groups							
Emerging Market and Middle-Income Economies	96	91.6	52.7	92.3	34.2	76.7	65.9
Low-Income Developing Countries	59	8.4	4.9	7.7	2.8	23.3	20.0
Heavily Indebted Poor Countries	39	2.9	1.7	2.1	0.8	12.1	10.4

[1]The GDP shares are based on the purchasing-power-parity valuation of economies' GDP. The number of economies comprising each group reflects those for which data are included in the group aggregates.
[2]Syria and West Bank and Gaza are omitted from the source of export earnings, and Syria is omitted from the net external position group composites because of insufficient data.

Table B. Advanced Economies, by Subgroup

Major Currency Areas		
United States		
Euro Area		
Japan		

Euro Area		
Austria	Greece	The Netherlands
Belgium	Ireland	Portugal
Cyprus	Italy	Slovak Republic
Estonia	Latvia	Slovenia
Finland	Lithuania	Spain
France	Luxembourg	
Germany	Malta	

Major Advanced Economies		
Canada	Italy	United States
France	Japan	
Germany	United Kingdom	

Other Advanced Economies		
Andorra	Israel	San Marino
Australia	Korea	Singapore
Czech Republic	Macao SAR[2]	Sweden
Denmark	New Zealand	Switzerland
Hong Kong SAR[1]	Norway	Taiwan Province of China
Iceland	Puerto Rico	

[1] On July 1, 1997, Hong Kong was returned to the People's Republic of China and became a Special Administrative Region of China.

[2] On December 20, 1999, Macao was returned to the People's Republic of China and became a Special Administrative Region of China.

Table C. European Union

Austria	France	Malta
Belgium	Germany	The Netherlands
Bulgaria	Greece	Poland
Croatia	Hungary	Portugal
Cyprus	Ireland	Romania
Czech Republic	Italy	Slovak Republic
Denmark	Latvia	Slovenia
Estonia	Lithuania	Spain
Finland	Luxembourg	Sweden

Table D. Emerging Market and Developing Economies, by Region and Main Source of Export Earnings[1]

	Fuel	Nonfuel Primary Products
Emerging and Developing Asia		
	Brunei Darussalam	Kiribati
	Timor-Leste	Marshall Islands
		Papua New Guinea
		Solomon Islands
		Tuvalu
Latin America and the Caribbean		
	Ecuador	Argentina
	Trinidad and Tobago	Bolivia
	Venezuela	Chile
		Guyana
		Paraguay
		Peru
		Suriname
		Uruguay
Middle East and Central Asia		
	Algeria	Afghanistan
	Azerbaijan	Mauritania
	Bahrain	Somalia
	Iran	Sudan
	Iraq	Tajikistan
	Kazakhstan	Uzbekistan
	Kuwait	
	Libya	
	Oman	
	Qatar	
	Saudi Arabia	
	Turkmenistan	
	United Arab Emirates	
	Yemen	
Sub-Saharan Africa		
	Angola	Benin
	Chad	Burkina Faso
	Republic of Congo	Burundi
	Equatorial Guinea	Central African Republic
	Gabon	Democratic Republic of the Congo
	Nigeria	Côte d'Ivoire
	South Sudan	Eritrea
		Ghana
		Guinea
		Guinea-Bissau
		Liberia
		Malawi
		Mali
		Sierra Leone
		South Africa
		Zambia
		Zimbabwe

[1]Emerging and Developing Europe is omitted because no economies in the group have fuel or nonfuel primary products as the main source of export earnings.

Table E. Emerging Market and Developing Economies by Region, Net External Position, Heavily Indebted Poor Countries, and Per Capita Income Classification

	Net External Position[1]	Heavily Indebted Poor Countries[2]	Per Capita Income Classification[3]		Net External Position[1]	Heavily Indebted Poor Countries[2]	Per Capita Income Classification[3]
Emerging and Developing Asia				North Macedonia	*		•
Bangladesh	*		*	Poland	*		•
Bhutan	*		*	Romania	*		•
Brunei Darussalam	•		•	Russia	•		•
Cambodia	*		*	Serbia	*		•
China	•		•	Turkey	*		•
Fiji	*		•	Ukraine	*		•
India	*		•	**Latin America and the Caribbean**			
Indonesia	*		•	Antigua and Barbuda	*		•
Kiribati	•		*	Argentina	•		•
Lao P.D.R.	*		*	Aruba	*		•
Malaysia	*		•	The Bahamas	*		•
Maldives	*		•	Barbados	*		•
Marshall Islands	*		•	Belize	*		•
Micronesia	•		•	Bolivia	*	•	•
Mongolia	*		•	Brazil	*		•
Myanmar	*		*	Chile	*		•
Nauru	*		•	Colombia	*		•
Nepal	•		*	Costa Rica	*		•
Palau	*		•	Dominica	•		•
Papua New Guinea	*		*	Dominican Republic	*		•
Philippines	*		•	Ecuador	*		•
Samoa	*		•	El Salvador	*		•
Solomon Islands	*		*	Grenada	*		•
Sri Lanka	*		•	Guatemala	*		•
Thailand	•		•	Guyana	*	•	•
Timor-Leste	•		*	Haiti	*	•	*
Tonga	*		•	Honduras	*	•	*
Tuvalu	•		•	Jamaica	*		•
Vanuatu	•		•	Mexico	*		•
Vietnam	*		*	Nicaragua	*	•	*
Emerging and Developing Europe				Panama	*		•
Albania	*		•	Paraguay	*		•
Belarus	*		•	Peru	*		•
Bosnia and Herzegovina	*		•	St. Kitts and Nevis	*		•
Bulgaria	*		•	St. Lucia	*		•
Croatia	*		•	St. Vincent and the Grenadines	*		•
Hungary	*		•	Suriname	*		•
Kosovo	*		•	Trinidad and Tobago	•		•
Moldova	*		*	Uruguay	*		•
Montenegro	*		•	Venezuela	•		•

Table E. Emerging Market and Developing Economies by Region, Net External Position, Heavily Indebted Poor Countries, and Per Capita Income Classification (continued)

	Net External Position[1]	Heavily Indebted Poor Countries[2]	Per Capita Income Classification[3]		Net External Position[1]	Heavily Indebted Poor Countries[2]	Per Capita Income Classification[3]
Middle East and Central Asia				Cameroon	*	•	*
Afghanistan	•	•	*	Central African Republic	*	•	*
Algeria	•		•	Chad	*	•	*
Armenia	*		•	Comoros	*	•	*
Azerbaijan	•		•	Democratic Republic of the Congo	*	•	*
Bahrain	•		•	Republic of Congo	*	•	*
Djibouti	*		*	Côte d'Ivoire	*	•	*
Egypt	*		•	Equatorial Guinea	•		•
Georgia	*		•	Eritrea	•	*	*
Iran	•		•	Eswatini	•		•
Iraq	•		•	Ethiopia	*	•	*
Jordan	*		•	Gabon	•		•
Kazakhstan	*		•	The Gambia	*	•	*
Kuwait	•		•	Ghana	*	•	*
Kyrgyz Republic	*		*	Guinea	*	•	*
Lebanon	*		•	Guinea-Bissau	*	•	*
Libya	•		•	Kenya	*		*
Mauritania	*	•	*	Lesotho	*		*
Morocco	*		•	Liberia	*	•	*
Oman	*		•	Madagascar	*	•	*
Pakistan	*		•	Malawi	*	•	*
Qatar	•		•	Mali	*	•	*
Saudi Arabia	•		•	Mauritius	•		•
Somalia	*	*	*	Mozambique	*	•	*
Sudan	*	*	*	Namibia	*		•
Syria[4]	...		...	Niger	*	•	*
Tajikistan	*		*	Nigeria	*		*
Tunisia	*		•	Rwanda	*	•	*
Turkmenistan	•		•	São Tomé and Príncipe	*	•	*
United Arab Emirates	•		•	Senegal	*	•	*
Uzbekistan	•		*	Seychelles	*		•
West Bank and Gaza	*		•	Sierra Leone	*	•	*
Yemen	*		*	South Africa	•		•
Sub-Saharan Africa				South Sudan	*		*
Angola	*		•	Tanzania	*	•	*
Benin	*	•	*	Togo	*	•	*
Botswana	•		•	Uganda	*	•	*
Burkina Faso	*	•	*	Zambia	*	•	*
Burundi	*	•	*	Zimbabwe	*		*
Cabo Verde	*		•				

[1]Dot (star) indicates that the country is a net creditor (net debtor).
[2]Dot instead of star indicates that the country has reached the completion point, which allows it to receive the full debt relief committed to at the decision point.
[3]Dot (star) indicates that the country is classified as an emerging market and middle-income economy (low-income developing country).
[4]Syria is omitted from the net external position group and per capita income classification group composites for lack of a fully developed database.

Table F. Economies with Exceptional Reporting Periods[1]

	National Accounts	Government Finance
The Bahamas		Jul/Jun
Bangladesh	Jul/Jun	Jul/Jun
Barbados		Apr/Mar
Bhutan	Jul/Jun	Jul/Jun
Botswana		Apr/Mar
Dominica		Jul/Jun
Egypt	Jul/Jun	Jul/Jun
Eswatini		Apr/Mar
Ethiopia	Jul/Jun	Jul/Jun
Haiti	Oct/Sep	Oct/Sep
Hong Kong SAR		Apr/Mar
India	Apr/Mar	Apr/Mar
Iran	Apr/Mar	Apr/Mar
Jamaica		Apr/Mar
Lesotho	Apr/Mar	Apr/Mar
Marshall Islands	Oct/Sep	Oct/Sep
Mauritius		Jul/Jun
Micronesia	Oct/Sep	Oct/Sep
Myanmar	Oct/Sep	Oct/Sep
Namibia		Apr/Mar
Nauru	Jul/Jun	Jul/Jun
Nepal	Aug/Jul	Aug/Jul
Pakistan	Jul/Jun	Jul/Jun
Palau	Oct/Sep	Oct/Sep
Puerto Rico	Jul/Jun	Jul/Jun
St. Lucia		Apr/Mar
Samoa	Jul/Jun	Jul/Jun
Singapore		Apr/Mar
Thailand		Oct/Sep
Tonga	Jul/Jun	Jul/Jun
Trinidad and Tobago		Oct/Sep

[1]Unless noted otherwise, all data refer to calendar years.

Table G. Key Data Documentation

Country	Currency	National Accounts					Prices (CPI)	
		Historical Data Source[1]	Latest Actual Annual Data	Base Year[2]	System of National Accounts	Use of Chain-Weighted Methodology[3]	Historical Data Source[1]	Latest Actual Annual Data
Afghanistan	Afghan afghani	NSO	2019	2016	SNA 2008		NSO	2020
Albania	Albanian lek	IMF staff	2020	1996	ESA 2010	From 1996	NSO	2020
Algeria	Algerian dinar	NSO	2019	2001	SNA 1993	From 2005	NSO	2020
Andorra	Euro	NSO and MoF	2020	2010	. . .		NSO	2020
Angola	Angolan kwanza	NSO and MEP	2020	2002	ESA 1995		NSO	2020
Antigua and Barbuda	Eastern Caribbean dollar	CB	2019	2006[6]	SNA 1993		CB	2020
Argentina	Argentine peso	NSO	2020	2004	SNA 2008		NSO	2020
Armenia	Armenian dram	NSO	2020	2005	SNA 2008		NSO	2020
Aruba	Aruban Florin	NSO	2020	2013	SNA 1993	From 2000	NSO	2020
Australia	Australian dollar	NSO	2020	2018	SNA 2008	From 1980	NSO	2020
Austria	Euro	NSO	2019	2015	ESA 2010	From 1995	NSO	2020
Azerbaijan	Azerbaijan manat	NSO	2020	2005	SNA 1993	From 1994	NSO	2020
The Bahamas	Bahamian dollar	NSO	2019	2012	SNA 1993		NSO	2019
Bahrain	Bahrain dinar	NSO and IMF staff	2020	2010	SNA 2008		NSO	2020
Bangladesh	Bangladesh taka	NSO	2019/20	2005/06	SNA 2008		NSO	2020/21
Barbados	Barbados dollar	NSO and CB	2019	2010	SNA 1993		NSO	2020
Belarus	Belarusian ruble	NSO	2020	2018	SNA 2008	From 2005	NSO	2020
Belgium	Euro	CB	2020	2015	ESA 2010	From 1995	CB	2020
Belize	Belize dollar	NSO	2020	2000	SNA 1993		NSO	2019
Benin	CFA franc	NSO	2019	2015	SNA 2008		NSO	2019
Bhutan	Bhutanese ngultrum	NSO	2019/20	2000/01[6]	SNA 1993		CB	2019/20
Bolivia	Bolivian boliviano	NSO	2020	1990	SNA 2008		NSO	2020
Bosnia and Herzegovina	Bosnian convertible marka	NSO	2020	2015	ESA 2010	From 2000	NSO	2020
Botswana	Botswana pula	NSO	2020	2016	SNA 2008		NSO	2020
Brazil	Brazilian real	NSO	2020	1995	SNA 2008		NSO	2020
Brunei Darussalam	Brunei dollar	MoF	2020	2010	SNA 2008		NSO and MoF	2020
Bulgaria	Bulgarian lev	NSO	2020	2015	ESA 2010	From 1996	NSO	2020
Burkina Faso	CFA franc	NSO and MEP	2020	2015	SNA 2008		NSO	2020
Burundi	Burundi franc	NSO and IMF staff	2019	2005	SNA 1993		NSO	2020
Cabo Verde	Cabo Verdean escudo	NSO	2019	2007	SNA 2008	From 2011	NSO	2019
Cambodia	Cambodian riel	NSO	2020	2000	SNA 1993		NSO	2020
Cameroon	CFA franc	NSO	2020	2005	SNA 2008		NSO	2020
Canada	Canadian dollar	NSO	2020	2012	SNA 2008	From 1980	NSO	2020
Central African Republic	CFA franc	NSO	2017	2005	SNA 1993		NSO	2020
Chad	CFA franc	CB	2017	2005	SNA 1993		NSO	2020
Chile	Chilean peso	CB	2020	2013[6]	SNA 2008	From 2003	NSO	2019
China	Chinese yuan	NSO	2020	2015	SNA 2008		NSO	2020
Colombia	Colombian peso	NSO	2020	2015	SNA 2008	From 2005	NSO	2020
Comoros	Comorian franc	MoF	2019	2007	SNA 1993	From 2007	NSO	2019
Democratic Republic of the Congo	Congolese franc	NSO	2020	2005	SNA 1993		CB	2020
Republic of Congo	CFA franc	NSO	2018	2005	SNA 1993		NSO	2019
Costa Rica	Costa Rican colón	CB	2020	2017	SNA 2008		CB	2020

Table G. Key Data Documentation *(continued)*

Country	Government Finance					Balance of Payments		
	Historical Data Source[1]	Latest Actual Annual Data	Statistics Manual in Use at Source	Subsectors Coverage[4]	Accounting Practice[5]	Historical Data Source[1]	Latest Actual Annual Data	Statistics Manual in Use at Source
Afghanistan	MoF	2019	2001	CG	C	NSO, MoF, and CB	2019	BPM 6
Albania	IMF staff	2019	1986	CG,LG,SS,MPC, NFPC	. . .	CB	2020	BPM 6
Algeria	MoF	2019	1986	CG	C	CB	2020	BPM 6
Andorra	NSO	2019	. . .	CG,LG,SS	C	NSO	2019	BPM 6
Angola	MoF	2020	2001	CG,LG	. . .	CB	2020	BPM 6
Antigua and Barbuda	MoF	2020	2001	CG	Mixed	CB	2020	BPM 6
Argentina	MEP	2020	1986	CG,SG,SS	C	NSO	2020	BPM 6
Armenia	MoF	2020	2001	CG	C	CB	2020	BPM 6
Aruba	MoF	2020	2001	CG	Mixed	CB	2020	BPM 6
Australia	MoF	2019	2014	CG,SG,LG,TG	A	NSO	2020	BPM 6
Austria	NSO	2019	2014	CG,SG,LG,SS	A	CB	2019	BPM 6
Azerbaijan	MoF	2020	2001	CG	C	CB	2020	BPM 6
The Bahamas	MoF	2019/20	2014	CG	C	CB	2020	BPM 5
Bahrain	MoF	2020	2001	CG	C	CB	2020	BPM 6
Bangladesh	MoF	2018/19	. . .	CG	C	CB	2019/20	BPM 6
Barbados	MoF	2019/20	1986	BCG	C	CB	2019	BPM 6
Belarus	MoF	2020	2001	CG,LG,SS	C	CB	2020	BPM 6
Belgium	CB	2020	ESA 2010	CG,SG,LG,SS	A	CB	2020	BPM 6
Belize	MoF	2020	1986	CG,MPC	Mixed	CB	2020	BPM 6
Benin	MoF	2019	1986	CG	C	CB	2019	BPM 6
Bhutan	MoF	2019/20	1986	CG	C	CB	2019/20	BPM 6
Bolivia	MoF	2020	2001	CG,LG,SS,NMPC, NFPC	C	CB	2020	BPM 6
Bosnia and Herzegovina	MoF	2020	2014	CG,SG,LG,SS	Mixed	CB	2020	BPM 6
Botswana	MoF	2020/21	1986	CG	C	CB	2020	BPM 6
Brazil	MoF	2020	2001	CG,SG,LG,SS,NFPC	C	CB	2020	BPM 6
Brunei Darussalam	MoF	2020	. . .	CG,BCG	C	NSO, MEP, and GAD	2020	BPM 6
Bulgaria	MoF	2020	2001	CG,LG,SS	C	CB	2020	BPM 6
Burkina Faso	MoF	2020	2001	CG	CB	CB	2019	BPM 6
Burundi	MoF	2020	2001	CG	Mixed	CB	2020	BPM 6
Cabo Verde	MoF	2020	2001	CG	A	NSO	2019	BPM 6
Cambodia	MoF	2019	2001	CG,LG	Mixed	CB	2020	BPM 5
Cameroon	MoF	2020	2001	CG,NFPC,NMPC	Mixed	MoF	2020	BPM 6
Canada	MoF	2020	2001	CG,SG,LG,SS,other	A	NSO	2020	BPM 6
Central African Republic	MoF	2019	2001	CG	C	CB	2017	BPM 5
Chad	MoF	2020	1986	CG,NFPC	C	CB	2013	BPM 5
Chile	MoF	2020	2001	CG,LG	A	CB	2020	BPM 6
China	MoF	2019	. . .	CG,LG,SS	C	GAD	2020	BPM 6
Colombia	MoF	2020	2001	CG,SG,LG,SS	. . .	CB and NSO	2020	BPM 6
Comoros	MoF	2020	1986	CG	Mixed	CB and IMF staff	2019	BPM 5
Democratic Republic of the Congo	MoF	2020	2001	CG,LG	A	CB	2020	BPM 6
Republic of Congo	MoF	2018	2001	CG	A	CB	2018	BPM 6
Costa Rica	MoF and CB	2020	1986	CG	C	CB	2020	BPM 6

Table G. Key Data Documentation *(continued)*

Country	Currency	National Accounts Historical Data Source[1]	Latest Actual Annual Data	Base Year[2]	System of National Accounts	Use of Chain-Weighted Methodology[3]	Prices (CPI) Historical Data Source[1]	Latest Actual Annual Data
Côte d'Ivoire	CFA franc	NSO	2017	2015	SNA 2008		NSO	2019
Croatia	Croatian kuna	NSO	2020	2015	ESA 2010		NSO	2020
Cyprus	Euro	NSO	2020	2010	ESA 2010	From 1995	NSO	2020
Czech Republic	Czech koruna	NSO	2019	2015	ESA 2010	From 1995	NSO	2019
Denmark	Danish krone	NSO	2020	2010	ESA 2010	From 1980	NSO	2020
Djibouti	Djibouti franc	NSO	2018	2013	SNA 2008		NSO	2020
Dominica	Eastern Caribbean dollar	NSO	2018	2006	SNA 1993		NSO	2020
Dominican Republic	Dominican peso	CB	2020	2007	SNA 2008	From 2007	CB	2020
Ecuador	US dollar	CB	2020	2007	SNA 2008		NSO and CB	2020
Egypt	Egyptian pound	MEP	2019/20	2016/17	SNA 2008		NSO	2019/20
El Salvador	US dollar	CB	2020	2014	SNA 2008		NSO	2020
Equatorial Guinea	CFA franc	MEP and CB	2020	2006	SNA 1993		MEP	2019
Eritrea	Eritrean nakfa	IMF staff	2018	2011	SNA 1993		NSO	2018
Estonia	Euro	NSO	2020	2015	ESA 2010	From 2010	NSO	2020
Eswatini	Swazi lilangeni	NSO	2019	2011	SNA 2008		NSO	2020
Ethiopia	Ethiopian birr	NSO	2019/20	2015/16	SNA 2008		NSO	2019
Fiji	Fijian dollar	NSO	2020	2014	SNA 2008		NSO	2020
Finland	Euro	NSO	2020	2015	ESA 2010	From 1980	NSO	2020
France	Euro	NSO	2020	2014	ESA 2010	From 1980	NSO	2020
Gabon	CFA franc	MoF	2019	2001	SNA 1993		NSO	2020
The Gambia	Gambian dalasi	NSO	2020	2013	SNA 2008		NSO	2020
Georgia	Georgian lari	NSO	2020	2015	SNA 2008	From 1996	NSO	2020
Germany	Euro	NSO	2020	2015	ESA 2010	From 1991	NSO	2020
Ghana	Ghanaian cedi	NSO	2019	2013	SNA 2008		NSO	2019
Greece	Euro	NSO	2020	2015	ESA 2010	From 1995	NSO	2020
Grenada	Eastern Caribbean dollar	NSO	2019	2006	SNA 1993		NSO	2020
Guatemala	Guatemalan quetzal	CB	2020	2013	SNA 2008	From 2001	NSO	2020
Guinea	Guinean franc	NSO	2018	2010	SNA 1993		NSO	2020
Guinea-Bissau	CFA franc	NSO	2017	2015	SNA 2008		NSO	2020
Guyana	Guyanese dollar	NSO	2020	2012[6]	SNA 1993		NSO	2020
Haiti	Haitian gourde	NSO	2019/20	2011/12	SNA 2008		NSO	2019/20
Honduras	Honduran lempira	CB	2019	2000	SNA 1993		CB	2019
Hong Kong SAR	Hong Kong dollar	NSO	2020	2019	SNA 2008	From 1980	NSO	2020
Hungary	Hungarian forint	NSO	2020	2015	ESA 2010	From 1995	IEO	2020
Iceland	Icelandic króna	NSO	2020	2015	ESA 2010	From 1990	NSO	2020
India	Indian rupee	NSO	2020/21	2011/12	SNA 2008		NSO	2019/20
Indonesia	Indonesian rupiah	NSO	2020	2010	SNA 2008		NSO	2020
Iran	Iranian rial	CB	2020/21	2011/12	SNA 1993		CB	2020/21
Iraq	Iraqi dinar	NSO	2020	2007	...		NSO	2020
Ireland	Euro	NSO	2020	2017	ESA 2010	From 1995	NSO	2020
Israel	Israeli new shekel	NSO	2020	2015	SNA 2008	From 1995	NSO	2020
Italy	Euro	NSO	2020	2015	ESA 2010	From 1980	NSO	2020
Jamaica	Jamaican dollar	NSO	2020	2007	SNA 1993		NSO	2019

Table G. Key Data Documentation *(continued)*

Country	Government Finance					Balance of Payments		
	Historical Data Source[1]	Latest Actual Annual Data	Statistics Manual in Use at Source	Subsectors Coverage[4]	Accounting Practice[5]	Historical Data Source[1]	Latest Actual Annual Data	Statistics Manual in Use at Source
Côte d'Ivoire	MoF	2020	1986	CG	A	CB	2019	BPM 6
Croatia	MoF	2020	2014	CG,LG	A	CB	2020	BPM 6
Cyprus	NSO	2020	ESA 2010	CG,LG,SS	A	CB	2020	BPM 6
Czech Republic	MoF	2019	2014	CG,LG,SS	A	NSO	2019	BPM 6
Denmark	NSO	2020	2014	CG,LG,SS	A	NSO	2019	BPM 6
Djibouti	MoF	2020	2001	CG	A	CB	2020	BPM 5
Dominica	MoF	2020/21	1986	CG	C	CB	2018	BPM 6
Dominican Republic	MoF	2020	2014	CG,LG,SS,NMPC	A	CB	2020	BPM 6
Ecuador	CB and MoF	2020	1986	CG,SG,LG,SS,NFPC	Mixed	CB	2020	BPM 6
Egypt	MoF	2019/20	2001	CG,LG,SS,MPC	C	CB	2019/20	BPM 5
El Salvador	MoF and CB	2020	1986	CG,LG,SS,NFPC	C	CB	2020	BPM 6
Equatorial Guinea	MoF and MEP	2019	1986	CG	C	CB	2017	BPM 5
Eritrea	MoF	2018	2001	CG	C	CB	2018	BPM 5
Estonia	MoF	2020	1986/2001	CG,LG,SS	C	CB	2020	BPM 6
Eswatini	MoF	2019/20	2001	CG	A	CB	2020	BPM 6
Ethiopia	MoF	2019/20	1986	CG,SG,LG,NFPC	C	CB	2019/20	BPM 5
Fiji	MoF	2020	1986	CG	C	CB	2020	BPM 6
Finland	MoF	2020	2014	CG,LG,SS	A	NSO	2020	BPM 6
France	NSO	2020	2014	CG,LG,SS	A	CB	2020	BPM 6
Gabon	IMF staff	2019	2001	CG	A	CB	2019	BPM 5
The Gambia	MoF	2019	1986	CG	C	CB and IMF staff	2019	BPM 6
Georgia	MoF	2020	2001	CG,LG	C	CB	2020	BPM 6
Germany	NSO	2020	ESA 2010	CG,SG,LG,SS	A	CB	2020	BPM 6
Ghana	MoF	2018	2001	CG	C	CB	2019	BPM 5
Greece	NSO	2020	ESA 2010	CG,LG,SS	A	CB	2020	BPM 6
Grenada	MoF	2020	2014	CG	CB	CB	2019	BPM 6
Guatemala	MoF	2020	2001	CG	C	CB	2020	BPM 6
Guinea	MoF	2019	2001	CG	C	CB and MEP	2019	BPM 6
Guinea-Bissau	MoF	2019	2001	CG	A	CB	2019	BPM 6
Guyana	MoF	2019	1986	CG,SS,NFPC	C	CB	2020	BPM 6
Haiti	MoF	2019/20	1986	CG	C	CB	2019/20	BPM 5
Honduras	MoF	2019	2014	CG,LG,SS,other	Mixed	CB	2019	BPM 5
Hong Kong SAR	MoF	2020/21	2001	CG	C	NSO	2020	BPM 6
Hungary	MEP and NSO	2020	ESA 2010	CG,LG,SS,NMPC	A	CB	2020	BPM 6
Iceland	NSO	2020	2001	CG,LG,SS	A	CB	2020	BPM 6
India	MoF and IMF staff	2019/20	1986	CG,SG	C	CB	2019/20	BPM 6
Indonesia	MoF	2020	2001	CG,LG	C	CB	2020	BPM 6
Iran	MoF	2018/19	2001	CG	C	CB	2020/21	BPM 5
Iraq	MoF	2020	2001	CG	C	CB	2020	BPM 6
Ireland	MoF and NSO	2020	2001	CG,LG,SS	A	NSO	2020	BPM 6
Israel	MoF and NSO	2019	2014	CG,LG,SS	...	NSO	2020	BPM 6
Italy	NSO	2020	2001	CG,LG,SS	A	NSO	2020	BPM 6
Jamaica	MoF	2019/20	1986	CG	C	CB	2019	BPM 6

Table G. Key Data Documentation (continued)

Country	Currency	National Accounts Historical Data Source[1]	Latest Actual Annual Data	Base Year[2]	System of National Accounts	Use of Chain-Weighted Methodology[3]	Prices (CPI) Historical Data Source[1]	Latest Actual Annual Data
Japan	Japanese yen	GAD	2020	2015	SNA 2008	From 1980	GAD	2020
Jordan	Jordanian dinar	NSO	2019	2016	SNA 2008		NSO	2019
Kazakhstan	Kazakhstani tenge	NSO	2020	2005	SNA 1993	From 1994	CB	2020
Kenya	Kenyan shilling	NSO	2020	2016	SNA 2008		NSO	2020
Kiribati	Australian dollar	NSO	2019	2006	SNA 2008		IMF staff	2019
Korea	South Korean won	CB	2020	2015	SNA 2008	From 1980	NSO	2020
Kosovo	Euro	NSO	2020	2016	ESA 2010		NSO	2020
Kuwait	Kuwaiti dinar	MEP and NSO	2020	2010	SNA 1993		NSO and MEP	2020
Kyrgyz Republic	Kyrgyz som	NSO	2020	2005	SNA 1993		NSO	2020
Lao P.D.R.	Lao kip	NSO	2020	2012	SNA 1993		NSO	2020
Latvia	Euro	NSO	2020	2015	ESA 2010	From 1995	NSO	2020
Lebanon	Lebanese pound	NSO	2019	2010	SNA 2008	From 2010	NSO	2020
Lesotho	Lesotho loti	NSO	2018/19	2012/13	SNA 2008		NSO	2020
Liberia	US dollar	IMF staff	2016	2018	SNA 1993		CB	2019
Libya	Libyan dinar	CB	2014	2007	SNA 1993		NSO	2020
Lithuania	Euro	NSO	2020	2015	ESA 2010	From 2005	NSO	2020
Luxembourg	Euro	NSO	2020	2010	ESA 2010	From 1995	NSO	2020
Macao SAR	Macanese pataca	NSO	2020	2019	SNA 2008	From 2001	NSO	2020
Madagascar	Malagasy ariary	NSO	2018	2007	SNA 1993		NSO	2020
Malawi	Malawian kwacha	NSO	2019	2017	SNA 2008		NSO	2020
Malaysia	Malaysian ringgit	NSO	2020	2015	SNA 2008		NSO	2020
Maldives	Maldivian rufiyaa	MoF and NSO	2020	2014	SNA 1993		CB	2020
Mali	CFA franc	NSO	2018	1999	SNA 1993		NSO	2020
Malta	Euro	NSO	2020	2015	ESA 2010	From 2000	NSO	2020
Marshall Islands	US dollar	NSO	2019/20	2003/04	SNA 2008		NSO	2019/20
Mauritania	New Mauritanian ouguiya	NSO	2018	2014	SNA 2008	From 2014	NSO	2020
Mauritius	Mauritian rupee	NSO	2020	2006	SNA 2008	From 1999	NSO	2020
Mexico	Mexican peso	NSO	2020	2013	SNA 2008		NSO	2020
Micronesia	US dollar	NSO	2017/18	2003/04	SNA 1993		NSO	2017/18
Moldova	Moldovan leu	NSO	2019	1995	SNA 2008		NSO	2020
Mongolia	Mongolian tögrög	NSO	2020	2010	SNA 1993		NSO	2020
Montenegro	Euro	NSO	2020	2006	ESA 2010		NSO	2020
Morocco	Moroccan dirham	NSO	2020	2007	SNA 2008	From 2007	NSO	2020
Mozambique	Mozambican metical	NSO	2019	2014	SNA 1993		NSO	2019
Myanmar	Myanmar kyat	MEP	2019/20	2015/16	...		NSO	2019/20
Namibia	Namibian dollar	NSO	2020	2015	SNA 1993		NSO	2020
Nauru	Australian dollar	IMF staff	2018/19	2006/07	SNA 2008		NSO and IMF staff	2019/20
Nepal	Nepalese rupee	NSO	2019/20	2000/01	SNA 1993		CB	2020/21
The Netherlands	Euro	NSO	2020	2015	ESA 2010	From 1980	NSO	2020
New Zealand	New Zealand dollar	NSO	2020	2009[6]	SNA 2008	From 1987	NSO and IMF staff	2020
Nicaragua	Nicaraguan córdoba	CB	2020	2006	SNA 1993	From 1994	CB	2020
Niger	CFA franc	NSO	2020	2015	SNA 2008		NSO	2020
Nigeria	Nigerian naira	NSO	2020	2010	SNA 2008		NSO	2020
North Macedonia	Macedonian denar	NSO	2020	2005	ESA 2010		NSO	2020
Norway	Norwegian krone	NSO	2020	2018	ESA 2010	From 1980	NSO	2019

Table G. Key Data Documentation *(continued)*

Country	Historical Data Source[1]	Latest Actual Annual Data	Statistics Manual in Use at Source	Subsectors Coverage[4]	Accounting Practice[5]	Historical Data Source[1]	Latest Actual Annual Data	Statistics Manual in Use at Source
	Government Finance					Balance of Payments		
Japan	GAD	2019	2014	CG,LG,SS	A	MoF	2020	BPM 6
Jordan	MoF	2019	2001	CG,NFPC	C	CB	2019	BPM 6
Kazakhstan	NSO	2020	2001	CG,LG	C	CB	2019	BPM 6
Kenya	MoF	2020	2001	CG	C	CB	2019	BPM 6
Kiribati	MoF	2019	1986	CG	C	NSO and IMF staff	2019	BPM 6
Korea	MoF	2019	2001	CG,SS	C	CB	2020	BPM 6
Kosovo	MoF	2020	...	CG,LG	C	CB	2020	BPM 6
Kuwait	MoF	2019	2014	CG,SS	Mixed	CB	2018	BPM 6
Kyrgyz Republic	MoF	2020	...	CG,LG,SS	C	CB	2019	BPM 6
Lao P.D.R.	MoF	2020	2001	CG	C	CB	2020	BPM 6
Latvia	MoF	2020	ESA 2010	CG,LG,SS	C	CB	2020	BPM 6
Lebanon	MoF	2020	2001	CG	C	CB and IMF staff	2019	BPM 5
Lesotho	MoF	2020/21	2001	CG,LG	C	CB	2020/21	BPM 6
Liberia	MoF	2019	2001	CG	A	CB	2019	BPM 5
Libya	CB	2019	1986	CG,SG,LG	C	CB	2017	BPM 6
Lithuania	MoF	2019	2014	CG,LG,SS	A	CB	2020	BPM 6
Luxembourg	MoF	2020	2001	CG,LG,SS	A	NSO	2019	BPM 6
Macao SAR	MoF	2019	2014	CG,SS	C	NSO	2019	BPM 6
Madagascar	MoF	2020	1986	CG	CB	CB	2019	BPM 6
Malawi	MoF	2019	2014	CG	C	NSO and GAD	2020	BPM 6
Malaysia	MoF	2020	2001	CG,SG,LG	C	NSO	2020	BPM 6
Maldives	MoF	2020	1986	CG	C	CB	2020	BPM 6
Mali	MoF	2019	2001	CG	Mixed	CB	2019	BPM 6
Malta	NSO	2020	2001	CG,SS	A	NSO	2020	BPM 6
Marshall Islands	MoF	2019/20	2001	CG,LG,SS	A	NSO	2019/20	BPM 6
Mauritania	MoF	2020	1986	CG	C	CB	2020	BPM 6
Mauritius	MoF	2020/21	2001	CG,LG,NFPC	C	CB	2020	BPM 6
Mexico	MoF	2020	2014	CG,SS,NMPC,NFPC	C	CB	2020	BPM 6
Micronesia	MoF	2017/18	2001	CG,SG	...	NSO	2017/18	BPM 6
Moldova	MoF	2019	1986	CG,LG	C	CB	2019	BPM 6
Mongolia	MoF	2020	2001	CG,SG,LG,SS	C	CB	2020	BPM 6
Montenegro	MoF	2020	1986	CG,LG,SS	C	CB	2020	BPM 6
Morocco	MEP	2020	2001	CG	A	GAD	2020	BPM 6
Mozambique	MoF	2020	2001	CG,SG	Mixed	CB	2019	BPM 6
Myanmar	MoF	2019/20	2014	CG,NFPC	C	IMF staff	2018/19	BPM 6
Namibia	MoF	2020/21	2001	CG	C	CB	2020	BPM 6
Nauru	MoF	2019/20	2001	CG	Mixed	IMF staff	2018/19	BPM 6
Nepal	MoF	2019/20	2001	CG	C	CB	2020/21	BPM 5
The Netherlands	MoF	2019	2001	CG,LG,SS	A	CB	2020	BPM 6
New Zealand	NSO	2020	2014	CG, LG	A	NSO	2020	BPM 6
Nicaragua	MoF	2020	1986	CG,LG,SS	C	IMF staff	2020	BPM 6
Niger	MoF	2020	1986	CG	A	CB	2020	BPM 6
Nigeria	MoF	2020	2001	CG,SG,LG	C	CB	2020	BPM 6
North Macedonia	MoF	2020	1986	CG,SG,SS	C	CB	2020	BPM 6
Norway	NSO and MoF	2020	2014	CG,LG,SS	A	NSO	2020	BPM 6

Table G. Key Data Documentation *(continued)*

Country	Currency	National Accounts					Prices (CPI)	
		Historical Data Source[1]	Latest Actual Annual Data	Base Year[2]	System of National Accounts	Use of Chain-Weighted Methodology[3]	Historical Data Source[1]	Latest Actual Annual Data
Oman	Omani rial	NSO	2020	2010	SNA 1993		NSO	2020
Pakistan	Pakistan rupee	NSO	2019/20	2005/06[6]	SNA 2008		NSO	2019/20
Palau	US dollar	MoF	2019/20	2018/19	SNA 1993		MoF	2018/19
Panama	US dollar	NSO	2020	2007	SNA 1993	From 2007	NSO	2020
Papua New Guinea	Papua New Guinea kina	NSO and MoF	2019	2013	SNA 2008		NSO	2019
Paraguay	Paraguayan guaraní	CB	2019	2014	SNA 2008		CB	2019
Peru	Peruvian sol	CB	2020	2007	SNA 2008		CB	2020
Philippines	Philippine peso	NSO	2020	2018	SNA 2008		NSO	2020
Poland	Polish zloty	NSO	2020	2015	ESA 2010	From 2015	NSO	2020
Portugal	Euro	NSO	2020	2016	ESA 2010	From 1980	NSO	2020
Puerto Rico	US dollar	NSO	2019/20	1954	. . .		NSO	2020
Qatar	Qatari riyal	NSO and MEP	2020	2018	SNA 1993		NSO and MEP	2020
Romania	Romanian leu	NSO	2020	2015	ESA 2010	From 2000	NSO	2020
Russia	Russian ruble	NSO	2020	2016	SNA 2008	From 1995	NSO	2020
Rwanda	Rwandan franc	NSO	2019	2017	SNA 2008		NSO	2019
Samoa	Samoan tala	NSO	2019/20	2012/13	SNA 2008		NSO	2019/20
San Marino	Euro	NSO	2019	2007	**ESA 2010**		NSO	2020
São Tomé and Príncipe	São Tomé and Príncipe dobra	NSO	2020	2008	SNA 1993		NSO	2020
Saudi Arabia	Saudi riyal	NSO	2020	2010	SNA 2008		NSO	2020
Senegal	CFA franc	NSO	2019	2014	SNA 2008		NSO	2020
Serbia	Serbian dinar	NSO	2020	2015	ESA 2010	From 2010	NSO	2020
Seychelles	Seychelles rupee	NSO	2020	2006	SNA 1993		NSO	2020
Sierra Leone	Sierra Leonean leone	NSO	2018	2006	SNA 2008	From 2010	NSO	2019
Singapore	Singapore dollar	NSO	2020	2015	SNA 2008	From 2015	NSO	2020
Slovak Republic	Euro	NSO	2019	2015	ESA 2010	From 1997	NSO	2020
Slovenia	Euro	NSO	2020	2010	ESA 2010	From 2000	NSO	2020
Solomon Islands	Solomon Islands dollar	CB	2019	2012	SNA 1993		NSO	2019
Somalia	US dollar	CB	2019	2013	SNA 2008		CB	2020
South Africa	South African rand	NSO	2020	2015	SNA 2008		NSO	2020
South Sudan	South Sudanese pound	NSO and IMF staff	2018	2010	SNA 1993		NSO	2019
Spain	Euro	NSO	2020	2015	ESA 2010	From 1995	NSO	2020
Sri Lanka	Sri Lankan rupee	NSO	2019	2010	SNA 2008		NSO	2020
St. Kitts and Nevis	Eastern Caribbean dollar	NSO	2019	2006	SNA 1993		NSO	2020
St. Lucia	Eastern Caribbean dollar	NSO	2020	2018	SNA 2008		NSO	2020
St. Vincent and the Grenadines	Eastern Caribbean dollar	NSO	2019	2006	SNA 1993		NSO	2020
Sudan	Sudanese pound	NSO	2019	1982	. . .		NSO	2019
Suriname	Surinamese dollar	NSO	2020	2015	SNA 2008		NSO	2020

Table G. Key Data Documentation *(continued)*

Country	Government Finance					Balance of Payments		
	Historical Data Source[1]	Latest Actual Annual Data	Statistics Manual in Use at Source	Subsectors Coverage[4]	Accounting Practice[5]	Historical Data Source[1]	Latest Actual Annual Data	Statistics Manual in Use at Source
Oman	MoF	2020	2001	CG	C	CB	2020	BPM 5
Pakistan	MoF	2019/20	1986	CG,SG,LG	C	CB	2019/20	BPM 6
Palau	MoF	2018/19	2001	CG	...	MoF	2019/20	BPM 6
Panama	MoF	2020	2014	CG,SG,LG,SS,NFPC	C	NSO	2020	BPM 6
Papua New Guinea	MoF	2019	1986	CG	C	CB	2019	BPM 5
Paraguay	MoF	2019	2001	CG,SG,LG,SS,MPC, NFPC	C	CB	2020	BPM 6
Peru	CB and MoF	2020	2001	CG,SG,LG,SS	Mixed	CB	2020	BPM 5
Philippines	MoF	2020	2001	CG,LG,SS	C	CB	2020	BPM 6
Poland	MoF and NSO	2020	ESA 2010	CG,LG,SS	A	CB	2020	BPM 6
Portugal	NSO	2020	2001	CG,LG,SS	A	CB	2020	BPM 6
Puerto Rico	MEP	2019/20	2001	...	A	...	...	...
Qatar	MoF	2020	1986	CG,other	C	CB and IMF staff	2020	BPM 5
Romania	MoF	2020	2001	CG,LG,SS	C	CB	2020	BPM 6
Russia	MoF	2020	2014	CG,SG,SS	Mixed	CB	2020	BPM 6
Rwanda	MoF	2019	1986	CG	Mixed	CB	2019	BPM 6
Samoa	MoF	2019/20	2001	CG	A	CB	2019/20	BPM 6
San Marino	MoF	2019	...	CG	...	Other	2019	BPM 6
São Tomé and Príncipe	MoF and Customs	2020	2001	CG	C	CB	2020	BPM 6
Saudi Arabia	MoF	2020	2014	CG	C	CB	2020	BPM 6
Senegal	MoF	2020	2001	CG	C	CB and IMF staff	2020	BPM 6
Serbia	MoF	2020	1986/2001	CG,SG,LG,SS,other	C	CB	2020	BPM 6
Seychelles	MoF	2020	1986	CG,SS	C	CB	2020	BPM 6
Sierra Leone	MoF	2019	1986	CG	C	CB	2018	BPM 6
Singapore	MoF and NSO	2020/21	2014	CG	C	NSO	2020	BPM 6
Slovak Republic	NSO	2019	2001	CG,LG,SS	A	CB	2019	BPM 6
Slovenia	MoF	2019	2001	CG,LG,SS	A	CB	2020	BPM 6
Solomon Islands	MoF	2019	1986	CG	C	CB	2019	BPM 6
Somalia	MoF	2019	2001	CG	C	CB	2019	BPM 5
South Africa	MoF	2020	2001	CG,SG,SS,other	C	CB	2020	BPM 6
South Sudan	MoF and MEP	2019	...	CG	C	MoF, NSO, MEP, and IMF staff	2018	BPM 6
Spain	MoF and NSO	2020	ESA 2010	CG,SG,LG,SS	A	CB	2020	BPM 6
Sri Lanka	MoF	2019	2001	CG	C	CB	2019	BPM 6
St. Kitts and Nevis	MoF	2020	1986	CG, SG	C	CB	2018	BPM 6
St. Lucia	MoF	2019/20	1986	CG	C	CB	2019	BPM 6
St. Vincent and the Grenadines	MoF	2020	1986	CG	C	CB	2019	BPM 6
Sudan	MoF	2019	2001	CG	Mixed	CB	2019	BPM 6
Suriname	MoF	2020	1986	CG	Mixed	CB	2020	BPM 6

Table G. Key Data Documentation *(continued)*

Country	Currency	Historical Data Source[1]	Latest Actual Annual Data	Base Year[2]	System of National Accounts	Use of Chain-Weighted Methodology[3]	Historical Data Source[1]	Latest Actual Annual Data
		National Accounts					Prices (CPI)	
Sweden	Swedish krona	NSO	2020	2020	ESA 2010	From 1993	NSO	2020
Switzerland	Swiss franc	NSO	2020	2015	ESA 2010	From 1980	NSO	2020
Syria	Syrian pound	NSO	2010	2000	SNA 1993		NSO	2011
Taiwan Province of China	New Taiwan dollar	NSO	2020	2016	SNA 2008		NSO	2020
Tajikistan	Tajik somoni	NSO	2019	1995	SNA 1993		NSO	2019
Tanzania	Tanzanian shilling	NSO	2020	2015	SNA 2008		NSO	2020
Thailand	Thai baht	MEP	2020	2002	SNA 1993	From 1993	MEP	2020
Timor-Leste	US dollar	NSO	2019	2015	SNA 2008		NSO	2020
Togo	CFA franc	NSO	2016	2016	SNA 1993		NSO	2019
Tonga	Tongan pa'anga	CB	2019/20	2016/17	SNA 1993		CB	2019/20
Trinidad and Tobago	Trinidad and Tobago dollar	NSO	2019	2012	SNA 1993		NSO	2020
Tunisia	Tunisian dinar	NSO	2020	2010	SNA 1993	From 2009	NSO	2020
Turkey	Turkish lira	NSO	2020	2009	ESA 2010	From 2009	NSO	2020
Turkmenistan	New Turkmen manat	IMF staff	2020	2006	. . .	From 2007	NSO	2020
Tuvalu	Australian dollar	PFTAC advisors	2019	2016	SNA 1993		NSO	2020
Uganda	Ugandan shilling	NSO	2020	2016	SNA 2008		CB	2020
Ukraine	Ukrainian hryvnia	NSO	2020	2016	SNA 2008	From 2005	NSO	2020
United Arab Emirates	U.A.E. dirham	NSO	2020	2010	SNA 2008		NSO	2020
United Kingdom	British pound	NSO	2020	2018	ESA 2010	From 1980	NSO	2020
United States	US dollar	NSO	2020	2012	SNA 2008	From 1980	NSO	2020
Uruguay	Uruguayan peso	CB	2020	2016	SNA 2008		NSO	2020
Uzbekistan	Uzbek som	NSO	2020	2015	SNA 1993		NSO and IMF staff	2020
Vanuatu	Vanuatu vatu	NSO	2018	2006	SNA 1993		NSO	2019
Venezuela	Venezuelan bolívar soberano	CB	2018	1997	SNA 1993		CB	2020
Vietnam	Vietnamese dong	NSO	2020	2010	SNA 1993		NSO	2020
West Bank and Gaza	Israeli new shekel	NSO	2020	2015	SNA 2008		NSO	2020
Yemen	Yemeni rial	IMF staff	2020	1990	SNA 1993		NSO, CB, and IMF staff	2020
Zambia	Zambian kwacha	NSO	2020	2010	SNA 2008		NSO	2020
Zimbabwe	Zimbabwe dollar	NSO	2019	2012	SNA 2008		NSO	2019

Table G. Key Data Documentation *(continued)*

Country	Government Finance					Balance of Payments		
	Historical Data Source[1]	Latest Actual Annual Data	Statistics Manual in Use at Source	Subsectors Coverage[4]	Accounting Practice[5]	Historical Data Source[1]	Latest Actual Annual Data	Statistics Manual in Use at Source
Sweden	MoF	2020	2001	CG,LG,SS	A	NSO	2020	BPM 6
Switzerland	MoF	2019	2001	CG,SG,LG,SS	A	CB	2020	BPM 6
Syria	MoF	2009	1986	CG	C	CB	2009	BPM 5
Taiwan Province of China	MoF	2020	2001	CG,LG,SS	C	CB	2020	BPM 6
Tajikistan	MoF	2019	1986	CG,LG,SS	C	CB	2019	BPM 6
Tanzania	MoF	2020	1986	CG,LG	C	CB	2020	BPM 6
Thailand	MoF	2019/20	2001	CG,BCG,LG,SS	A	CB	2020	BPM 6
Timor-Leste	MoF	2019	2001	CG	C	CB	2020	BPM 6
Togo	MoF	2020	2001	CG	C	CB	2020	BPM 6
Tonga	MoF	2019/20	2014	CG	C	CB and NSO	2018/19	BPM 6
Trinidad and Tobago	MoF	2019/20	1986	CG	C	CB	2020	BPM 6
Tunisia	MoF	2020	1986	CG	C	CB	2020	BPM 5
Turkey	MoF	2020	2001	CG,LG,SS,other	A	CB	2020	BPM 6
Turkmenistan	MoF	2020	1986	CG,LG	C	NSO and IMF staff	2020	BPM 6
Tuvalu	MoF	2019	. . .	CG	Mixed	IMF staff	2019	BPM 6
Uganda	MoF	2020	2001	CG	C	CB	2020	BPM 6
Ukraine	MoF	2020	2001	CG,LG,SS	C	CB	2020	BPM 6
United Arab Emirates	MoF	2019	2001	CG,BCG,SG,SS	Mixed	CB	2020	BPM 5
United Kingdom	NSO	2020	2001	CG,LG	A	NSO	2020	BPM 6
United States	MEP	2020	2014	CG,SG,LG	A	NSO	2020	BPM 6
Uruguay	MoF	2020	1986	CG,LG,SS,NFPC, NMPC	C	CB	2020	BPM 6
Uzbekistan	MoF	2020	2014	CG,SG,LG,SS	C	CB and MEP	2020	BPM 6
Vanuatu	MoF	2019	2001	CG	C	CB	2019	BPM 6
Venezuela	MoF	2017	2001	BCG,NFPC,SS,other	C	CB	2018	BPM 6
Vietnam	MoF	2020	2001	CG,SG,LG	C	CB	2020	BPM 5
West Bank and Gaza	MoF	2020	2001	CG	Mixed	NSO	2020	BPM 6
Yemen	MoF	2020	2001	CG,LG	C	IMF staff	2020	BPM 5
Zambia	MoF	2020	1986	CG	C	CB	2019	BPM 6
Zimbabwe	MoF	2019	1986	CG	C	CB and MoF	2019	BPM 6

Note: BPM = *Balance of Payments Manual*; CPI = consumer price index; ESA = European System of National Accounts; SNA = System of National Accounts.

[1] CB = central bank; Customs = Customs Authority; GAD = General Administration Department; IEO = international economic organization; MEP = Ministry of Economy, Planning, Commerce, and/or Development; MoF = Ministry of Finance and/or Treasury; NSO = National Statistics Office; PFTAC = Pacific Financial Technical Assistance Centre.

[2] National accounts base year is the period with which other periods are compared and the period for which prices appear in the denominators of the price relationships used to calculate the index.

[3] Use of chain-weighted methodology allows countries to measure GDP growth more accurately by reducing or eliminating the downward biases in volume series built on index numbers that average volume components using weights from a year in the moderately distant past.

[4] BCG = budgetary central government; CG = central government; LG = local government; MPC = monetary public corporation, including central bank; NFPC = nonfinancial public corporation; NMPC = nonmonetary financial public corporation; SG = state government; SS = social security fund; TG = territorial governments.

[5] Accounting standard: A = accrual accounting; C = cash accounting; CB = commitments basis accounting; Mixed = combination of accrual and cash accounting.

[6] Base year deflator is not equal to 100 because the nominal GDP is not measured in the same way as real GDP or the data are seasonally adjusted.

Box A1. Economic Policy Assumptions underlying the Projections for Selected Economies

Fiscal Policy Assumptions

The short-term fiscal policy assumptions used in the *World Economic Outlook* (WEO) are normally based on officially announced budgets, adjusted for differences between the national authorities and the IMF staff regarding macroeconomic assumptions and projected fiscal outturns. When no official budget has been announced, projections incorporate policy measures judged likely to be implemented. The medium-term fiscal projections are similarly based on a judgment about policies' most likely path. For cases in which the IMF staff has insufficient information to assess the authorities' budget intentions and prospects for policy implementation, an unchanged structural primary balance is assumed unless indicated otherwise. Specific assumptions used in regard to some of the advanced economies follow. (See also Tables B4 to B6 in the online section of the Statistical Appendix for data on fiscal net lending/borrowing and structural balances.)[1]

Australia: Fiscal projections are based on data from the Australian Bureau of Statistics, the FY2021/22 budget of the Commonwealth government, the FY2020/21 and FY2021/22 budget published by each state/territory government, the FY2021/22 budget published by some state governments (as of September 10), and the IMF staff's estimates and projections.

Austria: Fiscal projections are based on the 2021 budget, the Austria Stability Programme, and Austria National Reform Programme 2021. The new EU recovery funds have been incorporated in the projections.

[1]The output gap is actual minus potential output, as a percentage of potential output. Structural balances are expressed as a percentage of potential output. The structural balance is the actual net lending/borrowing minus the effects of cyclical output from potential output, corrected for one-time and other factors, such as asset and commodity prices and output composition effects. Changes in the structural balance consequently include effects of temporary fiscal measures, the impact of fluctuations in interest rates and debt-service costs, and other noncyclical fluctuations in net lending/borrowing. The computations of structural balances are based on the IMF staff's estimates of potential GDP and revenue and expenditure elasticities. (See Annex I of the October 1993 WEO.) Net debt is calculated as gross debt minus financial assets corresponding to debt instruments. Estimates of the output gap and of the structural balance are subject to significant margins of uncertainty.

Belgium: Projections are based on the 2020–21 Stability Program, the Draft Budgetary Plan for 2020, and other available information on the authorities' fiscal plans, with adjustments for the IMF staff's assumptions.

Brazil: Fiscal projections for 2021 reflect policy announcements as of May 31, 2021. Medium-term projections reflect full compliance with Brazil's constitutional expenditure ceiling.

Canada: Projections use the baseline forecasts from the Federal Budget 2021 and the latest provincial budgets. The IMF staff makes some adjustments to these forecasts, including for differences in macroeconomic projections. The IMF staff's forecast also incorporates the most recent data releases from Statistics Canada's National Economic Accounts, including quarterly federal, provincial, and territorial budgetary outturns.

Chile: Projections are based on the authorities' budget projections, adjusted to reflect the IMF staff's projections for GDP, copper prices, depreciation, and inflation.

China: After a large fiscal expansion estimated for 2020, a significant tightening is projected for 2021 based on the government's 2021 budget and the fiscal outturn to date.

Denmark: Estimates for the current year are aligned with the latest official budget numbers, adjusted where appropriate for the IMF staff's macroeconomic assumptions. Beyond the current year, the projections incorporate key features of the medium-term fiscal plan as embodied in the authorities' latest budget. Structural balances are net of temporary fluctuations in some revenues (for example, North Sea revenue, pension yield tax revenue) and one-offs (COVID-19–related one-offs are, however, included).

France: Projections for 2021 onward are based on the measures of the 2018–21 budget laws and the amendment to the 2021 budget voted in July 2021, adjusted for differences in revenue projections and assumptions on macroeconomic and financial variables.

Germany: The IMF staff's projections for 2021 and beyond are based on the 2021 budgets, the 2022 draft budget plan, and data updates from the national statistical agency (Destatis) and the ministry of finance, adjusted for differences in the IMF staff's macroeconomic framework and assumptions concerning revenue elasticities. The estimate of gross debt includes portfolios of impaired assets and noncore business transferred to institutions that are winding up as well as other financial sector and EU support operations.

Box A1 *(continued)*

Greece: Historical data since 2010 reflect adjustments in line with the primary balance definition under the enhanced surveillance framework for Greece.

Hong Kong Special Administrative Region: Projections are based on the authorities' medium-term fiscal projections of expenditures.

Hungary: Fiscal projections include the IMF staff's projections of the macroeconomic framework and fiscal policy plans announced in the 2020 budget.

India: Historical data are based on budgetary execution data. Projections are based on available information on the authorities' fiscal plans, with adjustments for the IMF staff's assumptions. Subnational data are incorporated with a lag of up to one year; general government data are thus finalized well after central government data. IMF and Indian presentations differ, particularly regarding disinvestment and license-auction proceeds, net versus gross recording of revenues in certain minor categories, and some public sector lending. Starting in FY2020/21 expenditure also includes the off-budget component of food subsidies consistent with the revised treatment of food subsidies in the budget. Staff adjust expenditure to take out payments for previous years' food subsidies, which are included as expenditure in budget estimates for FY2020/21 and FY2021/22.

Indonesia: The IMF staff's projections are based on moderate tax policy and administration reforms, some expenditure realization, and a gradual increase in capital spending over the medium term in line with fiscal space.

Ireland: Fiscal projections are based on the country's Budget 2021 and Stability Programme Update 2021.

Israel: Historical data are based on government finance statistics data prepared by the Central Bureau of Statistics. Projections are based on figures from the ministry of finance for the execution of the coronavirus fiscal package during 2020 and assumes partial implementation of the package for 2021.

Italy: The IMF staff's estimates and projections are informed by the fiscal plans included in the government's 2021 budget and amendments. The stock of maturing postal bonds is included in the debt projections.

Japan: The projections reflect fiscal measures already announced by the government, with adjustments for the IMF staff's assumptions.

Korea: The forecast incorporates the overall fiscal balance in the 2021 annual and supplementary budgets

and the medium-term fiscal plan announced with the 2021 budget, and the IMF staff's adjustments.

Mexico: The 2020 public sector borrowing requirements estimated by the IMF staff adjusts for some statistical discrepancies between above-the-line and below-the-line numbers. Fiscal projections for 2021–22 are informed by the estimates in the 2022 budget proposal; projections for 2023 onward assume continued compliance with rules established in the Fiscal Responsibility Law.

The Netherlands: Fiscal projections for 2020–26 are based on the IMF staff's forecast framework and are also informed by the authorities' draft budget plan and Bureau for Economic Policy Analysis projections. Historical data were revised following the June 2014 Central Bureau of Statistics release of revised macroeconomic data because of the adoption of the European System of National and Regional Accounts and revisions of data sources.

New Zealand: Fiscal projections are based on the Budget Economic and Fiscal Update 2021 and the IMF staff's estimates.

Portugal: The projections for the current year are based on the authorities' approved budget, adjusted to reflect the IMF staff's macroeconomic forecast. Projections thereafter are based on the assumption of unchanged policies.

Puerto Rico: Fiscal projections are based on the Puerto Rico Fiscal and Economic Growth Plans (FEGPs), which were prepared in August 2021, and are certified by the Financial Oversight and Management Board. The 2021 Fiscal Plan calls for a series of structural reforms, such as earned income tax credit benefits; the Natural Assistance Program; a lowering of barriers to entry for foreign firms; and investment in education, the power sector, and infrastructure. The new fiscal plan also pays particular attention to allocating strategic investment to emergency response and frontline service delivery, as the island is highly vulnerable to natural disasters and battling an ongoing pandemic. This plan represents an unprecedented level of fiscal support—over 100 percent of Puerto Rico's gross national product. The Fiscal Plan also focuses on the implementation of fiscal measures (centralization of fiscal authority, improvement of agencies' efficiency, Medicaid reform, pension reform, reduction of appropriations, enhanced tax compliance, and optimized taxes and fees) that will result in a smaller government deficit in the long term. The IMF staff's

Box A1 (continued)

fiscal projections rely on the information presented above as well as on the assumption that the fiscal position will deteriorate over time. Previous WEO submissions (prior to fall 2021) relied on the assumption of fiscal consolidation. Although IMF policy assumptions are similar to those in the FEGP scenario with full measures, the IMF staff's projections of fiscal revenues, expenditures, and balance are different from the FEGPs'. This stems from two main differences in methodologies: first, while IMF staff's projections are on an accrual basis, the FEGPs' are on a cash basis. Second, the IMF staff and the FEGP make very different macroeconomic assumptions.

Russia: Fiscal policy was countercyclical in 2020. There will be some degree of consolidation in 2021 in line with economic recovery, and the deficit is likely to come back to the fiscal rule's limit in 2022.

Saudi Arabia: The IMF staff's baseline fiscal projections are based on its understanding of government policies as outlined in the 2021 budget. Export oil revenues are based on WEO baseline oil price assumptions and staff's understanding of current oil policy under the OPEC+ (Organization of the Petroleum Exporting Countries, including Russia and other non-OPEC oil exporters) agreement.

Singapore: For FY2020 estimates are based on budget execution through the end of 2020. FY2021 projections are based on the initial budget of February 16, 2021. The IMF staff assumes gradual withdrawal of remaining exception measures in FY2022 and unchanged policies for the remainder of the projection period.

South Africa: Fiscal assumptions draw on the 2021 Budget. Nontax revenue excludes transactions in financial assets and liabilities, as they involve primarily revenues associated with realized exchange rate valuation gains from the holding of foreign currency deposits, sale of assets, and conceptually similar items.

Spain: Fiscal projections for 2021 include COVID-19–related support measures, the legislated increase in pensions, and the legislated revenue measures. Fiscal projections from 2022 onward assume no policy changes. Disbursements under the EU Recovery and Resilience Facility are reflected in the projections for 2021–24.

Sweden: Fiscal estimates for 2020 are based on preliminary information on the fall 2020 budget bill. The impact of cyclical developments on the fiscal

accounts is calculated using the 2014 Organisation for Economic Co-operation and Development elasticity[2] to take into account output and employment gaps.

Switzerland: The authorities' announced discretionary stimulus—as reflected in the fiscal projections for 2020 and 2021—is permitted within the context of the debt brake rule in the event of "exceptional circumstances."

Turkey: The basis for the projections in the WEO and *Fiscal Monitor* is the IMF-defined fiscal balance, which excludes some revenue and expenditure items that are included in the authorities' headline balance.

United Kingdom: Fiscal projections are based on the latest GDP data published by the Office of National Statistics on February 12, 2021, and forecasts by the Office for Budget Responsibility from November 23, 2020. Revenue projections are adjusted for differences between the IMF staff's forecasts of macroeconomic variables (such as GDP growth and inflation) and the forecasts of these variables assumed in the authorities' fiscal projections. Projections assume that the measures taken in response to the coronavirus outbreak expire as announced. It is also assumed that there is some additional fiscal consolidation relative to the policies announced to date starting in FY2023/24 with the goal of stabilizing public debt within five years. The IMF staff's data exclude public sector banks and the effect of transferring assets from the Royal Mail Pension Plan to the public sector in April 2012. Real government consumption and investment are part of the real GDP path, which, according to the IMF staff, may or may not be the same as projected by the UK Office for Budget Responsibility. Data are presented on a calendar year basis.

United States: Fiscal projections are based on the July 2021 Congressional Budget Office baseline, adjusted for the IMF staff's policy and macroeconomic assumptions. Projections incorporate the effects of the proposed American Jobs Plan; the American Families Plan; the Bipartisan Infrastructure Plan; the legislated American Rescue Plan; the Coronavirus Preparedness and Response Supplemental Appropriations Act; the Families First Coronavirus Response Act; the Coronavirus Aid, Relief, and Economic Security Act; and the

[2] Robert Price, Thai-Thanh Dang, and Yvan Guillemette, "New Tax and Expenditure Elasticity Estimates for EU Budget Surveillance," OECD Economics Department Working Paper 1174 (Paris: OECD Publishing, 2014).

Box A1 *(continued)*

Paycheck Protection Program and Health Care Enhancement Act. Finally, fiscal projections are adjusted to reflect the IMF staff's forecasts for key macroeconomic and financial variables and different accounting treatment of financial sector support and of defined-benefit pension plans, and are converted to a general government basis. Data are compiled using SNA 2008, and when translated into government finance statistics, this is in accordance with the *Government Finance Statistics Manual 2014*. Because of data limitations, most series begin in 2001.

Monetary Policy Assumptions

Monetary policy assumptions are based on the established policy framework in each country. In most cases, this implies a nonaccommodative stance over the business cycle: official interest rates will increase when economic indicators suggest that inflation will rise above its acceptable rate or range; they will decrease when indicators suggest inflation will not exceed the acceptable rate or range, that output growth is below its potential rate, and that the margin of slack in the economy is significant. On this basis, the London interbank offered rate on six-month US dollar deposits is assumed to average 0.2 percent in 2021 and 0.4 percent in 2022 (also see Table 1.1 in Chapter 1). The rate on three-month euro deposits is assumed to average –0.5 percent in 2021 and 2022. The rate on six-month Japanese yen deposits is assumed to average –0.1 percent in 2021 and 0.0 percent in 2022.

Australia: Monetary policy assumptions are based on the IMF staff's analysis and the expected inflation path.

Brazil: Monetary policy assumptions are consistent with the convergence of inflation toward the middle of the target range at the end of 2022.

Canada: Monetary policy assumptions are based on the IMF staff's analysis.

Chile: Monetary policy assumptions are consistent with attaining the inflation target.

China: Monetary policy is expected to be moderately tight in 2021, which will remain in place into 2022.

Denmark: Monetary policy is to maintain the peg to the euro.

Euro area: Monetary policy assumptions for euro area member countries are in line with market expectations.

Greece: Interest rates are based on the WEO London interbank offered rate, with an assumption of a spread for Greece. Broad money projections are based on monetary financial institution balance sheets and deposit flow assumptions.

Hong Kong Special Administrative Region: The IMF staff assumes that the currency board system will remain intact.

India: Monetary policy projections are consistent with achieving the Reserve Bank of India's inflation target over the medium term.

Indonesia: Monetary policy assumptions are in line with inflation within the central bank's target band over the medium term.

Israel: Monetary policy assumptions are based on gradual normalization of monetary policy.

Italy: The IMF staff's estimates and projections are informed by the actual outturn and policy plans by the Bank of Italy and the European Central Bank's monetary policy stance forecast from the IMF's euro area team.

Japan: Monetary policy assumptions are in line with market expectations.

Korea: The projections assume that the policy rate evolves in line with market expectations.

Mexico: Monetary policy assumptions are consistent with attaining the inflation target.

The Netherlands: Monetary projections are based on the IMF staff-estimated six-month euro London interbank offered rate projections.

New Zealand: Monetary projections are based on the IMF staff's analysis and expected inflation path.

Portugal: Monetary policy assumptions are based on the IMF staff's analysis, given input projections for the real and fiscal sectors.

Russia: Monetary projections assume that the Central Bank of the Russian Federation is adopting a moderately tight monetary policy stance.

Saudi Arabia: Monetary policy projections are based on the continuation of the exchange rate peg to the US dollar.

Singapore: Broad money is projected to grow in line with the projected growth in nominal GDP.

South Africa: Monetary policy assumptions are consistent with maintaining inflation within the 3–6 percent target band.

Spain: Monetary projection growth is in proportion to nominal GDP growth.

Box A1 *(continued)*

Sweden: Monetary projections are in line with Riksbank projections.

Switzerland: The projections assume no change in the policy rate in 2021–22.

Turkey: The baseline assumes that the monetary policy stance remains in line with market expectations.

United Kingdom: The short-term interest rate path is based on market interest rate expectations.

United States: The IMF staff expects the Federal Open Market Committee to continue to adjust the federal funds target rate in line with the broader macroeconomic outlook.

Box A2. Climate Change and Emissions Data in Figure 1.21

Data and estimates of historical greenhouse gas (GHG) emissions and nationally determined contributions (NDCs) come from the IMF's Climate Change Indicators Dashboard, coordinated by the IMF's Statistics Department. The *historical* GHG emissions reported in Figure 1.21, panel 1, exclude emissions and removals from land use, land-use change, and forestry. As such, they represent emissions of major GHGs due to human activity, especially in the energy sector. The estimate includes total emissions of (1) carbon dioxide emissions from energy use and industrial processes (for example, cement production); (2) methane emissions from solid waste, livestock, mining of hard coal and lignite, rice paddies, agriculture, and leaks from natural gas pipelines; (3) nitrous oxide; (4) hydrofluorocarbons; (5) perfluorocarbons; (6) sulphur hexafluoride; and (7) nitrogen trifluoride.

The 2019–30 GHG emissions *projected under business as usual*, excluding land use, land-use change, and forestry, represent an estimate of GHG emissions assuming that current trends in consumption and production technology continue to 2030. The projections are estimated using the Carbon Pricing Assessment Tool developed by IMF and World Bank staff. This tool estimates energy-related GHG emissions, holding non-energy emissions fixed at 2018 levels using projections of GDP, taxation regimes, global energy prices, along with assumptions on income, price elasticities, and rates of technological change. The economy-wide GHG emissions *projected under NDCs for 2030* (nationally determined contributions) reflect IMF calculations of individual countries' stated emission targets for 2030 (as of August 2021). The information is obtained from NDC submissions by countries under the United Nations Framework Convention on Climate Change.

The GHG emissions *target for well below 2°C warming cap in 2030* and *target for 1.5°C warming cap in 2030* are derived using pathways and carbon budgets adapted from the Intergovernmental Panel on Climate Change's "Special Report: Global Warming of 1.5°C" (commonly referred to as SR15; see IPCC 2018) and its "Sixth Assessment Report" (commonly referred to as AR6; see IPCC 2021). The 1.5°C target represents the emissions level in 2030 on pathway P2 ("no or limited overshoot") in SR15, adapted to correspond to the updated 1.5°C budgets in AR6, and scaled to GHGs according to the estimated

share of carbon dioxide in all GHGs, consistent with Representative Concentration Pathway (RCP) 2.6 (estimated in Matthews and others 2017). The "well below" 2°C target for 2030 is estimated using budgets achieving 1.8°C at the 80 percent confidence band (the inferred confidence level for scenario P2 for 1.5°C in SR15, given carbon budgets in AR6) and then scaled to total GHGs using the same assumed proportionate share of carbon dioxide in total GHGs for 1.5°C (85.9 percent in 2030).

Revenues from environmental taxes are defined as the revenues arising from charges levied on a physical unit of an item that has a proven negative impact on the environment (examples include taxes levied on a gallon of gasoline, airline tickets, and tons of carbon dioxide emissions). *Expenditures on environment* include government spending on a specified set of activities, as outlined by the framework of the *Classification of Functions of Government*, such as pollution abatement, protection of biodiversity, and waste management (IMF 2014).

References

International Monetary Fund (IMF). 2014. "Annex to Chapter 6, Classifications of Functions of Government." *Government Finance Statistics Manual*. Washington DC.

Intergovernmental Panel on Climate Change (IPCC). 2018. "Global Warming of 1.5°C (SR15)." An IPCC Special Report on the Impacts of Global Warming of 1.5°C above Pre-Industrial Levels and Related Global Greenhouse Gas Emission Pathways, in the Context of Strengthening the Global Response to the Threat of Climate Change, Sustainable Development, and Efforts to Eradicate Poverty [Masson-Delmotte, V., P. Zhai, H.-O. Pörtner, D. Roberts, J. Skea, P.R. Shukla, A. Pirani, W. Moufouma-Okia, C. Péan, R. Pidcock, S. Connors, J.B.R. Matthews, Y. Chen, X. Zhou, M.I. Gomis, E. Lonnoy, T. Maycock, M. Tignor, and T. Waterfield (eds.)]. In Press.

——. 2021. "Sixth Assessment Report (AR6) Contribution from Working Group I. Climate Change 2021: The Physical Science Basis." IPCC, Geneva.

Matthews, H. Damon, Jean-Sébastien Landry, Antti-Ilari Partanen, Myles Allen, Michael Eby, Piers M. Forster, Pierre Friedlingstein, and Kirsten Zickfeld. 2017. "Estimating Carbon Budgets for Ambitious Climate Targets." *Current Climate Change Reports* 3 (1): 69–77.

List of Tables[1]

[1] When countries are not listed alphabetically, they are ordered on the basis of economic size.

Table A1. Summary of World Output[1]
(Annual percent change)

	Average 2003–12	2013	2014	2015	2016	2017	2018	2019	2020	Projections 2021	2022	2026
World	**4.2**	**3.4**	**3.5**	**3.4**	**3.3**	**3.8**	**3.6**	**2.8**	**–3.1**	**5.9**	**4.9**	**3.3**
Advanced Economies	**1.7**	**1.4**	**2.0**	**2.3**	**1.8**	**2.5**	**2.3**	**1.7**	**–4.5**	**5.2**	**4.5**	**1.6**
United States	1.9	1.8	2.3	2.7	1.7	2.3	2.9	2.3	–3.4	6.0	5.2	1.7
Euro Area	0.9	–0.2	1.4	2.0	1.9	2.6	1.9	1.5	–6.3	5.0	4.3	1.4
Japan	0.7	2.0	0.3	1.6	0.8	1.7	0.6	0.0	–4.6	2.4	3.2	0.5
Other Advanced Economies[2]	2.7	2.4	3.0	2.1	2.2	2.8	2.4	1.8	–4.1	5.2	4.2	2.0
Emerging Market and Developing Economies	**6.6**	**5.0**	**4.7**	**4.3**	**4.5**	**4.8**	**4.6**	**3.7**	**–2.1**	**6.4**	**5.1**	**4.4**
Regional Groups												
Emerging and Developing Asia	8.7	6.9	6.9	6.8	6.8	6.6	6.4	5.4	–0.8	7.2	6.3	5.3
Emerging and Developing Europe	4.6	3.1	1.8	1.0	1.9	4.1	3.4	2.5	–2.0	6.0	3.6	2.6
Latin America and the Caribbean	3.9	2.9	1.3	0.4	–0.6	1.4	1.2	0.1	–7.0	6.3	3.0	2.4
Middle East and Central Asia	5.8	3.0	3.3	2.7	4.6	2.5	2.2	1.5	–2.8	4.1	4.1	3.7
Sub-Saharan Africa	5.7	4.9	5.0	3.2	1.5	3.0	3.3	3.1	–1.7	3.7	3.8	4.2
Analytical Groups												
By Source of Export Earnings												
Fuel	6.2	3.0	3.0	1.4	2.2	0.5	0.1	–0.3	–4.4	3.8	3.6	2.7
Nonfuel	6.6	5.4	5.0	4.7	4.8	5.3	5.1	4.1	–1.8	6.7	5.3	4.6
Of Which, Primary Products	4.9	4.1	2.1	2.8	1.8	2.9	1.9	1.2	–5.2	6.4	3.8	3.2
By External Financing Source												
Net Debtor Economies	5.4	4.8	4.5	4.1	4.1	4.7	4.6	3.4	–3.9	6.0	5.4	4.6
Net Debtor Economies by Debt-Servicing Experience												
Economies with Arrears and/or Rescheduling during 2016–20	4.9	3.4	2.4	1.1	2.6	3.3	3.5	3.5	–0.9	2.5	4.2	5.4
Other Groups												
European Union	1.3	0.0	1.7	2.5	2.1	3.0	2.3	1.9	–5.9	5.1	4.4	1.7
Middle East and North Africa	5.5	2.6	3.0	2.6	5.1	1.9	1.4	1.0	–3.2	4.1	4.1	3.4
Emerging Market and Middle-Income Economies	6.6	5.0	4.6	4.3	4.5	4.8	4.5	3.5	–2.3	6.7	5.1	4.3
Low-Income Developing Countries	6.2	5.8	6.1	4.6	3.8	4.9	5.1	5.3	0.1	3.0	5.3	5.6
Memorandum												
Median Growth Rate												
Advanced Economies	2.0	1.2	2.3	2.2	2.2	3.0	2.8	2.0	–4.6	5.3	4.1	1.9
Emerging Market and Developing Economies	4.8	3.9	3.8	3.3	3.4	3.7	3.5	3.0	–3.9	3.5	4.4	3.5
Emerging Market and Middle-Income Economies	4.2	3.4	3.2	3.0	2.9	2.9	2.9	2.3	–5.9	3.6	4.1	2.9
Low-Income Developing Countries	5.4	5.0	5.0	4.0	4.3	4.5	4.3	4.5	–1.0	2.9	4.6	5.0
Output per Capita[3]												
Advanced Economies	1.0	0.9	1.5	1.7	1.2	2.0	1.8	1.3	–4.9	5.0	4.3	1.4
Emerging Market and Developing Economies	4.8	3.5	3.1	2.8	2.9	3.3	3.3	2.3	–3.4	5.1	4.0	3.3
Emerging Market and Middle-Income Economies	5.1	3.7	3.2	3.0	3.3	3.6	3.5	2.5	–3.3	5.7	4.3	3.5
Low-Income Developing Countries	3.6	3.4	3.8	2.1	1.5	2.6	2.7	2.9	–2.1	0.7	3.0	3.4
World Growth Rate Based on Market Exchange Rates	**2.7**	**2.6**	**2.8**	**2.8**	**2.6**	**3.2**	**3.1**	**2.5**	**–3.5**	**5.7**	**4.7**	**2.7**
Value of World Output (billions of US dollars)												
At Market Exchange Rates	58,088	77,208	79,238	74,954	76,154	80,823	85,883	87,391	84,972	94,935	102,404	127,391
At Purchasing Power Parities	79,773	105,245	109,144	111,354	115,591	121,736	129,000	134,916	131,980	144,636	155,835	194,217

[1]Real GDP.
[2]Excludes euro area countries, Japan, and the United States.
[3]Output per capita is in international dollars at purchasing power parity.

Table A2. Advanced Economies: Real GDP and Total Domestic Demand
(Annual percent change)

	Average 2003–12	2013	2014	2015	2016	2017	2018	2019	2020	Projections 2021	Projections 2022	Projections 2026	Q4 over Q4[1] 2020:Q4	Q4 over Q4[1] Projections 2021:Q4	Q4 over Q4[1] Projections 2022:Q4
Real GDP															
Advanced Economies	**1.7**	**1.4**	**2.0**	**2.3**	**1.8**	**2.5**	**2.3**	**1.7**	**−4.5**	**5.2**	**4.5**	**1.6**	**−2.8**	**5.0**	**3.3**
United States	1.9	1.8	2.3	2.7	1.7	2.3	2.9	2.3	−3.4	6.0	5.2	1.7	−2.3	6.1	4.0
Euro Area	0.9	−0.2	1.4	2.0	1.9	2.6	1.9	1.5	−6.3	5.0	4.3	1.4	−4.4	4.9	3.0
Germany	1.1	0.4	2.2	1.5	2.2	2.7	1.1	1.1	−4.6	3.1	4.6	1.1	−2.9	4.1	1.9
France	1.2	0.6	1.0	1.0	1.0	2.4	1.8	1.8	−8.0	6.3	3.9	1.4	−4.3	4.5	2.6
Italy	−0.1	−1.8	0.0	0.8	1.3	1.7	0.9	0.3	−8.9	5.8	4.2	1.0	−6.5	5.6	2.9
Spain	1.1	−1.4	1.4	3.8	3.0	3.0	2.3	2.1	−10.8	5.7	6.4	1.5	−8.8	7.4	3.1
The Netherlands	1.2	−0.1	1.4	2.0	2.2	2.9	2.4	2.0	−3.8	3.8	3.2	1.6	−3.2	4.2	2.0
Belgium	1.7	0.5	1.6	2.0	1.3	1.6	1.8	1.8	−6.3	5.6	3.1	1.3	−4.9	5.0	2.2
Austria	1.6	0.0	0.7	1.0	2.0	2.4	2.6	1.4	−6.2	3.9	4.5	1.8	−5.7	6.0	4.3
Ireland	1.8	1.3	8.7	25.2	2.0	8.9	9.0	4.9	5.9	13.0	3.5	2.9	4.4	13.2	4.9
Portugal	−0.1	−0.9	0.8	1.8	2.0	3.5	2.8	2.7	−8.4	4.4	5.1	1.8	−6.8	4.8	2.3
Greece	−0.9	−2.7	0.7	−0.4	−0.5	1.3	1.6	1.9	−8.2	6.5	4.6	1.3	−6.8	2.7	11.2
Finland	1.4	−0.9	−0.4	0.5	2.8	3.2	1.1	1.3	−2.9	3.0	3.0	1.3	−1.8	2.9	3.3
Slovak Republic	4.7	0.7	2.6	4.8	2.1	3.0	3.6	2.5	−4.8	4.4	5.2	2.6	−2.7	4.5	3.6
Lithuania	4.0	3.6	3.5	2.0	2.5	4.3	3.9	4.3	−0.9	4.7	4.1	2.4	−1.1	4.6	5.3
Slovenia	1.9	−1.0	2.8	2.2	3.2	4.8	4.4	3.3	−4.2	6.3	4.6	2.9	−2.9	4.7	4.6
Luxembourg	2.3	3.7	4.3	4.3	4.6	1.8	3.1	2.3	−1.3	5.5	3.8	2.5	1.7	1.4	6.2
Latvia	3.5	2.3	1.1	4.0	2.4	3.3	4.0	2.0	−3.6	4.5	5.2	3.0	−1.8	2.7	7.5
Estonia	3.2	1.5	3.0	1.9	3.2	5.8	4.1	4.1	−3.0	8.5	4.2	3.2	−1.5	7.9	4.2
Cyprus	2.2	−6.6	−1.8	3.2	6.4	5.2	5.2	3.1	−5.1	4.8	3.6	2.6	−4.4	4.8	2.4
Malta	2.7	5.5	7.6	9.6	3.8	11.0	6.1	5.7	−8.3	5.7	6.0	3.3	−7.9	4.6	6.6
Japan	0.7	2.0	0.3	1.6	0.8	1.7	0.6	0.0	−4.6	2.4	3.2	0.5	−0.8	1.2	2.2
United Kingdom	1.4	2.2	2.9	2.4	1.7	1.7	1.3	1.4	−9.8	6.8	5.0	1.5	−7.3	7.2	2.2
Korea	4.0	3.2	3.2	2.8	2.9	3.2	2.9	2.2	−0.9	4.3	3.3	2.4	−1.1	5.0	2.3
Canada	1.9	2.3	2.9	0.7	1.0	3.0	2.4	1.9	−5.3	5.7	4.9	1.5	−3.1	4.9	4.0
Australia	3.1	2.1	2.6	2.3	2.7	2.4	2.8	1.9	−2.4	3.5	4.1	2.6	−0.9	1.2	5.6
Taiwan Province of China	4.4	2.5	4.7	1.5	2.2	3.3	2.8	3.0	3.1	5.9	3.3	2.1	4.9	3.1	4.1
Switzerland	2.0	1.9	2.4	1.6	2.0	1.7	2.9	1.2	−2.5	3.7	3.0	1.8	−1.8	4.8	0.5
Sweden	2.1	1.2	2.7	4.5	2.1	2.6	2.0	2.0	−2.8	4.0	3.4	2.0	−1.8	3.9	2.2
Singapore	6.6	4.8	3.9	3.0	3.3	4.5	3.5	1.3	−5.4	6.0	3.2	2.5	−2.4	3.8	2.5
Hong Kong SAR	4.5	3.1	2.8	2.4	2.2	3.8	2.8	−1.7	−6.1	6.4	3.5	2.8	−2.7	5.1	5.7
Czech Republic	2.8	0.0	2.3	5.4	2.5	5.2	3.2	3.0	−5.8	3.8	4.5	2.5	−5.3	5.6	2.0
Israel	4.1	4.8	4.1	2.3	4.5	4.4	4.0	3.8	−2.2	7.1	4.1	3.2	−0.1	5.8	2.4
Norway	1.6	1.0	2.0	2.0	1.1	2.3	1.1	0.9	−0.8	3.0	4.1	1.4	−1.1	4.3	2.0
Denmark	0.8	0.9	1.6	2.3	3.2	2.8	2.0	2.1	−2.1	3.8	3.0	1.8	−0.5	3.9	1.5
New Zealand	2.3	2.3	3.7	3.6	3.9	3.5	3.4	2.4	−2.1	5.1	3.3	2.4	0.1	3.1	4.8
Puerto Rico	−0.5	−0.3	−1.2	−1.0	−1.3	−2.9	−4.2	1.5	−3.9	−0.6	−0.3	−0.4	. . .	. . .	. . .
Macao SAR	13.2	10.8	−2.0	−21.5	−0.7	10.0	6.5	−2.6	−56.3	20.4	37.6	3.1	. . .	. . .	. . .
Iceland	2.4	4.6	1.7	4.4	6.3	4.2	4.9	2.4	−6.5	3.7	4.1	2.3	−5.4	3.8	4.7
Andorra	0.9	−3.5	2.5	1.4	3.7	0.3	1.6	2.0	−12.0	5.5	4.8	1.5	. . .	. . .	. . .
San Marino	−1.2	−0.8	−0.7	2.7	2.3	0.3	1.5	2.4	−6.5	5.5	3.7	1.3	. . .	. . .	. . .
Memorandum															
Major Advanced Economies	1.4	1.4	1.8	2.1	1.5	2.2	2.1	1.6	−4.9	5.3	4.7	1.4	−3.0	5.1	3.2
Real Total Domestic Demand															
Advanced Economies	**1.5**	**1.2**	**2.0**	**2.6**	**2.0**	**2.5**	**2.2**	**2.1**	**−4.5**	**5.2**	**4.7**	**1.6**	**−2.8**	**5.6**	**3.2**
United States	1.7	1.6	2.5	3.4	1.8	2.4	3.1	2.4	−3.0	7.1	5.4	1.6	−1.0	6.6	4.2
Euro Area	0.7	−0.5	1.3	2.3	2.4	2.3	1.8	2.4	−6.2	3.9	4.4	1.5	−6.5	4.9	3.0
Germany	0.8	1.1	1.7	1.4	3.1	2.6	1.7	1.8	−4.0	2.5	4.9	1.3	−4.0	5.2	2.2
France	1.4	0.8	1.5	1.5	1.4	2.5	1.4	2.1	−6.8	6.5	3.7	1.3	−3.8	5.4	2.1
Italy	−0.4	−2.7	0.1	1.2	1.8	1.8	1.3	−0.4	−8.4	5.8	4.4	1.1	−6.2	6.3	2.7
Spain	0.7	−2.9	1.9	4.1	2.1	3.3	3.0	1.6	−8.9	5.7	5.3	1.5	−6.7	6.3	3.0
Japan	0.4	2.4	0.3	1.1	0.3	1.1	0.5	0.5	−3.8	1.8	3.5	0.6	−1.1	2.2	2.0
United Kingdom	1.2	2.6	3.1	3.0	3.0	1.6	0.5	1.6	−10.5	7.3	5.4	1.5	−3.5	6.0	2.1
Canada	3.1	2.2	1.7	−0.2	0.4	4.1	2.2	1.5	−6.4	7.5	5.4	1.9	−3.6	7.1	3.8
Other Advanced Economies[2]	3.0	1.7	2.8	2.5	2.9	3.6	2.7	1.5	−2.7	4.2	3.6	2.6	−2.3	5.5	2.7
Memorandum															
Major Advanced Economies	1.3	1.4	1.9	2.4	1.7	2.2	2.1	1.8	−4.5	5.8	4.9	1.4	−2.1	5.7	3.3

[1]From the fourth quarter of the preceding year.
[2]Excludes the Group of Seven (Canada, France, Germany, Italy, Japan, United Kingdom, United States) and euro area countries.

Table A3. Advanced Economies: Components of Real GDP

(Annual percent change)

	Averages										Projections	
	2003–12	2013–22	2013	2014	2015	2016	2017	2018	2019	2020	2021	2022
Private Consumer Expenditure												
Advanced Economies	**1.6**	**1.7**	**1.2**	**1.8**	**2.4**	**2.1**	**2.2**	**2.1**	**1.6**	**−5.9**	**5.3**	**4.8**
United States	2.0	2.5	1.5	2.7	3.3	2.5	2.4	2.9	2.2	−3.8	8.2	3.9
Euro Area	0.8	0.9	−0.7	0.9	1.9	2.0	1.8	1.5	1.3	−7.9	3.2	5.9
Germany	0.7	1.2	0.4	1.1	1.9	2.4	1.4	1.4	1.6	−5.9	0.5	7.4
France	1.3	1.1	0.7	0.9	1.4	1.6	1.7	0.8	1.9	−7.2	4.1	6.0
Italy	0.0	0.1	−2.4	0.2	1.9	1.2	1.5	1.0	0.3	−10.7	4.2	5.0
Spain	0.8	0.8	−2.9	1.7	2.9	2.7	3.0	1.7	1.0	−12.0	5.9	5.1
Japan	0.7	0.3	2.6	−0.9	−0.2	−0.4	1.1	0.3	−0.3	−5.8	2.2	4.8
United Kingdom	1.2	1.4	2.6	2.3	3.0	3.4	1.1	1.4	1.1	−10.9	4.0	7.1
Canada	2.9	2.1	2.6	2.6	2.3	2.1	3.7	2.5	1.7	−5.9	5.2	4.9
Other Advanced Economies[1]	2.8	2.0	2.3	2.5	2.9	2.6	2.8	2.8	1.9	−5.7	4.0	4.4
Memorandum												
Major Advanced Economies	1.4	1.7	1.4	1.7	2.4	2.0	2.0	2.0	1.6	−5.6	5.6	4.9
Public Consumption												
Advanced Economies	**1.5**	**1.6**	**−0.1**	**0.6**	**1.8**	**2.1**	**0.8**	**1.5**	**2.3**	**1.9**	**3.5**	**1.2**
United States	0.9	0.9	−1.9	−0.8	1.6	1.9	0.0	1.2	2.0	2.0	2.0	1.5
Euro Area	1.4	1.3	0.2	0.8	1.3	1.9	1.1	1.1	1.8	1.4	3.3	0.3
Germany	1.4	2.2	1.4	1.7	2.9	4.0	1.7	1.0	3.0	3.5	2.9	−0.1
France	1.6	1.0	1.5	1.3	1.0	1.4	1.4	0.8	1.0	−3.2	5.3	−0.5
Italy	0.1	0.1	−1.1	−0.6	−0.6	0.7	−0.1	0.1	−0.8	1.6	1.4	0.8
Spain	3.5	1.3	−2.1	−0.7	2.0	1.0	1.0	2.3	2.0	3.3	3.2	0.8
Japan	1.3	1.6	1.5	1.0	1.9	1.6	0.1	1.0	1.9	2.8	2.3	1.9
United Kingdom	1.9	1.7	−0.5	2.0	1.8	1.0	0.7	0.6	4.0	−6.5	15.5	−0.2
Canada	2.2	2.2	−0.8	0.6	1.4	1.8	2.1	2.9	2.0	−0.3	7.9	5.2
Other Advanced Economies[1]	2.8	3.0	2.7	2.7	2.7	3.5	2.4	3.5	3.7	4.5	3.5	1.1
Memorandum												
Major Advanced Economies	1.1	1.3	−0.6	0.2	1.6	1.9	0.5	1.1	2.0	1.2	3.6	1.2
Gross Fixed Capital Formation												
Advanced Economies	**1.1**	**2.9**	**1.7**	**3.4**	**3.5**	**2.6**	**3.8**	**3.0**	**3.0**	**−3.7**	**6.4**	**5.8**
United States	1.4	3.9	3.6	5.1	3.7	2.1	3.8	4.4	3.1	−1.5	7.3	7.7
Euro Area	0.2	2.3	−2.3	1.4	4.7	4.0	3.9	3.0	6.5	−7.2	5.2	4.9
Germany	1.3	2.1	−1.3	3.2	1.7	3.8	2.6	3.4	1.8	−2.2	3.5	4.2
France	1.3	2.0	−0.7	0.0	0.9	2.5	5.0	3.3	4.1	−8.9	12.5	3.0
Italy	−1.9	1.4	−6.4	−2.2	1.8	4.0	3.2	3.1	1.1	−9.1	15.0	5.1
Spain	−1.6	3.0	−3.8	4.1	4.9	2.4	6.8	6.3	4.5	−9.5	6.4	9.9
Japan	−1.0	1.1	4.1	2.2	2.3	1.2	1.6	0.2	0.9	−4.2	1.5	2.0
United Kingdom	0.3	2.7	3.7	7.0	5.3	4.4	2.8	0.4	1.5	−8.8	6.0	5.5
Canada	4.2	1.6	1.4	2.3	−5.2	−4.7	3.3	1.8	0.3	−3.7	12.7	9.2
Other Advanced Economies[1]	3.4	2.5	2.6	2.6	2.2	3.0	4.9	2.1	0.4	−1.7	5.7	3.8
Memorandum												
Major Advanced Economies	0.8	2.9	2.1	3.7	2.7	2.2	3.3	3.1	2.4	−3.6	7.2	6.0

Table A3. Advanced Economies: Components of Real GDP *(continued)*
(Annual percent change)

	Averages		2013	2014	2015	2016	2017	2018	2019	2020	Projections	
	2003–12	2013–22									2021	2022
Final Domestic Demand												
Advanced Economies	**1.5**	**2.0**	**1.1**	**1.9**	**2.5**	**2.2**	**2.3**	**2.1**	**2.2**	**–4.0**	**5.2**	**4.3**
United States	1.7	2.6	1.4	2.7	3.1	2.3	2.4	3.0	2.4	–2.5	7.2	4.3
Euro Area	0.8	1.3	–0.8	1.0	2.3	2.4	2.1	1.7	2.6	–5.8	3.7	4.4
Germany	1.0	1.6	0.2	1.7	2.1	3.1	1.7	1.8	1.9	–3.0	1.7	4.9
France	1.4	1.3	0.6	0.8	1.2	1.8	2.3	1.4	2.2	–6.7	6.3	3.7
Italy	–0.4	0.4	–2.9	–0.4	1.4	1.6	1.5	1.2	0.2	–8.1	5.6	4.2
Spain	0.8	1.3	–2.9	1.6	3.1	2.3	3.3	2.7	1.9	–8.5	5.4	5.1
Japan	0.4	0.8	2.8	0.1	0.8	0.3	1.0	0.4	0.5	–3.8	2.3	3.7
United Kingdom	1.2	1.7	2.2	3.0	3.2	3.1	1.3	1.1	1.7	–9.7	6.6	5.3
Canada	3.0	1.9	1.6	2.1	0.3	0.5	3.3	2.5	1.4	–4.3	6.7	5.3
Other Advanced Economies[1]	2.9	2.3	2.4	2.6	2.7	2.9	3.4	2.4	1.7	–2.7	4.2	3.5
Memorandum												
Major Advanced Economies	1.3	1.9	1.2	1.9	2.3	2.0	2.0	2.1	1.8	–4.0	5.7	4.4
Stock Building[2]												
Advanced Economies	**0.0**	**0.0**	**0.0**	**0.1**	**0.0**	**–0.2**	**0.2**	**0.1**	**0.0**	**–0.4**	**0.1**	**0.4**
United States	0.0	0.1	0.2	–0.1	0.3	–0.5	0.0	0.2	0.1	–0.5	–0.1	1.1
Euro Area	–0.1	0.1	0.3	0.4	0.0	0.0	0.2	0.1	–0.1	–0.5	0.2	0.0
Germany	–0.2	0.1	0.8	0.0	–0.7	0.0	0.9	–0.1	–0.1	–0.9	0.7	0.0
France	0.0	0.1	0.2	0.7	0.3	–0.4	0.2	0.0	0.0	–0.2	0.3	0.0
Italy	–0.1	0.1	0.2	0.5	–0.1	0.2	0.2	0.1	–0.6	–0.3	0.1	0.1
Spain	–0.1	–0.1	0.1	0.2	–1.5	–0.1	0.0	0.3	–0.2	–0.5	0.3	0.2
Japan	0.1	0.0	–0.4	0.1	0.3	–0.1	0.1	0.1	0.0	–0.1	–0.3	0.0
United Kingdom	0.1	0.0	0.1	0.4	–0.1	–0.1	0.2	–0.7	0.1	–0.5	0.4	0.1
Canada	0.1	0.1	0.5	–0.4	–0.5	0.0	0.9	–0.2	0.2	–1.3	1.3	0.1
Other Advanced Economies[1]	0.1	0.0	–0.6	0.3	–0.1	0.0	0.2	0.3	–0.2	0.0	0.0	0.0
Memorandum												
Major Advanced Economies	0.0	0.0	0.2	0.1	0.1	–0.3	0.2	0.0	0.0	–0.5	0.1	0.6
Foreign Balance[2]												
Advanced Economies	**0.2**	**–0.1**	**0.2**	**0.0**	**–0.3**	**–0.1**	**0.1**	**0.0**	**–0.2**	**–0.1**	**–0.1**	**–0.1**
United States	0.1	–0.4	0.2	–0.3	–0.8	–0.2	–0.2	–0.3	–0.2	–0.3	–1.3	–0.4
Euro Area	0.3	0.1	0.3	0.1	–0.2	–0.4	0.4	0.1	–0.8	–0.3	1.3	0.1
Germany	0.4	–0.1	–0.5	0.7	0.3	–0.6	0.2	–0.5	–0.7	–0.8	0.8	–0.1
France	–0.2	–0.3	–0.1	–0.5	–0.4	–0.4	–0.1	0.4	–0.3	–1.1	–0.4	0.1
Italy	0.3	–0.1	0.8	–0.1	–0.4	–0.5	0.0	–0.3	0.7	–0.7	0.1	0.0
Spain	0.3	0.1	1.4	–0.5	–0.1	1.0	–0.2	–0.6	0.5	–2.2	0.2	1.2
Japan	0.2	0.0	–0.4	0.1	0.5	0.5	0.6	0.0	–0.5	–0.8	0.6	–0.3
United Kingdom	0.2	–0.2	–0.6	–0.9	–0.8	–0.4	0.8	0.1	–0.1	0.7	–0.4	–0.4
Canada	–1.2	–0.1	0.1	1.2	0.8	0.4	–1.1	0.1	0.3	0.5	–2.5	–0.6
Other Advanced Economies[1]	0.6	0.4	0.7	0.5	0.1	0.1	–0.3	0.2	0.6	0.8	0.9	0.4
Memorandum												
Major Advanced Economies	0.1	–0.2	0.0	–0.1	–0.4	–0.2	0.0	–0.2	–0.2	–0.4	–0.7	–0.3

[1]Excludes the Group of Seven (Canada, France, Germany, Italy, Japan, United Kingdom, United States) and euro area countries.
[2]Changes expressed as percent of GDP in the preceding period.

Table A4. Emerging Market and Developing Economies: Real GDP
(Annual percent change)

	Average 2003–12	2013	2014	2015	2016	2017	2018	2019	2020	Projections 2021	2022	2026
Emerging and Developing Asia	**8.7**	**6.9**	**6.9**	**6.8**	**6.8**	**6.6**	**6.4**	**5.4**	**−0.8**	**7.2**	**6.3**	**5.3**
Bangladesh	6.1	6.0	6.1	6.6	7.1	7.3	7.9	8.2	3.5	4.6	6.5	7.1
Bhutan	8.5	3.6	4.0	6.2	7.4	6.3	3.8	4.3	−0.8	−1.9	4.2	5.8
Brunei Darussalam	0.5	−2.1	−2.5	−0.4	−2.5	1.3	0.1	3.9	1.1	2.0	2.6	2.1
Cambodia	8.0	7.4	7.1	7.0	6.9	7.0	7.5	7.1	−3.1	1.9	5.7	6.6
China	10.5	7.8	7.4	7.0	6.9	6.9	6.8	6.0	2.3	8.0	5.6	4.9
Fiji	1.2	4.7	5.6	4.5	2.4	5.4	3.8	−0.4	−15.7	−4.0	6.2	3.4
India[1]	7.9	6.4	7.4	8.0	8.3	6.8	6.5	4.0	−7.3	9.5	8.5	6.1
Indonesia	5.8	5.6	5.0	4.9	5.0	5.1	5.2	5.0	−2.1	3.2	5.9	5.2
Kiribati	1.1	4.2	−0.7	10.4	5.1	0.9	3.8	3.9	−0.5	1.8	2.5	2.0
Lao P.D.R.	7.6	8.0	7.6	7.3	7.0	6.9	6.3	4.7	−0.4	2.1	4.2	5.8
Malaysia	5.1	4.7	6.0	5.0	4.4	5.8	4.8	4.4	−5.6	3.5	6.0	5.0
Maldives	6.6	7.3	7.3	2.9	6.3	7.2	8.1	7.0	−32.0	18.9	13.2	5.4
Marshall Islands	0.3	3.9	−1.0	1.6	1.4	3.3	3.1	6.8	−2.4	−1.5	3.5	1.6
Micronesia	0.1	−3.7	−2.3	4.6	0.9	2.7	0.2	1.2	−1.8	−3.2	0.6	0.6
Mongolia	8.2	11.6	7.9	2.4	1.2	5.3	7.2	5.2	−5.3	5.2	7.5	5.0
Myanmar	9.6	7.9	8.2	7.5	6.4	5.8	6.4	6.8	3.2	−17.9	−0.1	2.5
Nauru	...	31.0	27.2	3.4	3.0	−5.5	5.7	1.0	0.7	1.6	0.9	0.5
Nepal	4.2	3.5	6.0	4.0	0.4	9.0	7.6	6.7	−2.1	1.8	4.4	5.1
Palau	−0.3	−1.6	4.8	9.9	0.6	−3.3	2.2	−0.7	−8.7	−19.7	14.9	2.2
Papua New Guinea	4.6	3.8	13.5	6.6	5.5	3.5	−0.3	5.9	−3.9	1.2	4.0	2.7
Philippines	5.2	6.8	6.3	6.3	7.1	6.9	6.3	6.1	−9.6	3.2	6.3	6.5
Samoa	2.3	−0.4	0.1	4.3	8.1	1.0	−2.1	3.6	−2.7	−7.2	1.0	2.8
Solomon Islands	5.4	5.3	1.0	1.4	5.9	5.3	3.9	1.2	−4.3	1.2	4.4	2.9
Sri Lanka	6.7	3.4	5.0	5.0	4.5	3.6	3.3	2.3	−3.6	3.6	3.3	4.1
Thailand	4.4	2.7	1.0	3.1	3.4	4.2	4.2	2.3	−6.1	1.0	4.5	3.6
Timor-Leste[2]	4.9	2.1	4.4	2.9	3.4	−4.1	−1.1	1.8	−7.6	1.8	3.8	3.0
Tonga	0.1	0.3	2.0	1.2	6.6	3.3	0.3	0.7	0.7	−2.0	2.9	1.8
Tuvalu	0.0	3.8	1.7	9.4	4.7	3.4	1.6	13.9	1.0	2.5	3.5	3.7
Vanuatu	3.9	0.5	3.1	0.4	4.7	6.3	2.9	3.9	−6.8	1.2	3.0	2.7
Vietnam	6.6	5.6	6.4	7.0	6.7	6.9	7.2	7.2	2.9	3.8	6.6	6.9
Emerging and Developing Europe	**4.6**	**3.1**	**1.8**	**1.0**	**1.9**	**4.1**	**3.4**	**2.5**	**−2.0**	**6.0**	**3.6**	**2.6**
Albania[1]	4.7	1.0	1.8	2.2	3.3	3.8	4.1	2.2	−3.3	5.3	4.5	3.5
Belarus	7.1	1.0	1.7	−3.8	−2.5	2.5	3.1	1.4	−0.9	2.1	0.5	1.3
Bosnia and Herzegovina	3.1	2.4	1.1	3.1	3.1	3.2	3.7	2.8	−4.3	2.8	3.2	3.0
Bulgaria	3.8	0.3	1.9	4.0	3.8	3.5	3.1	3.7	−4.2	4.5	4.4	2.8
Croatia	1.4	−0.4	−0.3	2.4	3.5	3.4	2.8	2.9	−8.0	6.3	5.8	3.1
Hungary	1.3	1.9	4.2	3.8	2.1	4.3	5.4	4.6	−5.0	7.6	5.1	2.6
Kosovo	4.1	3.4	1.2	4.1	4.1	4.2	3.8	4.9	−5.3	6.0	4.5	3.5
Moldova	4.3	9.0	5.0	−0.3	4.4	4.7	4.3	3.7	−7.0	4.5	5.2	5.0
Montenegro	3.0	3.5	1.8	3.4	2.9	4.7	5.1	4.1	−15.2	7.0	5.6	2.9
North Macedonia	3.3	2.9	3.6	3.9	2.8	1.1	2.9	3.2	−4.5	4.0	4.2	3.6
Poland	4.2	1.1	3.4	4.2	3.1	4.8	5.4	4.7	−2.7	5.1	5.1	2.9
Romania	3.5	3.8	3.6	3.0	4.7	7.3	4.5	4.1	−3.9	7.0	4.8	3.5
Russia	4.8	1.8	0.7	−2.0	0.2	1.8	2.8	2.0	−3.0	4.7	2.9	1.6
Serbia	3.9	2.9	−1.6	1.8	3.3	2.1	4.5	4.2	−1.0	6.5	4.5	4.0
Turkey	5.6	8.5	4.9	6.1	3.3	7.5	3.0	0.9	1.8	9.0	3.3	3.3
Ukraine[1]	3.4	0.0	−6.6	−9.8	2.4	2.4	3.5	3.2	−4.0	3.5	3.6	4.0
Latin America and the Caribbean	**3.9**	**2.9**	**1.3**	**0.4**	**−0.6**	**1.4**	**1.2**	**0.1**	**−7.0**	**6.3**	**3.0**	**2.4**
Antigua and Barbuda	1.9	−0.6	3.8	3.8	5.5	3.1	7.0	4.7	−20.0	1.0	7.0	2.7
Argentina	5.6	2.4	−2.5	2.7	−2.1	2.8	−2.6	−2.1	−9.9	7.5	2.5	1.8
Aruba	0.1	6.4	0.0	3.6	2.1	5.5	1.3	−2.1	−22.3	12.8	7.5	1.4
The Bahamas	0.5	−3.6	2.3	1.6	0.1	1.6	2.8	0.7	−14.5	2.0	8.0	1.5
Barbados	0.7	−1.4	−0.1	2.4	2.5	0.5	−0.6	−1.3	−18.0	3.3	8.5	1.8
Belize	3.1	1.3	4.0	2.6	0.0	1.8	2.9	1.8	−14.0	8.5	5.4	2.0
Bolivia	4.5	6.8	5.5	4.9	4.3	4.2	4.2	2.2	−8.8	5.0	4.0	3.4
Brazil	3.8	3.0	0.5	−3.5	−3.3	1.3	1.8	1.4	−4.1	5.2	1.5	2.1
Chile	4.7	4.0	1.8	2.3	1.7	1.2	3.7	1.0	−5.8	11.0	2.5	2.5
Colombia	4.7	5.1	4.5	3.0	2.1	1.4	2.6	3.3	−6.8	7.6	3.8	3.5

Table A4. Emerging Market and Developing Economies: Real GDP *(continued)*
(Annual percent change)

	Average 2003–12	2013	2014	2015	2016	2017	2018	2019	2020	Projections 2021	2022	2026
Latin America and the Caribbean (continued)	**3.9**	**2.9**	**1.3**	**0.4**	**−0.6**	**1.4**	**1.2**	**0.1**	**−7.0**	**6.3**	**3.0**	**2.4**
Costa Rica	4.7	2.5	3.5	3.7	4.2	4.2	2.6	2.3	−4.1	3.9	3.5	3.3
Dominica	2.6	−1.0	4.8	−2.7	2.8	−6.6	3.5	7.5	−11.0	3.4	7.9	2.5
Dominican Republic	4.5	4.9	7.1	6.9	6.7	4.7	7.0	5.1	−6.7	9.5	5.5	4.9
Ecuador	4.7	4.9	3.8	0.1	−1.2	2.4	1.3	0.0	−7.8	2.8	3.5	2.8
El Salvador	2.0	2.2	1.7	2.4	2.5	2.3	2.4	2.6	−7.9	9.0	3.5	1.8
Grenada	1.6	2.4	7.3	6.4	3.7	4.4	4.4	0.7	−13.1	2.7	6.2	2.8
Guatemala	3.5	3.5	4.4	4.1	2.7	3.1	3.3	3.9	−1.5	5.5	4.5	3.5
Guyana	3.1	3.7	1.7	0.7	3.8	3.7	4.4	5.4	43.5	20.4	48.7	3.7
Haiti	2.0	4.3	1.7	2.6	1.8	2.5	1.7	−1.7	−3.3	−0.7	1.3	1.4
Honduras	4.3	2.8	3.1	3.8	3.9	4.8	3.8	2.7	−9.0	4.9	4.4	3.9
Jamaica	0.5	0.2	0.6	0.9	1.5	0.7	1.8	1.0	−10.0	4.6	2.7	1.6
Mexico	2.2	1.4	2.8	3.3	2.6	2.1	2.2	−0.2	−8.3	6.2	4.0	2.0
Nicaragua	3.8	4.9	4.8	4.8	4.6	4.6	−3.4	−3.7	−2.0	5.0	3.5	2.7
Panama	7.7	6.9	5.1	5.7	5.0	5.6	3.6	3.0	−17.9	12.0	5.0	5.0
Paraguay	4.1	8.3	5.3	3.0	4.3	4.8	3.2	−0.4	−0.6	4.5	3.8	3.5
Peru	6.2	5.9	2.4	3.3	4.0	2.5	4.0	2.2	−11.0	10.0	4.6	3.2
St. Kitts and Nevis	2.1	5.7	7.6	0.7	3.9	0.9	2.7	4.8	−14.4	−1.0	10.0	2.7
St. Lucia	2.7	−2.2	1.3	−0.2	3.8	3.5	2.9	−0.1	−20.4	3.5	13.1	1.5
St. Vincent and the Grenadines	2.2	1.8	1.2	1.3	1.9	1.0	2.2	0.5	−3.3	−6.1	8.3	2.7
Suriname	5.0	2.9	0.3	−3.4	−4.9	1.6	4.9	1.1	−15.9	0.7	1.5	1.0
Trinidad and Tobago	4.5	2.2	−0.9	1.5	−5.6	−3.0	0.1	−1.2	−7.9	−1.0	5.4	1.6
Uruguay[1]	5.2	4.6	3.2	0.4	1.7	1.6	0.5	0.4	−5.9	3.1	3.2	2.2
Venezuela	4.7	1.3	−3.9	−6.2	−17.0	−15.7	−19.6	−35.0	−30.0	−5.0	−3.0	. . .
Middle East and Central Asia	**5.8**	**3.0**	**3.3**	**2.7**	**4.6**	**2.5**	**2.2**	**1.5**	**−2.8**	**4.1**	**4.1**	**3.7**
Afghanistan[1]	9.2	5.7	2.7	1.0	2.2	2.6	1.2	3.9	−2.4	. . .	. . .	. . .
Algeria	3.6	2.8	3.8	3.7	3.2	1.4	1.2	0.8	−4.9	3.4	1.9	0.1
Armenia	6.9	3.4	3.6	3.3	0.2	7.5	5.2	7.6	−7.4	6.5	4.5	4.0
Azerbaijan	12.7	5.8	2.8	1.0	−3.1	0.2	1.5	2.5	−4.3	3.0	2.3	1.7
Bahrain	5.3	5.4	4.4	2.5	3.6	4.3	1.7	2.6	−5.1	2.4	3.1	3.1
Djibouti	4.3	5.0	7.1	7.7	6.9	5.1	8.5	7.5	1.0	5.0	5.5	6.0
Egypt	4.6	3.3	2.9	4.4	4.3	4.1	5.3	5.6	3.6	3.3	5.2	5.8
Georgia	6.6	3.6	4.4	3.0	2.9	4.8	4.8	5.0	−6.2	7.7	5.8	5.2
Iran	3.1	−0.2	4.6	−1.3	13.4	3.8	−6.0	−6.8	3.4	2.5	2.0	2.0
Iraq	16.1	7.6	0.7	2.5	15.2	−3.4	4.7	5.8	−15.7	3.6	10.5	3.1
Jordan	5.6	2.6	3.4	2.5	2.0	2.1	1.9	2.0	−1.6	2.0	2.7	3.3
Kazakhstan	7.2	6.0	4.2	1.2	1.1	4.1	4.1	4.5	−2.6	3.3	3.9	3.9
Kuwait	5.9	1.2	0.5	0.6	2.9	−4.7	2.4	−0.6	−8.9	0.9	4.3	2.7
Kyrgyz Republic	4.1	10.9	4.0	3.9	4.3	4.7	3.5	4.6	−8.6	2.1	5.6	3.8
Lebanon[1]	5.1	3.8	2.5	0.6	1.6	0.8	−1.7	−7.3	−25.0	. . .	. . .	. . .
Libya[1]	−0.8	−36.8	−53.0	−13.0	−7.4	64.0	17.9	13.2	−59.7	123.2	5.3	4.5
Mauritania	4.6	4.2	4.3	5.4	1.3	6.3	4.5	5.8	−1.8	2.7	5.0	4.2
Morocco	4.7	4.5	2.7	4.5	1.1	4.2	3.1	2.6	−6.3	5.7	3.1	3.4
Oman	3.8	5.1	1.4	4.7	4.9	0.3	0.9	−0.8	−2.8	2.5	2.9	2.6
Pakistan	4.8	3.7	4.1	4.1	4.6	5.2	5.5	2.1	−0.5	3.9	4.0	5.0
Qatar	13.9	5.6	5.3	4.8	3.1	−1.5	1.2	0.8	−3.6	1.9	4.0	4.2
Saudi Arabia	5.3	2.7	3.7	4.1	1.7	−0.7	2.4	0.3	−4.1	2.8	4.8	2.8
Somalia	. . .	1.9	2.4	3.5	2.9	1.4	2.8	2.9	−0.7	1.6	3.9	4.3
Sudan[3]	1.1	2.0	4.7	1.9	3.5	0.7	−2.7	−2.2	−3.6	0.9	3.5	6.5
Syria[4]	. . .	. . .	. . .	. . .	. . .	. . .	. . .	. . .	. . .	. . .	. . .	. . .
Tajikistan	7.5	7.4	6.7	6.0	6.9	7.1	7.3	7.5	4.5	5.0	4.5	4.0
Tunisia	3.9	2.8	2.9	1.2	1.2	1.9	2.7	1.0	−8.6	3.0	3.3	2.1
Turkmenistan[1]	12.2	0.5	4.6	1.5	−4.7	0.5	1.3	−7.7	−3.4	4.5	1.7	1.9
United Arab Emirates	4.6	5.1	4.3	5.1	3.1	2.4	1.2	3.4	−6.1	2.2	3.0	3.3
Uzbekistan	7.4	7.3	6.9	7.2	5.9	4.4	5.4	5.7	1.7	6.1	5.4	5.5
West Bank and Gaza	8.6	4.7	−0.2	3.7	8.9	1.4	1.2	1.4	−11.5	4.4	6.0	2.0
Yemen	2.3	4.8	−0.2	−28.0	−9.4	−5.1	0.8	1.4	−8.5	−2.0	1.0	5.5

Table A4. Emerging Market and Developing Economies: Real GDP *(continued)*

(Annual percent change)

	Average 2003–12	2013	2014	2015	2016	2017	2018	2019	2020	Projections 2021	2022	2026
Sub-Saharan Africa	**5.7**	**4.9**	**5.0**	**3.2**	**1.5**	**3.0**	**3.3**	**3.1**	**−1.7**	**3.7**	**3.8**	**4.2**
Angola	8.2	5.0	4.8	0.9	−2.6	−0.2	−2.0	−0.5	−5.4	−0.7	2.4	3.7
Benin	3.7	7.2	6.4	1.8	3.3	5.7	6.7	6.9	3.8	5.5	6.5	6.5
Botswana	4.5	11.3	4.1	−5.7	7.0	4.0	4.0	3.0	−8.5	9.2	4.7	4.0
Burkina Faso	6.1	5.8	4.3	3.9	6.0	6.2	6.7	5.7	1.9	6.7	5.6	5.3
Burundi	4.2	4.9	4.2	−3.9	−0.6	0.5	1.6	1.8	−1.0	1.6	4.2	4.8
Cabo Verde	4.8	0.8	0.6	1.0	4.7	3.7	4.5	5.7	−14.8	4.0	6.5	6.2
Cameroon	3.9	5.4	5.9	5.7	4.6	3.5	4.1	3.7	−1.5	3.6	4.6	5.6
Central African Republic	2.8	−36.4	0.1	4.3	4.7	4.5	3.8	3.0	1.0	−1.0	4.0	4.9
Chad	8.6	5.8	6.9	1.8	−5.6	−2.4	2.3	3.0	−0.8	0.9	2.4	3.8
Comoros	2.8	4.5	2.1	1.3	3.5	4.2	3.6	1.8	−0.5	1.6	3.8	4.4
Democratic Republic of the Congo	6.0	8.5	9.5	6.9	2.4	3.7	5.8	4.4	1.7	4.9	5.6	5.4
Republic of Congo	4.9	−0.7	6.7	−3.6	−10.7	−4.4	−4.8	−0.4	−8.2	−0.2	2.3	0.7
Côte d'Ivoire	1.8	9.3	8.8	8.8	7.2	7.4	6.9	6.2	2.0	6.0	6.5	6.0
Equatorial Guinea	9.5	−4.1	0.4	−9.1	−8.8	−5.7	−6.2	−6.0	−4.9	4.1	−5.6	−2.1
Eritrea	2.7	−10.5	30.9	−20.6	7.4	−10.0	13.0	3.8	−0.6	2.9	4.8	3.9
Eswatini	3.8	3.9	0.9	2.2	1.1	2.0	2.4	2.2	−2.4	1.5	1.7	2.2
Ethiopia[1]	9.7	9.9	10.3	10.4	8.0	10.2	7.7	9.0	6.1	2.0	. . .	. . .
Gabon	2.4	5.5	4.4	3.9	2.1	0.5	0.8	3.9	−1.8	1.5	3.9	3.5
The Gambia	2.9	2.9	−1.4	4.1	1.9	4.8	7.2	6.2	−0.2	4.9	6.0	5.6
Ghana	7.1	7.2	2.9	2.1	3.4	8.1	6.2	6.5	0.4	4.7	6.2	5.2
Guinea	3.4	3.9	3.7	3.8	10.8	10.3	6.4	5.6	7.1	5.2	6.3	5.4
Guinea-Bissau	3.1	3.3	1.0	6.1	5.3	4.8	3.4	4.5	−1.4	3.3	4.0	5.0
Kenya	4.7	3.8	5.0	5.0	4.2	3.8	5.6	5.0	−0.3	5.6	6.0	5.5
Lesotho	3.8	1.8	2.1	3.3	1.9	−2.7	−1.0	−1.5	−5.4	2.8	1.6	2.0
Liberia	2.9	8.8	0.7	0.0	−1.6	2.5	1.2	−2.5	−3.0	3.6	4.7	5.6
Madagascar	3.8	2.3	3.3	3.1	4.0	3.9	3.2	4.4	−6.1	2.9	4.8	4.9
Malawi	5.8	5.2	5.7	3.0	2.3	4.0	4.4	5.4	0.9	2.2	3.0	6.0
Mali	4.2	2.3	7.1	6.2	5.9	5.3	4.7	4.8	−1.6	4.0	5.3	5.0
Mauritius	4.3	3.4	3.7	3.6	3.8	3.8	3.8	3.0	−14.9	5.0	6.7	3.3
Mozambique	7.4	7.0	7.4	6.7	3.8	3.7	3.4	2.3	−1.2	2.5	5.3	13.9
Namibia	4.1	5.6	6.1	4.3	0.0	−1.0	1.1	−0.6	−8.0	1.3	3.6	2.5
Niger	5.0	5.3	6.6	4.4	5.7	5.0	7.2	5.9	3.6	5.4	6.6	6.0
Nigeria	7.7	5.4	6.3	2.7	−1.6	0.8	1.9	2.2	−1.8	2.6	2.7	2.7
Rwanda	7.7	4.7	6.2	8.9	6.0	4.0	8.6	9.5	−3.4	5.1	7.0	6.1
São Tomé and Príncipe	5.4	4.8	6.5	3.8	4.2	3.9	3.0	2.2	3.0	2.1	2.9	4.0
Senegal	3.5	2.4	6.2	6.4	6.4	7.4	6.2	4.4	1.5	4.7	5.5	5.4
Seychelles	3.0	6.0	4.5	4.9	4.4	5.0	1.3	1.9	−12.9	6.9	7.7	4.8
Sierra Leone	6.8	20.7	4.6	−20.5	6.4	3.8	3.5	5.5	−2.2	3.2	5.9	4.2
South Africa	3.4	2.5	1.4	1.3	0.7	1.2	1.5	0.1	−6.4	5.0	2.2	1.3
South Sudan	. . .	29.3	2.9	−0.2	−13.5	−5.8	−1.9	0.9	−6.6	5.3	6.5	4.4
Tanzania	6.5	6.8	6.7	6.2	6.9	6.8	7.0	7.0	4.8	4.0	5.1	6.0
Togo	3.0	6.1	5.9	5.7	5.6	4.3	5.0	5.5	1.8	4.8	5.9	6.5
Uganda	7.3	3.9	5.7	8.0	0.2	6.8	5.6	7.7	−0.8	4.7	5.1	6.8
Zambia	7.8	5.1	4.7	2.9	3.8	3.5	4.0	1.4	−3.0	1.0	1.1	1.5
Zimbabwe[1]	−0.3	2.0	2.4	1.8	0.5	5.0	4.8	−6.1	−4.1	5.1	3.1	3.0

[1]See the country-specific notes for Afghanistan, Albania, Ethiopia, India, Lebanon, Libya, Turkmenistan, Ukraine, Uruguay, and Zimbabwe in the "Country Notes" section of the Statistical Appendix.
[2]Data for Timor-Leste excludes projections for oil exports from the Joint Petroleum Development Area.
[3]Data for 2011 exclude South Sudan after July 9. Data for 2012 and onward pertain to the current Sudan.
[4]Data for Syria are excluded for 2011 onward owing to the uncertain political situation.

Table A5. Summary of Inflation
(Percent)

	Average 2003–12	2013	2014	2015	2016	2017	2018	2019	2020	Projections 2021	2022	2026
GDP Deflators												
Advanced Economies	**1.6**	**1.3**	**1.5**	**1.3**	**1.0**	**1.5**	**1.8**	**1.5**	**1.4**	**2.6**	**2.0**	**1.8**
United States	2.1	1.8	1.9	1.0	1.0	1.9	2.4	1.8	1.2	3.6	2.8	2.1
Euro Area	1.7	1.2	0.9	1.4	0.9	1.1	1.5	1.7	1.5	1.6	1.8	1.8
Japan	−1.1	−0.4	1.7	2.1	0.4	−0.1	0.0	0.6	0.8	0.4	0.5	0.4
Other Advanced Economies[1]	2.1	1.4	1.3	1.2	1.3	2.0	1.8	1.3	1.9	2.9	1.8	1.9
Consumer Prices												
Advanced Economies	**2.0**	**1.4**	**1.4**	**0.3**	**0.7**	**1.7**	**2.0**	**1.4**	**0.7**	**2.8**	**2.3**	**1.9**
United States	2.5	1.5	1.6	0.1	1.3	2.1	2.4	1.8	1.2	4.3	3.5	2.3
Euro Area[2]	2.1	1.4	0.4	0.2	0.2	1.5	1.8	1.2	0.3	2.2	1.7	1.7
Japan	−0.1	0.3	2.8	0.8	−0.1	0.5	1.0	0.5	0.0	−0.2	0.5	1.0
Other Advanced Economies[1]	2.3	1.7	1.5	0.5	0.9	1.8	1.9	1.4	0.6	2.2	2.0	1.9
Emerging Market and Developing Economies[3]	**6.4**	**5.4**	**4.7**	**4.7**	**4.3**	**4.4**	**4.9**	**5.1**	**5.1**	**5.5**	**4.9**	**3.9**
Regional Groups												
Emerging and Developing Asia	4.8	4.6	3.4	2.7	2.8	2.4	2.7	3.3	3.1	2.3	2.7	2.7
Emerging and Developing Europe	8.8	5.5	6.5	10.6	5.5	5.6	6.4	6.6	5.4	8.4	7.1	5.8
Latin America and the Caribbean	5.4	4.6	4.9	5.4	5.5	6.3	6.6	7.7	6.4	9.3	7.8	4.3
Middle East and Central Asia	7.9	8.3	6.4	5.6	5.7	6.9	9.5	7.3	10.1	11.7	8.5	6.4
Sub-Saharan Africa	9.1	6.5	6.4	6.7	10.3	10.6	8.3	8.2	10.3	10.7	8.6	6.4
Analytical Groups												
By Source of Export Earnings												
Fuel	8.2	8.2	5.6	5.6	7.6	6.4	8.4	6.4	8.9	11.5	8.8	7.1
Nonfuel	6.0	5.0	4.6	4.6	3.9	4.2	4.5	4.9	4.7	4.9	4.5	3.6
Of Which, Primary Products[4]	6.6	6.7	7.4	5.8	6.7	11.6	13.8	16.9	18.5	19.2	14.4	6.8
By External Financing Source												
Net Debtor Economies	7.2	6.2	5.8	5.7	5.4	5.8	5.6	5.4	5.9	7.0	5.8	4.6
Net Debtor Economies by Debt-Servicing Experience												
Economies with Arrears and/or Rescheduling during 2016–20	10.4	6.4	9.5	13.9	11.0	17.4	16.4	13.3	16.3	17.3	10.9	6.3
Other Groups												
European Union	2.4	1.4	0.4	0.1	0.2	1.6	1.8	1.4	0.7	2.4	1.9	1.8
Middle East and North Africa	7.6	8.7	6.3	5.6	5.5	7.0	10.7	7.5	10.5	12.7	8.6	6.7
Emerging Market and Middle-Income Economies	6.1	5.2	4.5	4.6	4.0	4.0	4.5	4.8	4.5	5.0	4.6	3.7
Low-Income Developing Countries	9.9	7.9	7.2	6.5	8.4	9.2	8.8	8.3	11.4	11.5	8.2	5.9
Memorandum												
Median Inflation Rate												
Advanced Economies	2.3	1.4	0.7	0.1	0.5	1.6	1.8	1.4	0.4	2.0	1.8	2.0
Emerging Market and Developing Economies[3]	5.3	3.7	3.2	2.6	2.7	3.3	3.1	2.6	2.8	3.6	3.7	3.0

[1]Excludes the United States, euro area countries, and Japan.
[2]Based on Eurostat's harmonized index of consumer prices.
[3]Excludes Venezuela but includes Argentina from 2017 onward. See the country-specific notes for Argentina and Venezuela in the "Country Notes" section of the Statistical Appendix.
[4]Includes Argentina from 2017 onward. See the country-specific note for Argentina in the "Country Notes" section of the Statistical Appendix.

Table A6. Advanced Economies: Consumer Prices[1]
(Annual percent change)

	Average 2003–12	2013	2014	2015	2016	2017	2018	2019	2020	Projections 2021	2022	2026	End of Period[2] 2020	Projections 2021	2022
Advanced Economies	**2.0**	**1.4**	**1.4**	**0.3**	**0.7**	**1.7**	**2.0**	**1.4**	**0.7**	**2.8**	**2.3**	**1.9**	**0.5**	**3.5**	**1.9**
United States	2.5	1.5	1.6	0.1	1.3	2.1	2.4	1.8	1.2	4.3	3.5	2.3	1.6	5.1	2.6
Euro Area[3]	2.1	1.4	0.4	0.2	0.2	1.5	1.8	1.2	0.3	2.2	1.7	1.7	−0.3	2.9	1.4
Germany	1.8	1.6	0.8	0.7	0.4	1.7	1.9	1.4	0.4	2.9	1.5	2.0	−0.7	4.0	1.2
France	1.9	1.0	0.6	0.1	0.3	1.2	2.1	1.3	0.5	2.0	1.6	1.3	−0.1	2.9	1.0
Italy	2.4	1.2	0.2	0.1	−0.1	1.3	1.2	0.6	−0.1	1.7	1.8	1.4	−0.3	1.7	1.8
Spain	2.7	1.4	−0.2	−0.5	−0.2	2.0	1.7	0.7	−0.3	2.2	1.6	1.7	−0.5	2.5	1.4
The Netherlands	1.8	2.6	0.3	0.2	0.1	1.3	1.6	2.7	1.1	1.9	1.7	1.9	0.9	1.8	1.8
Belgium	2.3	1.2	0.5	0.6	1.8	2.2	2.3	1.2	0.4	2.4	2.2	1.8	0.4	3.0	1.6
Austria	2.1	2.1	1.5	0.8	1.0	2.2	2.1	1.5	1.4	2.5	2.4	2.0	1.0	2.9	2.2
Ireland	1.7	0.5	0.3	0.0	−0.2	0.3	0.7	0.9	−0.5	1.9	1.9	2.0	−1.0	3.2	2.0
Portugal	2.3	0.4	−0.2	0.5	0.6	1.6	1.2	0.3	−0.1	1.2	1.3	1.4	−0.3	3.1	1.5
Greece	3.1	−0.9	−1.4	−1.1	0.0	1.1	0.8	0.5	−1.3	−0.1	0.4	1.9	−2.4	1.3	−0.1
Finland	1.9	2.2	1.2	−0.2	0.4	0.8	1.2	1.1	0.4	1.9	1.6	1.9	0.2	2.2	1.6
Slovak Republic	3.8	1.5	−0.1	−0.3	−0.5	1.4	2.5	2.8	2.0	2.4	3.0	2.0	1.6	3.5	2.5
Lithuania	3.6	1.2	0.2	−0.7	0.7	3.7	2.5	2.2	1.1	3.0	2.8	2.2	−0.1	3.0	2.8
Slovenia	3.0	1.8	0.2	−0.5	−0.1	1.4	1.7	1.6	−0.1	1.4	1.8	2.2	−1.1	2.2	2.1
Luxembourg	2.9	1.7	0.7	0.1	0.0	2.1	2.0	1.7	0.0	2.7	1.4	1.9	−0.4	1.3	1.7
Latvia	5.6	0.0	0.7	0.2	0.1	2.9	2.6	2.7	0.1	2.6	3.0	2.1	−0.5	5.0	2.3
Estonia	4.2	3.2	0.5	0.1	0.8	3.7	3.4	2.3	−0.6	3.8	4.9	2.1	−0.9	7.0	3.1
Cyprus	2.6	0.4	−0.3	−1.5	−1.2	0.7	0.8	0.6	−1.1	1.7	1.0	1.9	−0.8	2.0	1.0
Malta	2.5	1.0	0.8	1.2	0.9	1.3	1.7	1.5	0.8	0.7	1.8	2.0	0.2	1.6	1.7
Japan	−0.1	0.3	2.8	0.8	−0.1	0.5	1.0	0.5	0.0	−0.2	0.5	1.0	−0.9	0.7	0.4
United Kingdom	2.6	2.6	1.5	0.0	0.7	2.7	2.5	1.8	0.9	2.2	2.6	2.0	0.5	3.5	2.0
Korea	3.1	1.3	1.3	0.7	1.0	1.9	1.5	0.4	0.5	2.2	1.6	2.0	0.5	2.7	1.4
Canada	2.0	0.9	1.9	1.1	1.4	1.6	2.3	1.9	0.7	3.2	2.6	2.0	0.8	3.8	2.0
Australia	2.8	2.5	2.5	1.5	1.3	2.0	1.9	1.6	0.9	2.5	2.1	2.4	0.9	2.6	2.0
Taiwan Province of China	1.3	1.0	1.3	−0.6	1.0	1.1	1.5	0.5	−0.2	1.6	1.5	1.4	0.0	1.6	1.5
Switzerland	0.7	−0.2	0.0	−1.1	−0.4	0.5	0.9	0.4	−0.7	0.4	0.6	1.0	−0.8	0.9	0.6
Sweden	1.7	0.4	0.2	0.7	1.1	1.9	2.0	1.7	0.7	2.0	1.6	1.9	0.4	2.0	1.4
Singapore	2.5	2.4	1.0	−0.5	−0.5	0.6	0.4	0.6	−0.2	1.6	1.5	1.5	0.0	1.3	1.7
Hong Kong SAR	1.8	4.3	4.4	3.0	2.4	1.5	2.4	2.9	0.3	1.9	2.1	2.5	−0.9	2.6	2.4
Czech Republic	2.4	1.4	0.3	0.3	0.7	2.5	2.1	2.8	3.2	2.7	2.3	2.0	2.3	2.7	2.3
Israel	2.0	1.5	0.5	−0.6	−0.5	0.2	0.8	0.8	−0.6	1.4	1.8	1.6	−0.7	2.5	1.5
Norway	1.8	2.1	2.0	2.2	3.6	1.9	2.8	2.2	1.3	2.6	2.0	2.0	1.4	2.3	2.0
Denmark	2.0	0.5	0.4	0.2	0.0	1.1	0.7	0.7	0.3	1.4	1.6	2.0	0.4	1.4	1.6
New Zealand	2.6	1.1	1.2	0.3	0.6	1.9	1.6	1.6	1.7	3.0	2.2	2.0	1.4	3.6	1.9
Puerto Rico	3.1	1.1	0.6	−0.8	−0.3	1.8	1.3	0.1	−0.5	4.0	1.9	1.6	−0.1	4.0	1.9
Macao SAR	3.9	5.5	6.0	4.6	2.4	1.2	3.0	2.8	0.8	−0.3	2.0	2.5	−0.9	−0.3	2.0
Iceland	6.0	3.9	2.0	1.6	1.7	1.8	2.7	3.0	2.9	4.3	3.1	2.5	3.6	4.3	2.5
Andorra	2.5	0.5	−0.1	−1.1	−0.4	2.6	1.3	0.7	0.3	1.7	1.5	1.7	−0.2	2.3	1.7
San Marino	2.3	1.6	1.1	0.1	0.6	1.0	1.8	1.0	0.2	0.8	0.9	1.1	0.2	0.8	0.9
Memorandum															
Major Advanced Economies	1.9	1.3	1.5	0.3	0.8	1.8	2.1	1.5	0.8	3.0	2.5	2.0	0.6	3.9	2.0

[1]Movements in consumer prices are shown as annual averages.
[2]Monthly year-over-year changes and, for several countries, on a quarterly basis.
[3]Based on Eurostat's harmonized index of consumer prices.

Table A7. Emerging Market and Developing Economies: Consumer Prices[1]

(Annual percent change)

	Average 2003–12	2013	2014	2015	2016	2017	2018	2019	2020	Projections 2021	Projections 2022	Projections 2026	End of Period[2] 2020	End of Period Projections 2021	End of Period Projections 2022
Emerging and Developing Asia	**4.8**	**4.6**	**3.4**	**2.7**	**2.8**	**2.4**	**2.7**	**3.3**	**3.1**	**2.3**	**2.7**	**2.7**	**1.2**	**2.9**	**2.8**
Bangladesh	7.9	6.8	7.3	6.4	5.9	5.4	5.8	5.5	5.6	5.6	5.7	5.4	6.0	5.6	5.8
Bhutan	5.8	8.1	9.6	6.7	3.3	4.3	3.7	2.8	4.2	6.3	6.9	3.9	4.5	8.0	5.9
Brunei Darussalam	0.7	0.4	−0.2	−0.3	−0.4	−1.3	1.1	−0.4	1.9	2.5	1.5	1.0	2.0	0.7	0.7
Cambodia	6.0	3.0	3.9	1.2	3.0	2.9	2.4	2.0	2.9	2.5	3.2	3.0	2.9	2.7	3.2
China	3.0	2.6	2.0	1.4	2.0	1.6	2.1	2.9	2.4	1.1	1.8	2.0	−0.3	2.0	1.8
Fiji	4.2	2.9	0.5	1.4	3.9	3.3	4.1	1.8	−2.6	1.1	1.7	2.2	−2.8	1.4	1.8
India	7.6	9.4	5.8	4.9	4.5	3.6	3.4	4.8	6.2	5.6	4.9	4.0	4.9	5.5	4.9
Indonesia	7.2	6.4	6.4	6.4	3.5	3.8	3.3	2.8	2.0	1.6	2.8	3.0	1.7	2.0	3.4
Kiribati	2.0	−1.5	2.1	0.6	1.9	0.4	0.6	−1.8	1.8	3.3	4.1	1.4	1.5	3.7	3.2
Lao P.D.R.	6.9	6.4	4.1	1.3	1.6	0.8	2.0	3.3	5.1	4.9	3.7	3.1	3.2	4.3	3.1
Malaysia	2.4	2.1	3.1	2.1	2.1	3.8	1.0	0.7	−1.1	2.5	2.0	2.0	−1.4	2.5	2.0
Maldives	6.0	4.0	2.4	1.4	0.8	2.3	1.4	1.3	−1.6	1.4	2.3	2.0	−2.0	2.9	1.1
Marshall Islands	. . .	1.9	1.1	−2.2	−1.5	0.1	0.8	−0.5	−0.3	0.6	1.6	2.0	−0.3	0.6	1.6
Micronesia	4.2	2.1	0.7	0.0	−0.9	0.1	1.4	1.5	0.5	2.6	2.6	2.4	0.5	2.6	2.6
Mongolia	10.7	10.5	12.3	5.7	0.7	4.3	6.8	7.3	3.7	5.4	7.3	6.0	2.3	7.0	7.5
Myanmar	14.3	6.4	5.7	7.3	9.1	4.6	5.9	8.6	5.7	4.1	6.5	6.6	2.0	7.2	7.0
Nauru	. . .	−1.1	0.3	9.8	8.2	5.1	0.5	4.3	0.9	1.2	2.0	2.0	−0.9	1.2	1.4
Nepal	7.4	9.9	9.0	7.2	9.9	4.5	4.1	4.6	6.1	3.6	5.7	5.4	4.8	4.2	5.7
Palau	3.5	2.8	4.0	2.2	−1.3	1.1	2.0	0.6	0.7	1.0	1.0	2.0	0.6	1.0	1.0
Papua New Guinea	5.3	5.0	5.2	6.0	6.7	5.4	4.7	3.7	4.9	3.6	4.5	3.6	5.1	4.0	4.4
Philippines	4.6	2.6	3.6	0.7	1.3	2.9	5.2	2.5	2.6	4.3	3.0	3.0	3.5	3.3	2.9
Samoa	5.7	−0.2	−1.2	1.9	0.1	1.3	3.7	2.2	1.5	−3.0	2.7	2.6	−3.3	4.1	1.9
Solomon Islands	8.1	5.2	5.3	−0.6	0.5	0.5	3.5	1.6	3.0	2.4	3.5	2.0	−2.5	4.0	3.7
Sri Lanka	8.8	6.9	2.8	2.2	4.0	6.6	4.3	4.3	4.6	5.1	6.2	5.2	4.2	6.0	6.5
Thailand	3.1	2.2	1.9	−0.9	0.2	0.7	1.1	0.7	−0.8	0.9	1.3	1.9	−0.3	1.0	0.8
Timor-Leste	6.1	9.5	0.8	0.6	−1.5	0.5	2.3	0.9	0.5	1.6	2.5	2.0	1.2	2.0	3.0
Tonga	7.0	0.7	2.3	0.1	−0.6	7.2	6.8	3.3	0.4	1.4	4.7	2.9	−1.4	6.9	2.3
Tuvalu	2.5	2.0	1.1	3.1	3.5	4.1	2.2	3.5	1.6	2.5	2.7	3.0	0.1	2.5	2.7
Vanuatu	2.6	1.5	0.8	2.5	0.8	3.1	2.4	2.7	5.7	5.4	2.6	2.2	7.0	3.9	2.3
Vietnam	10.1	6.6	4.1	0.6	2.7	3.5	3.5	2.8	3.2	2.0	2.3	4.0	0.2	2.6	2.2
Emerging and Developing Europe	**8.8**	**5.5**	**6.5**	**10.6**	**5.5**	**5.6**	**6.4**	**6.6**	**5.4**	**8.4**	**7.1**	**5.8**	**6.4**	**8.5**	**6.5**
Albania[4]	2.8	1.9	1.6	1.9	1.3	2.0	2.0	1.4	1.6	1.9	2.3	3.0	1.0	2.1	2.2
Belarus	20.8	18.3	18.1	13.5	11.8	6.0	4.9	5.6	5.5	9.2	8.3	5.0	7.3	9.4	7.1
Bosnia and Herzegovina	2.7	−0.1	−0.9	−1.0	−1.6	0.8	1.4	0.6	−1.1	1.8	1.8	2.1	−1.1	1.6	1.6
Bulgaria[3]	5.2	0.4	−1.6	−1.1	−1.3	1.2	2.6	2.5	1.2	2.1	1.9	2.0	0.0	3.3	1.5
Croatia	2.8	2.2	−0.2	−0.5	−1.1	1.1	1.5	0.8	0.1	2.0	2.0	2.0	−0.7	2.9	2.1
Hungary	5.1	1.7	−0.2	−0.1	0.4	2.4	2.8	3.4	3.3	4.5	3.6	3.0	2.7	4.8	3.6
Kosovo	2.3	1.8	0.4	−0.5	0.3	1.5	1.1	2.7	0.2	3.1	3.6	2.0	0.1	5.4	2.6
Moldova	9.3	4.6	5.1	9.6	6.4	6.5	3.6	4.3	4.4	3.0	5.8	5.0	0.9	4.9	5.5
Montenegro	4.0	2.2	−0.7	1.5	−0.3	2.4	2.6	0.4	−0.2	2.0	1.5	1.7	−0.9	2.9	1.3
North Macedonia	2.2	2.8	−0.3	−0.3	−0.2	1.4	1.5	0.8	1.2	3.1	2.2	2.0	2.3	3.8	0.9
Poland	2.8	0.9	0.0	−0.9	−0.6	2.0	1.6	2.3	3.4	4.4	3.3	2.5	2.4	5.0	2.6
Romania	7.6	4.0	1.1	−0.6	−1.6	1.3	4.6	3.8	2.6	4.3	3.4	2.5	2.1	5.3	3.3
Russia	10.2	6.8	7.8	15.5	7.0	3.7	2.9	4.5	3.4	5.9	4.8	4.0	4.9	5.8	4.3
Serbia	9.1	7.7	2.1	1.4	1.1	3.1	2.0	1.9	1.6	3.0	2.7	2.8	1.3	4.1	2.0
Turkey	10.0	7.5	8.9	7.7	7.8	11.1	16.3	15.2	12.3	17.0	15.4	12.5	14.6	16.7	14.5
Ukraine[4]	10.7	−0.3	12.1	48.7	13.9	14.4	10.9	7.9	2.7	9.5	7.1	5.0	5.0	10.2	6.0
Latin America and the Caribbean[5]	**5.4**	**4.6**	**4.9**	**5.4**	**5.5**	**6.3**	**6.6**	**7.7**	**6.4**	**9.3**	**7.8**	**4.3**	**6.3**	**9.7**	**6.9**
Antigua and Barbuda	2.4	1.1	1.1	1.0	−0.5	2.4	1.2	1.4	1.1	1.6	2.0	2.0	2.8	2.0	2.0
Argentina[4]	9.2	10.6	. . .	. . .	. . .	25.7	34.3	53.5	42.0	. . .	. . .	. . .	36.1	. . .	. . .
Aruba	3.2	−2.4	0.4	0.5	−0.9	−1.0	3.6	3.9	−1.3	0.3	1.7	1.3	−3.1	1.7	1.6
The Bahamas	2.4	0.4	1.2	1.9	−0.3	1.5	2.3	2.5	0.0	3.0	4.2	2.5	1.2	5.0	3.5
Barbados	5.2	1.8	1.8	−1.1	1.5	4.4	3.7	4.1	2.9	2.5	4.4	2.3	1.3	3.2	2.5
Belize	2.5	0.5	1.2	−0.9	0.7	1.1	0.3	0.2	0.1	3.1	2.5	2.0	0.4	4.1	2.2
Bolivia	5.8	5.7	5.8	4.1	3.6	2.8	2.3	1.8	0.9	1.3	2.7	3.5	0.7	2.5	2.8
Brazil	6.3	6.2	6.3	9.0	8.7	3.4	3.7	3.7	3.2	7.7	5.3	3.1	4.5	7.9	4.0
Chile	3.2	1.8	4.7	4.3	3.8	2.2	2.3	2.3	3.0	4.2	4.4	3.0	2.9	5.5	3.4
Colombia	4.8	2.0	2.9	5.0	7.5	4.3	3.2	3.5	2.5	3.2	3.5	3.0	1.6	4.3	3.1

Table A7. Emerging Market and Developing Economies: Consumer Prices[1] *(continued)*

(Annual percent change)

	Average 2003–12	2013	2014	2015	2016	2017	2018	2019	2020	Projections 2021	Projections 2022	Projections 2026	End of Period[2] 2020	End of Period Projections 2021	End of Period Projections 2022
Latin America and the Caribbean (continued)[5]	**5.4**	**4.6**	**4.9**	**5.4**	**5.5**	**6.3**	**6.6**	**7.7**	**6.4**	**9.3**	**7.8**	**4.3**	**6.3**	**9.7**	**6.9**
Costa Rica	9.2	5.2	4.5	0.8	0.0	1.6	2.2	2.1	0.7	1.3	1.5	2.9	0.9	1.6	1.5
Dominica	2.3	0.0	0.8	−0.9	0.1	0.3	1.0	1.5	−0.7	1.5	2.0	2.0	−0.7	2.0	2.0
Dominican Republic	11.9	4.8	3.0	0.8	1.6	3.3	3.6	1.8	3.8	7.8	4.5	4.0	5.6	6.5	4.0
Ecuador	4.5	2.7	3.6	4.0	1.7	0.4	−0.2	0.3	−0.3	0.0	2.1	1.0	−0.9	1.8	2.2
El Salvador	3.6	0.8	1.1	−0.7	0.6	1.0	1.1	0.1	−0.4	3.6	2.9	1.4	−0.1	4.5	1.6
Grenada	3.2	0.0	−1.0	−0.6	1.7	0.9	0.8	0.6	−0.7	2.5	0.6	2.0	−0.8	2.5	0.6
Guatemala	6.2	4.3	3.4	2.4	4.4	4.4	3.8	3.7	3.2	4.8	4.5	4.3	4.8	4.6	4.3
Guyana	5.8	1.9	0.7	−0.9	0.8	1.9	1.3	2.1	0.7	3.2	2.7	3.1	0.9	3.4	2.8
Haiti	12.8	6.8	3.9	7.5	13.4	14.7	12.9	17.3	22.9	16.2	15.5	11.6	25.2	15.0	16.3
Honduras	7.1	5.2	6.1	3.2	2.7	3.9	4.3	4.4	3.5	4.6	3.7	4.0	4.0	4.1	4.0
Jamaica	11.4	9.4	8.3	3.7	2.3	4.4	3.7	3.9	5.2	5.6	6.3	5.0	5.2	6.0	6.5
Mexico	4.3	3.8	4.0	2.7	2.8	6.0	4.9	3.6	3.4	5.4	3.8	3.0	3.2	5.9	3.1
Nicaragua	8.7	7.1	6.0	4.0	3.5	3.9	4.9	5.4	3.7	4.1	3.6	3.5	2.9	4.1	3.5
Panama	3.6	4.0	2.6	0.1	0.7	0.9	0.8	−0.4	−1.6	1.4	2.0	2.0	−1.6	2.0	2.0
Paraguay	7.2	2.7	5.0	3.1	4.1	3.6	4.0	2.8	1.8	3.5	4.0	4.0	2.2	4.0	4.0
Peru	2.9	2.8	3.2	3.5	3.6	2.8	1.3	2.1	1.8	3.1	2.5	2.0	2.0	3.2	2.6
St. Kitts and Nevis	3.5	1.1	0.2	−2.3	−0.7	0.7	−1.0	−0.3	−0.6	−1.0	−0.5	2.0	−1.2	−0.8	−0.3
St. Lucia	2.8	1.5	3.5	−1.0	−3.1	0.1	2.4	0.5	−1.8	2.5	3.0	2.0	−0.4	3.8	1.8
St. Vincent and the Grenadines	3.3	0.8	0.2	−1.7	−0.2	2.2	2.3	0.9	−0.6	2.0	2.1	2.0	−1.0	2.2	2.0
Suriname	10.6	1.9	3.4	6.9	55.5	22.0	6.9	4.4	34.9	54.4	31.7	12.8	60.7	48.6	25.2
Trinidad and Tobago	7.4	5.2	5.7	4.7	3.1	1.9	1.0	1.0	0.6	1.0	0.0	1.4	0.8	1.2	1.4
Uruguay	8.5	8.6	8.9	8.7	9.6	6.2	7.6	7.9	9.8	7.5	6.1	4.5	9.4	7.2	5.8
Venezuela[4]	23.3	40.6	62.2	121.7	254.9	438.1	65,374	19,906	2,355	2,700	2,000	. . .	2,960	2,700	2,000
Middle East and Central Asia	**7.9**	**8.3**	**6.4**	**5.6**	**5.7**	**6.9**	**9.5**	**7.3**	**10.1**	**11.7**	**8.5**	**6.4**	**12.5**	**10.3**	**7.7**
Afghanistan[4]	11.2	7.4	4.7	−0.7	4.4	5.0	0.6	2.3	5.6	. . .	. . .	. . .	5.0	. . .	. . .
Algeria	4.3	3.3	2.9	4.8	6.4	5.6	4.3	2.0	2.4	6.5	7.6	5.4	3.5	7.6	7.2
Armenia	4.9	5.8	3.0	3.7	−1.4	1.0	2.5	1.4	1.2	6.9	5.8	4.0	3.8	8.0	5.2
Azerbaijan	7.8	2.4	1.4	4.0	12.4	12.8	2.3	2.7	2.8	4.4	3.2	3.2	2.7	4.5	3.2
Bahrain	2.2	3.3	2.6	1.8	2.8	1.4	2.1	1.0	−2.3	1.0	2.7	2.4	−1.6	2.5	3.0
Djibouti	4.3	1.1	1.3	−0.8	2.7	0.6	0.1	3.3	1.8	1.2	2.0	2.0	0.3	2.0	2.0
Egypt	9.4	6.9	10.1	11.0	10.2	23.5	20.9	13.9	5.7	4.5	6.3	7.1	5.7	4.9	7.0
Georgia	6.3	−0.5	3.1	4.0	2.1	6.0	2.6	4.9	5.2	9.3	5.4	3.0	2.4	13.1	3.2
Iran	17.0	34.7	15.6	11.9	9.1	9.6	30.2	34.6	36.4	39.3	27.5	25.0	48.7	30.0	25.0
Iraq	. . .	1.9	2.2	1.4	0.5	0.2	0.4	−0.2	0.6	6.4	4.5	2.0	3.2	6.4	3.1
Jordan	4.4	4.9	3.0	−1.1	−0.6	3.6	4.5	0.7	0.4	1.6	2.0	2.5	−0.3	2.5	2.0
Kazakhstan	8.5	5.8	6.7	6.7	14.6	7.4	6.0	5.2	6.8	7.5	6.5	4.0	7.5	7.5	5.8
Kuwait	3.8	2.7	3.1	3.7	3.5	1.5	0.6	1.1	2.1	3.2	3.0	3.0	3.0	3.2	3.0
Kyrgyz Republic	8.4	6.6	7.5	6.5	0.4	3.2	1.5	1.1	6.3	13.0	7.8	5.0	9.7	12.6	5.6
Lebanon[4]	3.6	4.8	1.8	−3.7	−0.8	4.5	4.6	2.9	84.9	. . .	. . .	. . .	145.8	. . .	. . .
Libya[4]	4.6	2.6	2.4	14.8	24.0	28.0	−1.2	0.2	2.8	21.1	8.0	5.0	2.8	21.1	8.0
Mauritania	6.7	4.1	3.8	0.5	1.5	2.3	3.1	2.3	2.3	2.7	3.8	4.0	1.8	3.5	4.0
Morocco	1.8	1.6	0.4	1.4	1.5	0.7	1.6	0.2	0.6	1.4	1.2	2.0	−0.9	1.1	1.2
Oman	3.8	1.2	1.0	0.1	1.1	1.6	0.9	0.1	−0.9	3.0	2.7	2.5	−0.9	3.0	2.7
Pakistan	9.8	7.4	8.6	4.5	2.9	4.1	3.9	6.7	10.7	8.9	8.5	6.5	8.6	9.7	9.2
Qatar	5.3	3.1	4.2	0.9	2.7	0.4	0.3	−0.7	−2.7	2.5	3.2	2.5	−3.4	6.5	0.1
Saudi Arabia	2.9	3.6	2.2	1.2	2.0	−0.8	2.5	−2.1	3.4	3.2	2.2	2.0	5.4	1.6	2.2
Somalia	. . .	. . .	. . .	. . .	. . .	. . .	. . .	. . .	. . .	. . .	. . .	. . .	4.8	4.3	4.0
Sudan[6]	13.6	36.5	36.9	16.9	17.8	32.4	63.3	51.0	163.3	194.6	41.8	8.0	269.3	115.5	27.0
Syria[7]	. . .	. . .	. . .	. . .	. . .	. . .	. . .	. . .	. . .	. . .	. . .	. . .	. . .	. . .	. . .
Tajikistan	10.5	5.0	6.1	5.8	5.9	7.3	3.8	7.8	8.6	8.0	6.5	6.5	9.4	8.0	6.5
Tunisia	3.7	5.3	4.6	4.4	3.6	5.3	7.3	6.7	5.6	5.7	6.5	5.0	4.9	6.8	6.1
Turkmenistan	6.3	6.8	6.0	7.4	3.6	8.0	13.3	5.1	7.6	12.5	13.0	10.0	8.9	16.0	10.0
United Arab Emirates	5.0	1.1	2.3	4.1	1.6	2.0	3.1	−1.9	−2.1	2.0	2.2	2.0	−2.1	2.0	2.2
Uzbekistan	11.7	11.7	9.1	8.5	8.8	13.9	17.5	14.5	12.9	11.0	10.9	5.1	11.1	10.6	10.2
West Bank and Gaza	4.0	1.7	1.7	1.4	−0.2	0.2	−0.2	1.6	−0.7	1.3	1.7	1.6	0.1	1.2	1.7
Yemen	11.4	11.0	8.2	22.0	21.3	30.4	27.6	12.0	23.1	40.7	31.5	8.4	35.0	45.0	22.3

Table A7. Emerging Market and Developing Economies: Consumer Prices[1] *(continued)*
(Annual percent change)

	Average 2003–12	2013	2014	2015	2016	2017	2018	2019	2020	Projections 2021	2022	2026	End of Period[2] 2020	Projections 2021	2022
Sub-Saharan Africa	**9.1**	**6.5**	**6.4**	**6.7**	**10.3**	**10.6**	**8.3**	**8.2**	**10.3**	**10.7**	**8.6**	**6.4**	**10.7**	**10.1**	**7.6**
Angola	23.3	8.8	7.3	9.2	30.7	29.8	19.6	17.1	22.3	24.4	14.9	6.8	25.1	22.0	11.0
Benin	3.4	1.0	−1.1	0.2	−0.8	1.8	0.8	−0.9	3.0	3.0	2.0	2.0	1.2	3.0	2.0
Botswana	8.7	5.9	4.4	3.1	2.8	3.3	3.2	2.7	1.9	5.8	5.0	4.3	2.2	6.1	5.0
Burkina Faso	2.7	0.5	−0.3	1.7	0.4	1.5	2.0	−3.2	1.9	3.0	2.6	2.5	2.3	2.7	2.6
Burundi	11.1	7.9	4.4	5.6	5.5	1.6	−4.0	−0.7	7.3	5.6	4.6	4.2	7.5	5.1	4.2
Cabo Verde	2.6	1.5	−0.2	0.1	−1.4	0.8	1.3	1.1	0.6	1.5	1.6	2.0	−0.9	1.5	1.6
Cameroon	2.4	2.1	1.9	2.7	0.9	0.6	1.1	2.5	2.4	2.3	2.0	2.0	2.1	2.1	2.0
Central African Republic	3.3	7.0	14.9	1.4	4.9	4.2	1.6	2.7	2.3	3.7	2.5	2.5	4.8	3.3	2.5
Chad	2.4	0.2	1.7	4.8	−1.6	−0.9	4.0	−1.0	4.5	2.6	2.8	3.0	3.0	2.3	4.8
Comoros	4.1	0.4	0.0	0.9	0.8	0.1	1.7	3.7	0.8	−1.0	1.2	2.0	−6.3	15.6	−0.1
Democratic Republic of the Congo	16.6	0.9	1.2	0.7	3.2	35.7	29.3	4.7	11.4	9.4	6.4	6.3	15.8	6.0	6.3
Republic of Congo	3.2	4.6	0.9	3.2	3.2	0.4	1.2	2.2	1.8	2.0	2.8	3.0	0.5	2.7	3.0
Côte d'Ivoire	2.8	2.6	0.4	1.2	0.7	0.7	0.4	0.8	2.4	3.0	2.5	2.0	2.0	2.0	1.6
Equatorial Guinea	4.8	3.2	4.3	1.7	1.4	0.7	1.3	1.2	4.8	0.5	3.1	3.0	−0.5	3.2	3.0
Eritrea	15.8	5.9	10.0	28.5	−5.6	−13.3	−14.4	−16.4	4.8	4.3	4.2	2.0	4.0	4.0	4.0
Eswatini	6.8	5.6	5.7	5.0	7.8	6.2	4.8	2.6	3.9	4.3	4.7	4.6	4.6	5.2	4.0
Ethiopia[4]	17.6	8.1	7.4	9.6	6.6	10.7	13.8	15.8	20.4	25.2	...	...	18.2	...	...
Gabon	1.4	0.5	4.5	−0.1	2.1	2.7	4.8	2.0	1.3	2.0	2.0	2.0	1.6	2.0	2.0
The Gambia	6.6	5.2	6.3	6.8	7.2	8.0	6.5	7.1	5.9	7.0	6.3	5.0	5.7	6.5	6.2
Ghana	12.7	11.7	15.5	17.2	17.5	12.4	9.8	7.1	9.9	9.3	8.8	6.0	10.5	10.2	8.4
Guinea	19.0	11.9	9.7	8.2	8.2	8.9	9.8	9.5	10.6	11.6	9.9	7.8	10.6	11.3	9.9
Guinea-Bissau	2.4	0.8	−1.0	1.5	2.7	−0.2	0.4	0.3	1.5	1.9	2.0	2.0	1.5	2.0	2.0
Kenya	8.5	5.7	6.9	6.6	6.3	8.0	4.7	5.2	5.2	6.0	5.0	5.0	5.8	5.2	5.0
Lesotho	6.2	4.9	5.4	3.2	6.6	4.4	4.8	5.2	5.0	5.8	5.3	5.5	6.5	5.4	4.9
Liberia	8.9	7.6	9.9	7.7	8.8	12.4	23.5	27.0	17.0	5.9	11.8	5.0	13.1	7.6	13.3
Madagascar	9.3	5.8	6.1	7.4	6.1	8.6	8.6	5.6	4.2	6.0	6.4	5.7	4.6	6.5	6.3
Malawi	9.4	28.3	23.8	21.9	21.7	11.5	9.2	9.4	8.6	9.5	9.0	5.0	7.6	9.5	8.1
Mali	2.5	−2.4	2.7	1.4	−1.8	1.8	1.7	−2.9	0.5	3.0	2.0	2.0	0.7	3.9	2.0
Mauritius	5.5	3.5	3.2	1.3	1.0	3.7	3.2	0.5	2.5	5.1	6.6	3.3	2.7	10.0	2.8
Mozambique	10.0	4.3	2.6	3.6	17.4	15.1	3.9	2.8	3.1	6.2	6.4	5.5	3.5	7.3	5.5
Namibia	6.0	5.6	5.3	3.4	6.7	6.1	4.3	3.7	2.2	4.0	4.5	4.5	2.4	4.0	4.5
Niger	2.2	2.3	−0.9	1.0	0.2	0.2	2.8	−2.5	2.9	2.9	2.5	2.0	3.1	3.0	2.5
Nigeria	12.1	8.5	8.0	9.0	15.7	16.5	12.1	11.4	13.2	16.9	13.3	11.5	15.8	15.0	12.6
Rwanda	8.6	4.2	1.8	2.5	5.7	4.8	1.4	2.4	7.7	2.4	4.9	5.0	3.7	3.5	5.2
São Tomé and Príncipe	16.7	8.1	7.0	6.1	5.4	5.7	7.9	7.7	9.8	8.3	7.8	4.4	9.4	8.4	6.2
Senegal	2.0	0.7	−1.1	0.9	1.2	1.1	0.5	1.0	2.5	2.4	2.0	1.5	2.4	3.1	0.9
Seychelles	8.0	4.3	1.4	4.0	−1.0	2.9	3.7	1.8	1.2	10.0	3.7	3.0	3.8	8.6	3.9
Sierra Leone	9.4	5.5	4.6	6.7	10.9	18.2	16.0	14.8	13.4	11.3	13.3	7.0	10.4	14.6	12.0
South Africa	5.5	5.8	6.1	4.6	6.3	5.3	4.6	4.1	3.3	4.4	4.5	4.5	3.2	5.0	4.5
South Sudan	...	0.0	1.7	52.8	379.8	187.9	83.5	51.2	24.0	23.0	24.0	11.3	87.7	8.0	8.0
Tanzania	8.5	7.9	6.1	5.6	5.2	5.3	3.5	3.4	3.3	3.2	3.4	3.5	3.2	3.2	3.4
Togo	2.4	1.8	0.2	1.8	0.9	−0.2	0.9	0.7	1.8	2.7	2.5	1.0	3.5	1.6	4.7
Uganda	9.5	5.5	4.3	3.7	5.2	5.6	2.6	2.3	2.8	2.2	5.0	5.0	2.5	1.8	5.0
Zambia	12.6	7.0	7.8	10.1	17.9	6.6	7.0	9.2	15.7	22.8	19.2	7.0	19.2	23.2	15.2
Zimbabwe[4]	3.9	1.6	−0.2	−2.4	−1.6	0.9	10.6	255.3	557.2	92.5	30.7	10.0	348.6	41.0	23.0

[1]Movements in consumer prices are shown as annual averages.
[2]Monthly year-over-year changes and, for several countries, on a quarterly basis.
[3]Based on Eurostat's harmonized index of consumer prices.
[4]See the country-specific notes for Afghanistan, Albania, Argentina, Ethiopia, Lebanon, Libya, Ukraine, Venezuela, and Zimbabwe in the "Country Notes" section of the Statistical Appendix.
[5]Excludes Venezuela but includes Argentina from 2017 onward. See the country-specific notes for Argentina and Venezuela in the "Country Notes" section of the Statistical Appendix.
[6]Data for 2011 exclude South Sudan after July 9. Data for 2012 and onward pertain to the current Sudan.
[7]Data for Syria are excluded for 2011 onward owing to the uncertain political situation.

Table A8. Major Advanced Economies: General Government Fiscal Balances and Debt[1]
(Percent of GDP, unless noted otherwise)

	Average 2003–12	2013	2014	2015	2016	2017	2018	2019	2020	Projections 2021	2022	2026
Major Advanced Economies												
Net Lending/Borrowing	−5.4	−4.3	−3.6	−3.0	−3.3	−3.3	−3.4	−3.8	−12.2	−10.0	−5.4	−3.6
Output Gap[2]	−1.9	−3.4	−2.7	−1.9	−1.6	−0.8	−0.1	0.1	−3.5	−0.9	1.5	0.6
Structural Balance[2]	−4.4	−3.2	−2.6	−2.3	−2.8	−3.0	−3.3	−3.8	−8.3	−7.9	−6.0	−3.9
United States												
Net Lending/Borrowing[3]	−6.5	−4.5	−4.0	−3.5	−4.3	−4.6	−5.4	−5.7	−14.9	−10.8	−6.9	−5.3
Output Gap[2]	−3.4	−5.1	−4.0	−2.5	−2.1	−1.3	0.0	0.7	−3.3	0.6	3.3	1.1
Structural Balance[2]	−4.6	−3.2	−2.7	−2.5	−3.5	−4.2	−5.2	−6.1	−10.7	−8.8	−8.3	−5.8
Net Debt	56.6	80.4	81.1	80.9	81.9	81.6	82.1	83.0	98.7	101.9	100.8	108.9
Gross Debt	77.7	104.5	104.5	104.9	106.9	106.0	107.1	108.5	133.9	133.3	130.7	133.5
Euro Area												
Net Lending/Borrowing	−3.3	−3.0	−2.5	−2.0	−1.5	−0.9	−0.5	−0.6	−7.2	−7.7	−3.4	−1.6
Output Gap[2]	−0.2	−3.1	−2.8	−2.2	−1.6	−0.6	−0.1	0.0	−4.3	−2.8	−0.6	0.1
Structural Balance[2]	−3.2	−1.0	−0.7	−0.6	−0.5	−0.5	−0.3	−0.5	−4.6	−5.9	−3.1	−1.7
Net Debt	60.9	76.0	76.2	75.0	74.6	72.4	70.6	69.3	80.7	82.8	80.9	78.4
Gross Debt	75.8	92.6	92.8	90.9	90.1	87.7	85.7	83.7	97.5	98.9	96.3	92.2
Germany												
Net Lending/Borrowing	−2.0	0.0	0.6	1.0	1.2	1.3	1.9	1.5	−4.3	−6.8	−1.8	0.5
Output Gap[2]	−0.2	−0.8	−0.3	−0.3	0.1	1.0	0.8	0.4	−2.6	−2.0	−0.3	0.0
Structural Balance[2]	−1.7	0.6	1.2	1.2	1.2	1.1	1.6	1.3	−3.1	−5.7	−1.6	0.5
Net Debt	57.0	58.8	55.2	52.5	49.6	45.7	42.9	40.8	50.1	54.4	52.9	46.0
Gross Debt	71.0	78.8	75.7	72.3	69.3	65.0	61.6	59.2	69.1	72.5	69.8	60.9
France												
Net Lending/Borrowing	−4.4	−4.1	−3.9	−3.6	−3.6	−3.0	−2.3	−3.1	−9.2	−8.9	−4.7	−3.4
Output Gap[2]	−0.3	−2.0	−2.2	−2.4	−2.6	−1.5	−0.8	0.0	−4.3	−2.2	−0.2	0.0
Structural Balance[2]	−4.2	−2.8	−2.5	−2.1	−1.9	−1.9	−1.6	−2.1	−6.3	−7.5	−4.6	−3.4
Net Debt	64.6	83.0	85.5	86.3	89.2	89.4	89.2	88.9	102.6	103.3	100.9	104.4
Gross Debt	74.2	93.4	94.9	95.6	98.0	98.3	98.0	97.6	115.1	115.8	113.5	116.9
Italy												
Net Lending/Borrowing	−3.4	−2.9	−3.0	−2.6	−2.4	−2.4	−2.2	−1.6	−9.5	−10.2	−4.7	−2.4
Output Gap[2]	−0.3	−4.1	−4.1	−3.4	−2.6	−1.6	−1.1	−1.3	−6.1	−4.9	−1.4	0.4
Structural Balance[2]	−3.7	−0.5	−1.0	−0.6	−1.3	−1.6	−1.7	−0.9	−5.9	−7.1	−3.8	−2.5
Net Debt	102.1	119.2	121.4	122.2	121.6	121.3	121.8	122.1	142.3	142.2	138.5	135.7
Gross Debt	111.6	132.5	135.4	135.3	134.8	134.1	134.4	134.6	155.8	154.8	150.4	146.5
Japan												
Net Lending/Borrowing	−6.8	−7.9	−5.9	−3.9	−3.8	−3.3	−2.7	−3.1	−10.3	−9.0	−3.9	−2.2
Output Gap[2]	−1.4	−1.9	−2.3	−1.5	−1.5	−0.5	−0.9	−1.5	−2.7	−2.4	−0.8	0.0
Structural Balance[2]	−6.3	−7.4	−5.6	−4.4	−4.3	−3.5	−2.7	−2.6	−9.2	−8.0	−3.6	−2.2
Net Debt	110.4	142.9	145.1	144.6	149.6	148.1	151.2	150.8	167.0	171.5	169.2	169.4
Gross Debt[4]	188.1	229.6	233.5	228.4	232.5	231.4	232.5	235.4	254.1	256.9	252.3	251.9
United Kingdom												
Net Lending/Borrowing	−5.4	−5.5	−5.5	−4.5	−3.3	−2.4	−2.2	−2.3	−12.5	−11.9	−5.6	−2.9
Output Gap[2]	0.3	−1.6	−0.5	0.0	0.0	0.2	0.0	0.1	−4.3	−2.1	−0.4	0.0
Structural Balance[2]	−5.6	−4.2	−4.9	−4.4	−3.3	−2.5	−2.3	−2.3	1.4	−5.6	−4.9	−3.1
Net Debt	48.8	75.9	77.9	78.2	77.8	76.8	75.9	75.3	91.8	97.2	95.2	99.9
Gross Debt	54.5	84.2	86.1	86.7	86.8	86.3	85.8	85.2	104.5	108.5	107.1	111.6
Canada												
Net Lending/Borrowing	−0.8	−1.5	0.2	−0.1	−0.5	−0.1	0.3	0.5	−10.9	−7.5	−2.2	0.4
Output Gap[2]	−0.1	0.0	1.0	−0.1	−0.9	0.4	0.6	0.4	−3.4	−1.0	0.8	0.0
Structural Balance[2]	−0.8	−1.5	−0.6	0.0	0.1	−0.3	0.0	0.3	−8.1	−6.6	−2.7	0.4
Net Debt[5]	27.2	29.7	28.5	28.4	28.7	26.0	25.6	23.4	34.7	34.9	32.5	22.2
Gross Debt	75.1	86.1	85.6	91.2	91.7	88.8	88.8	86.8	117.5	109.9	103.9	89.7

Note: The methodology and specific assumptions for each country are discussed in Box A1. The country group composites for fiscal data are calculated as the sum of the US dollar values for the relevant individual countries.
[1] Debt data refer to the end of the year and are not always comparable across countries. Gross and net debt levels reported by national statistical agencies for countries that have adopted the System of National Accounts 2008 (Australia, Canada, Hong Kong SAR, United States) are adjusted to exclude unfunded pension liabilities of government employees' defined-benefit pension plans.
[2] Percent of potential GDP.
[3] Figures reported by the national statistical agency are adjusted to exclude items related to the accrual-basis accounting of government employees' defined-benefit pension plans.
[4] Nonconsolidated basis.
[5] Includes equity shares.

Table A9. Summary of World Trade Volumes and Prices

(Annual percent change, unless noted otherwise)

	Averages		2013	2014	2015	2016	2017	2018	2019	2020	Projections	
	2003–12	2013–22									2021	2022
Trade in Goods and Services												
World Trade[1]												
Volume	5.6	3.0	3.5	3.8	2.9	2.2	5.6	3.9	0.9	−8.2	9.7	6.7
Price Deflator												
In US Dollars	5.1	−0.4	−0.6	−1.8	−13.3	−4.0	4.3	5.5	−2.5	−2.3	10.3	2.0
In SDRs	3.3	0.2	0.2	−1.7	−5.9	−3.4	4.6	3.4	−0.1	−3.0	7.4	1.1
Volume of Trade												
Exports												
Advanced Economies	4.6	2.6	3.0	3.8	3.7	2.0	4.9	3.6	1.2	−9.4	8.0	6.6
Emerging Market and Developing Economies	8.3	3.5	4.6	3.3	2.0	2.8	6.5	3.9	0.4	−5.2	11.6	5.8
Imports												
Advanced Economies	3.9	3.0	2.5	3.9	4.7	2.5	4.8	3.7	2.0	−9.0	9.0	7.3
Emerging Market and Developing Economies	9.8	3.2	5.1	4.3	−0.6	1.6	7.5	4.8	−0.9	−8.0	12.1	7.1
Terms of Trade												
Advanced Economies	−0.4	0.6	1.0	0.3	1.8	1.1	−0.2	−0.4	0.2	0.8	0.9	0.2
Emerging Market and Developing Economies	1.6	−0.5	−0.5	−0.6	−4.4	−1.6	1.5	1.1	−1.2	−1.0	1.6	−0.1
Trade in Goods												
World Trade[1]												
Volume	5.7	3.1	3.3	3.0	2.3	2.1	5.6	3.8	0.3	−4.9	10.5	6.0
Price Deflator												
In US Dollars	5.3	−0.7	−1.2	−2.4	−14.6	−4.8	4.9	5.8	−3.1	−2.8	11.8	1.8
In SDRs	3.5	−0.1	−0.4	−2.3	−7.2	−4.2	5.2	3.6	−0.8	−3.5	8.8	0.9
World Trade Prices in US Dollars[2]												
Manufactures	3.1	−0.2	−2.8	−0.4	−3.0	−5.1	0.1	2.0	0.5	−3.2	5.5	4.4
Oil	15.5	−4.8	−0.9	−7.5	−47.2	−15.7	23.3	29.4	−10.2	−32.7	59.1	−1.8
Nonfuel Primary Commodities	10.3	0.7	−5.8	−5.5	−17.1	−0.4	6.4	1.3	0.8	6.7	26.7	−0.9
Food	6.8	0.8	−0.3	−1.6	−16.9	1.5	3.8	−1.2	−3.1	1.7	27.8	1.9
Beverages	9.2	−0.2	−13.7	20.1	−7.2	−3.1	−4.7	−8.2	−3.8	3.5	14.1	5.8
Agricultural Raw Materials	6.5	−1.1	−4.4	−7.5	−11.5	0.0	5.2	2.0	−5.4	−3.3	17.0	0.2
Metal	15.3	1.3	−3.9	−12.2	−27.3	−5.3	22.2	6.6	3.7	3.5	49.7	−6.5
World Trade Prices in SDRs[2]												
Manufactures	1.4	0.3	−2.1	−0.3	5.3	−4.5	0.4	−0.1	2.9	−4.0	2.7	3.5
Oil	13.5	−4.2	−0.1	−7.5	−42.7	−15.1	23.6	26.7	−8.0	−33.3	54.8	−2.6
Nonfuel Primary Commodities	8.5	1.3	−5.1	−5.5	−10.0	0.3	6.6	−0.8	3.3	5.8	23.3	−1.7
Food	5.0	1.4	0.5	−1.5	−9.8	2.2	4.1	−3.3	−0.7	0.9	24.4	1.0
Beverages	7.4	0.4	−13.0	20.1	0.7	−2.5	−4.5	−10.1	−1.4	2.7	11.1	4.8
Agricultural Raw Materials	4.8	−0.5	−3.7	−7.5	−4.0	0.6	5.5	−0.1	−3.1	−4.1	13.8	−0.7
Metal	13.4	1.9	−3.1	−12.1	−21.1	−4.7	22.5	4.4	6.2	2.7	45.7	−7.4
World Trade Prices in Euros[2]												
Manufactures	0.0	0.4	−5.9	−0.4	16.2	−4.8	−1.9	−2.5	6.0	−5.0	0.8	3.3
Oil	12.0	−4.2	−4.1	−7.6	−36.8	−15.4	20.8	23.7	−5.2	−34.0	52.0	−2.8
Nonfuel Primary Commodities	7.0	1.3	−8.9	−5.6	−0.7	−0.1	4.2	−3.1	6.4	4.7	21.0	−2.0
Food	3.5	1.5	−3.5	−1.6	−0.5	1.8	1.7	−5.6	2.3	−0.3	22.1	0.8
Beverages	5.9	0.4	−16.4	20.0	11.1	−2.8	−6.6	−12.2	1.5	1.5	9.1	4.6
Agricultural Raw Materials	3.3	−0.4	−7.5	−7.6	5.9	0.3	3.1	−2.5	−0.2	−5.2	11.8	−0.9
Metal	11.8	1.9	−7.0	−12.2	−12.9	−5.0	19.7	1.9	9.4	1.5	43.0	−7.6

Table A9. Summary of World Trade Volumes and Prices *(continued)*
(Annual percent change, unless noted otherwise)

	Averages		2013	2014	2015	2016	2017	2018	2019	2020	Projections	
	2003–12	2013–22									2021	2022
Trade in Goods												
Volume of Trade												
Exports												
Advanced Economies	4.5	2.7	2.5	3.1	3.1	1.6	4.8	3.0	0.5	−6.4	9.3	5.6
Emerging Market and Developing Economies	8.2	3.5	4.5	2.6	1.5	2.7	6.5	3.8	−0.5	−2.0	11.2	5.2
Fuel Exporters	6.1	−0.3	1.1	−0.8	2.5	0.8	0.7	−0.8	−4.0	−6.6	0.0	4.4
Nonfuel Exporters	8.7	4.2	5.6	3.6	1.3	3.1	7.6	4.7	0.2	−1.2	12.8	5.4
Imports												
Advanced Economies	4.0	3.2	2.3	3.3	3.7	2.2	4.7	3.8	0.6	−5.8	11.1	6.8
Emerging Market and Developing Economies	9.9	3.4	4.7	2.7	−0.3	2.1	7.4	5.2	0.1	−4.3	10.9	6.3
Fuel Exporters	10.5	−0.8	5.8	4.2	0.0	−6.9	−0.9	−3.4	1.7	−10.8	0.6	2.4
Nonfuel Exporters	9.8	3.9	4.5	2.5	−0.4	3.5	8.6	6.3	−0.1	−3.5	12.1	6.7
Price Deflators in SDRs												
Exports												
Advanced Economies	2.4	0.4	0.4	−1.9	−6.4	−2.2	4.3	2.9	−1.4	−2.1	9.0	1.9
Emerging Market and Developing Economies	6.2	−0.5	−1.1	−3.1	−9.2	−7.0	7.0	5.1	0.2	−5.2	9.8	−0.2
Fuel Exporters	10.7	−3.0	−1.7	−7.4	−30.2	−10.8	15.7	15.4	−3.9	−22.3	32.0	−1.1
Nonfuel Exporters	4.9	0.1	−0.9	−1.8	−3.6	−6.3	5.5	3.2	1.0	−2.1	6.8	0.0
Imports												
Advanced Economies	2.9	−0.3	−0.6	−2.0	−8.1	−3.5	4.5	3.5	−1.5	−3.2	7.6	1.7
Emerging Market and Developing Economies	4.3	−0.1	−0.6	−2.8	−5.0	−5.5	5.8	3.7	0.4	−4.6	9.2	−0.6
Fuel Exporters	4.2	0.4	−1.5	−2.7	−2.4	−3.7	3.4	1.6	2.8	−2.7	9.7	0.7
Nonfuel Exporters	4.3	−0.2	−0.5	−2.8	−5.5	−5.7	6.1	4.0	0.1	−4.8	9.2	−0.7
Terms of Trade												
Advanced Economies	−0.5	0.6	1.0	0.1	1.8	1.4	−0.2	−0.6	0.2	1.1	1.3	0.2
Emerging Market and Developing Economies	1.8	−0.4	−0.5	−0.3	−4.4	−1.7	1.2	1.3	−0.2	−0.6	0.5	0.4
Regional Groups												
Emerging and Developing Asia	−1.2	0.7	1.1	2.4	8.5	0.2	−3.4	−2.3	1.2	4.5	−6.6	2.0
Emerging and Developing Europe	3.2	−1.1	−3.3	−0.6	−10.6	−6.2	2.9	4.4	0.3	−3.1	7.0	0.0
Latin America and the Caribbean	2.8	−0.3	−1.1	−2.5	−8.7	1.1	4.2	0.0	−0.1	0.5	5.8	−1.0
Middle East and Central Asia	4.6	−2.9	−0.8	−3.6	−24.5	−5.6	10.0	11.1	−4.7	−16.4	15.3	−3.1
Sub-Saharan Africa	4.6	−0.5	−0.8	−3.2	−14.8	−1.5	8.7	4.6	−2.6	−0.3	9.8	−2.5
Analytical Groups												
By Source of Export Earnings												
Fuel	6.2	−3.4	−0.2	−4.7	−28.5	−7.4	11.9	13.6	−6.6	−20.1	20.3	−1.8
Nonfuel	0.6	0.3	−0.4	1.0	2.0	−0.6	−0.6	−0.8	0.9	2.9	−2.2	0.7
Memorandum												
World Exports in Billions of US Dollars												
Goods and Services	16,453	23,960	23,385	23,802	21,132	20,752	22,881	25,063	24,618	22,123	26,785	29,063
Goods	13,056	18,545	18,563	18,637	16,199	15,741	17,447	19,110	18,544	17,201	21,205	22,806
Average Oil Price[3]	15.5	−4.8	−0.9	−7.5	−47.2	−15.7	23.3	29.4	−10.2	−32.7	59.1	−1.8
In US Dollars a Barrel	70.22	64.80	104.07	96.25	50.79	42.84	52.81	68.33	61.39	41.29	65.68	64.52
Export Unit Value of Manufactures[4]	3.1	−0.2	−2.8	−0.4	−3.0	−5.1	0.1	2.0	0.5	−3.2	5.5	4.4

[1]Average of annual percent change for world exports and imports.
[2]As represented, respectively, by the export unit value index for manufactures of the advanced economies and accounting for 83 percent of the advanced economies' trade (export of goods) weights; the average of UK Brent, Dubai Fateh, and West Texas Intermediate crude oil prices; and the average of world market prices for nonfuel primary commodities weighted by their 2014–16 shares in world commodity imports.
[3]Percent change of average of UK Brent, Dubai Fateh, and West Texas Intermediate crude oil prices.
[4]Percent change for manufactures exported by the advanced economies.

Table A10. Summary of Current Account Balances
(Billions of US dollars)

	2013	2014	2015	2016	2017	2018	2019	2020	Projections 2021	2022	2026
Advanced Economies	**239.4**	**237.6**	**283.9**	**372.7**	**491.7**	**412.6**	**336.5**	**173.8**	**245.5**	**200.3**	**442.7**
United States	−339.5	−370.0	−408.9	−397.6	−361.7	−438.2	−472.1	−616.1	−796.1	−868.0	−688.1
Euro Area	278.8	316.5	315.1	364.8	401.4	409.0	316.0	282.6	375.3	428.1	509.3
Germany	244.8	280.3	288.8	295.1	287.9	312.1	289.6	267.0	287.6	316.7	361.4
France	−14.3	−27.3	−9.0	−12.0	−19.8	−23.2	−7.9	−49.8	−49.0	−44.3	−24.6
Italy	23.7	41.1	26.1	48.7	50.6	52.6	64.3	66.9	78.8	80.8	93.0
Spain	27.6	23.3	24.2	39.1	36.4	27.4	29.8	8.8	6.0	22.2	22.1
Japan	46.0	36.8	136.4	197.8	203.5	177.8	176.5	164.4	176.9	178.5	203.8
United Kingdom	−136.2	−149.6	−147.4	−146.9	−100.4	−105.3	−87.6	−100.6	−104.6	−117.0	−120.6
Canada	−58.0	−41.9	−54.4	−47.2	−46.2	−40.3	−35.7	−29.9	10.6	4.6	−48.0
Other Advanced Economies[1]	343.7	354.7	356.5	336.5	339.6	337.0	358.4	406.4	504.0	488.9	484.2
Emerging Market and Developing Economies	**159.3**	**164.6**	**−73.6**	**−95.7**	**−24.6**	**−64.5**	**2.7**	**201.8**	**324.5**	**247.7**	**−222.4**
Regional Groups											
Emerging and Developing Asia	97.2	227.5	296.8	212.2	166.3	−51.3	92.6	338.7	249.6	236.8	4.0
Emerging and Developing Europe	−59.3	−11.0	34.2	−8.4	−19.8	66.3	51.7	4.3	66.3	43.0	−8.5
Latin America and the Caribbean	−172.8	−186.4	−172.3	−101.0	−94.6	−140.8	−102.7	0.7	−28.7	−52.9	−127.5
Middle East and Central Asia	332.9	198.8	−139.8	−145.5	−42.1	103.1	20.3	−92.7	79.3	75.4	−12.2
Sub-Saharan Africa	−38.6	−64.3	−92.4	−53.0	−34.4	−41.7	−59.2	−49.2	−42.0	−54.5	−78.2
Analytical Groups											
By Source of Export Earnings											
Fuel	426.7	251.3	−143.6	−97.1	38.2	192.5	76.3	−73.3	114.6	122.0	38.8
Nonfuel	−265.5	−84.8	72.0	3.5	−60.7	−254.8	−71.9	276.1	211.5	127.6	−259.1
Of Which, Primary Products	−90.3	−55.1	−64.1	−44.9	−57.6	−76.5	−45.2	1.7	−1.9	−18.9	−42.9
By External Financing Source											
Net Debtor Economies	−376.0	−366.1	−343.2	−262.7	−297.3	−373.5	−282.9	−89.7	−184.9	−242.9	−478.4
Net Debtor Economies by Debt-Servicing Experience											
Economies with Arrears and/or Rescheduling during 2016–20	−58.5	−54.1	−71.5	−67.6	−55.9	−46.7	−49.4	−29.2	−35.9	−36.4	−57.4
Memorandum											
World	**398.7**	**402.2**	**210.3**	**277.0**	**467.1**	**348.1**	**339.1**	**375.5**	**570.0**	**448.0**	**220.3**
European Union	433.2	451.9	442.9	472.1	501.1	506.8	450.5	425.3	516.4	567.9	655.9
Middle East and North Africa	326.8	190.1	−122.2	−120.5	−21.5	119.4	40.6	−78.0	82.6	90.0	18.5
Emerging Market and Middle-Income Economies	198.2	207.2	0.5	−55.6	8.9	−9.6	61.6	257.5	390.9	308.2	−131.8
Low-Income Developing Countries	−38.9	−42.6	−74.0	−40.1	−33.6	−54.8	−59.0	−55.7	−66.4	−60.4	−90.7

Table A10. Summary of Current Account Balances *(continued)*
(Percent of GDP)

	2013	2014	2015	2016	2017	2018	2019	2020	Projections 2021	Projections 2022	Projections 2026
Advanced Economies	**0.5**	**0.5**	**0.6**	**0.8**	**1.0**	**0.8**	**0.6**	**0.3**	**0.4**	**0.3**	**0.6**
United States	−2.0	−2.1	−2.2	−2.1	−1.9	−2.1	−2.2	−2.9	−3.5	−3.5	−2.4
Euro Area	2.1	2.3	2.7	3.0	3.2	3.0	2.4	2.2	2.6	2.7	2.7
Germany	6.6	7.2	8.6	8.5	7.8	7.8	7.4	6.9	6.8	6.9	6.7
France	−0.5	−1.0	−0.4	−0.5	−0.8	−0.8	−0.3	−1.9	−1.7	−1.4	−0.7
Italy	1.1	1.9	1.4	2.6	2.6	2.5	3.2	3.5	3.7	3.6	3.6
Spain	2.0	1.7	2.0	3.2	2.8	1.9	2.1	0.7	0.4	1.4	1.2
Japan	0.9	0.8	3.1	4.0	4.1	3.5	3.4	3.3	3.5	3.3	3.2
United Kingdom	−4.9	−4.9	−5.0	−5.4	−3.8	−3.7	−3.1	−3.7	−3.4	−3.4	−2.9
Canada	−3.1	−2.3	−3.5	−3.1	−2.8	−2.3	−2.1	−1.8	0.5	0.2	−1.8
Other Advanced Economies[1]	5.0	5.0	5.5	5.1	4.8	4.5	4.9	5.6	6.1	5.6	4.5
Emerging Market and Developing Economies	**0.5**	**0.5**	**−0.2**	**−0.3**	**−0.1**	**−0.2**	**0.0**	**0.6**	**0.8**	**0.6**	**−0.4**
Regional Groups											
Emerging and Developing Asia	0.7	1.5	1.9	1.3	0.9	−0.3	0.5	1.6	1.1	0.9	0.0
Emerging and Developing Europe	−1.3	−0.3	1.0	−0.3	−0.5	1.7	1.3	0.1	1.6	1.0	−0.1
Latin America and the Caribbean	−2.9	−3.1	−3.3	−2.0	−1.7	−2.6	−2.0	0.0	−0.6	−1.0	−1.9
Middle East and Central Asia	8.6	5.0	−4.0	−4.2	−1.2	2.7	0.5	−2.4	1.7	1.5	−0.2
Sub-Saharan Africa	−2.2	−3.5	−5.7	−3.5	−2.1	−2.4	−3.4	−3.0	−2.2	−2.7	−2.7
Analytical Groups											
By Source of Export Earnings											
Fuel	10.5	6.1	−4.0	−2.9	1.1	5.3	2.0	−2.0	2.7	2.7	0.7
Nonfuel	−1.0	−0.3	0.3	0.0	−0.2	−0.8	−0.2	0.9	0.6	0.3	−0.5
Of Which, Primary Products	−4.3	−2.7	−3.2	−2.3	−2.7	−3.7	−2.3	0.1	−0.1	−0.8	−1.6
By External Financing Source											
Net Debtor Economies	−2.7	−2.6	−2.6	−2.0	−2.1	−2.6	−1.9	−0.6	−1.2	−1.4	−2.1
Net Debtor Economies by Debt-Servicing Experience											
Economies with Arrears and/or Rescheduling during 2016–20	−5.2	−4.8	−6.6	−6.3	−5.5	−4.5	−4.4	−2.7	−3.0	−2.8	−3.2
Memorandum											
World	**0.5**	**0.5**	**0.3**	**0.4**	**0.6**	**0.4**	**0.4**	**0.4**	**0.6**	**0.4**	**0.2**
European Union	2.8	2.9	3.3	3.4	3.4	3.2	2.9	2.8	3.0	3.1	3.0
Middle East and North Africa	10.3	5.9	−4.3	−4.3	−0.7	3.8	1.2	−2.4	2.1	2.2	0.4
Emerging Market and Middle-Income Economies	0.7	0.7	0.0	−0.2	0.0	0.0	0.2	0.8	1.1	0.8	−0.3
Low-Income Developing Countries	−2.1	−2.1	−3.8	−2.1	−1.7	−2.6	−2.6	−2.4	−2.7	−2.2	−2.3

Table A10. Summary of Current Account Balances *(continued)*
(Percent of exports of goods and services)

	2013	2014	2015	2016	2017	2018	2019	2020	2021	2022	2026
									Projections		
Advanced Economies	1.6	1.6	2.1	2.8	3.4	2.6	2.2	1.2	1.5	1.1	2.0
United States	−14.7	−15.5	−17.9	−17.8	−15.1	−17.3	−18.7	−28.9	−31.1	−29.4	−18.3
Euro Area	8.2	8.9	9.7	11.2	11.3	10.6	8.3	8.1	. . .	. . .	. . .
Germany	14.4	15.8	18.3	18.5	16.5	16.6	16.0	16.0	14.8	15.0	14.2
France	−1.7	−3.1	−1.2	−1.5	−2.4	−2.5	−0.9	−6.6	−5.5	−4.5	−2.1
Italy	3.9	6.5	4.8	8.8	8.4	8.0	10.1	12.0	11.5	10.4	9.4
Spain	6.2	5.1	6.0	9.4	7.9	5.5	6.1	2.2	1.3	4.1	3.2
Japan	5.5	4.3	17.4	24.4	23.2	19.1	19.5	20.7	19.0	17.5	17.5
United Kingdom	−16.4	−17.3	−18.4	−19.2	−12.5	−11.9	−10.0	−13.7	−12.7	−12.4	−10.4
Canada	−10.4	−7.3	−11.0	−9.8	−8.9	−7.2	−6.4	−6.3	1.7	0.7	−6.2
Other Advanced Economies[1]	8.2	8.5	9.6	9.2	8.5	7.8	8.5	10.4	10.8	9.8	8.2
Emerging Market and Developing Economies	1.8	2.1	−0.8	−1.2	−0.3	−0.7	0.0	2.5	3.1	2.3	−1.7
Regional Groups											
Emerging and Developing Asia	2.5	5.7	7.8	5.8	4.1	−1.1	2.1	7.7	4.7	4.2	0.1
Emerging and Developing Europe	−4.0	−0.7	2.9	−0.7	−1.5	4.3	3.4	0.3	3.9	2.4	−0.4
Latin America and the Caribbean	−13.6	−15.0	−15.9	−9.6	−8.0	−11.1	−8.2	0.1	−2.1	−3.8	−7.5
Middle East and Central Asia	18.7	12.7	−10.4	−12.0	−3.3	6.6	1.4	−8.4	5.2	4.7	−1.1
Sub-Saharan Africa	−8.1	−14.1	−26.9	−16.6	−9.3	−9.9	−14.5	−14.7	−9.8	−12.2	−14.3
Analytical Groups											
By Source of Export Earnings											
Fuel	22.2	14.8	−10.8	−8.1	2.7	12.5	5.4	−7.1	8.0	8.2	2.1
Nonfuel	−3.8	−1.2	1.1	0.1	−0.9	−3.3	−0.9	3.8	2.4	1.4	−2.2
Of Which, Primary Products	−18.2	−11.4	−15.4	−10.9	−12.4	−15.4	−9.2	0.4	−0.3	−3.2	−5.9
By External Financing Source											
Net Debtor Economies	−9.7	−9.4	−10.1	−7.8	−7.7	−8.8	−6.6	−2.4	−4.0	−4.9	−7.5
Net Debtor Economies by Debt-Servicing Experience											
Economies with Arrears and/or Rescheduling during 2016–20	−16.6	−16.6	−27.9	−29.0	−21.0	−15.2	−15.9	−11.2	−11.8	−10.9	−12.6
Memorandum											
World	1.7	1.8	1.0	1.4	2.0	1.4	1.4	1.7	2.1	1.5	0.6
European Union	6.2	6.3	6.9	7.2	7.0	6.4	5.8	6.0	6.1	6.1	5.7
Middle East and North Africa	20.9	13.8	−10.1	−11.0	−2.0	8.6	3.1	−8.0	6.2	6.4	0.8
Emerging Market and Middle-Income Economies	2.4	2.7	0.1	−0.7	0.1	−0.1	0.7	3.4	4.1	3.0	−1.1
Low-Income Developing Countries	−7.6	−8.0	−15.4	−8.3	−6.0	−8.6	−8.6	−8.9	−9.3	−7.6	−8.4

[1]Excludes the Group of Seven (Canada, France, Germany, Italy, Japan, United Kingdom, United States) and euro area countries.

Table A11. Advanced Economies: Current Account Balance
(Percent of GDP)

	2013	2014	2015	2016	2017	2018	2019	2020	Projections 2021	2022	2026
Advanced Economies	**0.5**	**0.5**	**0.6**	**0.8**	**1.0**	**0.8**	**0.6**	**0.3**	**0.4**	**0.3**	**0.6**
United States	−2.0	−2.1	−2.2	−2.1	−1.9	−2.1	−2.2	−2.9	−3.5	−3.5	−2.4
Euro Area[1]	2.1	2.3	2.7	3.0	3.2	3.0	2.4	2.2	2.6	2.7	2.7
Germany	6.6	7.2	8.6	8.5	7.8	7.8	7.4	6.9	6.8	6.9	6.7
France	−0.5	−1.0	−0.4	−0.5	−0.8	−0.8	−0.3	−1.9	−1.7	−1.4	−0.7
Italy	1.1	1.9	1.4	2.6	2.6	2.5	3.2	3.5	3.7	3.6	3.6
Spain	2.0	1.7	2.0	3.2	2.8	1.9	2.1	0.7	0.4	1.4	1.2
The Netherlands	9.8	8.2	6.3	8.1	10.8	10.8	9.4	7.0	7.9	8.7	8.4
Belgium	1.0	0.8	1.4	0.6	0.7	−0.8	0.3	−0.2	0.0	−0.6	0.0
Austria	1.9	2.5	1.7	2.7	1.4	1.3	2.8	2.5	1.6	2.0	2.0
Ireland	1.6	1.1	4.4	−4.2	0.5	4.9	−19.9	−2.7	11.1	8.8	6.0
Portugal	1.6	0.2	0.2	1.2	1.3	0.6	0.4	−1.1	−1.7	−2.1	−1.1
Greece	−2.6	−2.4	−1.5	−2.4	−2.6	−3.6	−2.2	−7.4	−7.4	−5.1	−3.4
Finland	−1.8	−1.3	−0.9	−2.0	−0.8	−1.8	−0.3	0.8	−0.1	0.4	1.7
Slovak Republic	1.9	1.1	−2.1	−2.7	−1.9	−2.2	−2.7	−0.4	−0.9	−1.3	−0.8
Lithuania	0.8	3.2	−2.8	−0.8	0.6	0.3	3.3	8.3	6.7	4.7	−0.1
Slovenia	3.3	5.1	3.8	4.8	6.2	6.0	6.0	7.4	6.4	6.3	3.0
Luxembourg	5.4	5.2	5.1	4.9	4.9	4.8	4.6	4.3	4.7	4.3	4.1
Latvia	−2.8	−1.6	−0.6	1.6	1.3	−0.3	−0.6	3.0	−1.0	−1.1	−1.8
Estonia	0.3	0.7	1.8	1.2	2.3	0.9	2.0	−0.6	−1.8	−2.0	−3.3
Cyprus	−1.5	−4.1	−0.4	−4.2	−5.3	−3.9	−6.3	−11.9	−9.3	−7.4	−3.9
Malta	2.6	8.5	2.7	−0.6	5.6	6.1	5.5	−3.5	−2.4	−0.3	3.3
Japan	0.9	0.8	3.1	4.0	4.1	3.5	3.4	3.3	3.5	3.3	3.2
United Kingdom	−4.9	−4.9	−5.0	−5.4	−3.8	−3.7	−3.1	−3.7	−3.4	−3.4	−2.9
Korea	5.6	5.6	7.2	6.5	4.6	4.5	3.6	4.6	4.5	4.2	4.3
Canada	−3.1	−2.3	−3.5	−3.1	−2.8	−2.3	−2.1	−1.8	0.5	0.2	−1.8
Australia	−3.4	−3.1	−4.6	−3.3	−2.6	−2.1	0.7	2.7	3.6	1.3	−0.5
Taiwan Province of China	9.7	11.3	13.6	13.1	14.1	11.6	10.6	14.2	15.6	15.2	10.8
Switzerland	11.4	8.1	10.3	9.0	7.2	6.7	6.7	3.8	7.2	7.5	7.5
Sweden	5.2	4.2	3.3	2.4	3.0	2.6	5.5	5.7	4.8	4.3	3.0
Singapore	15.7	18.0	18.7	17.6	17.3	15.4	14.3	17.6	15.9	15.7	14.9
Hong Kong SAR	1.5	1.4	3.3	4.0	4.6	3.7	5.9	6.5	6.0	5.6	4.0
Czech Republic	−0.5	0.2	0.4	1.8	1.5	0.4	0.3	3.6	1.6	0.8	0.8
Israel	2.9	4.1	5.2	3.5	3.6	2.8	3.4	5.4	4.5	3.8	3.2
Norway	10.3	10.8	8.0	4.5	5.5	8.0	2.8	2.0	7.2	7.0	3.2
Denmark	7.8	8.9	8.2	7.8	8.0	7.3	8.8	8.2	7.0	6.8	6.5
New Zealand	−3.2	−3.1	−2.8	−2.1	−2.8	−4.0	−2.9	−0.8	−3.3	−2.5	−3.1
Puerto Rico	...	...	...	...	...	...	...	...	...	...	...
Macao SAR	39.3	32.7	23.3	26.5	30.8	33.1	33.6	−34.2	−18.5	8.9	31.5
Iceland	6.3	4.4	5.6	8.1	4.2	3.5	5.8	0.9	1.0	1.2	2.0
Andorra	...	...	...	...	...	...	18.0	14.3	14.7	15.7	18.2
San Marino	...	...	...	...	−0.1	−1.9	6.3	1.8	1.1	1.0	0.3
Memorandum											
Major Advanced Economies	−0.7	−0.6	−0.5	−0.2	0.0	−0.2	−0.2	−0.8	−0.9	−1.0	−0.4
Euro Area[2]	2.9	3.0	3.4	3.6	3.6	3.5	3.0	2.7	3.1	3.3	3.3

[1]Data corrected for reporting discrepancies in intra-area transactions.
[2]Data calculated as the sum of the balances of individual euro area countries.

Table A12. Emerging Market and Developing Economies: Current Account Balance

(Percent of GDP)

	2013	2014	2015	2016	2017	2018	2019	2020	Projections 2021	Projections 2022	Projections 2026
Emerging and Developing Asia	**0.7**	**1.5**	**1.9**	**1.3**	**0.9**	**−0.3**	**0.5**	**1.6**	**1.1**	**0.9**	**0.0**
Bangladesh	1.6	0.8	1.8	1.9	−0.5	−3.5	−1.7	−1.5	−1.1	−1.5	−2.2
Bhutan	−25.6	−27.1	−27.9	−30.3	−24.0	−19.1	−21.1	−12.2	−8.8	−12.0	2.1
Brunei Darussalam	20.9	31.9	16.7	12.9	16.4	6.9	6.6	4.5	4.6	5.5	13.7
Cambodia	−8.5	−8.6	−8.7	−8.5	−7.9	−11.8	−15.0	−12.1	−21.3	−16.1	−8.2
China	1.5	2.2	2.6	1.7	1.5	0.2	0.7	1.8	1.6	1.5	0.5
Fiji	−8.9	−5.8	−3.5	−3.6	−6.7	−8.4	−12.6	−13.4	−15.7	−8.7	−9.7
India	−1.7	−1.3	−1.0	−0.6	−1.8	−2.1	−0.9	0.9	−1.0	−1.4	−2.5
Indonesia	−3.2	−3.1	−2.0	−1.8	−1.6	−2.9	−2.7	−0.4	−0.3	−1.0	−2.2
Kiribati	−5.5	31.1	32.8	10.8	37.6	38.1	43.9	7.5	15.3	15.8	17.7
Lao P.D.R.	−26.5	−23.3	−22.4	−11.0	−11.1	−13.0	−9.1	−4.4	−6.2	−6.9	−6.5
Malaysia	3.4	4.3	3.0	2.4	2.8	2.2	3.5	4.2	3.8	3.7	3.4
Maldives	−4.3	−3.7	−7.5	−23.6	−21.6	−28.4	−26.5	−29.9	−15.9	−13.9	−8.1
Marshall Islands	−6.7	2.0	15.6	13.5	5.0	4.0	−25.9	16.2	3.6	0.4	−2.6
Micronesia	−9.9	6.1	4.5	7.2	10.3	21.0	17.0	3.0	1.2	1.1	−5.2
Mongolia	−37.6	−15.8	−8.1	−6.3	−10.1	−16.8	−15.4	−5.1	−8.5	−13.3	−8.4
Myanmar	−1.2	−4.5	−3.5	−4.2	−6.8	−4.7	−2.8	−3.4	−0.8	−1.0	−2.1
Nauru	49.5	25.2	−21.3	2.0	12.7	−4.6	10.6	4.0	3.4	5.8	1.4
Nepal	2.9	4.0	4.4	5.5	−0.3	−7.1	−6.9	−1.0	−8.3	−6.7	−3.8
Palau	−15.0	−19.6	−9.2	−13.7	−19.6	−15.9	−31.8	−45.5	−59.3	−44.0	−25.5
Papua New Guinea	−31.7	13.7	24.5	28.4	28.4	24.4	20.1	13.2	22.2	21.1	17.6
Philippines	4.0	3.6	2.4	−0.4	−0.7	−2.6	−0.8	3.6	0.4	−1.8	−1.8
Samoa	−1.5	−9.1	−2.8	−4.5	−1.9	0.9	3.1	1.0	−13.0	−5.6	−4.2
Solomon Islands	−3.0	−3.7	−2.7	−3.5	−4.3	−3.1	−9.8	−1.6	−5.8	−14.7	−10.5
Sri Lanka	−3.4	−2.5	−2.3	−2.1	−2.6	−3.2	−2.2	−1.3	−3.2	−2.9	−2.4
Thailand	−2.1	2.9	6.9	10.5	9.6	5.6	7.0	3.5	−0.5	2.1	3.0
Timor-Leste	171.4	75.6	12.8	−33.0	−17.7	−12.3	6.6	−17.3	−31.9	−44.4	−37.3
Tonga	−9.6	−6.3	−10.1	−6.5	−6.4	−6.3	−0.9	−3.9	−1.3	−8.2	−14.0
Tuvalu	−7.2	−3.7	−70.6	13.9	11.5	53.9	−16.9	3.8	−4.5	−4.6	−3.4
Vanuatu	−3.5	7.8	0.3	3.4	−4.4	12.2	16.0	3.3	−6.9	−8.0	−4.1
Vietnam	3.6	3.7	−0.9	0.2	−0.6	1.9	3.8	3.7	1.8	3.2	0.6
Emerging and Developing Europe	**−1.3**	**−0.3**	**1.0**	**−0.3**	**−0.5**	**1.7**	**1.3**	**0.1**	**1.6**	**1.0**	**−0.1**
Albania[1]	−9.3	−10.8	−8.6	−7.6	−7.5	−6.8	−7.6	−8.9	−8.6	−8.3	−7.9
Belarus	−10.0	−6.6	−3.3	−3.4	−1.7	0.0	−1.9	−0.4	0.4	−0.7	−1.0
Bosnia and Herzegovina	−5.3	−7.4	−5.1	−4.8	−4.8	−3.4	−3.1	−3.2	−3.9	−3.5	−3.3
Bulgaria	1.3	1.2	0.0	3.1	3.3	0.9	1.8	−0.7	0.5	0.3	0.4
Croatia	−1.1	0.3	3.3	2.2	3.5	1.8	3.0	−0.4	−0.1	−0.8	0.1
Hungary	3.5	1.2	2.3	4.5	2.0	0.3	−0.5	−0.1	0.6	0.9	0.7
Kosovo	−3.4	−6.9	−8.6	−7.9	−5.4	−7.6	−5.6	−7.1	−7.9	−6.7	−5.2
Moldova	−5.2	−6.0	−6.0	−3.5	−5.7	−10.4	−9.3	−6.7	−8.5	−9.6	−7.6
Montenegro	−11.4	−12.4	−11.0	−16.2	−16.1	−17.0	−14.3	−26.0	−21.0	−16.8	−11.6
North Macedonia	−1.6	−0.5	−2.0	−2.9	−1.0	−0.1	−3.3	−3.5	−2.1	−2.1	−2.5
Poland	−1.8	−2.6	−0.9	−0.8	−0.4	−1.3	0.5	3.4	2.3	1.6	0.0
Romania	−0.9	−0.3	−0.8	−1.6	−3.1	−4.6	−4.9	−5.2	−5.7	−5.5	−4.5
Russia	1.5	2.8	5.0	1.9	2.0	7.0	3.9	2.4	5.7	4.4	2.9
Serbia	−5.7	−5.6	−3.5	−2.9	−5.2	−4.8	−6.9	−4.3	−4.1	−4.4	−4.6
Turkey	−5.8	−4.1	−3.2	−3.1	−4.8	−2.8	0.9	−5.2	−2.4	−1.6	−1.9
Ukraine[1]	−9.2	−3.9	1.7	−1.5	−2.2	−3.3	−2.7	4.0	−0.7	−2.4	−4.0
Latin America and the Caribbean	**−2.9**	**−3.1**	**−3.3**	**−2.0**	**−1.7**	**−2.6**	**−2.0**	**0.0**	**−0.6**	**−1.0**	**−1.9**
Antigua and Barbuda	. . .	0.3	2.2	−2.4	−7.8	−14.5	−6.6	−8.0	−10.3	−9.9	−7.3
Argentina	−2.1	−1.6	−2.7	−2.7	−4.8	−5.2	−0.8	0.9	1.0	0.8	0.9
Aruba	−12.0	−4.8	3.9	4.6	1.0	−0.5	2.5	−13.1	−7.0	−4.7	2.8
The Bahamas	−14.4	−19.7	−13.5	−8.8	−12.7	−8.7	4.0	−18.1	−20.9	−15.8	−7.8
Barbados	−8.4	−9.2	−6.1	−4.3	−3.8	−4.0	−3.1	−7.3	−12.7	−8.4	−3.4
Belize	−4.6	−8.1	−10.1	−9.1	−8.5	−7.9	−9.3	−7.5	−8.2	−8.2	−8.1
Bolivia	3.4	1.7	−5.8	−5.6	−5.0	−4.5	−3.4	−0.5	−2.2	−2.8	−4.0
Brazil	−3.2	−4.1	−3.0	−1.4	−1.1	−2.7	−3.5	−1.8	−0.5	−1.7	−3.3
Chile	−4.8	−2.0	−2.4	−2.0	−2.3	−3.9	−3.7	1.4	−2.5	−2.2	−2.0
Colombia	−3.3	−5.3	−6.6	−4.5	−3.4	−4.1	−4.5	−3.4	−4.4	−4.0	−3.9

Table A12. Emerging Market and Developing Economies: Current Account Balance *(continued)*
(Percent of GDP)

	2013	2014	2015	2016	2017	2018	2019	2020	Projections 2021	2022	2026
Latin America and the											
Caribbean *(continued)*	**−2.9**	**−3.1**	**−3.3**	**−2.0**	**−1.7**	**−2.6**	**−2.0**	**0.0**	**−0.6**	**−1.0**	**−1.9**
Costa Rica	−4.8	−4.7	−3.4	−2.1	−3.6	−3.2	−2.1	−2.2	−3.0	−2.7	−2.5
Dominica	...	−5.4	−4.7	−7.7	−8.6	−42.4	−37.9	−24.5	−35.5	−24.9	−16.5
Dominican Republic	−4.1	−3.2	−1.8	−1.1	−0.2	−1.5	−1.3	−2.0	−2.0	−2.0	−2.0
Ecuador	−1.0	−0.7	−2.2	1.1	−0.2	−1.2	−0.1	2.5	1.7	1.7	2.0
El Salvador	−6.9	−5.4	−3.2	−2.3	−1.9	−3.3	−0.6	0.5	−2.8	−2.9	−3.6
Grenada	...	−11.6	−12.5	−11.0	−14.4	−15.5	−17.0	−22.2	−22.8	−20.6	−9.9
Guatemala	−4.2	−3.3	−1.2	1.0	1.1	0.9	2.3	5.5	4.3	3.0	1.5
Guyana	−9.9	−6.7	−3.4	1.5	−4.9	−29.0	−54.4	−14.5	−16.8	13.8	15.4
Haiti	−3.8	−5.0	−1.8	−1.9	−2.2	−2.9	−1.2	3.4	−0.3	0.2	−0.2
Honduras	−9.5	−6.9	−4.7	−3.1	−1.2	−5.7	−1.4	3.0	−3.0	−3.2	−4.0
Jamaica	−9.5	−8.0	−3.0	−0.3	−2.7	−1.6	−2.3	−0.1	−1.6	−3.7	−3.1
Mexico	−2.5	−1.9	−2.7	−2.3	−1.8	−2.1	−0.3	2.4	0.0	−0.3	−1.0
Nicaragua	−12.6	−8.0	−9.9	−8.5	−7.2	−1.8	6.0	7.6	4.1	4.0	0.7
Panama	−9.0	−13.4	−9.0	−7.8	−5.9	−7.6	−5.0	2.3	−3.7	−3.5	−2.6
Paraguay	1.6	−0.1	−0.4	3.6	3.0	0.1	−1.1	2.2	3.5	2.1	0.4
Peru	−5.1	−4.5	−5.0	−2.6	−1.3	−1.7	−0.9	0.8	0.4	0.1	−1.6
St. Kitts and Nevis	...	0.1	−8.3	−12.3	−10.5	−5.4	−4.8	−14.5	−11.3	−7.3	−5.7
St. Lucia	...	−2.5	0.0	−6.5	−1.0	2.2	6.1	−13.2	−13.5	−9.1	0.9
St. Vincent and the Grenadines	...	−26.1	−15.3	−13.9	−11.6	−12.1	−9.7	−16.0	−21.5	−13.4	−9.5
Suriname	−3.6	−7.4	−15.3	−4.8	1.9	−3.0	−11.3	9.0	3.4	−1.7	−1.6
Trinidad and Tobago	20.4	15.0	8.2	−3.5	6.3	6.9	4.4	0.1	13.2	18.8	13.3
Uruguay	−3.2	−3.0	−0.3	0.7	0.0	−0.5	1.3	−0.7	−1.3	−0.3	−2.0
Venezuela	1.8	2.4	−5.0	−1.4	6.1	8.8	7.8	−4.3	0.3	−0.7	...
Middle East and Central Asia	**8.6**	**5.0**	**−4.0**	**−4.2**	**−1.2**	**2.7**	**0.5**	**−2.4**	**1.7**	**1.5**	**−0.2**
Afghanistan[1]	1.4	6.5	3.7	9.0	7.6	12.2	11.7	11.2	...	...	...
Algeria	0.4	−4.4	−16.4	−16.5	−13.1	−9.6	−9.9	−12.7	−7.6	−5.5	−6.2
Armenia	−7.3	−7.8	−2.7	−1.0	−1.5	−7.0	−7.4	−3.8	−2.9	−4.0	−5.7
Azerbaijan	16.6	13.9	−0.4	−3.6	4.1	12.8	9.1	−0.5	7.8	7.7	4.3
Bahrain	7.4	4.6	−2.4	−4.6	−4.1	−6.5	−2.1	−9.3	−2.9	−2.9	−4.3
Djibouti	−30.8	23.9	29.2	−1.0	−4.8	14.2	16.9	10.7	−4.7	−3.0	1.6
Egypt	−2.2	−0.9	−3.7	−6.0	−6.1	−2.4	−3.6	−3.1	−3.9	−3.7	−2.6
Georgia	−5.6	−10.2	−11.8	−12.5	−8.1	−6.8	−5.5	−12.5	−10.0	−7.6	−5.5
Iran	5.8	2.8	0.4	3.2	3.3	5.9	0.6	−0.1	1.3	1.0	1.0
Iraq	1.1	2.6	−6.4	−7.5	−4.7	4.3	0.5	−10.8	6.2	4.0	−3.1
Jordan	−10.2	−7.1	−9.0	−9.7	−10.6	−6.9	−2.1	−8.0	−8.9	−4.4	−2.0
Kazakhstan	0.8	2.8	−3.3	−5.9	−3.1	−0.1	−4.0	−3.7	−0.9	−1.4	−3.2
Kuwait	40.3	33.4	3.5	−4.6	8.0	14.4	16.3	16.7	15.5	13.3	8.7
Kyrgyz Republic	−13.9	−17.0	−15.9	−11.6	−6.2	−12.1	−12.1	4.5	−7.7	−7.6	−6.4
Lebanon[1]	−28.0	−28.8	−19.8	−23.4	−26.3	−28.4	−27.6	−17.8	...	...	...
Libya[1]	0.0	−78.4	−54.3	−24.6	7.9	1.8	1.1	−12.2	19.2	15.4	18.4
Mauritania	−17.2	−22.2	−15.5	−11.0	−10.0	−13.3	−10.5	−7.6	−7.1	−8.9	−4.6
Morocco	−7.4	−6.0	−2.1	−4.1	−3.4	−5.3	−3.7	−1.5	−3.1	−3.3	−3.4
Oman	6.6	5.2	−15.9	−19.1	−15.6	−5.4	−5.5	−13.7	−5.8	−0.9	−0.3
Pakistan	−1.1	−1.3	−1.0	−1.8	−4.0	−6.1	−4.9	−1.7	−0.6	−3.1	−2.8
Qatar	30.4	24.0	8.5	−5.5	4.0	9.1	2.4	−2.4	8.2	11.6	8.6
Saudi Arabia	18.1	9.8	−8.7	−3.7	1.5	9.2	4.8	−2.8	3.9	3.8	−1.4
Somalia	−13.6	−8.3	−8.3	−9.3	−9.7	−7.6	−13.1	−17.2	−17.2	−15.6	−7.4
Sudan	−11.0	−5.8	−8.5	−6.5	−9.6	−14.0	−15.6	−17.5	−10.1	−9.4	−7.6
Syria[2]	...	...	...	...	...	...	...	...	...	...	...
Tajikistan	−10.4	−3.4	−6.1	−4.2	2.2	−5.0	−2.3	4.2	1.9	−1.9	−1.7
Tunisia	−9.7	−9.8	−9.7	−9.3	−10.3	−11.1	−8.4	−6.8	−7.3	−8.4	−7.4
Turkmenistan	−6.8	−6.6	−15.7	−24.2	−14.5	4.3	1.1	−2.6	0.6	−1.2	−5.3
United Arab Emirates	18.8	13.5	4.9	3.7	7.1	9.6	8.5	3.1	9.7	9.4	8.3
Uzbekistan	1.8	2.6	1.0	0.2	2.4	−6.8	−5.6	−5.0	−6.0	−5.6	−4.8
West Bank and Gaza	−14.8	−13.6	−13.9	−13.9	−13.2	−13.2	−10.4	−6.9	−9.5	−10.1	−9.7
Yemen	−3.1	−0.7	−6.2	−2.8	−1.4	−0.8	−3.9	−5.9	−8.8	−9.7	−9.7

Table A12. Emerging Market and Developing Economies: Current Account Balance *(continued)*
(Percent of GDP)

	2013	2014	2015	2016	2017	2018	2019	2020	Projections 2021	2022	2026
Sub-Saharan Africa	**–2.2**	**–3.5**	**–5.7**	**–3.5**	**–2.1**	**–2.4**	**–3.4**	**–3.0**	**–2.2**	**–2.7**	**–2.7**
Angola	6.1	–2.6	–8.8	–3.1	–0.5	7.3	6.1	1.5	7.3	5.7	1.6
Benin	–5.4	–6.7	–6.0	–3.0	–4.2	–4.6	–4.0	–3.9	–4.0	–4.3	–4.8
Botswana	4.5	10.9	2.2	8.0	5.8	0.7	–8.4	–10.6	–4.0	–1.9	4.2
Burkina Faso	–10.0	–7.2	–7.6	–6.1	–5.0	–4.1	–3.3	–0.1	–2.5	–4.1	–4.5
Burundi	–20.6	–15.6	–11.5	–11.1	–11.7	–11.4	–11.6	–10.4	–15.4	–14.4	–13.1
Cabo Verde	–4.9	–9.1	–3.2	–3.8	–7.8	–5.2	–0.4	–15.9	–13.2	–8.7	–2.8
Cameroon	–3.5	–4.0	–3.8	–3.2	–2.7	–3.6	–4.3	–3.7	–2.8	–2.2	–2.7
Central African Republic	–2.9	–13.3	–9.1	–5.3	–7.8	–8.0	–4.9	–8.6	–6.9	–6.1	–5.6
Chad	–9.1	–8.9	–13.8	–10.4	–7.1	–1.4	–4.8	–8.1	–5.2	–4.7	–3.4
Comoros	–4.0	–3.8	–0.3	–4.4	–2.1	–2.9	–3.3	–1.7	–4.1	–7.6	–6.9
Democratic Republic of the Congo	–9.5	–4.8	–3.9	–4.1	–3.3	–3.5	–3.2	–2.2	–2.1	–1.8	–1.3
Republic of Congo	10.8	1.0	–39.0	–48.7	–6.0	–0.1	0.4	–0.1	12.1	6.3	–5.2
Côte d'Ivoire	–1.0	1.0	–0.4	–0.9	–2.0	–3.9	–2.3	–3.5	–3.8	–3.4	–3.3
Equatorial Guinea	–2.4	–4.3	–16.4	–13.0	–5.8	–5.3	–6.1	–6.3	–4.2	–5.2	–17.4
Eritrea	2.3	17.3	20.8	15.3	24.0	15.4	12.1	10.9	12.4	12.7	10.1
Eswatini	10.8	11.6	13.0	7.9	6.2	1.3	4.3	6.7	1.4	–0.7	0.6
Ethiopia[1]	–5.9	–7.9	–11.5	–10.9	–8.5	–6.5	–5.3	–4.6	–2.9	. . .	. . .
Gabon	7.3	7.6	–5.6	–11.1	–8.7	–2.1	–0.9	–6.0	–3.8	–2.0	–2.4
The Gambia	–6.7	–7.3	–9.9	–9.2	–7.4	–9.5	–6.1	–3.6	–12.7	–13.3	–6.6
Ghana	–9.0	–6.8	–5.7	–5.1	–3.3	–3.0	–2.7	–3.1	–2.2	–3.5	–4.1
Guinea	–12.5	–14.4	–12.5	–30.7	–6.7	–19.5	–11.5	–13.7	–8.5	–11.2	–7.8
Guinea-Bissau	–4.3	0.5	1.8	1.4	0.3	–3.6	–8.8	–8.3	–5.5	–5.0	–3.9
Kenya	–7.8	–9.3	–6.3	–5.4	–6.9	–5.5	–5.5	–4.4	–5.0	–5.1	–5.0
Lesotho	–5.3	–5.2	–4.0	–6.7	–2.6	–1.4	–2.2	–2.1	–13.3	–9.6	–4.4
Liberia	–8.9	–34.7	–28.1	–22.9	–22.0	–21.5	–19.4	–17.5	–16.6	–20.5	–18.7
Madagascar	–6.5	–0.3	–1.6	0.5	–0.4	0.7	–2.3	–5.3	–5.8	–4.6	–3.4
Malawi	–5.9	–5.8	–12.2	–13.1	–17.8	–14.4	–11.9	–14.2	–15.8	–15.1	–14.3
Mali	–2.9	–4.7	–5.3	–7.2	–7.3	–4.9	–7.5	–0.2	–5.3	–5.0	–7.1
Mauritius	–6.2	–5.4	–3.6	–4.0	–4.6	–3.9	–5.4	–12.6	–18.6	–8.9	–4.3
Mozambique	–40.5	–36.3	–37.4	–32.2	–19.6	–30.3	–19.6	–27.2	–34.0	–23.0	–26.9
Namibia	–8.2	–9.4	–13.6	–16.5	–4.4	–3.4	–1.8	2.4	–7.3	–3.9	–0.4
Niger	–11.3	–12.1	–15.3	–11.4	–11.4	–12.6	–12.6	–13.5	–15.4	–16.1	–8.7
Nigeria	3.7	0.2	–3.1	1.3	3.4	1.5	–3.3	–4.0	–3.2	–2.2	–0.8
Rwanda	–7.5	–11.4	–12.7	–15.3	–9.3	–10.1	–12.1	–12.2	–13.4	–12.2	–6.8
São Tomé and Príncipe	–14.5	–20.7	–12.0	–6.1	–13.2	–12.3	–12.1	–14.1	–11.3	–7.5	–5.7
Senegal	–8.3	–7.0	–5.7	–4.2	–7.3	–8.8	–8.1	–10.2	–12.2	–11.6	–4.2
Seychelles	–11.9	–23.1	–18.6	–20.6	–19.6	–18.9	–16.1	–29.5	–28.9	–24.1	–15.6
Sierra Leone	–15.0	–9.4	–23.6	–9.4	–21.8	–18.6	–22.2	–16.7	–15.9	–14.3	–10.4
South Africa	–5.3	–4.7	–4.2	–2.6	–2.3	–3.2	–2.7	2.0	2.9	–0.9	–2.4
South Sudan	–3.9	–1.2	1.7	16.8	4.8	7.3	2.1	–5.8	–19.7	0.8	–4.2
Tanzania	–10.7	–9.8	–7.7	–4.2	–2.6	–3.1	–2.5	–1.8	–3.2	–3.8	–2.6
Togo	–9.0	–6.8	–7.6	–7.2	–1.5	–2.6	–0.8	–1.5	–2.7	–2.7	–1.6
Uganda	–5.7	–6.5	–6.1	–2.8	–4.8	–5.7	–6.4	–9.6	–8.9	–7.3	–10.2
Zambia	–0.8	2.1	–2.7	–3.3	–1.7	–1.3	0.6	10.4	13.5	14.9	13.2
Zimbabwe[1]	–13.9	–12.0	–8.0	–3.4	–1.2	–5.9	4.7	5.8	4.9	3.8	–2.2

[1]See the country-specific notes for Afghanistan, Albania, Ethiopia, Lebanon, Libya, Ukraine, and Zimbabwe in the "Country Notes" section of the Statistical Appendix.
[2]Data for Syria are excluded for 2011 onward owing to the uncertain political situation.

Table A13. Summary of Financial Account Balances
(Billions of US dollars)

	2013	2014	2015	2016	2017	2018	2019	2020	Projections 2021	Projections 2022
Advanced Economies										
Financial Account Balance	249.5	300.7	343.7	427.7	448.6	403.8	199.9	16.4	282.6	232.1
Direct Investment, Net	175.5	241.8	1.0	−313.7	324.5	−49.6	−86.6	47.4	7.4	103.3
Portfolio Investment, Net	−552.2	55.9	180.7	482.1	6.4	439.0	136.1	286.4	−31.2	−38.9
Financial Derivatives, Net	74.7	2.0	−85.7	35.9	21.9	51.8	29.2	109.6	44.5	53.6
Other Investment, Net	398.4	−139.0	21.3	44.3	−149.9	−165.0	54.9	−767.5	−90.8	−56.4
Change in Reserves	153.2	140.0	226.6	178.5	244.7	127.5	66.2	340.2	352.0	170.0
United States										
Financial Account Balance	−400.1	−297.1	−333.1	−363.6	−344.6	−348.4	−480.4	−653.0	−777.2	−870.3
Direct Investment, Net	104.7	135.7	−209.4	−174.6	28.6	−344.3	−180.0	100.4	−78.0	−108.3
Portfolio Investment, Net	−30.7	−114.9	−53.5	−195.0	−221.4	32.2	−190.6	−490.1	−237.4	−327.1
Financial Derivatives, Net	2.2	−54.3	−27.0	7.8	24.0	−20.4	−41.7	−5.8	−10.7	−11.9
Other Investment, Net	−473.2	−259.9	−37.0	−4.0	−174.1	−20.8	−72.7	−266.4	−449.0	−422.9
Change in Reserves	−3.1	−3.6	−6.3	2.1	−1.7	5.0	4.7	9.0	−2.1	0.0
Euro Area										
Financial Account Balance	379.1	368.7	319.2	308.8	387.6	358.6	224.2	292.9	...	...
Direct Investment, Net	9.9	88.6	281.1	119.7	49.0	162.0	−106.8	−207.2	...	...
Portfolio Investment, Net	−65.8	84.4	91.4	542.2	405.5	244.3	−46.7	690.3	...	...
Financial Derivatives, Net	2.0	49.7	126.3	13.4	25.9	47.1	1.2	0.6	...	...
Other Investment, Net	424.8	141.4	−191.5	−383.6	−91.4	−124.5	373.0	−205.8	...	...
Change in Reserves	8.3	4.6	11.8	17.1	−1.4	29.6	3.6	15.1	...	...
Germany										
Financial Account Balance	300.2	319.3	260.1	289.0	312.5	291.3	228.2	263.8	287.6	316.7
Direct Investment, Net	26.8	87.3	68.5	48.0	37.9	24.2	85.2	−0.7	39.2	47.1
Portfolio Investment, Net	210.0	179.9	210.5	220.0	229.6	181.5	82.2	48.8	113.9	99.1
Financial Derivatives, Net	31.7	51.2	33.7	31.7	12.6	26.6	27.5	113.1	43.0	36.3
Other Investment, Net	30.6	4.3	−50.2	−12.5	33.9	58.5	33.9	102.6	91.5	134.2
Change in Reserves	1.1	−3.4	−2.5	1.9	−1.4	0.5	−0.6	−0.1	0.0	0.0
France										
Financial Account Balance	−19.2	−10.3	−0.8	−18.6	−36.1	−28.4	−21.9	−59.9	−46.5	−41.9
Direct Investment, Net	−13.9	47.1	7.8	41.7	11.1	60.2	5.4	41.0	37.1	34.9
Portfolio Investment, Net	−79.2	−23.8	43.2	0.2	30.2	19.3	−76.9	−41.5	−22.1	−13.7
Financial Derivatives, Net	−22.3	−31.7	14.5	−17.6	−1.4	−30.5	4.1	−27.2	−18.5	−13.4
Other Investment, Net	98.1	−2.9	−74.2	−45.4	−72.6	−89.7	42.3	−36.8	−75.6	−55.0
Change in Reserves	−1.9	1.0	8.0	2.5	−3.4	12.3	3.2	4.6	32.6	5.4
Italy										
Financial Account Balance	32.4	73.0	43.1	36.2	53.8	31.5	52.1	56.0	81.7	95.0
Direct Investment, Net	0.9	3.1	2.0	−12.3	0.5	−4.9	1.6	10.7	−15.1	−16.2
Portfolio Investment, Net	−5.1	−2.2	105.7	154.8	95.0	142.0	−59.2	125.2	−75.6	−44.1
Financial Derivatives, Net	4.0	−1.9	1.2	−3.6	−8.2	−3.2	2.8	−3.3	−1.5	−0.5
Other Investment, Net	30.5	75.2	−66.5	−101.4	−36.5	−105.5	103.2	−81.2	153.2	155.8
Change in Reserves	2.0	−1.3	0.6	−1.3	3.0	3.1	3.6	4.6	20.7	0.0
Spain										
Financial Account Balance	41.2	22.8	31.8	39.2	40.0	39.3	27.9	19.7	28.8	45.2
Direct Investment, Net	−14.1	14.2	33.4	12.4	14.1	−15.8	11.2	17.9	20.0	20.9
Portfolio Investment, Net	−85.0	−8.8	12.0	64.9	37.1	28.3	−56.8	91.6	46.0	37.4
Financial Derivatives, Net	1.4	1.3	4.2	2.8	8.7	−0.9	−9.3	−4.9	0.0	0.0
Other Investment, Net	138.0	10.9	−23.3	−50.1	−24.0	25.1	82.0	−84.4	−50.5	−13.1
Change in Reserves	0.9	5.2	5.5	9.1	4.1	2.6	0.8	−0.4	13.2	0.0

Table A13. Summary of Financial Account Balances *(continued)*
(Billions of US dollars)

	2013	2014	2015	2016	2017	2018	2019	2020	Projections 2021	2022
Japan										
Financial Account Balance	−4.3	58.9	180.9	266.5	168.3	183.9	228.5	144.2	173.3	175.2
Direct Investment, Net	144.6	118.7	133.3	137.5	155.0	134.6	219.1	105.1	152.4	163.3
Portfolio Investment, Net	−280.4	−42.3	131.5	276.3	−50.6	92.2	87.4	37.0	−3.4	−25.1
Financial Derivatives, Net	58.1	34.0	17.7	−16.1	30.4	0.9	3.2	8.4	8.4	8.4
Other Investment, Net	34.6	−60.0	−106.7	−125.6	10.0	−67.9	−106.7	−17.2	−37.7	17.0
Change in Reserves	38.7	8.5	5.1	−5.7	23.6	24.0	25.5	10.9	53.6	11.5
United Kingdom										
Financial Account Balance	−127.4	−141.6	−158.2	−163.3	−87.5	−113.5	−105.8	−122.5	−107.5	−119.4
Direct Investment, Net	−11.2	−176.1	−106.0	−297.4	46.1	−23.9	−51.6	−53.2	31.1	27.5
Portfolio Investment, Net	−284.6	15.9	−230.1	−203.8	−126.2	−359.8	42.1	14.7	−168.6	−186.7
Financial Derivatives, Net	63.4	31.2	−128.6	29.3	13.3	11.2	11.3	37.9	5.5	6.1
Other Investment, Net	97.2	−24.4	274.3	299.8	−29.4	234.2	−106.6	−118.7	13.1	21.0
Change in Reserves	7.8	11.7	32.2	8.8	8.8	24.8	−1.1	−3.3	11.5	12.8
Canada										
Financial Account Balance	−57.2	−43.1	−51.8	−45.4	−44.2	−35.0	−38.6	−27.8	8.3	7.1
Direct Investment, Net	−12.0	1.3	23.6	33.5	53.4	19.2	31.1	22.3	1.3	51.9
Portfolio Investment, Net	−34.8	−32.8	−36.2	−103.6	−74.9	3.5	−2.4	−61.1	−98.2	7.3
Financial Derivatives, Net	...	...	...	...	...	...	...	...	...	...
Other Investment, Net	−15.2	−16.9	−47.8	19.1	−23.5	−56.1	−65.9	11.7	105.3	−52.1
Change in Reserves	4.7	5.3	8.6	5.6	0.8	−1.5	−1.3	−0.7	0.0	0.0
Other Advanced Economies[1]										
Financial Account Balance	376.0	297.6	295.3	325.4	306.7	339.7	320.1	368.8	513.2	494.9
Direct Investment, Net	31.2	−6.1	−102.5	−81.0	−163.2	15.2	−73.1	−2.2	−65.0	−33.8
Portfolio Investment, Net	141.0	174.0	324.7	247.6	151.3	368.5	305.1	270.0	294.0	295.7
Financial Derivatives, Net	−33.5	−22.3	−11.9	3.4	−5.5	32.1	23.0	7.2	12.8	19.1
Other Investment, Net	136.2	40.5	−90.8	4.6	109.9	−125.5	34.5	−213.4	66.1	81.5
Change in Reserves	101.3	111.5	176.0	150.2	213.1	49.5	30.7	307.0	204.6	131.8
Emerging Market and Developing Economies										
Financial Account Balance	−30.0	16.0	−304.3	−412.8	−260.2	−252.9	−144.4	67.8	394.4	298.4
Direct Investment, Net	−483.0	−428.3	−346.1	−258.7	−312.4	−375.3	−359.4	−341.5	−401.3	−433.0
Portfolio Investment, Net	−147.7	−88.8	130.0	−56.0	−207.7	−99.2	−55.4	−6.4	−92.2	−165.6
Financial Derivatives, Net	...	...	...	...	...	...	...	...	...	...
Other Investment, Net	60.5	408.3	471.6	385.1	85.4	97.6	96.6	308.0	161.6	323.3
Change in Reserves	544.4	96.0	−579.6	−483.7	177.2	127.0	170.0	76.3	715.4	554.2

Table A13. Summary of Financial Account Balances *(continued)*
(Billions of US dollars)

	2013	2014	2015	2016	2017	2018	2019	2020	Projections 2021	2022
Regional Groups										
Emerging and Developing Asia										
Financial Account Balance	27.7	153.6	72.1	−27.4	−57.7	−260.5	−53.0	166.2	248.1	236.7
Direct Investment, Net	−271.2	−201.6	−139.6	−26.2	−108.5	−169.8	−144.8	−167.7	−188.7	−202.2
Portfolio Investment, Net	−64.5	−125.2	81.7	31.1	−70.1	−99.5	−73.5	−96.9	−118.4	−184.1
Financial Derivatives, Net	−2.0	0.7	0.7	−4.6	2.3	4.7	−2.6	16.0	11.1	11.3
Other Investment, Net	−83.4	281.6	460.4	357.7	−79.9	−17.3	70.8	247.4	115.3	221.4
Change in Reserves	447.9	197.4	−330.7	−384.7	198.8	21.9	97.7	166.6	427.2	388.1
Emerging and Developing Europe										
Financial Account Balance	−66.8	−29.1	65.4	5.6	−19.6	99.3	63.1	19.4	104.5	76.3
Direct Investment, Net	−15.4	0.5	−22.0	−45.4	−28.8	−26.0	−51.0	−29.4	−38.8	−48.8
Portfolio Investment, Net	−38.0	23.2	54.9	−7.7	−34.4	13.3	−2.6	16.0	−1.4	−1.5
Financial Derivatives, Net	−0.9	5.8	5.0	0.4	−2.5	−2.8	1.6	−0.1	1.6	7.9
Other Investment, Net	−4.6	64.0	35.5	22.7	30.0	67.3	21.8	36.1	29.6	59.2
Change in Reserves	−7.6	−122.7	−7.9	35.6	16.2	47.6	93.3	−3.1	113.6	59.6
Latin America and the Caribbean										
Financial Account Balance	−197.5	−193.0	−192.0	−105.4	−108.9	−160.9	−122.9	−3.2	−25.4	−47.7
Direct Investment, Net	−151.4	−136.4	−136.1	−125.0	−121.3	−149.5	−115.0	−92.3	−121.7	−128.3
Portfolio Investment, Net	−100.0	−107.9	−46.8	−49.8	−38.0	−13.8	3.4	4.2	19.7	2.3
Financial Derivatives, Net	1.8	6.8	1.4	−2.9	3.9	4.1	4.9	5.7	8.0	8.4
Other Investment, Net	39.6	4.7	18.1	51.2	29.1	−15.6	16.5	67.9	14.6	42.4
Change in Reserves	12.5	39.8	−28.6	21.0	17.1	13.7	−32.7	11.2	53.9	27.5
Middle East and Central Asia										
Financial Account Balance	261.7	162.5	−182.2	−219.9	−29.0	110.6	24.5	−84.5	95.6	77.2
Direct Investment, Net	−22.8	−42.7	−10.7	−29.1	−16.4	−8.7	−20.1	−25.4	−28.1	−24.4
Portfolio Investment, Net	76.3	129.7	61.8	−12.2	−41.1	5.2	26.3	60.1	18.3	27.6
Financial Derivatives, Net	. . .	. . .	. . .	. . .	. . .	. . .	. . .	. . .	. . .	. . .
Other Investment, Net	119.0	68.2	−50.7	−36.3	106.1	82.7	12.4	−39.2	11.5	5.4
Change in Reserves	91.6	−9.6	−196.3	−150.6	−70.8	39.3	5.3	−89.3	104.7	78.7
Sub-Saharan Africa										
Financial Account Balance	−55.0	−78.0	−67.7	−65.8	−45.1	−41.3	−56.1	−30.1	−28.4	−44.1
Direct Investment, Net	−22.2	−48.2	−37.7	−33.0	−37.3	−21.3	−28.4	−26.7	−24.2	−29.3
Portfolio Investment, Net	−21.4	−8.6	−21.5	−17.5	−24.0	−4.4	−9.1	10.1	−10.5	−9.9
Financial Derivatives, Net	−0.8	−1.5	−0.3	0.9	0.3	−0.6	0.3	0.7	0.7	0.8
Other Investment, Net	−10.1	−10.2	8.3	−10.2	0.1	−19.5	−24.9	−4.1	−9.4	−5.1
Change in Reserves	0.0	−9.0	−16.1	−5.0	15.8	4.6	6.3	−9.1	16.0	0.2

Table A13. Summary of Financial Account Balances *(continued)*
(Billions of US dollars)

	2013	2014	2015	2016	2017	2018	2019	2020	Projections 2021	Projections 2022
Analytical Groups										
By Source of Export Earnings										
Fuel										
Financial Account Balance	308.3	186.7	−178.5	−180.8	19.3	179.4	68.1	−53.3	117.8	117.1
Direct Investment, Net	−2.5	−28.5	−9.7	−17.4	10.3	15.1	−4.9	−11.8	−14.5	−7.7
Portfolio Investment, Net	76.6	137.7	67.7	−10.0	−35.6	6.5	24.9	57.0	43.0	38.6
Financial Derivatives, Net	. . .	. . .	. . .	. . .	. . .	. . .	. . .	. . .	. . .	. . .
Other Investment, Net	156.8	94.9	−17.0	2.3	116.9	112.5	36.2	−14.4	−5.2	35.5
Change in Reserves	79.5	−34.6	−233.5	−164.3	−65.9	52.9	10.8	−94.0	104.6	59.9
Nonfuel										
Financial Account Balance	−338.3	−170.6	−125.8	−232.1	−279.6	−432.3	−212.4	121.2	276.6	181.3
Direct Investment, Net	−480.5	−399.8	−336.4	−241.3	−322.7	−390.3	−354.4	−329.7	−386.8	−425.3
Portfolio Investment, Net	−224.3	−226.4	62.3	−46.1	−172.1	−105.7	−80.3	−63.4	−135.2	−204.2
Financial Derivatives, Net	−1.9	11.8	6.8	−6.1	4.0	5.4	4.2	22.4	21.5	28.4
Other Investment, Net	−96.3	313.4	488.6	382.8	−31.5	−14.9	60.4	322.4	166.8	287.8
Change in Reserves	464.9	130.6	−346.1	−319.4	243.1	74.2	159.3	170.3	610.8	494.3
By External Financing Source										
Net Debtor Economies										
Financial Account Balance	−410.2	−366.7	−310.6	−273.4	−318.0	−369.6	−288.2	−79.0	−114.0	−187.3
Direct Investment, Net	−263.7	−274.9	−283.4	−295.7	−275.6	−316.4	−298.7	−245.4	−286.7	−316.9
Portfolio Investment, Net	−180.8	−200.1	−40.6	−58.6	−118.7	−20.3	−25.9	−32.6	−53.8	−87.6
Financial Derivatives, Net	. . .	. . .	. . .	. . .	. . .	. . .	. . .	. . .	. . .	. . .
Other Investment, Net	−43.0	−8.5	35.8	19.9	−13.3	−37.1	−67.1	49.4	−25.1	57.1
Change in Reserves	79.0	107.8	−20.3	75.4	86.4	4.4	105.4	142.0	243.5	145.2
Net Debtor Economies by Debt-Servicing Experience										
Economies with Arrears and/or Rescheduling during 2016–20										
Financial Account Balance	−52.8	−44.8	−65.7	−76.2	−47.2	−39.3	−46.3	−22.9	−17.9	−31.8
Direct Investment, Net	−14.7	−23.6	−37.4	−30.0	−21.9	−26.2	−29.9	−21.9	−22.0	−27.0
Portfolio Investment, Net	−11.7	−4.4	1.0	−9.0	−28.9	−16.3	−12.5	10.3	−21.6	−8.4
Financial Derivatives, Net	. . .	. . .	. . .	. . .	. . .	. . .	. . .	. . .	. . .	. . .
Other Investment, Net	−25.5	−6.0	−24.4	−37.0	5.4	−1.0	0.9	6.7	20.1	−7.8
Change in Reserves	−0.7	−10.5	−4.5	0.1	−1.4	4.6	−4.4	−17.3	6.4	12.6
Memorandum										
World										
Financial Account Balance	219.5	316.7	39.4	14.9	188.4	150.9	55.5	84.2	677.0	530.6

Note: The estimates in this table are based on individual countries' national accounts and balance of payments statistics. Country group composites are calculated as the sum of the US dollar values for the relevant individual countries. Some group aggregates for the financial derivatives are not shown because of incomplete data. Projections for the euro area are not available because of data constraints.
[1]Excludes the Group of Seven (Canada, France, Germany, Italy, Japan, United Kingdom, United States) and euro area countries.

Table A14. Summary of Net Lending and Borrowing
(Percent of GDP)

| | Averages | | | | | | | | Projections | | |
	2003–12	2007–14	2015	2016	2017	2018	2019	2020	2021	2022	Average 2023–26
Advanced Economies											
Net Lending and Borrowing	−0.6	−0.2	0.6	0.8	1.0	0.7	0.6	0.3	0.5	0.4	0.5
Current Account Balance	−0.6	−0.2	0.6	0.8	1.0	0.8	0.6	0.3	0.4	0.3	0.5
Savings	21.7	21.5	23.0	22.6	23.3	23.4	23.4	23.0	23.6	24.0	24.0
Investment	22.3	21.7	21.8	21.6	22.1	22.3	22.6	22.3	22.4	23.1	23.0
Capital Account Balance	0.0	0.0	−0.1	0.0	0.0	−0.1	−0.1	0.0	0.0	0.0	0.0
United States											
Net Lending and Borrowing	−4.3	−3.1	−2.3	−2.2	−1.8	−2.2	−2.2	−3.0	−3.5	−3.5	−2.8
Current Account Balance	−4.2	−3.1	−2.2	−2.1	−1.9	−2.1	−2.2	−2.9	−3.5	−3.5	−2.8
Savings	16.8	16.9	20.2	18.9	19.5	19.6	19.4	19.2	19.1	20.2	20.7
Investment	21.0	20.0	21.2	20.6	20.8	21.1	21.4	21.2	21.1	22.4	22.3
Capital Account Balance	0.0	0.0	0.0	0.0	0.1	0.0	0.0	0.0	0.0	0.0	0.0
Euro Area											
Net Lending and Borrowing	0.0	0.4	2.9	3.1	3.0	2.7	2.1	2.1	. . .	. . .	. . .
Current Account Balance	−0.1	0.3	2.7	3.0	3.2	3.0	2.4	2.2	2.6	2.7	2.8
Savings	22.7	22.6	23.8	24.3	24.9	25.4	25.8	24.6	25.6	25.8	25.9
Investment	22.0	21.3	20.4	20.7	21.3	21.9	22.8	21.9	22.4	22.5	22.6
Capital Account Balance	0.1	0.1	0.2	0.0	−0.2	−0.3	−0.2	0.0	. . .	. . .	. . .
Germany											
Net Lending and Borrowing	5.4	6.4	8.6	8.6	7.7	7.9	7.4	6.8	6.8	6.9	6.9
Current Account Balance	5.4	6.4	8.6	8.5	7.8	7.8	7.4	6.9	6.8	6.9	6.9
Savings	25.7	26.8	28.3	28.5	28.8	29.7	29.6	28.1	29.1	29.1	29.2
Investment	20.3	20.4	19.7	20.0	21.0	21.9	22.1	21.1	22.3	22.2	22.3
Capital Account Balance	0.0	0.0	0.0	0.1	−0.1	0.0	0.0	−0.1	0.0	0.0	0.0
France											
Net Lending and Borrowing	−0.2	−0.7	−0.4	−0.4	−0.8	−0.7	−0.2	−1.8	−1.6	−1.3	−0.8
Current Account Balance	−0.2	−0.7	−0.4	−0.5	−0.8	−0.8	−0.3	−1.9	−1.7	−1.4	−0.9
Savings	22.4	22.1	22.3	22.1	22.7	23.0	24.1	21.8	24.0	23.7	23.4
Investment	22.6	22.8	22.7	22.6	23.4	23.9	24.4	23.7	25.7	25.2	24.3
Capital Account Balance	0.0	0.0	0.0	0.1	0.0	0.1	0.1	0.1	0.1	0.1	0.1
Italy											
Net Lending and Borrowing	−1.5	−1.1	1.8	2.4	2.6	2.5	3.1	3.5	3.9	4.2	4.3
Current Account Balance	−1.6	−1.2	1.4	2.6	2.6	2.5	3.2	3.5	3.7	3.6	3.6
Savings	19.2	18.4	18.5	20.2	20.6	21.0	21.2	21.0	23.2	23.4	23.7
Investment	20.8	19.5	17.1	17.6	18.1	18.5	18.0	17.5	19.5	19.8	20.2
Capital Account Balance	0.1	0.1	0.4	−0.2	0.1	0.0	−0.1	0.0	0.1	0.6	0.7
Spain											
Net Lending and Borrowing	−4.9	−2.7	2.7	3.4	3.0	2.4	2.5	1.1	2.0	2.9	2.1
Current Account Balance	−5.4	−3.1	2.0	3.2	2.8	1.9	2.1	0.7	0.4	1.4	1.3
Savings	20.5	19.2	21.0	21.9	22.2	22.4	23.0	21.4	21.5	23.3	23.3
Investment	25.9	22.3	19.0	18.8	19.4	20.5	20.9	20.7	21.1	21.9	22.1
Capital Account Balance	0.5	0.4	0.6	0.2	0.2	0.5	0.3	0.4	1.6	1.5	0.8
Japan											
Net Lending and Borrowing	3.0	2.3	3.0	3.8	4.1	3.5	3.4	3.2	3.4	3.3	3.2
Current Account Balance	3.1	2.3	3.1	4.0	4.1	3.5	3.4	3.3	3.5	3.3	3.2
Savings	27.9	26.6	28.2	28.8	29.3	29.1	29.3	28.8	29.0	28.7	28.1
Investment	24.8	24.2	25.2	24.8	25.2	25.6	25.8	25.6	25.5	25.3	24.9
Capital Account Balance	−0.1	−0.1	−0.1	−0.1	−0.1	0.0	−0.1	0.0	−0.1	−0.1	−0.1
United Kingdom											
Net Lending and Borrowing	−2.8	−3.6	−5.1	−5.5	−3.8	−3.8	−3.1	−3.8	−3.5	−3.5	−3.1
Current Account Balance	−2.8	−3.6	−5.0	−5.4	−3.8	−3.7	−3.1	−3.7	−3.4	−3.4	−3.0
Savings	14.1	12.9	12.7	12.4	14.4	14.1	15.2	13.5	13.7	15.8	14.5
Investment	16.9	16.5	17.7	17.8	18.2	17.8	18.3	17.2	17.1	19.2	17.5
Capital Account Balance	0.0	0.0	−0.1	−0.1	−0.1	−0.2	0.0	−0.1	−0.1	−0.1	−0.1

Table A14. Summary of Net Lending and Borrowing *(continued)*
(Percent of GDP)

	Averages								Projections		
	2003–12	2007–14	2015	2016	2017	2018	2019	2020	2021	2022	Average 2023–26
Canada											
Net Lending and Borrowing	−0.5	−2.1	−3.5	−3.1	−2.8	−2.3	−2.1	−1.8	0.5	0.2	−1.3
Current Account Balance	−0.5	−2.2	−3.5	−3.1	−2.8	−2.3	−2.1	−1.8	0.5	0.2	−1.3
Savings	22.6	21.9	20.3	19.7	20.7	20.9	20.9	20.3	24.6	25.1	24.1
Investment	23.1	24.0	23.8	22.8	23.6	23.2	23.0	22.1	24.1	24.9	25.4
Capital Account Balance	0.0	0.0	0.0	0.0	0.0	0.0	0.0	0.0	0.0	0.0	0.0
Other Advanced Economies[1]											
Net Lending and Borrowing	4.0	4.1	5.1	5.1	4.8	4.7	4.9	5.6	6.1	5.6	4.9
Current Account Balance	4.0	4.2	5.5	5.1	4.8	4.5	4.9	5.6	6.1	5.6	4.9
Savings	30.4	30.5	31.0	30.4	30.8	30.3	30.3	31.6	32.4	32.0	31.3
Investment	26.1	26.1	25.2	25.2	25.7	25.7	25.3	25.6	25.7	25.9	25.9
Capital Account Balance	0.0	−0.1	−0.4	0.0	0.1	0.2	0.0	0.0	0.0	0.0	0.1
Emerging Market and Developing Economies											
Net Lending and Borrowing	2.6	1.7	−0.1	−0.2	0.0	−0.1	0.1	0.7	1.0	0.7	0.1
Current Account Balance	2.5	1.6	−0.2	−0.3	−0.1	−0.2	0.0	0.6	0.8	0.6	0.0
Savings	31.5	32.6	31.5	31.1	31.6	32.4	32.3	33.3	33.9	33.9	33.4
Investment	29.4	31.3	32.2	31.6	32.0	32.9	32.6	33.1	33.2	33.5	33.6
Capital Account Balance	0.2	0.1	0.1	0.1	0.1	0.1	0.1	0.1	0.1	0.1	0.1
Regional Groups											
Emerging and Developing Asia											
Net Lending and Borrowing	3.5	2.8	1.9	1.3	0.9	−0.3	0.5	1.6	1.1	0.9	0.4
Current Account Balance	3.4	2.7	1.9	1.3	0.9	−0.3	0.5	1.6	1.1	0.9	0.4
Savings	41.3	43.1	41.1	39.9	40.1	39.9	39.5	40.6	40.1	40.2	39.5
Investment	38.2	40.4	39.3	38.6	39.2	40.2	39.1	38.9	39.0	39.3	39.1
Capital Account Balance	0.1	0.1	0.0	0.0	0.0	0.0	0.0	0.0	0.0	0.0	0.0
Emerging and Developing Europe											
Net Lending and Borrowing	−0.3	−0.9	1.7	0.1	−0.2	2.2	1.8	0.8	2.4	1.8	0.8
Current Account Balance	−0.4	−1.0	1.0	−0.3	−0.5	1.7	1.3	0.1	1.6	1.0	0.2
Savings	23.1	23.1	24.6	23.5	24.0	25.5	24.2	24.0	25.9	25.4	25.1
Investment	23.3	24.0	23.6	23.7	24.5	23.5	22.8	23.9	24.1	24.4	24.9
Capital Account Balance	0.1	0.2	0.7	0.3	0.3	0.5	0.5	0.7	0.7	0.8	0.6
Latin America and the Caribbean											
Net Lending and Borrowing	−0.2	−1.7	−3.2	−2.0	−1.7	−2.6	−1.9	0.1	−0.5	−0.9	−1.6
Current Account Balance	−0.3	−1.7	−3.3	−2.0	−1.7	−2.6	−2.0	0.0	−0.6	−1.0	−1.6
Savings	20.9	20.2	16.3	16.6	16.2	16.4	16.7	17.4	18.9	19.0	18.7
Investment	21.2	22.0	21.0	18.3	18.2	19.1	18.7	17.8	19.5	20.1	20.6
Capital Account Balance	0.1	0.1	0.0	0.0	0.0	0.0	0.0	0.1	0.1	0.1	0.1
Middle East and Central Asia											
Net Lending and Borrowing	8.8	8.1	−3.6	−4.0	−1.2	2.8	0.6	−2.3	1.8	1.6	0.3
Current Account Balance	9.1	8.3	−4.0	−4.2	−1.2	2.7	0.5	−2.4	1.7	1.5	0.3
Savings	36.0	36.0	24.4	23.9	26.7	29.2	28.9	26.6	30.9	30.4	28.9
Investment	28.5	29.6	29.9	29.6	29.8	28.5	30.7	31.3	30.2	30.0	29.7
Capital Account Balance	0.2	0.1	0.1	0.1	0.0	0.0	0.0	0.0	0.1	0.1	0.1
Sub-Saharan Africa											
Net Lending and Borrowing	1.6	−0.4	−5.3	−3.1	−1.7	−2.0	−3.0	−2.5	−1.8	−2.3	−2.5
Current Account Balance	0.4	−1.2	−5.7	−3.5	−2.1	−2.4	−3.4	−3.0	−2.2	−2.7	−2.8
Savings	20.6	20.2	17.0	18.0	18.5	19.3	19.6	19.9	21.1	20.8	21.2
Investment	20.4	21.6	22.3	21.2	20.7	21.6	23.2	23.1	23.3	23.5	24.1
Capital Account Balance	1.2	0.8	0.4	0.4	0.4	0.4	0.4	0.4	0.5	0.4	0.3

Table A14. Summary of Net Lending and Borrowing *(continued)*
(Percent of GDP)

	Averages								Projections		
	2003–12	2007–14	2015	2016	2017	2018	2019	2020	2021	2022	Average 2023–26
Analytical Groups											
By Source of Export Earnings											
Fuel											
Net Lending and Borrowing	11.8	10.2	–3.9	–2.8	1.0	5.3	2.0	–2.0	2.6	2.6	1.1
Current Account Balance	12.0	10.3	–4.0	–2.9	1.1	5.3	2.0	–2.0	2.7	2.7	1.2
Savings	38.6	37.6	23.9	24.7	27.7	31.7	31.6	28.9	34.1	33.5	31.2
Investment	28.0	29.2	31.3	28.1	28.9	28.5	31.9	34.1	32.6	32.2	31.4
Capital Account Balance	0.2	0.1	–0.1	0.0	0.0	0.0	0.0	0.0	0.0	0.0	0.0
Nonfuel											
Net Lending and Borrowing	1.1	0.3	0.4	0.1	–0.1	–0.7	–0.1	1.0	0.7	0.5	–0.1
Current Account Balance	0.9	0.2	0.3	0.0	–0.2	–0.8	–0.2	0.9	0.6	0.3	–0.2
Savings	30.4	31.8	32.6	31.9	32.1	32.5	32.4	33.8	33.8	34.0	33.7
Investment	29.6	31.7	32.4	32.0	32.3	33.3	32.7	33.0	33.2	33.7	33.9
Capital Account Balance	0.2	0.1	0.2	0.1	0.1	0.1	0.1	0.1	0.1	0.1	0.1
By External Financing Source											
Net Debtor Economies											
Net Lending and Borrowing	–1.1	–2.1	–2.3	–1.8	–1.9	–2.3	–1.7	–0.4	–0.9	–1.1	–1.7
Current Account Balance	–1.5	–2.4	–2.6	–2.0	–2.1	–2.6	–1.9	–0.6	–1.2	–1.4	–1.9
Savings	23.4	23.4	22.2	22.2	22.4	22.6	22.6	23.1	23.2	23.3	23.5
Investment	25.0	25.8	24.9	24.3	24.5	25.1	24.6	23.8	24.5	24.8	25.5
Capital Account Balance	0.3	0.3	0.3	0.2	0.2	0.2	0.2	0.3	0.3	0.3	0.2
Net Debtor Economies by Debt-Servicing Experience											
Economies with Arrears and/or Rescheduling during 2016–20											
Net Lending and Borrowing	–0.9	–2.9	–6.2	–6.1	–5.1	–4.1	–4.1	–2.3	–2.7	–2.5	–2.9
Current Account Balance	–1.7	–3.5	–6.6	–6.3	–5.5	–4.5	–4.4	–2.7	–3.0	–2.8	–3.1
Savings	21.2	19.8	15.7	15.0	16.2	17.6	16.5	15.3	16.2	17.2	18.1
Investment	23.2	23.4	22.4	21.8	22.4	21.9	21.9	18.4	19.7	20.4	21.7
Capital Account Balance	0.8	0.6	0.4	0.3	0.4	0.3	0.3	0.4	0.3	0.3	0.2
Memorandum											
World											
Net Lending and Borrowing	0.3	0.4	0.3	0.4	0.6	0.4	0.4	0.5	0.7	0.5	0.3
Current Account Balance	0.2	0.4	0.3	0.4	0.6	0.4	0.4	0.4	0.6	0.4	0.3
Savings	24.7	25.4	26.3	25.9	26.6	27.0	27.0	27.2	27.8	28.1	28.0
Investment	24.5	25.1	25.9	25.4	26.0	26.5	26.6	26.6	26.8	27.3	27.5
Capital Account Balance	0.1	0.0	0.0	0.0	0.0	0.0	0.0	0.0	0.1	0.1	0.1

Note: The estimates in this table are based on individual countries' national accounts and balance of payments statistics. Country group composites are calculated as the sum of the US dollar values for the relevant individual countries. This differs from the calculations in the April 2005 and earlier issues of the *World Economic Outlook*, in which the composites were weighted by GDP valued at purchasing power parities as a share of total world GDP. The estimates of gross national savings and investment (or gross capital formation) are from individual countries' national accounts statistics. The estimates of the current account balance, the capital account balance, and the financial account balance (or net lending/net borrowing) are from the balance of payments statistics. The link between domestic transactions and transactions with the rest of the world can be expressed as accounting identities. Savings (S) minus investment (I) is equal to the current account balance (CAB) (S – I = CAB). Also, net lending/net borrowing (NLB) is the sum of the current account balance and the capital account balance (KAB) (NLB = CAB + KAB). In practice, these identities do not hold exactly; imbalances result from imperfections in source data and compilation as well as from asymmetries in group composition due to data availability.
[1]Excludes the Group of Seven (Canada, France, Germany, Italy, Japan, United Kingdom, United States) and euro area countries.

Table A15. Summary of World Medium-Term Baseline Scenario

	Averages				Projections		Averages	
	2003–12	2013–22	2019	2020	2021	2022	2019–22	2023–26
	Annual Percent Change							
World Real GDP	**4.2**	**3.1**	**2.8**	**−3.1**	**5.9**	**4.9**	**2.6**	**3.4**
Advanced Economies	1.7	1.9	1.7	−4.5	5.2	4.5	1.7	1.8
Emerging Market and Developing Economies	6.6	4.1	3.7	−2.1	6.4	5.1	3.2	4.5
Memorandum								
Potential Output								
Major Advanced Economies	1.7	1.2	1.4	−1.3	2.5	2.3	1.2	1.8
World Trade, Volume[1]	**5.6**	**3.0**	**0.9**	**−8.2**	**9.7**	**6.7**	**2.0**	**3.9**
Imports								
Advanced Economies	3.9	3.0	2.0	−9.0	9.0	7.3	2.1	3.3
Emerging Market and Developing Economies	9.8	3.2	−0.9	−8.0	12.1	7.1	2.3	5.0
Exports								
Advanced Economies	4.6	2.6	1.2	−9.4	8.0	6.6	1.3	3.3
Emerging Market and Developing Economies	8.3	3.5	0.4	−5.2	11.6	5.8	2.9	4.5
Terms of Trade								
Advanced Economies	−0.4	0.6	0.2	0.8	0.9	0.2	0.5	0.3
Emerging Market and Developing Economies	1.6	−0.5	−1.2	−1.0	1.6	−0.1	−0.2	−0.6
World Prices in US Dollars								
Manufactures	3.1	−0.2	0.5	−3.2	5.5	4.4	1.7	1.6
Oil	15.5	−4.8	−10.2	−32.7	59.1	−1.8	−1.4	−3.3
Nonfuel Primary Commodities	10.3	0.7	0.8	6.7	26.7	−0.9	7.8	−0.3
Consumer Prices								
Advanced Economies	2.0	1.5	1.4	0.7	2.8	2.3	1.8	1.9
Emerging Market and Developing Economies	6.4	4.9	5.1	5.1	5.5	4.9	5.1	4.1
Interest Rates				*Percent*				
Real Six-Month LIBOR[2]	0.2	−0.9	0.5	−0.5	−3.1	−2.4	−1.4	−0.4
World Real Long-Term Interest Rate[3]	1.4	−0.2	−0.2	−0.3	−2.2	−1.4	−1.0	−0.2
Current Account Balances				*Percent of GDP*				
Advanced Economies	−0.6	0.6	0.6	0.3	0.4	0.3	0.4	0.5
Emerging Market and Developing Economies	2.5	0.2	0.0	0.6	0.8	0.6	0.5	0.0
Total External Debt								
Emerging Market and Developing Economies	28.2	30.6	30.6	32.6	31.3	30.4	31.2	29.4
Debt Service								
Emerging Market and Developing Economies	9.2	11.0	10.9	11.4	10.8	10.7	11.0	10.5

[1]Data refer to trade in goods and services.
[2]London interbank offered rate on US dollar deposits minus percent change in US GDP deflator.
[3]GDP-weighted average of 10-year (or nearest-maturity) government bond rates for Canada, France, Germany, Italy, Japan, the United Kingdom, and the United States.

WORLD ECONOMIC OUTLOOK
SELECTED TOPICS

World Economic Outlook Archives

I. Methodology—Aggregation, Modeling, and Forecasting

II. Historical Surveys

III. Economic Growth—Sources and Patterns

IV. Inflation and Deflation and Commodity Markets

V. Fiscal Policy

VI. Monetary Policy, Financial Markets, and Flow of Funds

VII. Labor Markets, Poverty, and Inequality

VIII. Exchange Rate Issues

IX. External Payments, Trade, Capital Movements, and Foreign Debt

X. Regional Issues

XI. Country-Specific Analyses

XII. Climate Change Issues

XIII. Special Topics

The following remarks were made by the Chair at the conclusion of the Executive Board's discussion of the Fiscal Monitor, Global Financial Stability Report, *and* World Economic Outlook *on September 28, 2021.*

Executive Directors broadly agreed with staff's assessment of the global economic outlook, risks, and policy priorities. They welcomed the continuing recovery, despite the resurgence of the pandemic driven by more contagious new variants of the virus and the ongoing supply shortages that brought the inflation risk to the forefront. Directors acknowledged that economic divergences, especially between advanced economies and low-income countries, brought on by the pandemic seem more persistent, a reflection of differentiated vaccine access and early policy support. In this context, Directors highlighted the importance of global cooperation to ensure universal access to vaccines and a strong financial safety net. To ensure a successful exit from the crisis, these efforts will need to be coupled with sound policy frameworks and ambitious domestic reforms, which would facilitate new growth opportunities, including from digitalization and green technology, while confronting climate change and rising inequality.

Directors concurred that uncertainties around the baseline projections remain large and that the risks to growth outcomes are tilted to the downside. They stressed that the economic outlook continues to depend heavily on the path of the health crisis and the speed at which widespread vaccination can be reached. Directors also acknowledged that the uncertainty surrounding inflation prospects—primarily stemming from the path of the pandemic, the duration of supply disruptions, and how inflation expectations may evolve in this environment—is particularly large. They noted that while inflation expectations appear well-anchored, inflation risks could prompt a faster-than-anticipated monetary normalization in advanced economies. Higher debt levels and large government financing needs in many countries are also a source of vulnerability, especially if global interest rates were to rise faster than expected.

Directors highlighted that policy choices have become more difficult, confronting multidimensional challenges—subdued employment growth, rising inflation, food insecurity, the setback to human capital accumulation, and climate change—with limited room to maneuver. They stressed that multilateral efforts to avoid international trade and supply chain disruptions, speed up global vaccine access, provide liquidity and debt relief to constrained economies, and mitigate and adapt to climate change continue to be essential. Directors further agreed that it is crucial to ensure that financially constrained countries can continue essential spending while meeting other obligations, and highlighted the expected contribution of the recent General Allocation of Special Drawing Rights in providing the much-needed international liquidity. At the national level, Directors agreed that policy priorities should continue to be tailored to local pandemic and economic conditions, aiming to overcome the still-evolving health crisis and promote an inclusive recovery while protecting the credibility of policy frameworks. As the recovery progresses, policymakers will need to shift to measures that aim to reverse scarring from the crisis.

Directors noted that fiscal policy should remain supportive but needs to be well-targeted, carefully calibrated, and tailored to country-specific circumstances. In countries with high levels of vaccination and low funding costs, fiscal policy should gradually shift from pandemic-fighting emergency measures toward promoting a transformation to more resilient and inclusive economies. In countries with lower vaccination rates and tighter financing constraints, health-related spending and protecting the most vulnerable will remain top priorities. As countries converge back to precrisis GDP trends, the focus should shift toward ensuring fiscal sustainability, including through establishing credible medium-term fiscal frameworks, which would also promote fiscal transparency and sound governance practices. Given likely long-lasting negative impacts on budget revenues in developing economies, further efforts will be needed to mobilize revenues in the medium term and improve expenditure efficiency. While recognizing that the international community provided critical support to alleviate fiscal vulnerabilities in low-income countries, Directors noted that more is needed, including through debt relief in the context of early and timely implementation of multilateral initiatives, such as the G20 Common Framework.

Directors concurred that monetary policy should remain accommodative where there are output gaps, inflation pressures are contained, and inflation expectations are consistent with central bank targets. However, they noted that central banks should be prepared to act quickly if the recovery strengthens faster than expected or if inflation expectations are rising. Directors stressed that transparent and clear communication about the outlook for monetary policy is critical at the current juncture to avoid de-anchoring of inflation expectations and prevent financial instability.

Directors noted that financial vulnerabilities continue to be elevated in several sectors—including nonbank financial institutions, nonfinancial corporates, and the housing market—masked in part by the very substantial policy stimulus. They highlighted that a prolonged period of extremely easy financial conditions, while needed to sustain the economic recovery, may result in overly stretched asset valuations and further fuel financial vulnerabilities. Directors agreed that policymakers should act preemptively to address vulnerabilities and avoid a buildup of legacy problems. They should also tighten selected macroprudential tools to tackle pockets of elevated vulnerabilities while avoiding a broad tightening of financial conditions.

Directors agreed that some emerging and frontier markets continue to face large financing needs. While the outlook for capital flows has improved and monetary conditions remain still broadly accommodative, a sudden change in the monetary policy stance of advanced economies may result in a sharp tightening of financial conditions, adversely affecting capital flows and exacerbating pressures in countries facing debt sustainability concerns. They concurred that the policy response in these countries will need to be centered on implementing structural reforms, rebuilding buffers, and strengthening financial market governance and infrastructure.